THE WIFE OF ROSSETTI

HER LIFE AND DEATH

by

VIOLET HUNT

With Thirty Illustrations

"My life is so miserable I wish for no more of it."

LONDON

JOHN LANE THE BODLEY HEAD LIMITED

First published in 1932

1329

Printed in Great Britain by R. Clay & Sons, Ltd., Bungay, Suffolk.

Dedicated with sincerest respect and admiration to THOMAS J. WISE, who has helped me with counsel and afforded me documentation from the serried rows of his garner, in my task of collecting and interweaving the delicate strands of a short and tenuous life, like a Victorian lady's gossamer veil, caught and impaled on the thorns of this troublesome world.

INTRODUCTION

THE truth about Rossetti has been told, more or less: the truth about the woman he married, never. For the first time, brushing away the decent coverlet of leaves with which Rossetti's admirers have covered his reputation, I seem to have laid bare much that is painful, wild and unexpected but, at the same time, something beautiful, heroic even, and all that is pitiful.[1] For surely the struggle of youth, avid of honours and joy, to do good work whether one lives or dies—preferably lives—is implicit in the stories of Eleanor Elizabeth Siddall and her husband and those he led against the Sanhedrim of old, mild but evil men who had sat down heavily in the High Places of British Art and persistently stifled all effort to see things truly and well. Eleanor's first sitting was to one of the Band and she was sitting to another on the day she died.

She was born exactly a hundred years ago, and all the persons, nearly, that I knew well in youth had known her and were full of the legend, reinforced and cemented by her tragic death, which constitutes the dark stain on Pre-Raphaelite annals. Like another Iphigeneia, she was sacrificed and slain that the P.R.B. might conquer and live,[2] with her red hair for gonfalon. Her blood served for the anointing of the corner-stone, for the solemn ratification of this cult and its acceptance by a backward nation, which culminated in the exhibition, one Spring, of Burne-Jones' *Mermaid* with her divine sneer—a Blessed Damozel of the Depths—on the walls of the Royal Academy and the curt resignation of the last of the Pre-Raphaelites (second swarm) the very next year, from The Accursed Thing! Perhaps—who

[1] Puissant even now is the posthumous charm wielded by this pair, so that people say to me, " Don't put the searchlight on Rossetti, pray leave the bloom on Lizzy ! "

[2] " All the world and his wife has seen Millais's *Black Brunswicker* and Mr. Hunt's *Temple* and is beginning to think it rather hard that a new Pre-Raphaelite picture should not be produced once a month."—*Illustrated London News.*

knows—the violent gesture of this so mild man was intended to avenge her ?

"Strange and sad her story," said Mrs. Howitt who knew her fairly well (no one knew her very well—not even her "dear little Georgy") and her life "like a short and troubled dream." Respecting the details of that story there has been a conspiracy of silence, kept up until to-day, when there is hardly anybody left who knows at all.

But now, according to a member of her family—set, dignified and reticent as they all were and are—it has come to form part of the educational curriculum. Children in Board Schools are taught[1] that the wife of the painter Rossetti, reproductions of whose works adorn the walls of their school-house, committed suicide, while a distinguished German professor has made this young woman, whose features have come to stand for the Pre-Raphaelite ideal in the eyes of the world, the subject of a thesis, read before the youth of Jena.

Virtuous, static, almost characterless except for a natal obstinacy, something of the sharpness and sourness immanent in those born under the banner of a lost cause, her history is that of the eleven years during which her orbit coincided with that of Gabriel Rossetti and the Pre-Raphaelites. No saliences, certainly no sins;[2] her merits not in any way on the surface. No one knew anything about the soul that might have looked out of those eyes, under lids heavy with doom, had she been willing to raise them for you. Not Georgy, nor Bessie, Emma, Mary or Barbara could tell what lay under that silence, behind that haughty sweep of the upper lip that was not all sweetness, or knew what source of secret pride or unblessed knowledge it was that reared her fine throat with its upward lift, like a lark's, about to sing. . . .

If anyone, it might have been William Allingham, who neither denied nor pried but accepted her secretness ; seeing her always as Little Bridget who had been stolen away by the fairies, come back from seven long years in the keeping of creatures known to be soulless, with their implicit, careless knowledge of things it is safe for mortals not to know. He never expected her to be chatty on their long walks to Highgate and back on summer evenings—after seeing their friends the Howitts and the Patmores. Did Little Bridget

---

[1] See note 2, p. vii.

[2] "I have never heard any fault attributed to *her*." Letters of the Honourable Mrs. Twisleton, of America.

on her return to her parents dare to tell everyone what she had seen and heard while she was among the Good People, the queernesses, the languors and lapses of that land where the sun never shines and the wind never blows and all things are seen in the faery underlight, as it were through a piece of smoked glass? Better far had Lizzy married William Allingham who understood her, or run away with Algernon Swinburne [1] practising the same strange withdrawal of personality under a mask of satyrdom, instead of Gabriel Rossetti, to whom " sonnets meant insomnia," subject to nervous breakdowns and hallucinations [2] even before he took to drugs, and with a suicide in his family.[3] And as for hers, nervous people all of them! Young Lydia could not sleep unless she half sat up in bed, or bear the usual constriction of stays. Harry was weak-minded and Clara died insane. (People said that it was because they all wore their hair too long.)

Nowadays one would simply call her an eccentric.

Compared with his wife, Dante Gabriel Rossetti was more or less normal, self-protective, even stable in mutability. Capricious without being flighty, wayward as genius is wayward but knowing full well how far in perversity he meant to go, obstinate and domineering but incapable of sulks and sourness, full of swagger but entirely without pretentiousness. Of his habit lazy and lolling; the intensity of his moral outlook, as a fire that burns straight, belied the supineness of his bearing. Like the lover of Arabella in 'Tis Pity, he conquered but did not fight. Even dour, carping " Scotus," the discoverer of his genius, while resenting the implications of this overlordship, felt the fascination that made everyone place " glorious Gabriel " in a different position *qua* morality from themselves and be willing to lay down their lives for him.[4] In the great heart of Hunt was such love for his friend—though always between them the meeted rivalry of the purist and the sensualist; [5] with their great counter pictures of

---

[1] Lady Jane was quite frightened of it.

[2] See the voice that called to him on the morning of his twenty-third birthday. And a child of his was epileptic.

[3] In August 1821 John William Polidori died "from a subtle poison of his own composition." A verdict of Natural Death was returned. *See* Dict. Nat. Biography.

[4] Some wag changed a letter but, indeed, P.R.B. devotion for Gabriel ran to that.

[5] In his heart of hearts Hunt considered Rossetti " a painter without passion " and his " Blessed Damozel " but " a brawny wench." While Fanny was " the large-throated, disagreeable woman he painted so much."

the kept lady in the Victorian drawing-room and the "twisted one"[1] at the bridge head—that when the moral and monetary crash came and most of them streamed out to the Antipodes to look for gold, he hesitated long to join the exodus (to the Promised Land in his case), for "I do not know what I should do away from Gabriel." He could have borne it had he had the assurance that Gabriel was somewhere in the same land with him, but "to have the dark world between—" *that* he would not "bring to pass easily, or anticipate the cold desolateness of Death's valley." In Palestine he heard of his friend's little treacheries and, without bitterness, stroked his golden beard and bade the Arabs fetch him the day's model, the wretched beast bound with the phylactery of all the crimes men do under the sun, wandering, outcast, on the stony beach of the Moabitish Sea.

Selfish, Gabriel liked to help and often used his marvellous business capacity in the service of what Ruskin contemptuously called "the smaller fry that followed in his wake." After fascinating big buyers for himself he would attend to the others, and the tales of his business transactions show many picturesque *revirements* of conduct in the man who liked to be paid in guineas and saw to it, but who was sometimes seen emptying his pockets into the laps of beggars; who told his friends to "go to the drawer and take whatever was wanted," and wrote to Brown on a certain occasion, bidding him not to be annoyed at sight of enclosed,[2] "which would be quite idle with me" and could be refunded when Cromwell or the portraits went home.

It had suddenly struck him that Brown, after some great "botheration" or other, must be inconvenienced. Brown refused it.

Ruskin, with the percipience of the sex-stultified, got Rossetti best—"a great Italian living in England" instead of in a Catholic country where a man may wipe out a crime or a peccadillo in the confessional and die, leaving pious wishes and penances to be liquidated by gifts and candles and the prayers of women[3] after his death. He was doing the best he could in this austerer land, the "could" shortened by the strength of his animal passions, due corollary of the Colour-Sense which is such precious bane. Hampered in his art by lack of mastery of the medium,

---

[1] *Defence of Guenevere.*
[2] A cheque.
[3] "Dear Old Antique" (as he called his mother) and Christina did that for him.

D. G. ROSSETTI

From an oil painting by
William Holman Hunt

he knew it, with the sad, inward eye of the artist turned on the faults that clipped his wings. Out loud he prided himself on his neglect of the usual processes for clearing, collocating and adjusting the clotted mass of the raw findings of genius. And his were very clotted—"The simple, the natural, the naïve were insipid in his mouth";[1] he demanded the strongest savours in Art and Literature—not so much perhaps in Life!

He did not love Nature or encourage her appeal, except in so far as he could bring her into romantic relation with himself. Lush, tree-shadowed, bewitched country inspired him with the lovely melancholy which was, as artists say of pictures, the " eye " of his poetry; wooded groves where he could feign to see the red blood of a suicide staining and the tears of a mourner drenching the secret stream and its banks, the alder over the dark green leaves that carpet the floor of our English woods—

> With tear-spurge wan, and bloodwort burning red.

He means wood-spurge. Without even knowing its name he remembers that this plant has a cup of three. He took all that in, sitting with Scott once on Brignal Banks (which he chooses to call Willow Wood), his forehead between his knees, his eyes wide open, in some dreadful agony of remembrance

> From perfect grief there need not be
> Wisdom or even memory.

With bravura he carried off his narrowness, his lack of all interest in ethics, the why and the wherefore of our existence. He was not sure if the earth moved round the sun, and what matter if it did not? Without a bean's worth of faith he lays claim to the female Intercession that Catholics invoke—

> O Mary Mother, be not loth
> To listen, Thou whom the stars clothe.

Surely the first a-moral person to exist delightfully in those austere Victorian fields, and managing to get a strain of mysticism as well as sensuality into his pictures, live to see his Magdalens and Belcolors nicely housed on the walls of sober, righteous and respectable patrons, his naked figures of Love into reredos or triptych and the light shining on their limbs through stained-glass windows in churches all over the country! For this man, who later was accused of " wheeling his nuptial

[1] Allingham

couch into the street," was devout in youth, brought up by a mother who went to church regularly but who could never bear to hear the lesson read that tells of the organized slaughter of the Priests of Baal by Elijah, or bring herself to believe that Socrates would be condemned by Him to eternal torment, wrote, when he was nineteen, two poems which may be said to hold as much as he chose to assimilate of his mother's religious training, *The Blessed Damozel* and *Jenny*. From early youth his two principal motor ideas, apart from self, were of redemption, through the intercession, and the remission of sins through the tears and prayers of a Saviour Woman. And the reciprocity must be mutual. Antedating the tactics of Butler and Gladstone, he and his friends started the Rescue Work of the 'fifties, patrolling the streets solemnly every night in parties of two or three, expostulating, preaching and getting themselves laughed at.

His sisters were obsessed all their lives long with this idea of moral salvage :[1] careful, delicate females without the zest of the hunt to inspirit them, reading aloud to sulky fallen women in grey-walled Homes at Highgate and in Portobello Road. Christina's own earthly passion was frustrate : her Prince made no Progress—" Too late for Joy, the Bride was dead." Her *saudades*,[2] as her friend Howell called it, found expression and gained zest in the act of cherishing all wretched, despoiled and hunted things. Like many old maids she was devoted to animals, furry, feathered and the smaller the better. Once in Regent's Park she had looked out of her window at dawn and seen a wave of yellow light sweep up from the trees and fill the still dreaming glades. . . . It was all the canaries escaped from all the cages in London and agreed among themselves never to go back to captivity. Her brother always meant to paint it.

Had she cared more for humans the catastrophe of 1874 might have been averted and the soul of a brother been saved from the Purgatory she steadily believed in. One wonders if she had time to think of this on that night in Spring when, a maiden lady, bonnetless, she went out, to deal double raps at a physician's door and get him to come and put Gabriel out of his laudanum sleep, procured from the dregs of a bottle first used ever so many years ago. A saint, doubled regrettably with a dis-

---

[1] Reading of Dickens' Martha and her thoughts of suicide had helped to put the idea in their heads, not to speak of Little Em'ly, " found."

[2] *Saudades*. Portuguese word for rueing—remorse.

agreeable woman, she had the justness, the intuitive taste of the peasant Marie Claire together with the passion of Sœur Marie Angélique who had been La Vallière. She had sent away Collinson, whom she loved, for religious reasons, but, meeting him in the street a month afterwards, fainted away on William's arm and dropped her painting for good as a mortification. Her motives were misconstrued by one near to her :—

" Christina finds Art interferes with the legitimate exercise of anguish and insists on going on dreaming of a lifelong ill," said the ever-candid relation.

Olive-skinned, with deep brown eyes that showed sometimes the white over the pupils—sign of her inherent malady—Christina had much temperament. Quiet, still and brooding, she had plumbed depths that Lizzy never knew and there was more passion in her little finger than in the other's whole white body.

" It is over at last, the terrible pain." Now, broken and shaken in her own esteem, she haunted the portals of convents and imposed on herself penances for a contemplated sin. "There's blood between us, Love, my Love. . . ." Not blood but a wife. For Collinson,[1] when she threw him over a second time, consoled himself.

The secret has been well kept, but with poets, murder will soonest out. She could never, in verse, keep off the subject, so dreadful then to the lay mind that no one had the moral hardihood to read between the lines.[2]

" For there's no love like a sister's. . . ." Maria did not, like Laura to save Lizzy, hold converse and traffic with goblin men on the hillside and eat their delicious, deadly fruits or, like Meredith's beauty of Bath,[3] need to hang herself as a deterrent on the threshold which the delinquent must pass. But for a week of nights the kind, sonsy creature crouched on the mat by the house door and saved her sister from the horrors of an elopement with a man who belonged to another.

The fits of peculiar sadness that Ruskin observed in both Gabriel and Lizzy he may have set down to their lineage—scions both of a family—Gabriel's certainly—which had in the past expended its energies in political effort. Maybe the physical disabilities entailed by the proscription and subsequent wanderings of the father, as a fugitive, had diminished in the

---

[1] Collinson, a P.R.B., had married the Sister of an R.A. (one of the worst).
[2] Of her brother's preface to *Goblin Market*.
[3] He told me he had founded *The Story of Chloe* on this incident.

son the power of resistance to what may come, fostered his dreadful *laisser-aller, laisser-faire*, his withdrawal from the decisions of life other than the arrangement of a few lines and colours—more colours than lines—on a canvas or a piece of Whatman paper, and his brutal envisagement of matters pertaining to the emotions—has a hunted patriot a right to any but political ones? He had a low opinion of women—" Yes, they are ever so much nicer when they have lost their virtue." [1] Stunners all : divided broadly into useful, approachable Blessed Damozels and women " nascent for Hell." He had no " Cousin Nell " [2] to set against Jenny : he was not, as a matter of fact, acquainted with any woman who would have been called " a lady " in those days and chose to attribute to them all the morality of servant-girls.[3] He spoke slightingly of Brown's Emma and, called to account, apologised in uncomplimentary terms—" I regard *all* women as being absolutely loose-tongued and unreliable, so that to suggest such qualities in one of them does not seem to me particularly disrespectful."

Lizzy had breeding—her every gesture shows it. But simple, unsuggestible, obstinate as a child, in the wrong places, though Gabriel could sweep her off her feet in his hustle, charm her with his voice that lulled the tempest and rode the storms she raised. Yet, even convinced, she could not accommodate herself to his meretricious adaptations, jesuitical reservations, or realise, for the artist, the need of variety as a stimulus to invention,—by a sort of immoral *tour de main* confounding the sensations, the sensibilities evoked by one model with those set up by another— as in the tales of Masuccio and Bandello where a lover enjoys two women in the same night. She could not forgive those apt processes of substitution in the moral and artistic order which, instead of shocking and estranging, in the end please and convince. The Arch of Marius at Saint Rémy de Provence is

---

[1] So he told Frederick Shields.

[2] My cousin Nell is fond of fun,
And fond of dress, and change, and praise,
. . . .
My cousin Nell is fond of love
And she's the girl I'm proudest of.
Who does not prize her, guard her well?

[3] All his life he preferred to find his loves among the proletariat—the daughters of carpenters, blacksmiths and livery-stable keepers. To the one " real " lady who came within his provenance he did not propose, and she would not have taken him.

subtly irregular : the Maison Carrée at Nîmes looks so well because it has one column less on the south side.[1] The Madonna adored by both Ruskin and Proust is black, and a head painted by Rossetti, for which Mrs. Morris sat, is so distinctly Semitic in cast and feature that it might stand for Naaman's little Syrian maid.

Her last words were prompted by jealousy, not the dislike of being left by herself, for she took a positive pleasure in loneliness ; see her wilful claustrations in Chatham Place, her resort to the wildwood at Scalands and Matlock, lying like a hunted animal in the long grass. Fanny, in the end, had grown to be a habit, so there is some other reason to seek for suicide. Her jealousy was not of Janey—that was spared her—or of " My Lady Audley," unobtainable or Annie Miller, giddy but equally so.[2] All of them were good to paint ; he wanted something coarser to live with, more like Byron's Marianna Segati—" Vacca tua, Eccellenza ! " Fanny ! William Bell Scott introduced him to her.

William Bell Scott, " the Northern Vitruvius," or " Scotus " as his friends called him, always said that it was he who really discovered Gabriel.

Artist as well as poet : when the cards were shuffled by Sir Henry Cole, he had left off being a Stunner—so said Kenny Meadows, who invented the phrase—and taken the place of Bellenden Kerr in Newcastle as Head of the School of Design. He didn't paint much more but resigned himself to be Pictor Ignotus, " a painter without recognition," taking the privilege of lashing his erstwhile competitors in the race with a bitterness they did not relish and hit back.[3] He was married to a

[1] The Soldiers' Memorial at Hyde Park Corner is not quite rectangular.

[2] Grant Allen saw the making of a novel in the whole affair but he never wrote it. Annie Miller is the one Pre-Raphaelite heroine who has, perhaps out of consideration for these two men, been sedulously " kept dark " ; references to her in P.R.B. memoirs are scanty, though, in the 'sixties and 'seventies, her name was on every one of their tongues.

[3] Scotus—" impressive as a truthful and understanding person can be—and that is little or nothing," says Patmore, who ticked off people rather well. Rossetti always gave him " the impression of tenacity rather than intensity." " Impressive in his way but, as to his output, a *null* he is and ever will be," said Carlyle. Rossetti's own mild contribution was, " Scott warps things ! " together with a nice sketch of his Stunner, whose connection with him was purely honorific though it saddened poor little Mrs. Laetitia.

woman who had been very pretty[1] and who was always a "character"—Miss Laetitia Norquoy, the daughter of a rich Ceylonese tea-planter.

Fanny—or Sarah—Cox (afterwards Hughes), like Lizzy, was of good family stock. The Hyltons dated from long before the Conquest, the family originating in the mythological union of one of Odin's ravens with a Saxon maiden. Her uncle quartered the arms of Hylton of Hylton Castle. One Thomas Hilton was bailiff of "Roon" when Joan was burnt. Her mother, a Hylton, and her father, a Cornforth, were both heir to estates lost through attainder. She had a great-uncle living in her native town of Darlington, old Tommy Bowes, who could never eat butcher's meat because it reminded him of the smell of roasting rebels in the market-place. Twice a Jacobite, she was also allied to the Vanes. One of the daughters of old Richard Hylton had married the son of Albinia, posthumous daughter of Sir Harry Vane, begotten in the Tower the night before his execution (after the premeditated fashion of the Abbesse de Jouarre in the prison of the Abbaye). And Albinia's son, styling himself the Honourable Harry Vane, left a dole to the poor of Darlington.

Elizabeth Hylton, great-grandmother of Sarah Cox, was a queer, obstinate, romantic figure about whom Rossetti, with his predilection for the hard-bitten North, its legends, its savage romance, was never tired of hearing. He prized Fanny's tales of the beautiful ancestress who, in her youth, lived in a "hall-house"[2] —that is to say, a house into which you did not burst at once into the living-room, because it had a porch built in front of it—at the spot where Westmorland, Cumberland and Durham meet.

She was the daughter of "a retired captain in the army"— periphrasis used to denote persons who did not exist for their country's good such as Catholics and Jacobites. The Earl of Seaforth had taken part in the 'Fifteen and, pardoned, lived in exile. But his son Lord Fortrose came out in

---

[1] Conscious that her value was deeply impaired by the illness which deprived her of her looks and half her wits, Miss Norquoy offered to release him from his engagement but he gallantly refused. So she early accepted the existence of a "noble and queenly rival"—so her husband naïvely puts it—"and had faith in us both." Rightly enough. Alice Boyd was a sweet woman, a sister of Hugh Spencer Boyd, Scott's dead friend, whose spirit-messages got through and converted Scott to Spiritualism. Alice Boyd had inherited a castle in Ayrshire and shares in a rich seam of coal.

[2] Hall-House—a gentleman's mansion. Teesdale Glossary.

the 'Forty-five, and his wife too. Elizabeth Hylton was living with her and her daughters at Coxhoe Hall near Durham, where a certain John Cornforth was bailiff, when, like a Suffragette of our own day, Lady Fortrose chose to take part in her husband's campaign—"leading some few of the Mackenzies" while he was with Lord Loudoun and Mr. Mackintosh, whose wife also was helping him to be in two places at once.[1]

Elizabeth Hylton looked after the children while their mother was leading armies, but she would not go to France with them afterwards, for she had fallen in love with the son of the bailiff and married him nine years later, when all was quiet again.

The Cornforths, a splendid yeoman stock, had held property in the neighbourhood of Darlington since the fourteenth century and their name figures in most of the leases, with their dangling seals, of lands, and messuages in the neighbourhood. They had been in rebellion too.[2] A Cornforth of Blackwell was in the Rising of the North. William Cornforth of Manfield was a fine rider and the terror of all the horse-thieves and smugglers who infested Weardale.[3]

Fanny Cox inherited her good sense and efficiency from her mother's family, whose name she adopted professionally, but she had all the passion of her remoter ancestress, whom, so she had been told, she resembled, an immensely fine woman with blue eyes and the yellow hair of the family. One of his schoolfellows remembered the long hair of Freeman Hylton hanging down his back in ringlets, in the manner of a wig in Charles II's time. His sister had it too. She was the life of the rustic Academy at Denton, near by Hylton, remembered for her little frauds, promising apricots, peaches and such rare fruit from her ancestral acres in order to get her sums done for her. The Hylton garden boasted nothing but plums and apples : her father had obtained a decree by which he had recovered his estate but, as so often happened with lands long forfeited, the revenue was not equal to the charges and the last Baron of Hylton had large ideas. . . . He italianated his house and died.

[1] *London Gazette*, March 2nd, 1746 : "If this be a contrivance it may save or lose their heads, according as the word WIFE is understood."

[2] Quietly and warily, they contributed to all the local Doles by which the good Catholics compensated for heady evil deeds in those days and so saved their souls and estates alive. There was the Sober Dole—a Cornforth Christian name—the Forster Dole, distributed with the much larger Cornforth Dole.

[3] There is a place called Cornforth's Leap which he negotiated on his celebrated charger that he fed on bread and beer when unable to get a feed of corn for it.

Fanny had managed to get hold of the Hylton seal (pointed, elliptic, a lozenge with a chevron between three *fleurs de lys*) and divers lockets and portraits. She had seen the family cradle before the last Baron sold it and the chrism-cloth of red, silver and gold thread in which all the Hyltons were baptised. She cut up for Rossetti some splendid brocade dresses and satins " that stood alone," and adapted to her own use the " visiting dresses " of Mary Ann Hylton, the promiser of peaches, who died unmarried of consumption before she was twenty-five.[1]

Rossetti found the brocade scraps useful, and impressive the legends of Hylton, its derelict corridors full of raddled pillars, its music gallery with ceiling painted by Vercelli, through which the north wind now whistled and where the good wife churned amid life-sized statues of Venus, Cupid and Minerva. But he who wrote *Jan Van Hunks* was as deeply interested in the plebeian annals of the Cornforths and would savour on his tongue the queer names of their properties—Towneland, Malande, Stickbitchland —and enjoy Fanny's description of the family mansion in Black-wellgate, where she had stayed as a girl, the house door, with a cruciform knocker, clamped with iron, that would have resisted an invasion by the Scots, and the " colour " of the wood, dark, rich and shiny like petrified oil. There was a well in the middle of the house in case of siege and the ghost, Old Pinckney, roamed o' nights in his red nightcap, so that no one liked to be afoot after nightfall.[2]

" Little things touch secret springs—" and Mr. Scott came to be responsible for that ill-starred clumsy picture which procured Rossetti's quarrel with Hunt and led his steps to the Place of the Gnashing of Teeth where his ruin was finally consummated.

A bright lad in Edinburgh, walking back from Portobello one night, Scott had come across a poor, starved street-walker called Rosabell Bonalley. She was of a French colony there and, *en tout bien, tout honneur* (Scott was the most cantankerous but the most chivalrous of men), he gave her supper and sent her home. Not long after he wrote a poem called *Mary Anne* and published it in a magazine.

[1] The male blood of the Hyltons died out with Henry Hylton, a spirit merchant in Barnard Castle, with blue eyes and a golden beard ; and a midshipman, R.N., ridiculously yellow-haired too—" the last leaves on a blasted tree."

[2] Things are altered. The house is now an inn—The Fleece.

Another youth in London read it and wrote enthusiastically to the author. It was the beginning of a life-friendship between the two men. Mr. Gabriel Charles Rossetti suggested a volume and promised to illustrate the poem as soon as he could " beg, buy or steal the copper to etch it on." He posted to Newcastle three of his own magazine attempts, giving Scott the chance to say afterwards that he had " made " him. Perhaps he did? For Rosabell proved to be the very navel, the hub, of Rossetti's particular complex in its first and last expression. In order to get the background he took Chatham Place. The model for it was already in his eye. So we get Rosabell Bonalley of Portobello with the face of Fanny Hughes of Wapping,[1] the fine and the abject : the piteous and the unregenerate : the spiritual and the sumptuous—crouching by the Bridge, sick and averse, while the lover she has left for the voluptuary, pulls her chin round like a policeman about to move on a vagrant and, in so doing, recognises his old sweetheart " gone on the town." The subject of this picture with its touching legend [2] was so near the inner core of the painter's feeling that he seemed to be inhibited from finishing it. Gabriel's " Bridge Picture " ended by becoming an imposthume, a dreary responsibility that his friends often spoke of as they might of a deformed bastard child that a doting father will cling to. Fanny was its mother—poor Fanny with her strayed aitches—" I know I don't say h'it right ! " —came to suit him better than the other woman brooding in her still preciosity at Chatham Place or lying kicking on the Browns' hearthrug in her paroxysms of rage.

Found, or *The Drover*, or *The Bridge Picture*, or *Lost*, as Mr. Leatheart called it, first commissioned in 1853, was " married " to three people—McCracken, Leatheart and Graham. Its last mate was Samuel Bancroft, Jun., of Rockford, Wilmington, Del. It needed a bridge, a cart, a countryman, a calf and a harlot. Fanny sat for the harlot. Brown sat for the countryman and got him the calf, and Millais got him the cart. " A dreadfully difficult subject," says Ruskin discreetly. He hated it and it may have been his fault that it was never finished, to the lifelong vexation of the four gentlemen who at different times

---

[1] Rossetti's portraits are never likenesses. He makes Meredith look like Howell and Howell like the Angel Gabriel, while into Fanny's smug face (as seen in the photograph she sent to Mrs. Hemblen) he put all the pathos and tragedy begotten of her stormy days with her " incumbrance "—a drunkard and a waster.

[2] " I remember thee, the kindness of thy youth and the love of thy betrothal."

commissioned it. The last commission, given in 1859, was for three hundred and fifty guineas. After Rossetti died Burne-Jones touched it up and sent it off to America.

At the top of the tree, with an income of four figures thanks to Charles Augustus Howell, scorning academic honours (Jenny Morris told me that Mr. Rossetti had said that, if the Royal Academy were to elect him at any time, he would immediately put the matter into the hands of his solicitor), two short sentences concerning the author of *The Blessed Damozel* spoken in my hearing stand out in my mind. I have never forgotten them and the emphasis with which they were delivered. Sitting at the round, rickety, varnished table in the house on the canal, from which the albums were shoved aside for the tea-tray at which Miss Sarianna Browning presided, I heard Mr. Browning say in his so loud and guttural voice, " I never can forgive Rossetti! "

And another crashing sentence came from between the patriarchally bearded lips of Mr. Holman Hunt in answer to my mother's question, as he stood in the studio in Warwick Road (where the big flats are now), mixing his paints with Jordan water out of a bottle. " No, I never see Gabriel now . . . his life is so bad." And then, " He behaved very ill to the poor girl he married.[1] . . . Just before her end he went to see her and promised to marry her if only she would get well. . . . They had been growing more and more apart. . . ." His voice trailed off—as if the subject disgusted him.

I did so want to know, not so much about her, as about him—the man who had written the poem I had learned to repeat before I could read. One dark rainy evening, walking after painting hours with my father near our house, I asked him to tell me about Mr. Rossetti. With a seriousness quite inexplicable to me and rather appalling, he answered, " I cannot. You had better ask your Mamma, or Professor Ellis. He is the only man who knows anything about him now."

Pressed, he gave his reason, using the same expression that Mr. Hunt had used—Victorian for " that kind of thing."

Yet I remembered Sunday mornings, sometimes, when I was let walk with my nurse as far as I could go—and sent back while my parents went on to breakfast with Mr. Rossetti. I

[1] These long engagements have the worst effect on women. Tennyson's Emily spent most of her after marriage life on a *chaise longue*.

heard about it afterwards, when he had gone down into the long, stuffy night of chloral. He would open the door himself in his dirty Chinese dressing-gown, unshaven, unwashed, and receive them and cherish them as he alone knew how. Nothing romantic about him but the soft Italian voice and the wonderful eyes, with the bar of Michelangelo across the brows, so that she who afterwards described him to me, said that one could refuse him nothing.

But soon the walks stopped. Fanny was his housekeeper *en titre* and *à domicile*, so gentlemen could not take their wives there any more.

Ruskin was the only person, so far as I am aware, who never, after Mrs. Rossetti's death, committed himself to an opinion either about her or her husband. Just as he never spoke of his own Effie excepting perhaps a veiled allusion—"one other person of whom I do not suppose you are thinking "—in a savage letter to Miss Octavia Hill forty years or so after.

But there is one voice raised in defence of Gabriel. It comes from Germany and is reinforced by a member of Gabriel's own family.

" I cannot get rid of the idea that this so renowned Miss Siddal, because she was cold and self-centred, had a monstrously evil influence on Rossetti's development." So says Professor Levin Schücking, and, in answer to his request for corroboration, the other admits that " he is not far wrong. Of course Miss Siddal was a disagreeable and acid person with a very cold temperament." But he grants her " immense and devastating charm and a remarkable character to set against her terrible bad temper," which made her life with his distinguished relation " a series of violent scenes one after another."

She was " pretentious," the Professor goes on to suggest, " easily offended, touchy, self-contained, cold and unemotional." But, on the other hand, Rossetti had " little use for the gentler virtues." Still, he " gave the gold of his purest feelings, receiving as it were, copper coins in exchange." Doctor Schücking quotes her two terrible letters which seemingly are all that have been preserved and comes to the conclusion that, " Once they were married, disillusionment was sure to follow."

Worse. Suicide. To the Professor this act must have appeared some sort of an outrage on Art, like throwing a bomb at a fine public building. What ! Saddle a great painter with the pangs of remorse; better far the *chemise Isabelle* or the obedience of Fair Helen, fording the stream on foot at the side of her mounted lover—

> I pray to God, Childe Waters,
> You never will see me swim.

(But he did and they got through somehow and, that night, she " had her young son born " and the Childe married her because she had been so good.)

It is certain that their two morbidities crashed. Lizzy was far too ill to marry. He felt the reluctance of the healthy male to beget his children on a phthisical subject, condemned to the deadliest forms of relief for pain. She could not, actually, eat without " taking something," or lie down when the attack was on.

She taught him to drug: Stillman, who is generally considered responsible for this, only provided him with a neater, more modern remedy for remorse.

One windy autumn afternoon at the Scotts' I was bored in the drawing-room and strayed out by the queer underground kitchen-study way into the garden, all nettles and weeds and straggling things as tall as I was, long grass unmown pressing up against the windows of an old stable and some sheds, with half red, half white panes broken in places. . . . I looked in through a crack and saw the great derelict picture *Dante's Dream* which, for the present, Mr. Scott was housing for his distinguished neighbour a few yards further down the road. The danger was that he might spoil it by re-touching. He was now unfit to handle it.

Then I went in; to Mamma and Mr. Scott and his two Egerias in the dining-room with the great bow window, its window-boxes full of wilted plants that gave on the bridge and the little bit of garden nestling just under it. Miss Boyd got up suddenly and went to the window, which was open, for it was a mild evening. Mrs. Scott said "Tea!" but she did not come away and we joined her and looked out. In the whole street there was only one man and he was immediately under the sill. I could have leant out and touched his head. His itinerary along the Embankment parapet had been broken by the bridge and the bit of More's Garden. He had his *pardessus* [1] " hugged up," as these North-

---

[1] I have it now. It fell to a relation of mine.

country people said, over his face so that he looked like a monk.

"Gabriel!" Mrs. Scott exclaimed.

No one, much, saw him now except a young adorer from Liverpool who had driven Watts [1] away, and his old friend Frederick Shields, who tempered the narcotic with water whenever he got the chance. And there was a spiritualist fellow who called now and again. As for women, only Janey Morris (" Scarecrow," as she chose to call herself since her illness) and the beautiful Miss Herbert who came up from Brighton once to see him, for old sake's sake. She was shown into the dining-room, with its long table and heavy brocade cloth reaching to the ground and, when she had waited a few minutes alone, out crept her host from under it, on all-fours. She never came again.

After using up all his best Delft plates as missiles, even Fanny left him, though, like King Charles for Nelly, he had a last word for her and the suggestion of a cheque to be sent—as many a time before. "I am writing to tell The Elephant that she may expect you at 36 Royal Avenue. When you or she tell me . . . I will disgorge—my leading function in life being to do so."

Like Browning, I never can forgive Rossetti.

My sources for this Life are chiefly oral, from the circumstances of my childhood and early girlhood, spent much in the company of the actors in the scenes I am attempting to describe, wandering o' mornings in and out of their houses with messages and, older, with a good book in my hand which I did not read, hearkening as a servant waiting at table might, to words that I only half understood. The Cloud of Witnesses have set down, many of them, afterwards what they judged meet of their garnered memories, in chastened, more academic language, instead of giving the hot sentences that come from the entrails as well as the heart: *le mot cru* as well as *le mot juste*. Allingham did not count Fanny's lost aitches or William Rossetti, moved by brotherly love and consideration for posterity, cross Gabriel's t's. For the painful and

---

[1] I never shall forget Watts' vexation when Hall Caine got in first with his " Life " and " fingered the bloom off Gabriel."

homely sensations procured in persons present at the exhumation of the poems I refer them to Mr. Virtue Tebbs' account of this ceremony. The exact terms of the message to her husband written in pencil on a bit of paper pinned that night in February to the front of Lizzy's nightgown were never given to the public by Mr. Madox Brown who found them. Nor did he publish or even finish the sonnet, wrung from him by the sight of her lying there. In the appendix of this volume will be found a draft of one of a whole Sequence embodying a later experience of the author's. In the margin, scrawled in pencil, are the letters D.G.R. Emotion remembered, in what could never be tranquillity, for the fiery Father of the Pre-Raphaelites!

Gradually, in the process of time, the details of some of these happenings drifted into volumes in which the Faithful strove to justify or condemn their idol's behaviour. I give the names and the publishers of some of these books that enshrine modified versions of sentences that came hot, blurted out in Pre-Raphaelite simplicity and directness, from lips now sealed in death. For, with nearly all the persons concerned in this ancient woe, I have held converse in my degree, except with the chief protagonist, who died before I was born. Her husband I have seen in the street, but his head was muffled up, as it were in a monk's cowl. But I remember well his sister Christina and her broad bosom in dove-coloured silk wreathed in black lace. And his brother William, with his bald head and red lips. I remember Morris' Viking eyes and Mrs. Morris' hair, her ghostly beauty like a blasted tree or a sprig of mistletoe; and Georgy Jones like a little brown bird, and Effie Millais, a handsome Scotch lassie, dressed in her *criarde* crocus gowns. I remember Brown's flowing beard, Hunt's darling snub nose and Browning's guttural voice and Millais' hoarse one, a year before he died. And Mr. Scott's wigs, that he changed monthly to simulate growth, and Theodore Watts with his walrus moustache and gipsy eyes. He never let me see " My Swinburne."

Listening humbly, not putting in my word, so as to get all I could without frightening them by the expression of my almost elfish interest in Pre-Raphaelitism, its errors and its glory, to Mr. Holman Hunt, painting away in my father's studio : to Millais, smoking endless shilling pipes there or walking round and round me in his own to see how I " came " in my Greek dress : to my Corsican governess, home from sitting to Rossetti.

Taken all round, the most fruitful sources of information were talk with and perusal of the diaries and letters of those dear arch-gossips, Mr. and Mrs. Bell Scott, Mr. and Mrs. Virtue ("Virtuous") Tebbs, Mr. and Mrs. George Boyce and Mr. and Mrs. Frederic Stephens. My debt to Mr. and Mrs. Allingham tops all the others. To them I owe most of the details of the domestic life of one who had, alas, but little feeling for it. I have been thrown generous scraps from the store of Messrs. Ricketts and Shannon, Mr. Arthur Waugh, Sir William Rothenstein and Sir Hall Caine, but they had, all the time, memoirs in them, which the public have absorbed by now. So had poor, disappointed Theodore Watts (later Dunton), estopped by the last named, from writing *his* version of Rossetti's life. But he let himself go in the company of my mother and me every Sunday evening for many years.

To Mr. William Rossetti I am deeply indebted for the result of meetings at the house of Mary Robinson in Earl's Terrace and his own in Euston Square (to which he makes flattering reference in his Recollections), showing and lending me sketches and MSS. of which his sister-in-law's escritoire had been full.

And to all these that follow my best thanks.

For John Ruskin, universal godfather to the P.R.B., who sponsored a sister of mine, to his cousin Miss Lucy Richardson. To another distant relation, Mrs. Joan Severn, her husband Arthur and a relation of his, Sir Charles Newton. To Ruskin's pupil, Miss Constance Hilliard, and Miss Grace Allen, daughter of the clever carpenter to the estate (who eventually became Ruskin's publisher and whose mother occupied a position of trust in the household at Herne Hill), and her uncle John Hobbes. And another of Ruskin's valets, the sinister Mr. Crawley. To old Anne for the ghost story of Bowerswell. To my grandfather the Reverend James Raine, Sir George Otto Trevelyan and one of Ruskin's lawyers, Mr. Albert Fleming.

And, of all people, to Sir John Millais, whose verdict on his wife's ex-husband was kind and almost tender.—"A very good fellow!"—as he turned the pages of my birthday book.

To Robert Browning and his sister Sarianna and his son Pen and their friends Monsieur Milsand and Miss Henriette Corkran. This lady published her memoirs, but did not, oddly enough, enliven them with the wonderful stories she told me. To Mrs. Sutherland Orr, her father Doctor Leighton and her brother, the President of the Royal Academy.

To Sir John Swinburne of Capheaton ("Cousin John"), and his second wife, and Sir Hubert and Lady Swinburne for a night in Swinburne's old home.

To the late Mrs. Vane Thomas, who brushed the hair of Pre-Raphaelite ladies, for Morris and life at Kelmscott.

To Mrs. Lockwood Kipling, Lady Poynter, Miss Edith Macdonald and their only brother Harry. To Harry's college friend Wilfred Healey and his second wife Josephine, for Burne-Jones and life in Kensington Square and The Grange.

To Mr. Ford Madox Brown and his wife Emma and his daughter Lucy (Mrs. William Rossetti), his second daughter Catherine (Mrs. Hueffer), and his son Nolly, who died young, and their servant, old Charlotte.

To the Deverell family, and especially to Mrs. Wykeham Deverell, the wife of Mr. Deverell's eldest son and sister-in-law of Walter, Spenser, Margaretta and Maria. She gave me leave to use the letters included in an unpublished memoir by herself, of Walter Deverell, now in the Fitzwilliam Museum at Cambridge.

To Madame Bodichon (Barbara Leigh-Smith), Madame Belloc (Bessie Parkes), Mrs. Alaric Alexander Watts (Anna Mary Howitt) and their maid, Henrietta Blackadder and to Mr. Leigh-Smith (who lives there now), for the life at Scalands Gate and a sight of the room where Rossetti proposed, and to Mrs. Kennedy for letting me go over the Cottage where the engagement was broken off.

To Mrs. Stillman (Marie Spartali) and to the Greek Colony (as we used to call it), staunch patrons of the P.R.B. To the Ionides sisters, Chariclea, Aglaia and Euterpe and, above all, to their brother Luke.

To Mr. H. T. Wells and his sister Augusta; Mr. Briton Riviere; Sir Luke Fildes; Lord De Tabley and Lord Lovelace.

To George Meredith and his friend Edward Clodd.

To Mrs. Richmond Ritchie and her sister-in-law, Pinkie.

To Sir George Donaldson.

To Sir Harry Johnstone.

To Mr. William De Morgan.

To Mr. and Mrs. Joseph Pennell, Mrs. Russell Barrington, Mrs. Felix Moscheles, Mr. George du Maurier, Mrs. Jopling Rowe, Sir John and Lady Simon, Sir Leslie Stephen, Mr. Frederic Leyland, Miss Bell and Miss Heaton.

To my father's *confrères* of the Old Water-Colour Society, Sir John Gilbert, Messrs. Harry Hine, Inchbold, Henry Wallis and Arthur Hughes, and his friends J. McNeil Whistler and John Brett, R.A.

For much local and family history I am indebted to Mr. W. R. Freemantle, of Barbot Hall, Masbro', and Dr. John Stokes, and to Mr. W. G. Wells of Sheffield for an introduction to these gentlemen.

To Mr. S. M. Ellis for all sorts of help.

To Mr. James Laver.

To Mr. Sydney Cockerell.

For permission to use photographs of Chatham Place, to the Librarians, respectively, of the Guildhall and County Hall. To the Rev. E. G. O'Donoghue, author of the standard history of Bridewell, for a visit to the Court Room and much data.

To Dr. G. C. Williamson.

To Mr. Errol Sherson.

To Mr. Lionel Tebbs and Miss Evelyn Tebbs for the use of photographs out of their family album.

To Messrs. Maggs and Messrs. Tregaskis for permission to read letters in their possession.

To Professor Levin Schücking, of Leipzig, for—perhaps—the only adverse criticism of my heroine.

And, above all, to Miss Elizabeth Eleanor Higgins, Mrs. Rossetti's great-niece (who has been good enough to make out and attest her pedigree for me), and to her mother, daughter of Lydia. And to Mrs. George Button, her aunt, who has kindly allowed me to have reproduced the daguerreotype which appears as the frontispiece of this volume, the only likeness I have ever seen done from life.

LIST OF ILLUSTRATIONS

xxix

THE WIFE OF ROSSETTI

PART I

CHAPTER I

I

MODELS! Models! And more Models! was the constant cry of painters in the early 'fifties, and especially of Pre-Raphaelites who did not care, as the Royal Academicians did, to "work from feeling." If young Deverell had not needed a model for his Viola, Elizabeth Eleanor Siddall would not have met Gabriel Rossetti, who was to make her and her red hair famous for ever.

Walter Howell Deverell, who found her for his friend, was a son of the Head Master of the Government School of Design at Somerset House.

She was one of the four beautiful daughters of a cutler and watchmaker in the Borough. Elizabeth Eleanor, named after her mother, a Miss Evans of Hornsey, worked with a milliner in Cranbourn Alley. Another daughter, Lydia, a fine girl, " helped " her maternal aunt Mrs. Day, who kept a tallow-chandler's shop in Pentonville. The youngest, Clara, perhaps the best-looking of all, was too young to go out to work. Annie, the eldest, was already married to a Scotchman and does not come into this story.

Elizabeth Eleanor got up very early every morning, crossed the river and walked to her work at Mrs. Tozer's, in Cranbourn Alley.[1] Her hours were long, for she was not supposed to leave till eight o'clock, after she and the other young ladies had taken the stands out of the window and put the bonnets back into cardboard boxes aligned on the high shelves that ran all round the walls of the workroom behind the shop, where the girls sat and sewed all day. It was small and darkish, even by daylight, lighted only by one window which looked out on a sodden plot of grass where Mrs. Tozer hung her sheets to dry.

[1] A little bit of it is left.

B

Mrs. Tozer's bonnet shop had quite a name and Mrs. Tozer's girls were of the smartest, and the young men found it worth while to line up—say twenty minutes before eight—and help their particular Fair to undress the window. This had been the way before the new street had been made and driven right through the alley. A stroll through the narrow paved passage was a recognised form of amusement for idle young men about town or down from the Universities. The agreed chances of "so many pretty faces to be seen flitting about among the bonnets on a summer's day" made Cranbourn Street—you put yourself in bad odour with the young ladies if you called it Alley —a rake's harvest and field of operations. A hundred years before Walter Deverell discovered Elizabeth Eleanor, His Grace of Kingston was congratulating himself on stealing a pretty milliner thence and taking her down to Thoresby. She went willingly, it was what she was there for; the goods sold by these accessible houris represented but the *décor* of seduction. "A Cranbourn Alley article" was synonymous for something cheap and vulgar. It thereby follows that when Mrs. Walter Ruding Deverell, of Somerset House, wife of the Secretary of the School of Design, let young Walter persuade her to go there for a new bonnet, she had, surely, some other object in view than the furtherance of a son's furtive amour.

2

The Schools of Design, dotted all over the country, had been founded, in the interests of the recent iron, coal and steam expansion, to teach artisans to draw and provide fodder for manufacturers who did not see why they should continue to stamp the patterns designed by foreign artists, on home wares, all British. Three or four Royal Academicians from the great, state-subsidised art centre, in Trafalgar Square, were kind enough to give up their time on certain evenings to assist Messrs. Platt of Leeds, Messrs. Pott of Sheffield and their like, to compete with each other in the mass production of hideous things and flood the country of their birth with indigenous horrors instead of imported ones. "Fictile fabrics" of all kinds; "Rafaelle" ware, ormolu—and gilt made to look like ormolu, chased—and chaste —goblets or decanters presenting nude nymphs whose lower members turned politely to leaves or shells or both—a kind of crinoline *nature*—were turned out by the hundred. Soon work-

2

men were supposed to take a pride in their hateful work; they grew souls and Mr. Ruskin was called in to lecture to them. "You must not follow art *without* pleasure : you must not follow it *for* pleasure ! " And, to please the omnipotent art critic, " adjacent to the red glare of the furnaces," Mr. Platt, it was claimed, permitted " a small section of nature to wear her garment of refreshing green " in the shape of a garden.

But all was not well, money was wasted, good patterns were not available and people began to blame what they called " the plunging blindness of the Administration." There were " continual kick-ups " in the committee at Somerset House, commented on with derisive hoots by the friends of the starving Madox Brown in his rival school at Camden Town. Questions were asked in the House, Royal Commissions appointed; but the thing went on until bustling Mr. Cole, with his horse-sense, came in and smashed it all to fragments, to be made up again in a different pattern of horror, after the Great Exhibition in Hyde Park.

But, while it lasted, it afforded a pleasant home to the Deverells, clever, gay, sprightly and sociably inclined, all of them except the father.

Mr. Ruding Deverell, a native of Bristol, had been Classical Master in an American University, and his eldest son, Walter Howell, had been born in Charlottesville, Virginia. When he was two years old the family returned to England and lived in a small house near Buckingham Gate until the Secretaryship of the School of Design was offered to Mr. Deverell by Lord Granville, connoting a salary of two hundred and fifty a year and rooms in Somerset House overlooking the river.

When the great gates in the Strand were closed the big courtyard in front was " as quiet as the sands of Arabia," [1] and it was supposed to be haunted. Bells rang in the night. Mrs. Deverell, in bed, called to her son to fetch her a glass of water from the kitchen, but before he returned there was a bang on the bedtable and a glassful was handed to her. Young Spenser, a budding mathematician, interested in Bessemer's theory of wave-propelling, had written a manual on the subject and was reading it in bed. After he had folded up the manuscript and put out the candle he distinctly heard someone beside him turning over the pages. . . .

A D'Évrolles had come in with the Conqueror and was in the

[1] So says Crabbe.

3

Roll of Battle Abbey. Broad lands in Somerset still bear the name. Goodall, R.A., who painted Mr. Ruding Deverell, always declared that he was one of the handsomest men he ever saw. Pale, with light yellow hair combed in an upward roll over a high forehead, small eyes, a long straight nose, an expression at once wistful, acute and obstinate. He was tyrannical and unkind. A "determined Atheist," [1] he would not allow his children to go to church with their mother, whom, however, he could not prevent attending Divine Worship.

Mrs. Dorothy Margaretta Deverell, *née* Phillips,[2] in her fifties, her health already mined by worry, her black hair combed smoothly down till it merged in rapids of ringlets under her ears, with black eyebrows finely drawn, had imported the Jewish strain which showed faintly in her eldest son's beautiful face but hardly at all in Wykeham and Spenser or Maria and Margaretta.

Young Walter had not been intended for the Arts. His rich Uncle Travel did not approve of it. He was sent into Scotland to a private tutor and placed, when he was sixteen, in a London solicitor's office. He would have liked to be an actor; the whole family had a bent that way. In James Street they had rented a stable next door and used the stable-boys as scene-shifters and the stable lanterns as footlights. But in Somerset House it was different. Mr. Deverell did not approve of theatricals and once, when they had put on *The Taming of the Shrew* with Walter as Petruchio, Margaretta as Katherine and Miss Clementina Black as Bianca, no one saw them play, for Papa, getting wind of the performance, had the great doors on to the Strand closed so that none of the invited could drive or walk in.

Though Walter wanted to be an actor, he was sent to Carey's, whence he passed into the Academy Schools. Then he was appointed Assistant Master of the School of Design, armed with testimonials from Messrs. Redgrave, Horsley, Dyce and J. R. Herbert.

When he was but eighteen he had a picture accepted and hung. *Reposing after the Ball* was quite in the approved style of Academy "fill-ups" : his next subject had been in the prevailing Germanophile fashion which had set in with the betrothal of the

[1] See William Rossetti.
[2] The Phillipses had originally been bankers in Haverford West; a Phillips of the Queen's Body Guard had been through the Mutiny and, disobeying orders, once saved a position and got thanked for it.

4

WALTER HOWELL DEVERELL
From an oil painting by W. Holman Hunt

Queen. And now he was painting a subject from Shakespeare's *Twelfth Night*,[1] portraying himself as the handsome Duke Orsino—as why should he not? His friend Gabriel Rossetti, devoid of personal vanity, had posed unprotesting, except at the exertion, for the Jester and now Walter wanted a model for Viola.

He was one of the handsomest fellows in London, after the Director. Mr. Dyce was forty; young Deverell only twenty and looking younger, like a page of the Middle Ages, a Cherubino without the vice. His beauty was of the type that could only, it seemed, be described in contradictory adjectives :—" Little Deverell, lovely yet manly, with his effeminate, alluring face." " Not properly to be termed feminine—say troubadourish," was his friend William Rossetti's contribution. " Silky without being effeminate," said Mr. William Bell Scott, one of his father's *confrères*. They were all agreed on his charm, his " manliness mixed with warmth," his exquisite manners, his affectionate nature. . . .

Careless in dress, his collar mostly unbuttoned, often one of his Pre-Raphaelite Brothers, meeting him, would be seen securing it in the middle of the road while he waltzed round and round, like a pony being saddled. Yet women followed him in the street, as they pursue their favourite actors nowadays, racing round turnings, waiting at corners to catch another glimpse of his beautiful face. The wife of Hughes the porter, who sold crayons and sheets of drawing-paper to the students, watched for his goings out and his comings in, but he never gave her so much as a look out of his dark eyes as she stood, wantonly waiting, at the door of the Schools, her hearty pink face and yellow hair framed against the dark arch. She seemed to have no particular work to do, but was always ready to joke with the young " Academinions " (as they were called in the Schools), cracking nuts with her strong white teeth as they passed in and out. Once she flung a whole handful of shells in Gabriel Rossetti's face, who took it in good part since the hussy was handsome.

The women students all went to Gower Street, but Walter did not care for girls : they chased *him*. He had no sweetheart. His mother was his best friend and chosen companion, unexacting, reasonable and kind, willing to go with him and

[1] It was the very picture Scott bought for love of him after his death (from a dealer in Newcastle, where it had drifted) for a song.

purchase an *outré* bonnet that she could never wear, to help him to get hold of a good model.

Gabriel Charles Rossetti, whom he had met at Carey's, was his greatest friend; after him, in estimation and intimacy, came two other youths, William Holman Hunt and John Everett Millais.

They had all three gone up together to the Academy Schools, but Rossetti had left in a pet because, quite soon, Hunt and Millais had got into the Life while they kept him at friezes and bas-reliefs. Anxious to get on quickly he asked his grandfather Polidori, a rich merchant, to pay for lessons from Mr. Brown—always called Kind Brown or Old Brown, though he was only twenty-seven, but already a widower. Young Rossetti admired his work tremendously. Flattered by the youth's appreciation, Brown took him on—rather doubtfully : " We'll see what we can make of him ! "

Brown's " manner " was characteristic of the school to which the lads later gave a name. Although he hadn't enough to eat and time was of dreadful importance to him he would spend hours over a hand or a forearm and make a dress before he painted it, cutting out tabards and fabricating liripipes, spending hours sewing with his own hand *fleurs-de-lis* in calico over a surcoat for the Black Prince. He set his pupil down to paint some old verdigrised bottles stacked in a corner of the studio. Gabriel made them serve as a foreground for a sort of lazy, leering Lilith. The lessons were not a success. Gabriel had left Brown and Clipstone Street after a couple of lessons and set up with Hunt in Cleveland Street. Hunt was only a year older, but he had managed to get into the Life before he left the Academy and he tried to give Gabriel a hint or two. That did not last either. Now Gabriel was working alone in Newman Street, over a " hop-shop," which meant the noise of music and dancing below, so that he could not get a night's rest and went back regularly to share his brother's bed in Charlotte Street.

3

Mrs. Deverell knew all about Gabriel Rossetti's people—had made it her business, since Walter went there so much. They were Italian refugees, living somewhere near Portland Place, the neighbourhood where that kind of person mostly congregated, making a living by teaching, the usual way adopted by people

FORD MADOX BROWN
From a photograph

who have escaped from a country by the skin of their teeth, leaving their earthly goods behind them. There was much sympathy for Italians in England just then. The attempt at revolution last year, the prison stories, Father Gavazzi's and Mazzini's lectures made the study of Italian fashionable. Mr. Uwins, R.A., had had an Italian to teach his sister, and Mr. Swinfen Jervis, M.P., the youngest Rossetti girl for his daughter Agnes. Cavaliere Gabriele Rossetti himself gave lessons at half a guinea an hour. He was by way of being a poet : Mrs. Deverell had once heard him improvise at a party at the Turkish Ambassador's. His wife was three-parts English—her maternal grandmother had been a Pierce. In a word, they were good citizens and quite respectable. Mrs. Deverell had asked Pistrucchi about them. Sir Isaac Goldsmid, who was on the Council of the University College where the father lectured, had interested himself in one of the boys and talked to Mr. Wood of the Excise about him, and she believed he kept the family now, for the father seemed to be going blind. They attended Trinity Church, Marylebone, sitting under Dr. Penfold, with occasional visits to Christ Church, Albany Street. One of the curates, Mr. Burrows, was a great friend of the eldest daughter, Maria. She was not so pretty as the younger one, Christina, but, with a kind of espièglerie about her ugliness, seemed more likely to marry, for the Collinses, Charles and his brother Wilkie, admired her and so did Mr. Street, an architect.

These good people had no access to the Classes except through teaching, but they were, Walter informed her, of noble blood and would have been somebodies in Italy now if all had gone well. He cunningly contrived to spread over this family that he so affected, the aroma of lost causes. The old gouty teacher of languages who took snuff and bit his nails to the quick styled himself " Of Vasto, Ammone," a town or district in the Abruzzi. He maintained that he was of the family of the Counts of Della Guardia, whilom magnates of the place,[1] but, somehow, a later Della Guardia, a blacksmith, had come to be called Rossetti— Red Skin.[2]

---

[1] His brother Joseph was a notary of good repute in Nice and did business for Lady Mary Coke, of Aubrey House, Campden Hill. His son was married to an Englishwoman, a certain Lillas Moses, aunt of the Incumbent of Denton near Darlington, the Reverend John Birkbeck. Thus early did the Rossetti blood invade England.
[2] The same derivation has been given to Ruskin's patronymic.

Though Mrs. Rossetti rose at seven and kept no servant, cleaning down the house, preparing her husband's Italian dishes herself, they saw plenty of company. Counts, Princes, Kings even, together with Red Revolutionaries, drank tea and ate bread-and-butter and teased the squirrel and Maria's cat Zoë. Louis Naundorf, who claimed to be Louis the Seventeenth of France, would be discussing her escape over the Beresina with Mademoiselle de St. Elme, whose lover had been one of Napoleon's marshals. There was a descendant of the Queen of Cyprus, Caterina Cornaro, the subject of a poem of Browning's that Gabriel was illustrating. Present very often was a Babylonian Princess and a man who had married a Queen.

There were to be found, naturally, more Italians in the Casa Rossetti than English, and hardly any French, for Mr. Rossetti hated them. Ida de St. Elme was a Russian really. There was Doctor Cypriani Potter and Doctor Elliotson,[1] who called himself the family doctor but, as he refused to take a fee, was not often called in professionally. Of Italians there was Paganini and Madame Pasta and young William's two distinguished godfathers, Michael Costa and General Carrascosa. There was Aspa, too, a piano-tuner from Broadwood's, Sangiovanni a brigand, Sarti a plaster-cast vendor, Parodi a dancing master, Rolandi a bookseller, Faro a coal-dealer and, among out-and-out revolutionaries, Giuseppe Mazzini and Mr. Panizzi holding a post in the British Museum.[2]

Used to mixed society of this sort young Gabriel's manners were good, almost distinguished. He was polite to everyone and very kind to his mother and sisters. So was Millais to his family. Mrs. Deverell had not heard of Hunt's mother, but he had a sister Emily, who painted too and often procured models for him. They were all nice lads enough, but she would have preferred that her son should consort with his peers, like Robert Leslie and the young Constables, sons of Academicians. Hunt's father was a warehouseman in the City and that of Millais a professional, or semi-professional, flute-player. Frederic Stephens was the son of an official in the Tower. Collinson, who was engaged to Gabriel's pretty sister, was the son of a bookseller in the Midlands, and Tom Woolner, of a letter-sorter in a Suffolk post office, while the two

[1] Dr. John Elliotson, Thackeray's friend, professor of the practice of medicine to the London University in 1831. Hypnotist. The first to use the stethoscope.
[2] A visiting list that was not likely to impress the rather exigent parents of Miss Siddall.

8

WILLIAM MICHAEL ROSSETTI
From a photograph

Tuppers lived with their father, a printer, in South Lambeth. Jacob Bell, who was rich, got his money out of a chemist's shop in Marylebone.

It was not good for her delicate boy to imitate Gabriel, who never went to bed till two or three in the morning or got up till he had to, so kept him up late. They sat up, night after night, in this study or the other, talking, or starting at half-past twelve for a moonlight walk. They would go and wake up the Dormouse, as they called Christina's young man, and drag him half-dressed, half-asleep and protesting, supporting his arms, as far as Putney or Wimbledon. Not to places where they shouldn't go—Mrs. Deverell would say that for them. They were all strictly anti-Bohemian and had forsworn rowdyism. They neither smoked, drank nor swore, as a protest against Bohemia, saturated with tobacco, spirits and oaths. They were too poor to be dissipated as well as too earnest; not one of them had a banking account and Mrs. Deverell or little Mrs. Howitt cashed their cheques for them when they were lucky enough to earn any. They had one dummy between the three, carted about in cabs, looking most indecent, from studio to studio, so that they risked being taken for Wainewrights. They did not spend much money on food: Rossetti, a coarse eater, only wanted enough. When lobsters were cheap, one for supper was a treat. Tea was the great meal,—with slices of bread-and-butter, beer or perhaps sherry-cobbler—at the Collins' in Hanover Terrace or at Millais' in Gower Street, in a magnificent apartment 19 ft. by 20 ft. And there was the Howitts', at Highgate, but that was a long cross-country journey only helped by the omnibus. And Jacob Bell's people gave dances, but sometimes the night fixed for them turned out "intensely sloshy" and their footwear being rather uncertain they did not attend. Or, maybe, the dress-suit was at the pawnbroker's. (As Rossetti said, "Avuncularism tied" one, rather.)

But, as children prefer the dirtiest doll, the mudpie in the road to the rocking-horse in the parlour, the garret at the top of the Rossettis' house was found to be the pleasantest, most suitable place to meet in. There was no carpet and only three, or perhaps four, chairs with bursting seats and one rickety table. Small and frowsty, and, if William persuaded the window to open, ten to one Gabriel would come in and say, out of Poe: "Oh, lady bright, Can it be right? This window open to the night?" and shut it. Once in, out they never came—half a dozen of

9

them packed in behind closed doors. Anyone eavesdropping would hear, on Saturday nights especially, when the Literary Society met, an even murmur of voices, musical, strident, passionate or academic, declaiming from behind it. They would be reading aloud out of their pet poets, or bits they had got by heart. Their memories held in solution all the verse in the world. Ballad refrains, tags of plays, stanzas and lines of poetry from this or that author mixed with the tenor of their daily lives, as little flakes of spume float on the dark surface of a stream or fly in the air overhead, like white cotton grass over the moor in summer. They would go murmuring—did they lose a pencil or notebook—" Oh, what is gone we fancied ours ? Oh, what is lost that never may be told ? " out of Allingham. Or, " What is it that they say and do ? " out of the same author when there was a noise in the kitchen.

When Gabriel gave them

> Dark, deep and cold the current flows
> Unto the sea where no wind blows,
> Seeking the land which no one knows,

by Ebenezer Elliott, a cold air seemed to blow into the room, the way he chanted it. Or some of the eerie felicities of his most recent find, an Irishman from Ballyshannon, whose poems he knew by heart.

> Up the airy mountain,
> Down the rushy glen,
> We daren't go a hunting
> For fear of Little Men.
>
> They stole Little Bridget
> Long years ago.

The journeys of the old king of the fairies

> . . . going up with music
> On cold starry nights
> To sup with the Queen
> Of the cold Northern Lights.

And *For Annie* and *The Haunted Palace* by the American, Poe, or translations from Hugo's *Les Burgraves* :—

> Love on, who cares !
> Who cares, love on !

And some new version, for he made many, from Bürger's *Lenore* :—

> Oh, Mother! Mother! What is Heaven?
> Oh, Mother, what is Hell to me?
> With him, with him is Blessedness
> And without William, Hell to me!

And later, when the maiden gets her impious wish and is riding behind the ghostly horseman, home to her marriage bed

> . . . still, cool and clean,
> Six boards and one across them,

> The dead ride quick . . .
> Darling, dost fear the dead?

it put the rest of them into a cold sweat.

It was not all high-falutin'. Rossetti had a grotesque thing, *Jan Van Hunks*, which William would not let him publish. Johnnie Tupper, who was going in for the law, wrote poems, which William considered "bordered on the ultra-peculiar." But his parodies provided them with one of their best catch-words :—

> And all who paint as Sloshua did
> Shall have their sloshy fingers frozen.

"Mr. Sloshy-Slosh" signified an artist who painted like Sir Joshua or in the way recommended in his lectures to the students. "Gentlemen, if you *have* genius, industry will improve it; if you have none, industry will supply its place." Industry, quotha! Think of that, from a President of the Arts! Oh, those hide-bound dodderers, self-elected members of the great public Art Service of England, swimming complacently, like the crusted carp at Versailles, on their calm unrippled ponds, pompous and omnipotent in the palace of Trafalgar Square, must be pulled down, deposed, deprived of their privileges— eight pictures on the line for sure—in favour of the earnest, patient outsiders who had no less difficulty than they in finding models to paint from and a great deal more in finding places wherein to paint them.

When they were not holding meetings they were wandering about the streets looking for a room advertised To Let, with a North Light that would do for a study—people had not yet taken to Italianising the word.[1] When the boys had found some barrack or other, squalid but possessed of an apartment with a

---

[1] In 1866, there were only four apartments in London built expressly for painting in : Hook's, Frith's, Hodgson's and someone else's.

window at the right angle for the sun, they were jubilant, moving each other in, giving a hand with the furniture so as to dispense with the services of Crocker's van, and making a day of the induction of the lucky lessee.

It was almost as difficult to find models as studios, female models especially, and the wives and sisters of R.A.'s, even, knew the agonies of constraint and the growing stiffness that soon turns into positive pain. Rossetti and his friends commandeered the services of their relations ruthlessly, using them in every capacity except those in which Dummy was available, and *he* generally monopolised her. *The Carpenter's Shop* of Millais is quite a family party and *The Girlhood* includes portraits of nearly all the Rossettis, including Christina. William was of general utility, posing for spare parts, feet, hands, forearms—anything! He had a fine head and sat to Hunt for that of Colonna in *Rienzi*. Gabriel, though restless, had to take his turn : he sat for Rienzi himself and to Brown for *Chaucer* and to Deverell for the Jester in *Twelfth Night*. Millais took him for the guest,[1] with the villainous lip propped against the drinking cup, in *The Marriage Feast of Lorenzo and Isabella*. Brown's wife was his model all the time : he had found her at Stratford when she was sixteen. Friends too ; Hannay, ex-Consul from Barcelona, sat for the head of Valentine in *The Two Gentlemen*, and his brother, the police magistrate, for somebody in another picture. Frederic Stephens, for Ferdinand in *Ariel and the Fairies*, stood from ten in the morning till six at night and had to be supported down from the *estrade* and stayed with brandy before he could go home. Deverell, " beautiful as the morning," sat for the page in *Chaucer* and for Claudio in Hunt's *Isabella visiting her Brother in Prison*, but never to Rossetti, who, working largely from imagination, was more independent of models than the others. They instituted search-parties for models, turning out in groups of twos and threes so as to cover the pavement and not let a likely one slip past them. Rescue of the Fallen, so fashionable just now, they took in their stride, expostulating, pleading. . . . Millais, small-eyed, sandy-haired, but with an ingratiating lisp ; Deverell, extremely good-looking, were generally spokesmen, and led a band each. They lost nobody for want of asking, but their funds were scanty and the willing beauties were seldom of a type that they admired. Gabriel always wanted red hair—which you had, of course, to

[1] He really did not like Rossetti ; " Queer fish ! " he would say.

12

call auburn when you were wheedling them to sit—and you had to be very tactful, praising their faces and making it plain that that was all you wanted, and only for one or two sittings. Sometimes they were haughty, or even fierce : that was better than when they were common. Walter did not dare tell his mother of an incident that befell him and Gabriel and Collinson. Coming out of Marshall's they spied a most lovely girl, beautifully dressed and looking so like a Duchess that they almost feared to ask her. But she had stopped on the way to her carriage and asked pleasantly what they would give her for sitting. And when Deverell explained that they were poor and that the whole figure came expensive, so that they would only ask her to sit for the face, her reply left them in doubt as to whether she was really a Duchess, for she said, if she sat at all, she would sit for quite another portion of her frame if they liked. He had had such a shock that he had not slept for a week and swore that he would never ask a girl to sit again for any part of her.

<h1 style="text-align:center">4</h1>

And they had what boys generally do have, a secret society or two. There was a Mutual Suicide Association and the Literary Evenings. And a very much more important one they had started earlier in the year. It included Gabriel Charles Rossetti, William Holman Hunt and John Everett Millais (the founders), plus Thomas Woolner, Frederic Stephens (a nominee of Hunt's), James Collinson (Gabriel's fellow-student in the R.A. Schools) and William Michael Rossetti. Brown had been invited but he had declined. Too old ! They had let in Collinson [1] because he was engaged to Gabriel's sister Christina, and William Rossetti, who wasn't an artist, because he was methodical, and could act as secretary. It was to be nothing less than a revolution in art.

Something really had to be done about the derelict state of painting in this country, betrayed by George III, who had surrendered the common heritage of all into the hands of a few interested old dodderers and given them a palace to house their daubs in. Untrammelled and uncriticised, they used their self-appointed privilege to hound a few great artists to madness and death and, if they survived this treatment, to keep their work off

[1] " Oh, Collinson was nothing ! He had about as much in him as that old hen ! " So Hunt in 1903, to my mother, pointing to such an object in the garden.

the walls,[1] or if they hung them, prevent them from being seen, keeping all the good places for themselves.

To strengthen their case against the Academy the boys would adduce the sneers of the old mad poet William Blake; Hazlitt's bitter epigrams, " The marring of artistic effect is the making of the Academy," and criticisms of the great past-President's " hasty, washy, indeterminate manner of painting, neglectful alike of severe form and accurate detail " (this was a quotation from one of the unpublished and uncompleted manifestos of the society) " and lavish of unctuous vehicles. . . ." This was why they called him " Sloshua," and all R.A.'s and their wives by the generic names of " Mr. and Mrs. Sloshy-Slosh." All painters on the wrong tack—" excessive in all that is low and to the public taste." The things of Mr. Armitage, the religious fellow, were exactly like the picture bricks that their little sisters played with, just portraits of Mrs. Sloshy-Slosh, whom Mr. Armitage had taken, Gabriel said, out of a harem and who always dressed like it, in Eastern veils and yashmaks. And what of Mr. Constable, who prepared his landscapes every year, regularly going down to Bergholt and slashing a bough of a tree, in a foreground of a view he meant to paint next year, to ensure its being a nice brown when he wanted it? And Mr. Etty, the " voluptuous painter " who was called the English Titian! Walter's mother protested. Who could help liking Mr. Maclise, such a hard worker, and Mr. Dyce, so clever and handsome, and Mr. Horsley, whom you never would have taken for an artist unless you were told, for he looked more like a lawyer? Mrs. Deverell never could resist the President's Irish voice and Mr. Ward's imitations. She liked Mr. Stanfield, so burly and sincere, and the two Chalons, so gentle and inoffensive, who loved each other so dearly that they never even cared to marry, and dear old Sir William Boxall, and Mr. Uwins, with his blue eyes and feathered eyebrows, so tactful, and who never made mischief, which was awfully convenient in a collection of men associated together in the choice and collection of the Nation's Art. Talking as if it were a club!

[1] The P.R.B. should be living at this hour! What would Hunt, Rossetti and Millais say, nowadays, when a self-appointed Hanging Committee judges pictures, that have probably taken a man at least a year to paint, at the rate of two hundred an hour, " in a sun-flooded room," spending actually three seconds or so on " each gilt frame," more important, the phraseology of the *Daily Telegraph* would seem to imply, than the picture and certainly simpler of adjudication? But, in this Year of Grace 1932, no artistic effort has been " given more than three or four seconds." See *Daily Telegraph*, April 2nd.

They had no business to be there at all, looking like lawyers and painting like Poor Poll, and keeping better men out. It was no use, Gaza must fall and a David seemed to have been found in Ruskin, but, meantime, men must live . . . and to live by art and prosper was well-nigh impossible unless you were a member of the abominable junta. The only thing to do was to start a thing of one's own.

5

One evening in Gower Street, in August, Gabriel had got hold of a volume of engravings belonging to Mr. Millais who bought books : *Pitture a Fresco del Camposanto di Pisa designata da Guiseppe Rossi de incise del Professori Cav. G. Lasinio Figlio. Firenze MDCCCXXXII*, rather good reproductions of some wonderful frescoes that were rotting off the walls of the Campo Santo. There were only one or two that were any good ; the rest were just horrible, devils and tortured souls—sinners with their entrails outside, neatly twisted into collars and girdles, scorpions flying through the air, holding in their claws babies that had died unbaptised, the devil sitting below in the caves of Hell, damn well pleased. One plate, at least, was worth looking at—*The Triumph of Death*. Knights and ladies on horseback, falcon on wrist, chattering, linking along, leaning over each other's saddle-bows, out on a jolly hawking expedition as people did when times were fairly quiet and it was safe to go unarmed any distance outside the town. And suddenly holding their noses, while the horses paw and prod the ground and refuse to go on, for right in front of them, under their feet almost, there are three open stone coffins reposing among the flowers, holding the bodies of Kings that have died long ago, all in an advanced state of decomposition.

One peg is as good as another on which to hang up the coat, the oriflamme of revolution. They had to find a phrase to place the Movement, give it a name and attract the attention of the public and puzzle the Philistines. They would go back to the fourteenth century, the age of innocence in Art, now grown so sophisticated and overlaid with all sorts of bunkum. It was a good thing for a new Society to be advertised as reverting to an earlier state of things, to a time when people were pious and reverent, modestly painting what they saw and all they saw, as well as they could. Not presuming to select, giving all the

15

tourelles of a castle, the machicolations in the walls and the number of steps up to the bastions and, outside, rendering faithfully the hind in the brake and the steer in the meadow and the eyes of the daisies in the grass and the embroidery in the trains of the maids that brushed them, as they walked abroad in the Spring.

" I vote we call ourselves the Pre-Raphaelite Brethren," said Rossetti. Painting as artists did before old Raphael, who was a very bad painter really; all his ideas swamped in manipulation till he came to be a sort of Dumas—fashionable—and got so many orders that he had to have assistants, so that all sorts of stupid conventions grew up. . . .

6

Mrs. Deverell had heard about this Pre-Raphaelite business from other quarters. Her eldest son Wykeham had been to tea with the mother of Freddy Stephens in The Tower, and had never been so surprised in his life as when he was given his tea in a cup without a handle. And Mr. Scott told her husband that, when young William was staying with him in St. Thomas' Street, Mrs. Scott had commented on the absence of the word *Esquire* on the letters he got there, replaced by the initials *P.R.B.*, and asked him what that signified? Oh—shyly—the name of a club that his brother and some friends had planned out . . . they wanted to start a new line . . . Art was getting so stale in England !

Just a bit of bravado—a boy's cap flung over a church steeple— and Mr. Scott wasn't so sure that it wouldn't stay on, either !

There was certainly something in that elder brother of Bill's, who had written to tell him how much he admired *Rosabell*. Mr. Scott had been so struck with the three poems of his which accompanied the letter that, when he was in town last Christmas, he had made a point of getting hold of the address of the house where the poet lived with a man called Hunt, to see what he was doing. The other man was a painter too. The drawing master, tapping with a big stick he always carried, up the stairs of a house in Cleveland Street, had come to a room on the second floor, bare, with maroon walls and one window—not even a north light. Two young men were sitting as far as they possibly could get from each other in the small room, painting away in this newly invented style of theirs—absurdly photographic—

16

WILLIAM BELL SCOTT
From a photograph

neglecting no detail. There was a fly crawling on a leaf near the body of Rienzi in Hunt's picture and Rossetti was putting in the common watering-pot used by St. Joachim and the pattern of the Virgin's piece of embroidery. Mr. Scott recognised the portrait of a shy girl he had just seen in Charlotte Street. Obviously, Hunt could paint and Rossetti could not. Yet he was more struck with his picture than with that of the other. Good, solid, journeyman's work, Hunt's : Rossetti's a mixture of hopeless dilettantism and positive genius.

Later Scott saw the work of the other members of the band. The teacher in him saw at once that young Millais had *nothing* to learn in the way of technique; it was obvious that his essay in Pre-Raphaelitism was just a lark to show he could do anything he liked. Hunt knew his job and would get there; Millais was *already* there. Rossetti, perhaps, would *never* get there, though the best of the three. And Millais would leave the two tyros as soon as he tired of playing tricks with painting ! For a little handful of unaccredited youths would never be able to stand against the Royal Academy. The Academicians were perfectly aware of that and were watching the antics of Millais, their crack student, with amusement—betting on his integrity, so to speak ! He was far too sensible to back any but a winning horse. Of the Brethren, the two business men, Millais and Rossetti, well knew the power of the dealer and the critic ; either of these, properly handled, can make an artist's fortune.

William could string sentences together and Gabriel managed to get him on the staff of the *Spectator*, pledged not to fling too much abuse at the Academy (for no journal could afford to be at loggerheads with the great painted money-box into which the Nation put so many shillings every year). Also young Walter Deverell, of " great but impatient ability," was a member of the enemy's camp and must be got into the confraternity somehow. Gabriel believed in his genius, but Hunt, who never stuck at the naïve explicit, said he was no good.

They were to proclaim their principles in every way they could, force their women to dress like the ladies in the pictures of the Primitives, design and have made, proper furniture—run a shop, maybe—and all pledge themselves to patronise no other. They would take a house and live all together, with the letters P.R.B. on the bell, on the coffee-pot and on every surface where there was room. Rossetti, when he had toothache, used up all the notepaper in the house designing the P.R.B. monogram.

For the rest of his working day or, at any rate, until the death of Lizzy, this artist chose to see Life through a stained-glass window, without *repoussé*, without relief, as it were with the thin hem of iron enclosing the colour, bordering the outlines of the figures. He had certainly acquired a strong bias for the mediæval convention in the course of his early reading of German, Italian and French romances, and the niggling, painstaking habit he got obviously from Madox Brown, his first master. Brown was the true Founder[1] of the Pre-Raphaelite Cult, or Band. Brown's worst enemy, Ruskin, who hated mediævalism, knew it and always hated both Brown and the younger man, Morris, who encouraged his " pet " protégé in that heresy.

[1] In 1906 they were still fighting about who had been the Founder of the little dead society, and Holman Hunt and Stephens quarrelled *à la mort* about it.

CHAPTER II

I

IF it had not been for an Irish poet called William Allingham the chances were that Rossetti would never have met his Stunner and best model.

Allingham was an Officer of Customs in Donegal; his job, signing ships' papers, paying off seamen, visiting lonely stations on the coast and noting wrecks off the wild headlands. In the exercise of his duties he would be tramping over miles of tricksy rabbit warren and fields patterned with monoliths, gnome-like surface rocks, and stones that " walked " at night and, in his ears, " The Sound "—the noise, day and night, of the great waterfall at Ballyshannon—" *Time itself* made audible "— So he gave Rossetti one of his best lines.

For Literature possessed him too. He would pace, after work, along the village street, concentrated, though seeming not to attend, on the shy girls at cottage doors, singing ballads which he would take down, add to and finish or, if they were improper, refine. He would save up his pocket-money so as to be able to go over to England for a month or two of frenzied life, armed with introductions from publishers to Leigh Hunt, and Tennyson, and Thackeray, and to a certain clerk in the British Museum who yielded him the introduction of his life. C. K. Dighton Patmore, who liked his verses but did not like him, handed him over to Rossetti, who liked him tremendously and especially as a poet. So did Gabriel's Lizzy. She always sent him her love and Gabriel always forgot to give it in his letters. Not that Gabriel was jealous, though Allingham was well-built, had a thoughtful brow, crisp curly hair and the dark blue-grey eyes that go to make up what is known as the Celtic glamour, and a lovely voice with a *soupçon* of brogue. He was the best of listeners and became at once a favourite member of the circle, concerned equally with them in the great Publisher, Editor and Art-Critic Chase, those shy, cantankerous birds to be caught and caged by aspirants for literary and artistic honours.

He had been appointed Sub-controller, with a salary of a hundred and twenty pounds a year, in his own native town. He was to have a holiday first. The cholera in London had frightened him : he came over later in the year, put up at The Norfolk and went out to present his letters of introduction, keeping the Rossettis for the last.

First to Patmore, in his neat little house by the railway bridge in Camden Town. Patmore took him for a walk to Highgate Cemetery and showed him the Catacombs, exciting everybody just now. The deep, circular basin, dark at noon-day, with the private mausoleums ranged round, each with its tall door, strong as if to ward off an untimely rising of the dead and contesting of wills, made the poet think of " the grand family funerals," in a book he had just bought off a stall by Edgar Allan Poe, and that

> . . . sepulchre, remote, alone
> Against whose portals she had thrown
> In childhood, many an idle stone. . . .
>
> Some tomb, from out whose sounding door
> She ne'er shall force an echo more.

There was a picture—the little child playing at the side of its destined grave, all unwitting ! Allingham fancied he could hear, as he stood in the circular alley below the level of the terrace, queer noises :—" The echo," Patmore said. Ah no, " *it was the dead that groaned within.*" He would not have missed this new sight of London for anything, but he was glad to come out of the circle to the world above—of the dead too, but properly buried under kind annealing earth. There were, Patmore said, any amount of Rossetti's relations lying there— mostly on the mother's side—Polidoris. And if there was time he wanted to take Allingham to a place close to the western wall of the cemetery which people did not fancy for their Beloveds, cheaper, neglected, overgrown and damp at all times. It was supposed to be haunted—some idea of its being reserved for suicides. There was an aspen, thin, forlorn. . . . But the hour was not born when one of these men would attend, hat in hand, at a distance, to see a Rossetti laid lonely to her fiercely snatched-at rest. They just stuck to the broad gravel walk bordered by " gay tombs," all scraped and whitened, shaded by

20

WILLIAM ALLINGHAM
From a photograph

shrubs, pruned so that they need not hide the " In Memorys "
and " Requiescats " of decent, cared-for obsequies.

2

Later Mr. Allingham found Mr. Carlyle at home, eager to
talk of the Brotherhood, which he had heard about from
Mazzini. Carlyle " liked their sincerity." [1] A great concession
from him !

And then to Newman Street, the plum of the day. There
they all were, except Millais and young Deverell, in Rossetti's
new study over the " Hop-Shop." [2]

On the easel a picture, cold and pure : white walls, white
sheets, white maiden in a hard, stone-like bed without any
bedclothes—Mary Virgin would have left them off " because
Bethlehem was such a hot place "—shyly squeezing herself
against the wall, glaring up at the Angel. The treatment was
so refined that Christina had been willing to sit for the female
figure.

Old Gabriel looked just the same, like a changeling, born
old, and those wonderful eyes, and between them " the bar of
Michel Angelo," the ridge or wrinkle that is one of the signs of
genius. The one pockmark on his cheek was more obvious—
he had had smallpox in youth. His voice was softer than ever,
with more authority to it. . . . William was there, with his red
lips and the big anchor-seal dangling from his fob that he had
not lost (he never lost anything), as nearly as possible bald and
going in for a wig. Then, as always, mild and ancillary, though
he talked much louder than Gabriel.

There was the dear old Maniac with his golden beard grown
and his violet eyes deeper and his button-nose that was too
small even to be *retroussé*, his air of a child born into a world he
didn't understand, with stories to tell that he could never
conveniently bring to an end. He was talking now of the
P.R.B. and how *his* " initiatory programme " had called forth
Gabriel's " amplification of the idea " ; and Gabriel, so sure of
his own dominance, was listening without contradicting him.

[1] He had been told that they copied the thing as it was or invented it as they
supposed it might have been—" Some sense in that ! "

[2] The landlord had asked them thirty pun' a year for it, but clever Gabriel
had managed to beat him down to twenty-eight, because of the noise of the
dancing below.

21

"Holy Hunt," a really good if rather dull man, Allingham thought, prodigiously honest and straightforward. He had not joined Rossetti in this studio but, perhaps a little resenting the latter's kingship, had stayed in Bayswater with Collinson, who refused to use the Initials or entertain in his turn. He never saw the fun of anything and was doubly disconsolate just now because he had got religion and Miss Rossetti had jilted him. Woolner was there, ginger-haired and short-nosed, *not* keeping his humble family dark, for he was *not* ashamed of it.

Stephens, Millais and Deverell were out hunting for models in Tottenham Court Road, so there was plenty of room. Gabriel had some new "bits" to show—but they were not seats. Allingham was given the only good one in the place. The host lounged in a torn and frayed basket-chair into which, with his wide hips, he fitted so exactly that it seemed to have become part of him. The others squatted about wherever they could find an unencumbered though dusty spot and began to read aloud to each other. Gabriel politely began with Mr. Allingham's latest, *The Maids of Elfin Mere* (which Gabriel was going to illustrate), about the three weird maidens, Nixes or Loreleis, "like three white lilies, calm and clear," who came up out of the mere into the pastor's cottage and began to sing "to a pulsing cadence" till it struck eleven and they departed as they came. The pastor's son, to keep them, one night put the clock back; they missed their hour and, without saying one word, left the room "like three doves on snowy plume." And next day the people heard cryings on the shore and saw on the water three bloodstains spread out and fade and dwindle. . . .

And *The Dream* :—

> I heard the dogs howl in the moonlight night
> And I went to the window to see the sight.
>
> All the dead that I ever knew
>   Going by one and two by two,
> Born in the moonlight of the lane
>   And quenched in the heavy shadow again.
>
> And one moving ridge they made
>   Across the moonstream from shade to shade.

And then he read the poem *Rosabell*, which had made him and Mr. Scott acquainted, and then Sir Henry Taylor's *Hesterna Rosa*, of which he was doing a water-colour :—

> Quoth tongue of neither maid nor wife
>   To heart of neither wife nor maid,
> " Lead we not here a jolly life
>   Between the sun and the shade ? " . . .
>
> " Thou wag'st, but I am sore with strife
>   And feel like flowers that fade."

After that they began on *bouts rimés*. Rossetti gave the rhymes : *scorn, forlorn, corn, morn ; alone, own* and *sown*. His, of course, was the best :—

> She bowed her head among them all, as one
>   By one they rose and went.   A little scorn
> She showed, a very little, more forlorn
>   She seemed because of that. . . .
>
>   . . . the free-hearted corn
> Kissed by the hot air freely all the morn
>   Is better than the weed which has its own
> Foul glut in secret. . . .

Just chance rhymes, but see how the innocent youths turned them at once into line with their crusade against London's nightly pandemonium of harlotry !   And, while the verses were being read out, handsome Deverell and handsome Millais came in—disappointed ; they had had no luck that night, had saved none nor picked up a single model. . . .

The moan of Scott's *Rosabell*, the way Gabriel gave it, remained with Allingham :—

> I am forsaken, not a wheel
>   Rings on the street's hard stones !
> .   .   .   .
> Down the wet pavement gleam the lamps . . .
> .   .   .   .
> And every lamp on every street
>   Lights *their* wet feet down to death,

as he crept down the wooden staircase and turned out into the streets ; he knew that the two handsomest young fellows in London and, he'd wager, the most innocent, had been patrolling all the evening, accosting and probably being accosted.   For respectable women did not go out at night unattended or, if obliged, took care not to be spoken to.   He was not afraid of Millais, mad on his profession, with the great safe alternative, love of sport.   Or even for little Deverell, who was proof against " light loves in the portal " and the coarse solicitations of the porter's wife, and managed to evade the subtler wiles of women of his own class. Or for Hunt, who had revealed religion like a violet ray behind the whole of his lovely life.

But for Gabriel——

3

On his way to Surrey Street Allingham crossed the Haymarket, where the " Jennys " were supposed to parade " on market nights in the rain and wet." The hay had been cleared away many years before; but the young poet saw plenty of " improper persons brilliantly walking, under a mild, muffled moon " and, before he got back to his hotel, had composed the poem to the tags given by William (*glare, despair, while* and *smile*) which he had failed to accomplish a while ago in Rossetti's rooms. . . . Not bad !

> Along the street in the midnight glare
> The sinners crowd in gay despair,
> Soft women who retain awhile
> Their heavenly form and tender smile,
> When all within has sunk to wreck,
> *Awhile, awhile, a little while !*

The night after, he went to the ballet and, falling in love with a *coryphée*, followed her home from the stage door as far as her garden gate, but no further. That night he could not sleep. Bad thoughts ! He suppressed them and his fancy for Miss Fowlinski, after a bouquet or two which Gabriel, romantic, delivered for him in St. John's Wood—but he went on falling in love during the brief space of his stay in London. There was a girl in Cranbourn Alley, nay, there were two— Jeannet—he never knew her surname—and a handsome, haughty creature called Ellen Britten. He had come across them one day when he went to the Panorama, because it was of Killarney, and then for a look round the shops—something for the girls at home. . . . Jeannet and Ellen were in the biggest and most important shop—all sold pretty much the same class of thing. After that he took to hanging about in the passage to watch the graceful shapes flitting about under the sullen glare of the gas, turned low—for you don't need to see much just to put the things away. He made their acquaintance and was told that he might come along of an evening and help ; Mrs. Tozer's young ladies might make what hay they liked so long as it was not made among the millinery. The bandboxes into which the bonnets were put to rest for twelve hours must be properly filled with softest tissue-paper and laid on high shelves until morning. The gentle susurration of whispers, the soft crushing of the thin crumpled sheets that made beds for the bonnets was an agreeable and novel sensation for one fresh from the wilds of Donegal, where nobody puts hats away because nobody covers their head at all. Jeannet said he might call on a Sunday at her home in Waterloo Road, where she lived with Miss Britten. They went part of the way home with a Miss Siddall who also lived over the water. She was timid and afraid of being spoken to.

Allingham did not admire Miss Siddall except for her complexion. Gentle, with the manners of a lady, she did not say much—probably had very little to say, always seemed in a dream. He preferred the lively French style of Jeannet and, one Sunday, he took a penny ride over the river, rang the little tinkly bell of her house and waited. Jeannet came to the door, showed her eyes and the tip of her nose and explained that she could not let him in " for ladies were sitting without their dresses for the heat " and, besides, Miss Britten was out. After that she was always out and he abandoned her for another charmer at Mrs. Jarvis' in Ryder Court, same street. In the end he dropped both, but he just remembered " Miss Sid," as the girls called her, because of her rather stuck-up manner. And Deverell, next night, bemoaning his failure to find a model for his Viola, someone pretty who was thin enough to look nice in boy's clothes, heard from Allingham that there was a Stunner who would just do for him if he could get her to sit.

4

Next day, after tea, they started for the Alley, the slow-moving, stolidly dreaming, poet and the eager stripling intent on the picture that was to admit him to the Brotherhood. Past the church with its wide churchyard, through Dirty Lane and Green Street into Leicester Square and the domed building in bastard Byzantine, where they had lectures every hour, past the house that Hogarth had lived in, half of which Monsieur Jacquière was running as an up-to-date hotel and restaurant, past an anatomical machinist's, an iron-founder's, a builder's, a surgeon's, a seal engraver's and a Lending Library and new offices, till they came to the Hôtel de Provence, that the wonderful French cooking at the Sablonière was ousting in public favour. . . . Allingham remembered it all by the light of what happened afterwards.

In Cranbourn Alley, though it was dark, the blinds were not down, for it was a pretty sight and enticing for the passers-by to see the little milliners going about inside with one eye on Mrs. Tozer and the other cocked over their shoulders on the delights of outside and the eager faces against the pane. Then Allingham pointed out the Stunner they had come to see, standing under a naked, noisome gas-jet, reaching up to a high shelf against the wall. The light seemed to be shining through each particular hair [1] on her head, so soft and loose it was in arrangement as it were the wings of an oriole, framing a face that, when she turned it towards the window, was the very face for Viola or any beauty of old story. . . .

Allingham offered to take Deverell in and introduce him to the damsel—it was what he had come for—but Walter shied. She looked such a lady . . . and he had vowed that never again would he ask any woman to sit after the catastrophe outside Marshall's. He would not care to have Mrs. Tozer and her young ladies think he had come to take her out for a walk, like all the other young men. The end of it was, he said he might perhaps get his mother to come and choose a bonnet— ten bonnets—here to-morrow and get into conversation with her. . . .

Allingham did not think that the young lady, though more modest-looking than most, would need much persuasion. And that opulent chevelure would be a difficulty for Viola : she would have to stow it away somewhere, somehow, under a tarbosch, which she might object to doing. . . .

Hair and all she would just have suited Rossetti; but for some reason or other William Allingham did not want her to be put into stock, not just at present.

In the square they arranged a programme. Walter would bring his mother next day to buy a bonnet and persuade the girl to sit, and he must promise to keep her to himself—at any rate for the run of Viola.

[1] Golden hair has always been potent in its appeal to all. Ladies, " *belle et blonde et coloriées*," have always used it as an amatory weapon. Sarah Marlborough, to anger her husband, cut off hers he so admired, laid it along a chair in an ante-room where he must see it and waited, trembling. There was no reconciliation : the great general came, said nothing and was gone. But after his death she found the lock of hair wrapped up among his best possessions.

ELIZABETH ELEANOR SIDDALL, 1855
From a drawing by D. G. Rossetti

"Yet, Tragedy would creep in." Allingham, the seer,[1] said afterwards that, as he and Deverell walked away southwards again, passing between the Places of the Beginning and the End—Mrs. Tozer's shop and the Sablonière Hotel—he was possessed for one moment of the knowledge of all that his stricken friend, lying on the burnt, brown grass in Lincoln's Inn Fields, told him one day thirteen years later. He went home to his hotel and wrote *The Cold Wedding.*

> White favours rest
> On every breast!
> And yet, methinks, we seem not gay.
> The church is cold,
> The priest is old—
> And who will give the Bride away?
>
> The Bride in white
> Is clad aright
> Within her carriage closely hid.
>
> (*The wedding bells, how slow they swing!*)
>
> A match most fair
> This silent pair
> Now to each other given for ever.
> .   .   .   .   .   .
> Now, delver, stand
> With spade in hand,
> All mutely to discharge thy trust;
> .   .   .   .   .   .
> Ere she was born
> That vow was sworn;
> And we must lose into the ground
> Her face we knew:

For the bridegroom, in Allingham's poem, was Death.

[1] Allingham, on his death-bed, Nov. 18, 1889, "I am seeing things that you know nothing of."

CHAPTER III

I

A FEW days later the beautiful red-haired girl passed under the archway in the Strand, where another fair woman, whose hair was auburn and who knew—how do these sort of people get to know?—that this was Mr. Walter's new model, stood arms akimbo, looked her up and down and jeered at the goldilocks that one of the students—the one she disliked—was going to make the fashion.

Mrs. Tozer had been easily squared, but Walter's mother had had to go all the way down to Kent Road to ask Mrs. Siddall's permission for her daughter to sit. She had done this partly to please Walter and partly out of curiosity to see where "Miss Sid" got her style from, for one had always heard that the lowest of the low and the vilest of the vile congregated in that part of the world on the other side of the river! Feeling that she could negotiate this sort of thing better alone, she went in her hired brougham across the bridge, past the Elephant, bidding her man drive quickly as far as the triple corner of Kent Street, New Kent Road and Bermondsey Road and then go slowly on watching the numbers. She had never been on this side of the river in her life though she had heard Kennington and Newington spoken of as "pretty places," and, indeed, after they had passed the Bricklayer's Arms the road widened and became half rural, with residential houses interspersed with shops on either side and behind them, on the east, nothing much but tanneries and rope-walks and market gardens stretching, she supposed, all the way to the river.

Number Eight Kent Place was by the side of Searle's,[1] and opposite a fine building which her coachman informed her was the Asylum for Deaf and Blind Children. The door they wanted was in Jane Place, and there was a little pocket-hand-kerchief of a garden in front.

[1] A furniture dealer.

28

The mother, presumably, who opened the door with the air of a duchess, while effacing herself against the wall like a servant to let her visitor pass in, was handsome, with the same coloured hair as her daughter but of a more refined shade—pale, pale gold. Her manner was perfect, a trifle too haughty, perhaps, but refined, giving you nothing to take hold of. She led the way to the parlour and did not wipe a chair for her visitor; there was no need; everything was spotlessly clean though the room was small and dark. The fiddle in the corner which caught Mrs. Deverell's eye and seemed a good thing to begin on, belonged, Mrs. Siddall said, to her husband, who was in his shop a little further up the road, where he exercised the profession of an optician and cutler. A handsome, weak-looking boy slipped out of the room as she came in and was told severely to go and see if his father didn't need him. A handsome bold-eyed girl, almost a child, was introduced as "my daughter Clara—or Kate"—some name like that, Mrs. Deverell didn't remember, for with her raven locks she would be no use to Walter, mad, like Rossetti, just now on red hair.

She quite believed what her son had told her and what Mrs. Tozer had implied, that Miss Siddall was of good class though her people had come down in the world—through no fault of their own. The little sitting-room had an air of proud, not wanton, destitution, the furniture,—quite good, some of it—had the sharp clear angles that constant polishing will give, and off the round table in the middle, with a red morocco leather book stamped with some sort of crest,[1] lying on it, she would have eaten her dinner without a qualm. She tried to make out this crest and the names on the framed samplers hanging on each side of the old, dark, oil-painting, of a gentleman. The fiddle in the corner—yes, Mr. Siddall was fond of music. It was his hobby now and had been his work. They had not always lived in this part—oh no! There was a place called Hope, not far from Sheffield, where the family had owned property since the seventeenth century. They said, locally, that until the old family came back to Hope Hall, ill-luck would pursue anyone else that lived there. And so it had. But her husband had come to London on purpose to see to his rights and had afforded ever so many lawyers' fees so that he might in the end come to his own.

[1] Was it Per Bend Vert and Gules, an Eagle displayed? See Lysons' *Britannica*.

It sounded as if the father was ruining himself and his family with litigation. Mrs. Deverell, in no hurry and anxious to help Walter as much as she could, drew her story out of this proud, retiring woman by degrees. How she was Welsh, a Miss Evans, how Charles had met her soon after he came to London and married her in Hornsey—where she had been staying—five weeks from the date of their meeting, and taken her to live in the house higher up the road where the business was now carried on. Her husband was an optician, his father had been a cutler, his grandfather a scissors-maker. Nice distinctions to which Mrs. Deverell listened patiently with her object in view.

Number Five had a nice garden up to the tan-yard and a view of the masts at Wapping. All her children—she had had seven—except Annie, the eldest, had been born there. Her husband was sorry to leave Sheffield and Queen Street Independent Chapel where he was Choir Master, but when he came to live in the Euston Road he played the organ in the Chapel there, and they had been very glad of him. He was fond of poetry and read aloud in the evenings while they sewed and the mother played the violin. "Our Liz" was a great reader too. She had begun to write poetry when she was eleven and was always scribbling when she came home from the shop, sitting up in her bedroom in the cold. Mrs. Deverell asked, didn't she have a fire? Her mother said Yes she could have had one but they didn't want to encourage her to sit up there alone.

Mrs. Siddall was hard—hard as nails and sharp as the cutlery she lived by; but she allowed herself to be wheedled by Mrs. Deverell's motherly address and position as wife of a Government Official and made no difficulty about letting her daughter sit, so long as Mrs. Tozer, who had been very good to "Liz," was willing to spare her. A relation of hers, Mrs. Hill of St. Paul's Terrace, Pancras—she had not seen much of her since she left off living in the Euston Road—had a daughter, Emma, who was sitting to a painter—perhaps Mrs. Deverell knew him—for everything he did, and this Mr. Brown was educating her to make her his equal, and then he would marry her. Mrs. Deverell thought she *had* heard her son mention the name. Emma Matilda had the same coloured hair as Liz only rather darker, corn-coloured. . . . Liz would sit to Mrs. Deverell's son with pleasure.

There was, at present, no talk of payment. Mrs. Deverell

did not touch on it. Walter must settle that. A little present, perhaps, when the picture was finished?

The compact with Allingham was faithfully observed— Gabriel Rossetti never saw Elizabeth Siddall until Walter Deverell and he set up together in Red Lion Square. None of the Brethren did, except Woolner and Stephens, who came to Somerset House to interview Hughes the porter about some copies of *The Germ* that he had undertaken to get off, together with the paper and pencils he supplied to the students. Stephens did not think Walter's model worth mentioning, nor Woolner the sculptor, to whom her colouring did not appeal. She disliked both of them and came to hate Woolner.

2

The Deverells moved to Kew, Heathfield House,[1] with a ceiling by Verrio, or Vanloo or somebody. Walter kept his under-mastership at the Schools and went backwards and forwards into town every day. Without his father's knowledge he had rigged up a makeshift studio in a disused coach-house at the bottom of the garden, with a gate giving on to the Mortlake Road. There was no provision for heating and the silly little stove he put in was always going out. When it rained the water came in through the roof and had to be caught in pails; but his new model never complained when a great drip came on her head, and sat for hours without asking for a rest. As painters will, he forgot to remind her. He did not notice that now and then she took drops for a little cough she had. Because of the family tyrant, she came and went by the back gate in Mortlake Road, without meeting or disturbing anyone. When they knew she was there, one of the Deverell girls, " Gret " or Maria, would make a merit of " sending the model her tea on a tray," which generally arrived cold. But their mother, not very well herself, would now and again put on her goloshes and go down the path to the end of the garden and watch the model as she sat, and even read aloud to her if Walter did not mind it.

" Miss Sid," as they came to call her, looked older than she said she was. More handsome than pretty, tall without being weedy, well-formed, with big white arms and neck almost too

---

[1] Now Adam House, near the Green, on the high-road to Richmond.

columnar. Her eyes were blue, the colour of agate, egg-shaped, rather Eastern, pale and unsparkling, like the pools left by the tide on the shore of a yellow beach that but languidly reflect the blue of the sky over them, and prominent, so that she could not have worn a veil without fretting the eyelids. She had no eyebrows to speak of. Her upper lip was short and there was a cleft in the lower one. In repose the face seemed full of character, not all of it good, bearing at times an expression described by Mrs. Deverell, who ordinarily never used the word, as sensual and at the same time starved—a saint's mouth or a sinner's? . . .

The matron, who had buried a daughter, considered Miss Siddall's vivid colouring a bad sign and said a girl like that ought never to have been put to Mrs. Tozer's. Those places were regular breeding-grounds of consumption. She would not be surprised if the mischief had begun already. No, Miss Siddall must not think of going on with that job. As a second shop-hand she had been getting twenty-four pounds a year, exclusive of board and lodging. Her friend Jeannet got nearly double, but she had served her full apprenticeship. And indeed and indeed the hours were terribly long—six in the morning till eight at night : sometimes in a full season Liz was not home till daylight. Mrs. Tozer put upon her a bit because she happened to be a friend of her mother's.

Obviously, she could make more as a model than as a milliner. Models were paid a shilling an hour, that is to say, five shillings for a morning's sitting and seven-and-six for the whole day. Mrs. Deverell had asked Isabel Frith. In the Schools they were paid at a higher rate . . . varying . . . in the R.A. Schools it ran to half-a-crown.

Miss Siddall's hair, of course—not her eyes, too pale, or her nose, too round—was her best asset as far as painters were concerned. But then, the colour wouldn't suit every taste. She did it very cleverly, without a net or pads, and so that it covered the ears properly. (Mr. Tennyson was supposed to have brought in that fashion ; he said women's ears, in general, were so ugly that they had to be covered.)

Walter disapproved of the step she proposed to take, but what alternative could he suggest? Her talent for stringing verses would not keep her and she would be no use on the stage, though she had a good figure, because of her voice—slightly sibilant, turning into the faintest little hiss whenever she got excited or tired with talking too long. She did not ever talk much, perhaps from a fear of betraying this peculiarity.

There really seemed nothing Walter could do for her but marry her, and he had not enough to marry on. His father would have opposed it and his mother too. He was as weak as wax in the hands of that good lady. And, moreover, he felt queerly, unaccountably ill at times. The doctor had advised him to take a rest, but he only worked the harder. Honourable to excess, he did not consider himself justified in taking a step that would involve another person's happiness until his malady, if malady there was, had declared itself.

3

She was a good model, taking poses readily and maintaining them. In the rests she read hard out of the books Walter lent her; at home they called it waste of time. He tried her with *The Idylls of the King*, but she had read everything of Tennyson's she could get hold of, ever since she had found a poem of his written on the paper round a pound of butter. That was the way, said he, many manuscripts went. Landladies sold them as waste-paper or lit the fires with them. Gabriel had found the maid at Charlotte Street using up some of his translations from the Italian poets in that way.

He amused her by quoting Tupper's verses about the Club Magazine :—

> Come, Early Christians, bring a knife
> And cut these woeful pages down !
> You would not have them haunt the town,
> Where butter and where cheese is rife ?

For of course the P.R.B. had had to have an organ. Something like the old *Keepsakes* and *Annuals*. Out of forty alternative titles that of *The Germ* was chosen. It was to comprise forty pages, with two etchings, to be sold at a shilling and come out monthly. By Christmas Eve fifty copies were in the printers' hands. Millais, though he had caught a bad cold sleeping on his truckle bed in *The Carpenter's Shop* (Meux's Brewery), had his illustration ready and Gabriel his story too, though he had put off beginning it till the very last and, excessive in all things, had had to sit up all night to finish it. They had not been allowed to have the Letters printed on the cover—somehow their innocent swagger had antagonised John

D

33

Bull already. But the Brethren, going round to leading book-sellers with copies in hand, had not done badly. Hughes, the porter, sold fifty, and Stephens by January had disposed of thirty copies, and Hunt had managed to get off twelve out of the sixteen he had undertaken, on the way from his new studio in Prospect Place to Newman Street.

4

But it died. On the seventeenth day of February next year Millais, backed by his redoubtable and hard-headed mother, got his way, and in committee it was decided not to bring out another number. And the housemaid at Somerset House lit her fires of a morning with the little booklets which fetch nowadays several pounds a copy.

In a last kick and flicker, posters were pasted and sandwich men walked up and down the gutters in front of the fine folk attending the Private View of the Royal Academy on Whit Monday, announcing "The Germ's" brilliant and enduring qualities.

Two works by the Brethren attained the honours of hanging : Hunt's *Rienzi* and Millais' *Christ in the House of His Parents*,[1] and, drawing the whole venom of the critics, suffered the brunt of the stone-slinging of the accredited Philistines of our isles. The critics, Kingsley, Chorley, S. C. Hall and Frank Stone— called the Hammer of the Pre-Raphaelites, who could quote the sermons of Savonarola at them—were unanimous. Abuse, contrasting with the praise and soft-sawder dealt out, almost by the yard, to the pictures of accredited men and R.A.'s.[2]

They were lost—for the time. Ruskin had not yet come forward to speak up for the infant iconoclasts, the baby destroyers of the images in the Temple of Crudities ; and, with all the power of his eloquence, reasoned, crushing and subtle, raise his

---

[1] Dickens wrote, "The loathsome minuteness of 'The Carpenter's Shop,' the hideous, wry-necked, blubbering, red-haired boy and his common-looking mother . . . who would have disgraced the lowest gin shop in London." It is to be supposed that the ex-bootblacking factory boy from Day and Martin's knew what he was talking about, writing superior in the midst of his own lovingly chosen floral wall-papers and carpets.

[2] Of Mr. Sydney Cooper's "Hawking"—"a small picture exceedingly sweet in colour "—or Mr. Stothard's "Sleeping Nymph," among other detailed merits "charmingly coloured." While Rossetti was castigated for his "unintelligent imitation of the technicalities of Old Art, his golden Glorys and other infantine absurdities."

protest in their favour, dealing his tremendous indictment of England's art politics.[1] For a moment Ruskin was less a critic than a man, unskilled, inapt, much puzzled, in the throes of an undesired wedlock and the practice of its duties. He was in Venice with his Stunner, who was making it all very difficult for him.

5

Gabriel Rossetti must have met his by now—even painted from her. The little water-colour, *Rosso Vestita*, is the image of her, and so is *Beatrice at a Marriage Feast denying Dante her Salutation* and *Guardami ben, ben son, ben son Beatrice*—and every other Beatrice after that.

He admired her then, certainly—loved her, when? William " could not say," of this brother of his, so lacking in sense of proprietorship or possessiveness in anything—" tin " or " digs " ; models or mistresses, pictures, china or lead pencils, albeit he freely borrowed such, at times convenient to himself but not perhaps to others. But though he assumed an umbrella easily he was equally willing to lend his and, if he slept in a friend's bed, was eager enough to put him up whenever he had a place of his own. The Sid he permitted to pose for them all without a murmur. For the moment he was not ready for her, unprepared for the sudden éclosion of sentiment which broke out into the passion which ended by wrapping them both in an everlasting coat of flame, like Dante's doomed lovers in Hell. As animals intending to mate will approach each other, describing wide but gradually narrowing arcs, so humans, whose sexual peripatetics are determined by the higher nerve-centres, will seek to prolong the pleasantly harrowing ante-period : will simulate indifference, suggest dislike, even blackening [2] the object of their unconscious preoccupation.

---

[1] Italy in her great period knew her great men and did not despise their youth. " It is reserved for England to insult the strength of her noblest children, to wither their warm enthusiasms early into the bitterness of patient battle and to leave to those whom she should have cherished and aided no hope except in resolution, no refuge but in disdain."—*Modern Painters*.

[2] See the rancorous remarks made to his confidant, by Keats about a lady called Charmian, though nevertheless he " would like her to ruin him " !

Miss Siddall's second sitting was to Hunt, in boy's clothes, for what was farcically called *Two Gentlemen and a Half*. She was the half—*Silvia in the Forest of Arden*, otherwise Knole Park. And she was thus brought acquainted with a girl—" good-hearted to the core, with the makings of an intelligent woman in her "—whom Hunt was having educated with a view to espousal should she prove herself fit. Miss Siddall took a dislike to Miss Miller there and then and would not go down to Sevenoaks for ' a kind of ' picknick the Brethren were having that October, real girls sitting under real trees, and staying all together at Mrs. Hearnden's, at Number Five, High Street.

Generous and rich, inasmuch as he was able to live at home, Rossetti lent Hunt enough to go on with and found him a buyer for *The Christian Missionary*, at one hundred and sixty pounds, so that he declined an offer of the post of draughtsman to the Mosul Expedition and, pursuing the straight and Pre-Raphaelite way, started on *Claudio and Isabella*, going across the water every morning to Lambeth to get the prison cell for it. It was six months since he had made any money whatever, but he had found a sovereign in the stuffing of an armchair, which tided him over for a bit. Woolner had got a nice commission for a medallion of Wordsworth and hoped to " get " Carlyle. Gabriel Rossetti talked of " cutting " art altogether and applied for the post of telegraph clerk on the North-Western Railway, but gave it up on finding that he didn't know anything about the use of the little needles diddling about in front of his eyes—nor wanted to learn. He didn't like people to know how poor he was, so sat grouting alone all day in his wretched study where the rain came in, complaining of toothache—and took laudanum for it, as anyone would.

William was now the chief breadwinner of the family. Old Mr. Rossetti's eyesight was failing and his engagements for lessons fell off so that a move to a house at a lower rental was indicated where they could live according to their principle, that " No butcher or baker or candlestick maker," in the words of the nursery rhyme, " had a claim unpaid." William found one near Mornington Crescent, where his mother and sisters pro-

WILLIAM HOLMAN HUNT
From a photograph

posed to open a day-school. It was not far from their relations; the Polidori aunts who were fairly well off and had not much else to do with their money.

William kept his mother and sisters mostly on his screw from the Board of Trade, and by reviewing. Schooled by his brother, he framed his articles "so as not to show too much family bias" here or there. He was to put Hunt first and "not defend my mannerisms—they are absurd and merely superficial." He had to hunt up the dealers, see them and bring them to the picture market, "but not with too much officiousness." He was to look up "the Demon Dunlop" and get hold of White, "that shining, baldpate, deep old file," mostly to be come across at Jullien's Promenade Concerts. Or the pensive pork-packer of Belfast, Francis McCracken ("Crack" or "the Kraken" by analogy with the Sea Serpent), whom Rossetti never did see in the flesh, "a real scoundrel," but who had got a little money. And always be civil, which was not difficult, to Barbara Leigh-Smith, whose brougham had C-springs, and to her friends the Howitts, who got his poems into magazines for him. And, William, look to it—"Lady Bath's cheque *not* to hand!"

Lady Bath had bought *The Girlhood*. She was the conquest of Maria's bow and spear; while Tom Seddon, passionately adjured by Patmore, brought a most productive M.P. who commissioned a window in the Welsh church that a cousin of his had been given the job of rebuilding.

Always clamouring for loans—the loan of a bed, or half a one, the loan of a pair of trousers (he particularly affected Brown's best), the loan of "tin" to pay somebody for something, models, rent in arrears, colours at Roberson's, charities—he was never half so hard up as some of those he borrowed from, Brown or Hunt or Allingham, or Hannay, poor dear, who was never at home in the daytime, but went out before the people of the house were up and never came back until they had gone to bed. Gabriel was never without a bed to lie on except in that year when the school in Arlington Street failed and the family separated, some going to Somersetshire to try another "lay" and the rest into lodgings. As young men go, he had plenty of pocket-money, for he earned it easily, in spurts, and spent it in the same way. He just wanted it wherewith to support his tempestuous generosities, purchasing power to back his daily quest of curios, old ivories, china, netsuke, jade, scraps of silk and brocade—what poor Allingham, touring the second-hand shops with him for hours, called " bits of strangeness." He already had the soul of the *brocanteur*, the tic that became a mania for the acquisition of pictures that Howell forged and pawned and stole, for jewellery that his women wore and lost, for china that servants broke or mistresses used as missiles.[1]

8

He exaggerated his depression as he exaggerated his poverty. His friends, aware that a dentist could have dealt with his toothache and his blue devils been chased away by fresh air, got him at last down to Sevenoaks, where it would do him good to play hide-and-seek in the Park with Eliza Cook and Ledru Rollin. But he would not play. He found a good background for *Rachel and Leah*. He wrote canzoni in the evenings and in the day painted out of doors, with an umbrella tied to his buttonhole, copying a leaf. Neither the leaf nor the umbrella would stay still and those men made him get up at seven! After exactly a week he returned by coach, to find that the " hop-shop " below his studio had " absquatulated " without paying its rent, so that the landlord had distrained on him and seized his furniture.

As he had not yet begun to collect in earnest, the damage was less serious for him than for William, who lost all the books he had lent his brother at various times. Gabriel was taken by Brown into his studio, but he had to go and sleep at home. By December Deverell found a study for them both at twenty shillings a week or four guineas a month, three rooms on the first floor—one with a window that could be cut right up to the ceiling for the painting light. So January of next year found them installed in Number Seventeen, Red Lion Square, with the obelisk in the middle and the stone watch-houses at each corner like family vaults, the middle all white and yellow with lilies and marigolds, and low-boughed trees under whose shade Deverell meant to set Rosalind to witness the encounter between Jacques and Orlando in the Forest of Ardennes. Another projected Shakespeare subject of Walter's was *Laertes and*

[1] The last woman he ever pretended to care for he put out of doors because of her onslaughts on his Delft, and there is, or was, a blue enamel snake with ruby eyes in a haystack, or in the stomach of the cow that ate the hay—*und weiter* (lost by Miss Rosalind Howell).

Ophelia. He must have a try at Ophelia too. And Miss Siddall was to do her hair high and curl it and pose as the Lady of Quality dancing, if not for her life, for her purse, on Hounslow Heath with Claude Duval. He finished this in October and gave it to Stephens, but the others, including *The Flight of an Egyptian Ibis*, he never even began. Rossetti finished the *Rosalind* and altered the face of Celia. Why?

CHAPTER IV

I

NEXT year, fortified by rustication and hard living, cheered on by pals' backing, still potent in fraternity, they meant to have another try at the R.A. William Rossetti, in his news letter to Allingham in Ireland, has hope for next year's Academy. Millais would have three pictures, *The Woodman's Daughter*, illustrating a poem by their valued friend Patmore, very, *very* P.R.B., *Mariana*, not so very, and *The Daughters of the Sons of Noah*—hangers like scriptural subjects. Hunt's *Two Gentlemen*, William in his capacity of critic opined, would certainly take the shine out of his critics " as well as out of any R.A.'s work that may happen to hang near it."

But *The Woodman's Daughter* was put in the Octagon Room, called the Condemned Cell, equal to an artistic sentence of death. Hunt was " abominably shirked off "—the same place he had been in before with *Rienzi*. Millais came off best, he had two " on the line." [1] But the critics were dead against. Shirley Brooks walked about all day calling attention, with a loud sniff, to this or that outrageous picture : that little monkey Chorley was likewise in ecstasies of amusement while poor Mrs. Jones, near her time, had to be supported to a settee, and, even with the Howitts, friendly to the P.R.B. and useful in the Press, it was " The Woodman's quaint children . . . strange and naïve in treatment. . . ."

Hunt would hang about the R.A. to hear what people were saying. His poor old father was jeered at on his way to and from the City. Scurrilous letters and pamphlets were freely received by the Brethren and their relations. One Professor in the Schools had trained his pupils to hiss daily at the contemptuous references to the P.R.B. which he introduced shamelessly into the body of his discourses. Another wrote to a mutual friend that Mr. Millais must expect to be cut in the

[1] Keeper Jones, Head of the Antique, cherished an affection for his early pupil.

street by all decent-minded people. The President issued a pronunciamento to the effect that this was the last year that he and the Hanging Committee " would admit this new and outrageous school of painting on their walls."

And the Club, in January, held its sad little first anniversary meeting, as arranged at Millais' house in the study where, over a year ago, Rossetti had picked up the Lasinio book. The scene was the same. Tea was still provided in the study for Johnny and his friends by his handsome, decided mother, with her thin lips and deep-lidded eyes under the curls, surmounted, but not confined, by a none too clean cap. They passed some dull regulations and then Millais proposed that " we no longer call ourselves P.R.B. because of the misapprehension the name excites." Better to " let our converts be known only by their works." That was too much : they could not bear it. His motion was not passed : it was decided to make some more attempts to nobble the Press. Doctor Westland Marston was Editor of an important Journal, *The Critic*, and they all attended a party at his villa in Camden Town. Mrs. Deverell took Miss Siddall, who did her credit. Of her two dresses, a grey and a black silk, both made by herself, the young lady chose to wear the black and looked, so Mr. Madox Brown said, like a queen on about three pounds.

But Westland Marston and the other critics were not propitiated. Patmore had suggested to the greatest critic of all, that he should "write something kind about the Pre-Raphaelites." Ruskin was not sure he liked them very much. He thought the face of Silvia in *Two Gentlemen* horrid (little witting that she who was to be his Princess Ida had sat for it !) and was quite sorry that the wives of Noah had *not* been drowned. His letter in *The Times* was useful, if a little grudgingly worded :—" The admirable though *strange* pictures of Mr. Millais and Mr. Hunt."

The little group dispersed [1]; " some stayed isolated ; the majority drifting back into the ordinary and more profitable ways of life and art." [2] And Gabriel's sister used her poetical talent and her excruciating wit (that turned to acid in her old age) on the hapless, hopeless venture of her brothers.[3]

[1] Hunt, sadly, " I am now only P.R.B., but can't use the letters as there *are* no P.R.B.'s in the plural."

[2] Mrs. Oliphant.

[3] So rivers merge in the perpetual sea—
So luscious fruit must fall when over ripe—
And so the consummated P.R.B.

The faithful Allingham, on his arrival in town, went straight to Burlington House. All round him he heard the comments of "the despicable public," a ground-swell of disapproval that had not gone down since the opening day, and he was considerably depressed.

That night he dined with Thackeray in Kensington Square—quite a small party, Mrs. Carmichael-Smyth, Father Prout, Miss Anny and a Mr. Cole, much concerned with the Great Exhibition to come, and a young painter who was studying in Berlin, very handsome, rather Jewish-looking, wearing purple stockings, called Frederic Leighton. They talked Art. But, of the P.R.B., not a word !

Next day he went to Red Lion Square and rang the bell of Number Seventeen, looking wistfully up at the window on the first floor in which he imagined Gabriel and Walter to be working. A maid opened the door—" Mr. Rossetti has gone away. Mr. Deverell is ill." Scribbling something on a card he gave it to her and walked sadly away down the steps.

Someone had left the garden gate unlatched and he wandered up and down the strip of grass, noting that the trees were faded already, dry as the summer dust that whirled round the square and as pale, the leaves flapping like old tattered banners whose web had " perished " and their warp decayed, left in a church where no man comes to pray. London squares are always empty and yet he felt that there were people there ! [1]

He went on to Thirty-five, Arlington Street, Camden Town, where he understood the Rossettis had recently moved, a wide, elegant road, with Highgate Hill, of a dull blue like the background of an Italian picture, at the end of it. He rang the bell of a two-storied house with an area, whence a servant put her head up to ask what he wanted. " Mr. William is at the play. Mr. Gabriel don't live here."

As a last resort he looked for Gabriel at Brown's, who lent his study so often that there was never any knowing to whom it

---

[1] . . . a place
Where one might think to find a din
Of doubtful talk and a live flame
Wandering, and many a shape whose name
Not itself knoweth and old dew,
And your own footsteps meeting you,
And all things going as they came.

really belonged, except that Brown paid the rent. Gough, the model, coming to the door with a candle in his hand, lit him to the enormous study where Brown was lounging by a stove with a jar of shag and a bottle of whisky, alone; but Allingham had thought as he came in that he had seen Gabriel looking down at him over the banisters with an " expression almost diabolic. . . ."

It *was* Gabriel. He came down, lit a pipe and was as urbane as ever, with perhaps some slight sign of effort. In answer to an inquiry about Deverell's illness—" Sick unto death, I think ! " adding, cheerfully, that Deverell's family had left Somerset House for the country. He asked how Miss Siddall was. Pretty well for her. She had sat to Hunt for Silvia and was going to sit to Millais for Ophelia. Millais had refused to go to Switzerland with the Ruskins and was off to Cheam with Hunt, where he had found a river for Ophelia to drown in. Of course the model couldn't be asked to get into that, but Millais' mother had invented a sort of bath arrangement filled with hot water, you could put an ordinary lamp under. The Sid didn't object to lying in it for an hour or so, drowning in a splendid old dress with silver embroidery which he had picked up in a " cag-mag shop " for four pounds.

She lived in town now, to be nearer her engagements. He gave Allingham her professional card with the address, and, he added, " You must spell the name with only one *l* and one *d*. She is a Sidal of Hope."

3

Next day he took Allingham to the Exhibition and, among the fountains, statues and models of ships, at a refreshment table attended by pretty Stunners, told him all about the ancestors of Miss Siddall (whose name was in future to be spelt Siddal). Her family coat was Three Birds and the word Honour, but they had a right to quarter that of Greaves (Per Bend Vert and Gules : an Eagle displayed) so her mother said. Scott, who had been making inquiries, said it was mostly true. The Siddals—or the Greaves—went back to the seventeenth century —Slade Hall near Manchester and later of Hope in Derbyshire, near Castleton, an old market town lying in an angle of Hope Dale. Hope Hall, Scott said, was now a public-house, but the churchyard was full of authentic tombs, with the name on them

43

spelt in all sorts of ways, according to the literacy or the whim of the stonecutter. A Norman name, of course—Sudel or Suddel—there were some of their family tombs in the churchyard at Ovington in the County of Durham.

And according to the Hope registers, the son of Jacobus Sidall et Anna Grant de Hope married into a much older family still, that of Greaves. There was a Greaves, a knight of Beeley, in the time of Henry III, but, about the time when Queen Anne came to the throne, a descendant of his settled at Swarkeston—the bridge south of Derby, Allingham must remember, where the Pretender's Highlanders insisted on going back when they might have been in London ere night. (And what a good thing if they had : the Stuarts, bad as they were, had some feeling for art and *we* could have controlled them !) Rachel Greaves, the heiress of Crook Hall at Hathersage, married Christopher Siddal, but somehow or other her money did not avail Christopher. He was the first to let the family down, becoming a bankrupt, probably because of the failure of the flax industry ?

Lizzy had got hold of some of the papers to show to her Gabriel, such as the Auditors' assignment. . . . "*All creditors . . . for good and charitable reasons agree to accept and take the remaining sum of money . . . proceeding from the sale of . . .*" The poor man seemed to have sold a piece of land, at his disposal, to a rascally firm of solicitors and migrated to Sheffield, where he let them add another *l* to his name and ceased to be romantic, his children no longer christened and married in the church on the hill, or, dying, their names inscribed on tombstones in the church garth. Sheffield henceforth held their bones. There were some of them alive there. Christopher Siddal was Miss Siddal's grandfather, and her aristocratic bearing and the Roman nose of her sister were thereby accounted for, together with her brother Harry's deficiency . . . ? These old families in their decadence had jolly well to pay for the prime.

Rossetti talked of her all the time. She was now definitely his Stunner ; her beauty had become the legend which the egotistic man of genius goes about to create round his own. And one begins to hear the faintly adverse criticisms of the sheep-like followers, daring to look over the hedge. Doctor Marshall suggested that Miss Siddall—they long persisted in that spelling—was one of Rossetti's " swans " and, like Petruchio bent on annoying Caterina, saw " no more beauty in her Than

44

CHARLES CROOKES SIDDALL
From a photograph

without candle may go dark to bed." (But then Marshall liked fat women and spoke admiringly in his lectures of " the well-cushioned female.") Her complexion he thought fine but misleading—no indication of health. None of the others admired her, while Arthur Hughes, who saw her at Somerset House, struck, like Miss Howitt, by her " unworldly simplicity and purity of aspect," said that she looked " a good little girl who probably read her Bible and said her prayers every night."

Her manner did not vary with her new circumstances and she did not go the way to make the new people like her or feel at ease with her, confounding and puzzling them all by an obstinate withdrawal of personality, assumed, perhaps, in the beginning as a defence and continued unconsciously until the end. Not friendly or chatty, but, like Beatrice, denying them nearly everything but her Salutation ; turning off the talk the moment it became personal to herself. As much as to say—but she was too well brought up to say it—that her " mind and feelings were her own." Why not ? It is the privilege of the meanest. She permitted herself to indulge in sarcasm, perhaps that was why Christina could not get on with her—two of a trade. But nobody could have called her ill-natured as they did Christina. Described in popular style, she was " flighty "— the usual complaint against servants under Victoria.[1] Born and bred in a slum ; but recently stationed behind a counter in a second-rate milliner's shop ; translated with some suddenness into a society excessively sophisticated, yawning with pitfalls for the unlettered and unlessoned, this young woman, sprung from a race whose wits are as sharp as the scissors they fabricate, did not care to give points to ridicule by talking freely until she had got her bearings. Looking like a Madonna, she had the sapience of the gutter-child. And a little embittered ! Except Mrs. Deverell no society woman noticed her much. Gabriel's family did not welcome her and William Rossetti owns that he was not in her society " as much as might be expected." His descriptions of her appearance breathe an almost personal antipathy. He gives a list of her points ; item, a good figure, a lofty neck, regular features, brilliant complexion, hair, abundant, of a coppery colour " that some people would call *red* "—and did. Her upper lip was wrong. Her manners were good. After detailing her parentage or as much of it in his opinion as will bear telling, he asks leave to say " once for

[1] It was the word Swinburne used at the inquest to describe her behaviour.

45

all " that she did know " how to behave in company and committed no faults of speech." And she had every claim to be called a lady. He had never heard of her pretensions to Family, or he discounted them. She had, he fancied, no religion.

She never found time to sit to anyone but Gabriel now. Her sitting to Millais in December for Ophelia was the fulfilling of an engagement made long ago. Gabriel was not afraid that Millais would flirt with her—his study was full of sketches of Mrs. Ruskin done from memory, after the fateful day when she and her husband had driven over to fetch Johnny to dinner in Camberwell and the love that fell between them was so obvious that even the servants marvelled.

Miss Siddal came to Mr. Rossetti from Weymouth Street, Number One, where she lived in rooms over a Mr. Barbour's, a surgeon (the lodgings were kept by a member of the family and were quite, quite respectable), either to Newman Street or to Highgate, where the Howitts, connected with so much of the romance of Gabriel Rossetti's life (his playtime, if he ever had any), lived.

4

Taken all round, father, mother and daughter, the Howitts were charming people. William Howitt had left off being a Friend and became connected with *The People's Journal* and *Household Words*, which Mrs. Howitt, little, grey and charming, author herself of pleasant books for children,[1] helped him to edit. They entertained their friends simply, as Quakers use, and their connection with journalism procured publication for a first poem, *Sister Helen* (" by an artistic friend of ours "), in the *Düsseldorfer Album*, edited by a brother-in-law. They went away a great deal, and then Mrs. Howitt allowed " Mr. Gabriel " to use the studio at the bottom of the garden as often and for as long as he liked.

Fifty-two was a bad year for nerves. Etna was in eruption. In September there was an earthquake, it rained all the time, and in October there was a terrific storm. Cold by November, with a display of the Aurora which tallied with what Mrs. Howitt called " spiritualistic experiments made by persons interested in the new electro-biological discoveries." Mr.

---

[1] Mrs. Howitt's best known work is *Will You Walk into my Parlour? said the Spider to the Fly.*

Howitt had sailed for the Gold Fields with Bernhard Smith at the beginning of the year and his wife and daughter were eking out defective postal communication with the other side by resort to the "Rapping Spirits," obtaining "most wonderful results." Night after night they would sit with their intimates, Gabriel and Lizzy, Eliza Cook, Bessie Parkes, Miss Coutts and Miss Barbara Leigh-Smith, in the parlour of the lonely little house, and the damp would come in cold from the Ponds, and the dogs, about eleven, would begin to bark horribly and incessantly, which everyone knows augurs ill for those whose nearest and dearest are beyond the uses of telegraphy. Gabriel Rossetti would tell ghost stories—how young George Frederick Watts, returning to town after a dinner with the Ionides at Tulse Hill, saw and spoke to a woman in the shrubberies whom he thought to be one of the ladies of the house out for a lark . . . but she was indoors at the time! And accounts of the séances that he and Blanchard were attending at the Academy in Sloane Street, describing D. D. Home, his eyes, inferior and pale by day but, by night, "like little phosphorescent lights that come together and dart away again." . . . And Barbara Leigh-Smith would say pettishly, "I do not like death, I tell you!" in her downright way, as if confiding to them an unshared singularity.

Cousin to Florence Nightingale: the eldest daughter of Benjamin Leigh-Smith, she acted as mother to his other children, commanding his house in Blandford Square, his servants and the well-hung carriage which the two Rossetti boys thoroughly appreciated. Her attention had been called to Gabriel by Ruskin's *Edinburgh Lectures* and she had sent the poor penniless lad a copy—"Just a slight but very friendly mention of *you*—on page 16." She was a year older than he (which, in Victorian apprehension, counted as ten years). He thought her "a really jolly fellow, with her golden hair, her breeches, her enthusiasms and her tin," summing up her advantages with Rossettian shrewdness, for, "kind, indefatigable and invaluable," her father allowing her three hundred a year: she regarded money as "the power to do good." Handsome and healthy, she liked to live in a draught and in the country wore a costume tending towards that appropriated so long and so unjustly by the male. But in London she conformed, though her dress was made of plain material without fuss or furbelows. Chignonless, she wore a plain band of velvet round her braided hair.

She was not averse to male society but made no concessions to the pretensions of men (so anxious to reserve all the comfortable ways of living for themselves), devoting herself and her wealth to the removal of the disabilities that the law of England laid on women, more especially on poor clergymen's daughters and girls forced, without equipment, to become governesses. The first Suffragette, in a word !

She had built herself, near Hastings, a small house of red brick in the style of an old Sussex cottage—a forerunner of Morris' protest against Victorian ugliness—constantly inviting the young women engaged with her in The Cause to come there and recuperate. Anna Mary Howitt's room was crowded with Catholic emblems. Bessie Parkes, her second best friend, ran down very often and, at different times, Miss Coutts, Miss Meteyard, Emily Faithfull, Marian Evans and Eliza Cook inscribed their names on the red glazed bricks of the mantelpiece [1] in the living-room.

[1] It is covered with names.

CHAPTER V

I

THE ferment set up by the nightly search for models to paint and women to save, in Rossetti and Hunt, which left Millais, less morbid than the one and less didactic than the other, unaffected, was actually responsible for the first rift among the Brethren. Hunt, intending to contribute his illustration of the problem, was beginning *The Awakened Conscience*—Miss Annie Miller's conscience—for it was she who posed for the kept woman, standing up starkly in a drawing-room full of jardinières and antimacassared chairs, overcome by hearing one of the songs [1] of her innocence strummed by her lover at the piano behind her, while the cat pulls over the what-not table and eats her canary out of the overturned cage. " Rooms like this " *were* strange to Hunt : he had set his Jenny—or Rosabell—down, for lack of unholy knowledge, in a room no more lasciviously furnished than his mother's best parlour.

Rossetti had not yet begun *Found*, but he could not bear anyone else to handle that subject. He must counter Hunt : Hunt was not to have it all his own way !

Brown, who had had some luck—" McCrack " had bought the *Chaucer* for sixty-three pounds and he had been offered the place of Head Master at the North London School of Design—had taken a room in Heath Street, and was painting *Work* from out the window of a four-wheeled cab. His marriage was not yet announced. Emma and the child still lived at Hendon, but she came every day in the bus to see him and

---

[1] Oh ! don't you remember sweet A-a-lice, Ben Bolt,
　Sweet Alice with hair so brown ?
She wept with delight, when you gave her a smile,
　And trembled with fear at your frown.
In the old churchyard, in the valley, Ben Bolt,
　In a corner obscure and alone,
They have fitted a slab of granite so grey,
　And sweet Alice lies under the stone.

receive the clerical instruction that would eventually make her fit to be introduced to his friends. He wanted Gabriel to come to Hampstead too and do his *Rescue* picture; he would find him a cart, and a calf new from the cow, and himself pose for the countryman—out of doors, so that Gabriel might get "the healthy blue that flesh assumes in the open air."

No. *Found* was emphatically a town subject; he had to get the antithesis of Rosabell's countryman-lover coming across his lost sweetheart in urban degradation.

He saw his Rosabell crouching by one of the London bridges, and not long since he had gone with Woodward to the site for the new Crown Insurance Offices which the architect had been commissioned to do (in Venetian Gothic). There he had noticed a residential square or place, built in quadrangle form, tallish houses on both sides of the street ending in the bridge. From the corner block you could throw a stone out of window on to people's heads, and on that side he meant to have his rooms. He had settled it all as he waited for Woodward seeing his Commissioners. He would (" Yes, if you get up early enough," said Brown) see the sun rise on the river (" And smell it ! "). No, a great waterway like the Thames created a draught and blew the miasma away. So convenient. The river steamers served Chatham Place and at the corner were stairs where you could take a boat. Plenty of windows, though the tax was still on. Would Brown go with him to see it ? No, better take William—more practical ! Brown saw that the place had caught the fellow's imagination and that his mind was made up. So did the landlord, another artist, Edward Duncan of the Old Water Colour Society, realise that the young fellow with the inward, concentrated face was set on these particular rooms. He closed with him and drove a fairly hard bargain for the premises just vacated by the Newfoundland and Colonial Schools Society. By November Gabriel was giving parties there.

2

Chatham Place, in the precinct of Bridewell with a jurisdiction of its own, was first called Pitt and then Chatham *Square*. It represented a sort of spatulate widening of the new street that had been cut through the slums of Blackfriars when the last bit of The Ditch was covered over, leading to the fine new bridge built across to the Surrey side. Residences for

By kind permission of the Librarian of the Guildhall

No. 14 CHATHAM PLACE FROM THE
RIVER. THE BALCONY ROOM ×

gentlemen, set down amid the low-browed squalor, the higgledy-piggledy buildings of Bridge Street, Queen Street and the adjacent wharves. On each floor were three windows, arched, ogival, two on each side of the house door which looked like a window too. Each house had its little plot of cat-ridden garden (Never, Boyce, who succeeded him, used to say, were there so many cats as huttered about St. Bride's!) enclosed in low green palings with serrated top, boasting a green gate no higher than a man's knee. There was a lamp-post to every three blocks and one with two burners came just outside the door of Number Fourteen.

Chatham Place was purely residential at first; people were not afraid to sleep in its airs and successfully reared children there,[1] but it seemed now more or less given up to Societies and legal and other offices. The sun shone on the brass plates, polished every morning, of lawyers, auctioneers and accountants, insurance and colonial offices, land and immigration buildings, and even a Society devoted to the Proper Observance of the Lord's Day. One side of Number Fourteen gave straight on the river, the cowering wharves, the slippery sets of stairs, the greasy baulks, the line of them criss-crossed by black cranes and red sails. One could trace the long curved line of the bridge and its stone balustrade which "returned" to the recesses formed over the Ionic columns and pilasters placed upon the cutwaters of the piers. Both ends widened handsomely into quadrant corners, with easy flights of steps leading down to the water. And if one looked up one would see St. Paul's, under repair, with scaffolding about it, dominating all.

The merit of Chatham Place was the view: its disadvantage the smell, of which Gabriel Rossetti was more or less unconscious; the odour of the disjecta of Vasto, so to speak, in his blood probably outdoing that of the Fleet Ditch at its best. There were romantic compensations. He liked to think he was living on Church property and therefore accursed; that the roadway beneath his windows was once a stream on which navies used to ride and known in its later stage as the River of Dead Dogs, whose stench was so strong that the monks of Whitefriars, over the water, used to complain that it overcame the smell of frankincense on their altars.

[1] Emma Lyon was Doctor Buff's nursemaid at Number Eight before she ran away with Greville and made her fortune, and Miss Dinah Mulock lodged as late as 1843 with her father in the very house Gabriel Rossetti first thought of taking.

Though it was nearly a hundred years since the Fleet River had been covered over, the coal wharves, the copper, the lime and the iron wharves and, worst of all, the Gas Light Company's wharf, just behind, made a stink combined with that of the grey, tireless, universal mud splayed over the flats at low tide, that sent many of his friends, less resistant than he, away from his parties with a sick-headache. As 'twere an iceberg, the lower part of the house—vaults and cellars that held God knows what, only *not* wine—was out of all proportion to the habitable apartments. There was a nice balcony to his end window looking on the river, where chairs could be placed, and he and his friends could sit outside and watch the stream of people going across the bridge. From a big window at the back he could see the Temple trees and gain the relief of green from so much grey and blue.

William and he were taken as co-tenants at a rental of forty pounds per annum, to be paid quarterly, but the younger brother's name alone appears in the earlier directories. The sisters, who until the time of Gabriel's marriage called it "William's," entertained their vicars and pet curates at tea on the balcony. But William never slept there; he disliked the place—there was not really room for him among the easels and folios, and he *had* a nose!

The accommodation (*vide* William) comprised " a spacious " painting-room, " a commodious " living-room, a small but very light bedroom and an ill-lit passage full of dusty book-shelves between those two last apartments. In taking this suite Gabriel obviously did not, at that time, contemplate marriage.

All the furniture he bought had to be second-hand : one could find nothing new nowadays that was even tolerable. Knock-kneed couches and commodes stained deep with the crusted rime of ages he would cover with a *nappe*—in the mediæval sense of the word—pieces of Eastern brocade that lit up a corner here and there and scraps of Genoa velvet that made a rich monotone of shadow in another. Lamps, statuettes, bas-reliefs were propped on spindly *étagères* or corner cupboards whose keys had long been lost so that the doors, after being carefully " put to," would yawn open suddenly at you. " Truck " (so Mrs. Birrell[1] called it) which had doubtless, as " Mr. Riz-

---

[1] The tenant of the ground floor of Chatham Place who " did " for Mr. Rossetti. He calls her Mrs. Burrell: Mr. Allingham Mrs. Birrell: and the Coroner called her Mrs. Birrill. I have gone by Mr. Allingham's spelling.

zetty" said, graced—or disgraced—the palaces of the Borgias or the Visconti. She wouldn't give a bob for anything in the rooms. And on the walls, nearly covering them, squares and oblongs of coagulated mud, framed in faded gold that he called pictures, and mirrors that no one could see themselves in, but that ghosts would certainly look out of, if you were fool enough to stare into them !

He furnished as he went along : he was not afraid of empty spaces or unpeopled corners, aware of the value of due alternations of dark and light. The dark is the playtime of the painter's eye, demanding, exulting in clarity all day : pleased to rest of an evening on the bat's-wing shadows that gather so quietly in the corners, the expanses of velvety gloom on which the images collected in the day's stress are spilled and spread to group themselves anew. " The little candle that sheds its beams but a little way " procures a delightful chiaroscuro : artists like Rembrandt did not dread the dark. Fancy if the Magi had been able to see the Christ Child clearly by the light of an electric bulb attached to the headstall of the manger in a stable, which nowadays would have been more like a cheerful bathroom ! Could the Raven have ejaculated his " Never More ! " with such awful incidence from the bust over the door if his listener could have studied the outlines of the ungainly fowl that preached to him of misspent opportunities ? No, dirt is a part of our Mother Earth, and a layer of it softens the harsh edges of things. The maid attached to the chambers was bidden leave things alone and not touch. She obeyed. His key was always put, when he went out, under the centre mat. Mrs. Birrell, slightly deaf, when surprised at her avocations on the ground floor and questioned, got into the way of answering, " Upstairs for Mr. Rizzetty," for this one of her gentlemen— they were all gentlemen—saw more people, was more popular than the Lord's Day Observance Society and the Prudential Mutual Life Society and kept more company than Mr. Keates, Consulting Chemist, or Mr. Simon Rendall, Solicitor.

By November he had ceased to form part of the household at Arlington Street. He was not on good terms with either Christina or his father, who had come back from Frome no better and nearly blind—" threatening soon to go under-ground with beloved Polidori." He was worrying his son on minor points, objecting to his present signature—wishing him to leave out Gabriel and sign himself Dante only—and

53

annoyed with him for the delay in the production of his Italian translations. The son, slightly annoyed and harassed, did not go to see him very often nowadays.

Number Fourteen was not even ready; the dilapidations not properly made good by the last tenant—" The window seems an endless job ! "—and he had only one lamp to arrange things by, but still he offers " tea and squalor at six on Thursday— and a bed," though that might be on the floor, or a share of his own. He has already asked some men he met at Stephens' on Sunday, Millais, Hunt and Deverell, and is going to ask the two Seddons and Collins and perhaps Hannay, if he "can get the room decent by then." One of the Seddons defaulted, but the others—including young Deverell, looking terribly ill—kept faith. It was a man's party, so The Sid did not go. It was the last time Gabriel saw Walter Deverell.

3

The first quarter's rent is due and he does not know where to turn for the money and is adjuring William to get it—some of it—anything up to twelve pounds (which was two pounds over)—from a Polidori. Soon a cheque from Aunt Charlotte comes to hand. Then, " my beastly foot keeps me away from settling in altogether " so that he continues to occupy a room in Arlington Street, William being away at Hastings with papa in lodgings on the parade over which the three families of Rossetti, Brown and Cave Thomas had a retainer. He seeks Brown's advice continually. " Will Brown come in late after School and he will give him half his bed if he likes ? " For Hampstead was then afar and unget-at-able after eleven when the buses stopped, and Brown could hardly afford a cab— except to paint from.

" Gabriel is a myth and seldom visible to the naked eye, but I suppose we are all painting pretty hard in the daytime and don't know where to find each other o' nights," said one of the Brethren charitably. Their Chief was behaving like a newly-made bridegroom, denying himself to visitors and refusing invitations. Mr. Edmund Blanchard and Mr. Hannay called but did not find the key under the third mat and, though they heard voices, they knew better than to ring. Brown wrote asking Gabriel to dine and go with him to the Photographic Exhibition, but he declined for he had promised to take " my

54

ELIZABETH ELEANOR SIDDALL
From a drawing by D. G. Rossetti

pupil" to the last Jullien concert of the season. But would not Brown come and see " dear Guggums' [1] drawings at Chatham Place instead "? For, discovering some sort of aptitude, he had made her take up painting so that she might have something to do when he was not with her and an excuse for coming to his studio so often—the light was better than in Weymouth Street.

Sometimes he sat to her, his legs thrust straight out on the seat of the chair on which she propped her little baby easel under the studio gas, five burners like sausages on a stand, flaring, hissing, making the most uncanny shadows in the low-ceiled room. Tea was brought up to them by Mrs. Birrell for six-pence, and Lizzy would shut the door and minister to Gabriel lying on an extempore couch of three chairs; he never stood when he could sit or sat when he could lie down. They would work on until they heard the click of the lamplighter's rod " setting the two seedy flames astir " that burned there outside and he, and even Lizzy perhaps, grew hungry. Then they would go out and have dinner at some chop-house near by—Anderton's or the Green Dragon or the Howard or De Keyser's hotel, which occupied two of the houses in Chatham Place and was slowly invading it altogether. But it was rather too grand for them and too expensive. And after dinner he would see her home to Weymouth Street, light up and begin to draw her again, she sitting huddled in the wicker armchair (the vulgarity of whose curves would have kept it out of Chatham Place even at a gift), racked with a pain she could not, Victorianly, name.

Like most Italians he could digest anything so long as it was succulent and there was enough of it; but the bane of Bohemia, which is indigestion, was her's and probably responsible for most of her inexplicable attacks.

Her dislike of modelhood dated from those days when she had been smuggled into Somerset House, and with the con-nivance of Deverell's mother because his father was not to know. And later on, in Red Lion Square, when Walter's brother Spenser and his sisters Margaretta and Maria, and wild Eustacia Davies and demure Harriett Hogarth over from Heston, had invited themselves to picnic teas with the " Pre-Raffs " as a great excitement and she had sat mum on the *estrade*, free to take a book, while the four swished up and down in their crino-lines, giggling and chattering about the ghost, treating her, perforce, as if she were one.

[1] Her newest pet name, taken from his own " Gug."

55

It would have been in the nature of an insult for the artist to introduce his paid model to his lady friends.

She had resented men coming in and out and talking freely as if she wasn't there; Woolner's stories of his investigations, conducted by him to please Darwin, into the average suscepti- bilities of models—how far down, for instance, they would blush the first time they stripped for the Altogether. Moreau had known one who had actually blushed all over. And the landlord's insolent stipulation with regard to women employed on his premises for artistic purposes.[1]

Gabriel worked her very hard, never asked her if she was tired as Mr. Deverell used to do; even beginning afresh after she had owned to fatigue. When he did grant her a moment's relaxation and she fell by accident into some new and gracious posture, bringing out fresh beauties of line and contour, he would exclaim—" Just stop like that ! " and begin a fresh drawing. . . .

Meek, unconscious dove—the shrewish turn developed later— she complied easily with all his demands, to please him, doing her hair in different ways, natural-seeming but all as com- plicated as might be, whorls and arabesques of gold falling around, and sheltering her cheeks; elaborate yet loose, a leaning tower that never fell, so cunningly was its gradient engineered. . . .

In order to be ready to pose to Gabriel at any time she had informed Walter that she had not now time to go to Kew to sit for him. Time ! She had all the time in the world. Long since she had dropped Jeannet and Ellen Britten : Mrs. Deverell, who used to take her to parties, was dead, and Emma, as Gabriel said, was " pinnacled in the intense inane " out Hendon way until she should be educated enough to be presented to them all.

Lizzy had not introduced her sweetheart to her mother : why should she ? He had not taken her to see his ! To keep Lyddy and Clara quiet she had told them in the strictest con- fidence which she knew would be abused, that she was engaged to be married. And now and then she caught The Paragon or The Wellington at the corner and went across the river to see her people without telling Gabriel. But for the most part she would sit in the window-seat and look across to where her old home lay, over there under the Surrey Hills that one could see quite plainly, of a quiet blue on a clear evening—the " Sunny

---

[1] " Models to be kept under some restraint, as some gentlemen and artists sacrifice the dignity of art to the baseness of passion."

'ills " Mrs. Birrell called them. She saw again, as in a picture, the long, low, tiled roofs of the rope-walks, red-tiled, under which the men walked with bent backs, twisting the strands, the poplars and alders hanging over the little canals and ditches in Grange Road and Halfpenny Hatch and the green fields stretching behind their house with its own long garden, all the way to Deptford and Wapping. She, who never now did more than board one omnibus after another, used to tramp with her sisters and brothers all the way to Champion Hill and Penge ! It was still there, the sign of the bright-coloured Elephant with the Castle on its back and the two red grocers' teapots outside Mrs. Rose's, the Swan Tavern with the big white bird and the horses coming up to drink all day in the trough outside The World Turned Upside Down—as hers was. And the old man without arms and legs who sat outside the Asylum for the Blind, and the blind man who drew on the pavement outside the Bricklayers' Arms.

But she did not forget, for she never could—she saw his eyes now whenever she closed her own—the big man in farmer's clothes who used to come out of his shop and carry her across the street, when it was muddy, to save her pretty shoes . . . holding her with his bloody hands. . . . This Mr. Greenacre used to obsess her, though she thought of him less since she had found her vocation. She had been told so often that she had genius that she now believed it. Brother William, a competent critic, had declared that she was " of uncommon capacity and various aptitudes " ; her talent for water-colour painting may have struck him as being one of them.

Gabriel, of course, said and swore that she was wonderful and had her little things framed and hung up as finished productions. Christina, vexed by what she considered her own " non-competence in anything," took some drawing lessons from Madox Brown, but, with the tactlessness that relations use, her brother forbade her " to attempt to rival The Sid in *painting !* " He made this reservation, for well he knew how great Christina was, with her little poems scribbled on odds and ends of note-paper on the corner of her washstand at the rate of sometimes three a day !

Though she had not been to Albany Street, Miss Sid had met the sisters in Chatham Place—planned carefully. " Tell Christina, if she will come here on Thursday, Lizzy will be here," so Gabriel writes to William, adding that he will be glad if she *will*

57

come, as he has told Lizzy of her wish to do so. A welcome relenting that periodically occurred whenever Christina's almoner for the moment had recommended Good Will to All Men and even to prospective sisters-in-law. But whenever the two girls met in Chatham Place or at Brown's, Christina, " speaking sparingly—working at worsted ever," managed to give Lizzy pain and her brother umbrage. The cold, deliberate insolence, her attitude of " pushing away " of which her brother-in-law complains, were her protective armour against the cruel glances askance dealt from those large, heavy-lidded eyes full of the dove's crooning passion. Christina, though deeply religious, was still earth-bound. . . .

CHAPTER VI

I

THE Liverpool award of prizes had done much for the P.R.B. "People are, in fact, affected towards us," said Hunt, who had sold *Claudio and Isabella* and paid off his debt to the old Millais'. Johnny was successful with a portrait of Mrs. Ruskin in *The Order of Release*. Pre-Raphaelitism had already "become too laborious" for him ;[1] and not even a business proposition, so his mother said. And poor Walter Deverell had exhibited two pictures, for both of which Lizzy had posed, *Twelfth Night* and *The Marriage of Rosalind and Orlando*. The rumours of his ill-health that had been going about appeared to have no foundation. But Gabriel had looked unwell for some time, so Scotus said when he came up to town that Spring to see the R.A. Exhibition and Gabriel's picture.[2] He stayed in Chatham Place and fell ill himself.

Gabriel had a boil of which he could not get rid in spite of Maria's poultices, but did not connect Scott's ailing and his own with Chatham Place. Yet all the papers that year were full of the state of the river and questions were asked in Parliament. His mother put her finger on the spot at once, but he silenced her by telling her that a doctor who came to a party in Chatham Place had "liked the situation very much"—and, by the way, his boil was better.[3]

[1] George Moore : *Impressions and Opinions.*
[2] He was painting *Giotto occupied on the Portrait of Dante,* in his hand a pomander, made in the shape of Katherine of Aragon's badge—the grenada or open pomegranate. People carried them in the Middle Ages, to deaden the effluvia of uncharted detritus and drainage matter. Such an object Théroigne de Méricourt, when she rode the cannon to Versailles, wore fixed in the head of her cane, to neutralise the smell of the Sacred People.
[3] Like many artists he did not notice smells. The divine furore of composition is an antidote to attacks of that kind. As one lights a fire in an infected area to purify the air, so the artist, burning with the creative fever, is unconscious of outside stimuli, good or bad, for the time. I have seen my father sitting at his easel, planted on the roof of a pigstye, contentedly painting away for a week of mornings.

In June, however, he told her that he was going to Scott's for a week or two, " as I keep getting ill," to see if the fresh air and bathing would cure his boil. "Tynemouth is only half-an-hour from Newcastle by rail so that I can go out for the day and bathe." [1]

Borrowing a carpet bag from someone, he took the train and travelled from 7 a.m. to 9 p.m., arrived in Newcastle and drove to St. Thomas Street in time for supper, full of his woes and with his carbuncle for Mrs. Scott to nurse—she gathered that Miss Sid was not good at poulticing.

From Newcastle, in a letter marked Private, he informed his brother that she might be working at Chatham Place, perhaps sleeping there, " so please don't encourage anyone to go near the place " except " McCrack," who was to be allowed to see certain works by arrangement. Lizzy would pick up his letters and forward them.

2

Mr. McCracken did not go to Chatham Place after all and, even if he had, would not have been shocked if the artist's pretty model had opened the door to him. The other tenants, meeting her on the stairs, thought of her as Mr. Rossetti's mistress. Mrs. Birrell, though perfectly civil, probably thought so too—for gentlemen, even the most hard-working, do not care as a rule to live without female society of a kind. Lizzy was probably the first woman to live by herself in a bachelor's flat. Stiff, haughty and fearless, looking not in the least professional—model or mistress—she just took her clothes, her baby easel and her big workbox to Gabriel's rooms and stayed there, living for days without speaking to a single human creature except the caretaker and her daughter. She went out for her meals or brought in something in a bag. There was no provision for cooking at Number Fourteen, even if she had known how.

She coughed a little, but not enough to keep her awake at night and, if it did, she would lie still, inventing and remembering poetry, listening to the various night-sounds, shouts, cries, screams even, but was not afraid " with any amazement," for nothing had happened to her as yet and she feared little except

[1] Tynemouth is the Lido of Newcastle which is as smelly as Blackfriars and was just then getting ready for its epidemic of cholera in the autumn. Though Gabriel did not bathe at Tynemouth or anywhere else, he did carry out the other part of his programme and walked twelve miles in one day—for the last time.

earthquakes, which mostly occurred abroad. But this *was* a queer house to be alone in. The foundations were so many times in the twenty-four hours, actually in the water: in the night, when you heard it best—or worst—weltering about the corner stones—back and forth—" the blind wave feeling round his long sea wall, In silence . . ." from her favourite poet. He had happened to mean a particular cave by the sea,[1] she had been told, hollowed out of the base of a black basalt cliff, at the end of a quiet bight where the fishes go to spawn . . . somewhere in Yorkshire. It fitted here.

3

Gabriel came back full of complaints. Newcastle was a beastly place. Nor had he been a success. He had kicked Scott's dog and abused Scott's admirable and beloved brother David, but he had written *Sister Helen* and painted *Carlisle Wall*.

To return, he had entrained at Newcastle for Coventry, and thence to Stratford, where he had sat upon a hillside and (in a sonnet) " seen the gold air and the sunset fade, And the last bird fly into the last light." And then (see his bread-and-butter letter) " back to the accursed circle, bones and skulls rattling, goblins mumbling, owls beating their obscene wings." Maybe he was receiving some Freudian information of the obscure root of his *malaise*. But he put it down to the incidence of the rent and disappointment over McCracken's not having turned up.

The first thing he saw when he let himself in was the portrait of herself which his clever sweetheart had been doing while he was away, for a surprise. He lifted the canvas from the floor. She had exaggerated her defects: the too prominent eyelids, the mouth pursed like that of a nursery governess. He almost laughed—but he never laughed—though it was a fine performance for one who had only just begun to handle oils. The poise of the head was amiss; the artist, doubled with the model, had had to crane backwards at every stroke and then resume the position. He alone knew how to pose her the right way, in the attitude she at once took on when told to let herself go, surprising

---

[1] Was it Lear's too—the wave that

> . . . keeps eternal whisperings around
> Desolate shores and with its nightly swell
> Gluts twice ten thousand caverns.

in so young a girl, as of a woman whose lover has kissed her
" until she be wearied out," assuming the aspect of passion
jaded, yet eager for a renewal of love, her pale eyes, " as of a dove
that sickeneth," hid " in the sweet dimness of her loosened hair's
downfall." The hair that people had jeered at, jeered at still,
and that perversely had bound him to her for ever, as a man and
an artist, so that when he painted her or wrote of her, upsurged
in him all his old tenderness.

That bewitched, inhibited man, Ruskin, knew it and told him
often how much more " beautifully and subtly " he worked when
Lizzy sat to him. " She cures you of your worst faults when you
only look at her."

But she was no good at nursing, so he went back to Arlington
Street to be tended by sister Maria. Scott invited him back to
Hexham, but now it would be too hot in Newcastle. He spent
the next three weeks mostly in bed at his people's house. The
boil gave way to Maria's treatment, so that he left off his poultices, got out of bed, came down to the parlour and was wearying
to get back to his study. He had an idea that the housekeeper
and Lizzy between them had kept McCrack away.

4

She worked at her portrait and by August it was finished—
" A perfect wonder ! " Gabriel said, helped a little with the
colour, and was going to send it to the Exhibition. . . . " She
has been very ill though, lately."

This is the first discernible waft of the wings of Azrael the
Angel of Death.[1] Emma Brown did not at all like the look of
her young friend. Near the Browns, at Twenty-four Sussex
Lodge, Finchley Road, a friend of the Howitts had come to
live whose daughters played with his little Cathy. Not quite
an ordinary doctor; he was a Homœopath, a Swedenborgian
and a bit of a crank, and published poems which he said he had
been " constrained to write without his own volition." [2]

Gabriel quite approved of Emma's taking Lizzy to see
Dr. Wilkinson. He did not particularly want to call in the
family doctor.

[1] About August 25th, 1853.
[2] What Gabriel always called the " Bogie Poems." It was Garth Wilkinson
who introduced Blake to the reading world.

ELIZABETH ELEANOR SIDDALL
From a drawing by D. G. Rossetti

Wilkinson did not send Mrs. Brown out of the room, for he did not think Miss Siddal would stand it. He indicated an armchair and she assumed the position in which she could sit the longest. Big-faced, quiet, tall and straight as a spear, gentle and deliberate in manner, Wilkinson considered her. Fatefully roseate, perniciously lovely, she waited until he should tell her her fate, sitting very still, with half-closed eyelids, head pressed back into the swelling cushion that almost hid her cheeks on both sides. The contour of the bosom was dissimulated under the plaited folds of her dress, the whole languid torso masked by its sheath of pliable whalebones converging to the low-placed, pointed waist. But he could see that there was no such constriction as ladies use. He noted the long thin feet pushed out from under her skirts, crossed on the footstool he had advanced for her. She did not use them much—they were as thin as her hands. He noted those, flabby and blue-veined, and the shape of the arms—like little Lyddy's, fine, but in her case out of proportion to the rest, lying supported on the arms of the chair.

" Move them ! " he ordered, and the sheaf of fingers was clasped and fell again into her lap as if she would never lift them again.

Long legs, long fingers, long throat, dullish prominent eyes, luxuriant hair—all characteristic of one type of what we now colloquially call T.B. Distinct curvature of the spine ! He asked the usual questions about her way of life, and experienced the same difficulty as William Rossetti did in getting anything out of her, though she did not, of course, permit herself to be " flighty " with him. Her life was still her own, though death was implicit in it. Both she and Wilkinson, approaching the theme from different angles and avenues, knew this. The poet in the doctor got at the deep, dark kernel of inward knowledge that every human being possesses about himself.

She was vocal enough about the unhealthiness, the cold and damp of her old home, which had doubtless encouraged the illness ; the stagnant canals and cluttered-up hatches and the mixed smells of the avocations practised by the inhabitants of the region ; parchment, glue, size and chemical works, and how the Mumpers who made brooms, always said that the Plague, which had been so bad hereabouts, still lingered. She was too loyal to her parents and to Millais to mention her fireless bedroom and tell of that P.R.B. experiment on the body of a hapless

woman in Gower Street, but she owed no loyalty to Mrs. Tozer
—there was no need to blink facts there. But of the crescent
horror of her childhood, which grew with her growth instead of
fading out with puberty and the onrush of fresh images,[1] she
told him nothing. Her class is notoriously shy of doctors.

Garth Wilkinson recommended change and a *confrère* of his,
Doctor Hailes of Hastings. She must not *think* of working for
the present.

But Gabriel, getting a nice commission from Routledge to
illustrate a selection of her own dear Border Ballads, to be
chosen by her own dear Allingham, handed over some of her
favourites to see what she could do with them. " She ought not
to paint, but *this*, of course, she must do." At least she was
taking her codliver oil.

She had refused to tell him in detail what the doctor had said,
—he put no faith in Mrs. Brown's version, who would ?—and,
like many another artist, confronted with circumstances which
he humanly conceived himself powerless to avert, took refuge
in a cynicism which haply belied his real feelings. " Models
suffer from sitting still when they are consumptive," and " always
contrive to look their worst when wanted to look their best," and
other such thankless speeches, came from his lips. Like a priest
serving the altar who should suddenly see the Madonna swoon
from her pedestal, deprived for the nonce of her good offices and
intercessions, so he, suddenly saddled with the care and protection
of an invalid, was unable to adopt the ancillary attitude and leave
his own comfort out of the question. What was *he* to do ? He
had any amount of commissions to fulfil. Going away just now
was an impossibility. There was " McCrack's " commission,
with which he was getting on, and the Plint arrears. He had
not time to take her to the seaside, and even if he had had time,
no money for lodgings, and the rent was due here and, instead of
setting to and painting a picture to raise it, he was making and
sending Scott caricatures of his landlord tearing his hair, with
a scrip of objurgation issuing from his mouth !

6

Partly out of rivalry of Christina, Lizzy was writing verse that
she made no attempt to publish nor Rossetti for her. The

[1] William Rossetti, in his so brief account of his sister-in-law, considers the
memory of the murderer's very touch as worth recording. He realised its Freudian
signification and once, at the Robinsons', he told me all about it.

poems were not quite good enough; like her drawings, frustrate, without force, mere imitations of her Master, down to his great idea of Inter-Redemption. But her version of the Rescue-Complex was as the little lecture of Browning's Pippa to the whores of Venice as against the tremendous implications of *Jenny* and *The Blessed Damozel*.

She herself is the protagonist throughout. She has died, and wingèd angels have borne her up to the Judgment Seat to tell the Christ, bending down, her woes. And later, these angels "her lover's soul shall bring" while she stands by singing and they play among themselves. She sings because she is glad, she knows that all will be well and they are both to be received into Eternal Life, when "he and she and Angels three Before God's Face shall stand" at last.

She will go first, of course, but Gabriel is not to grieve or weep bitter tears that might prevent her soul from passing, but to sit meekly at her side and "watch her young life flee." And when she is dead he is to distinguish her in the throng of spirits floating past. . . . They are represented so, flying across a starry heaven in the Lasinio book that old Mr. Millais had given to Gabriel, which was now in the little passage-room full of books that nobody ever dusted.

She worked up her poems, much as Swinburne did, inserting and erasing, like him, on long sheets of blue post paper, altering and re-altering them: urgently Pre-Raphaelite in her attempt to get the one lonely word, because it is the only one, and the little intimate detail amid the rhetoric which will bring the situation before us. Her range of subjects suggests Edgar Allan Poe, of whose verse she had heard so much repeated. "Gone, gone for ever like the tender dove, That left the ark, alone." The buried shepherd's grave, grass-grown, "where his lambs could come and bleat over him." Like Poe, who said he stayed for fourteen nights in the churchyard where his lost Lenore was buried, Lizzy's thought, after her visit to the doctor, dwelt on "grey headstones and green moss—pale church-grass waving in the wind" that is blowing the brown leaves over, or kissing the dust from off the tombs with faint carven effigies of the dead prone along their surfaces—

> Lying alone
> With hands pleading earnestly
> All in white stone.

CHAPTER VII

I

WILLIAM ALLINGHAM came over in October
and, visiting the circle at Highgate, the Seddons,
the Tebbs, Patmore and the Howitts, was told of
Miss Siddall's state of health, of which they could
not get Gabriel to take enough notice. Barbara Smith, deep-
toned, gave him instructions how to find Gabriel in his
new digs.

Gabriel was painting, but he quickly took his picture off the
easel and turned it to the wall. It was not *Found*. He had left
that aside in a temper—in two tempers. He was annoyed with
Hunt for another reason than *The Awakened Conscience*, and with
Johnny Millais too. The pair had managed to collar Ruskin,
who refused to recognise dear old Brown at all, and whose
acquaintance he himself seemed so far unable to make. Yet Hunt
(and Halliday) had been staying with him that autumn in a
lonely cottage in the Highlands, where the Professor had installed
himself, his young wife and a beautiful young man, leaving them
alone together while he went to Edinburgh to give his lectures.
Halliday had remonstrated with him, in view of the appointments
of the cottage. There was not room to swing a cat in it and
meals were sent round from the inn. Millais had twice run
away from temptation, and returned. He was going back now.
He had only come up to receive his Academy Diploma, and Hunt
was staying in London, putting off his journey to the East
because he was trying to get Johnny to go too and keep out of
mischief.

Millais would not go, Gabriel told Allingham. Something
else, more important than a woman to him, was keeping him
back. A friend!

2

" If you want to see Deverell alive you had better go soon, for
he is very bad."

66

Deverell had been ailing for the last six months, but had insisted on going on with his work; his brothers and sisters were dependent on him since his father's death. His complaint was now found to be Doctor Bright's disease of the kidneys. By October people had begun to guess the truth. Woolner, returning from the Antipodes, wrote that he hoped that " maybe Hunt would be back too " (Hunt, who had not yet gone), and the Brethren would all meet and enjoy themselves again—" poor Deverell excepted."

Misfortune dogged the poor lad. After his father died a little sister was struck with paralysis and lost the use of her arm for life. Then he, the breadwinner, got ill. The move from the Strand to Kew had necessitated going backwards and forwards to his job in all weathers, walking home in the rain or travelling in draughty third-class carriages. Gabriel begged him to use one of the rooms in Number Fourteen, " but he keeps off coming to me because of some sketches he wants to make for his next picture." [1]

He did not know his danger but, in November, Dr. Marshall, who was by way of attending the Pre-Raphaelites for nothing, confirmed the verdict of Deverell's own doctor. There was a chance for him if he would only take reasonable care but, the way he was going on, he had only two months to live. Rossetti had repeated his offer of Chatham Place, " so much more cheerful than Kew "—but Deverell had answered coldly that he must not think of moving just now.

He was never again to darken its doors, but if we are to believe Stephens and Lizzy, his fleeting thought travelled there in the moment of death.

In those last weeks he turned to Hunt and Millais, though it was Rossetti he had loved. Millais, the only one of the P.R.B. to win the fight of their juvenescence, was now but faintly putting up the other great fight in which he did not win. " He won't go back to Glenfinlas," they said—but he did. Returning to London on Christmas Day he went to church three times— and next week dined with his enchantress at Herne Hill. Yet, in love, ambitious and hard at work, he found time to sit with his sick friend, reading aloud to him, beating up help. . . . He begged for Deverell of Ruskin, whose portrait he was painting, whose wife he was stealing, of kind Mrs. Combe for comforts for the sick man. He deplored the apathy of those about Walter, the servant incompetent and the young sister not much use.

[1] *The Doctor's Visit.*

67

" Last night she went out to a dance and was not back till twelve
o'clock,"[1] so that when Millais got to Margaretta Terrace, where
they had moved, the fire was out and the patient leaning un-
covered half out of bed. He could only touch toast and milk
and was wasting away. Millais thought it time he saw a clergyman, but they dared not tell him because he was fretting over the
fate, in the event of his death, of his people.

They let him know one cold February morning that he could
not live through the day. Wishing a little fretfully that he had
been told before, he supposed he was " man enough to die," and
died as his father had made him live, an agnostic, without
benefit of clergy. He had not been able to hear what was said
to him for some days before, but, when Rossetti came uninvited,
he rose up in bed and kissed him.

Rossetti wished that he had been able to go oftener but
supposed that the patient would not have been allowed to see
him? " Pity! He might have had something to say to me!"
He might, indeed.

Lizzy, with Frederic Stephens, had been leaning out of the
window in Chatham Place on that snowy morning, watching
through the curtain of snowflakes the people going over the
bridge. Gabriel was inside working. Stephens had said suddenly, " There goes Deverell!"

It was the very moment he died alone in the room, the nurse
away and Millais waiting in the parlour.

3

At the funeral were Brown, Stephens, Munro and of course
Millais, but Gabriel averred that he " could not trust his excit-
able nature." He was invited to a party that very evening but
did not know if he " would be in spirits to go to it." He kindly
undertook to finish a picture the dead man had left on the easel,
so that the family would get the money, and kept his word, taking
licence to alter " what I do not quite like in the face of Celia," for
which Lizzy had sat.

His letters to his intimates gave colour to inevitable inferences
with regard to the triple relation of Walter, Lizzy and himself.
" Him whose heart has so often beat with mine in the longing
which Death could only end for either!" And to Scott,
" May God bless him and bless you and me!" There was no

---

[1] *Life of John Everett Millais.*

doubt that this couple were, both of them, deeply disturbed and distressed by the death of that pale, piteous man, and the woman at once began to manœuvre for position, and none of them blamed her—certainly not Brown.

Once Gabriel's model—now his pupil; a slight step, but no nearer than that, in five years !

Living in rooms by herself, spending the rest of her time in the company of one man, closeted with him alone for hours, for days, for nights, using his chambers when he was away . . . sleeping in his bed . . . yet unable to point to a ring on her third finger, she had every excuse for seeking to get the situation regularised and for using Walter Deverell in the assault on Gabriel's emotions.

The long sheets of blue post with their clauses and erasures were stamped with a new morbidity: full of talk of " her ghostly connections " that was to distress Acland and Ruskin so deeply.

> Unsummoned, he returned to me,
> The great strong heart that loved me so.

Nay, but summoned, he did not come. The Sid was to be seen constantly at The Tables, her long white hands posed on the shining mahogany and her chin upturned in the intense yearning for spiritual communion, now at the house of the Howitts', now at Home's Séances in Sloane Street and elsewhere. But she never " got " him : she knew she never would, except through her own death.

> Soon I'll return to thee
> Hopeful and brave
> When the dead leaves
> Blow over thy grave.

> Soon must I leave thee
> This sweet summer tide.
> That other is waiting
> To claim his pale bride.[1]

He wasn't, that was the worst of it.

A duel, silent but to the death began, between these two. As a means to the end, perhaps unconsciously, she encouraged Rossetti's complex, reading up Dante, adapting her appearance to mediæval standards—in the house, that is. In those days even Gabriel, so frowsty at home, would have been quite upset at seeing a lady without gloves in the street. She walked herself

[1] *Rossetti*, Evelyn Waugh.

sick, she got her feet wet, she sat till she dropped, she missed her meals, she asked nothing in return except marriage; she yielded everything (except that which mediæval romancers call *la chose*). And Gabriel Rossetti wanted that from a woman among other things. Her Victorian airs, her mediæval rigours stimulated his lazy libertinism; he thought only of abolishing so much pride!

Strong in her carefully held virginity, tempting in her rose-white purity, the English girl was not afraid to be alone day in, day out, with this imperious, hot-blooded Italian. That long, proud neck of hers, that tall, high-breasted figure, those cheerless eyes made for chastity, those carefully careless bandeaux of golden hair, like the nymph's " unloosened zone," suggesting uses other than art to which beauty could be put. . . .

But so cruel, this meek unconscious dove! Her attitude, like that of the mediæval ladies, of whom she read with Gabriel, towards their lovers—withholding *le don de l'amoureuse merci*, but condescending to play with them, placing them in ridiculous positions, exchanging clothes and personalities with their waiting-maids, getting them ducked in ponds or beaten with rods, adopting, according to mediæval chroniclers, even more vulgar expedients, hiding them in cellars or up chimneys to be discovered there by irate husbands and given over before their eyes to the coarsest of revenges. . . . Or, like the high-born damsel of whom Brantôme tells us, who had her lover imprisoned and once a day visited him, lazily undressing herself before the bars of his cage.

Dante never possessed the Florentine; perhaps he never wanted to, but the constant companionship of one who had some of the sensuality of the consumptive, ill, but beautiful and desirable, was exacerbating to nerves that surrender might have assuaged and set the mind of the artist free, letting him make of her the spaniel he could kick instead of the Blue Bird he could not snare. His brusqueries, even brutalities, were sign of nervous disarray when she was present, the revolt of him who was used to sex-submission. . . .

" My mind and my feelings are my own . . ."

And my body too! Such obstinacy in withdrawal annoyed and stimulated; brought out some sort of Sadic twist in him and drove him to reprisals. To her, who did as Patmore says all women may, " on her sweet self set her own price," she denied the gift within her provenance.

He was starving her out, wilfully, perhaps? The idea of

downing so much pride possessed him until he actually came to want her because she was recalcitrant.

And her rigours paved the way for Annie Miller and Fanny.

4

It was reserved for William Allingham to drive Rossetti into the formal engagement to which his friends had almost ceased to look forward.

In February of this year he gave up his post in the Customs and came to London to make a living by literature. He had secured work on *Household Words* through his friendship with Dickens, and Hepworth Dixon of *The Athenæum* was well affected towards him. Wearing his outlandish blue cloak that matched his eyes he secured a room in Southampton Row, left a note at Rossetti's and, on his return, found an invitation from him to Chatham Place that evening—saying that the writer had not slept for nights and that Lizzy was rather bad again.

It was a man's party—Stephens, Hannay, Patmore, Halliday, but not Millais—" out of the way, love-making." There was George Price Boyce, an architect who had just become a landscape painter, Whitley Stokes, C.I.E., LL.D., a Celtic scholar, George Sala, a journalist, and Cayley, Christina's admirer—and William, of course. There was whisky-punch, oysters and tea and smell—the river was getting more and more objectionable. The last guest did not clear off till two, and then the host, in his horror of being left alone, offered to see Allingham home. Noting, counting carefully as usual the " forlorn " women in the Strand, they came to his rooms and for a long time stood together at the window watching the blue stars going in and the dawn coming up under a thick stretch of reddish-brown cloud till in the clear soft light the outlines of the Lombardy poplar just in front were made out and Rossetti, with a deep blowing sigh, went back (he said) to paint all night—when there was no night left—forgetting to shut the house door behind him !

After that they were together for the greater part of each day— Allingham and Gabriel and Boyce (a very nice fellow), visiting divers places of amusement. The Crystal Palace, in its new home at Sydenham—paint-pots still about and workmen daubing it red and blue on a sort of Alhambra model—Regent's Park, to watch the water-fowl rushing about in the kindly air ; Rossetti nervous,

71

making patterns in the gravel all the way with the point of his umbrella. They dined at a new place Rossetti had found in Bankside, Southon's, where a " cordial Stunner " waited, and supped at another chop-house where there was a " *Belle (pas) Sauvage* " with whom Gabriel chose to impute a flirtation to Allingham.

On St. Patrick's Day, the sun setting as a red globe as they hung over the Bridge, Gabriel took him across it into Southwark to show him some old Chaucerian houses, and to where Lizzy's people lived—in the bad street " full of Broom Men and Mumpers," whatever they might be. Gabriel showed him the house—he had never been in it. Once or twice Allingham fancied Gabriel was going to begin about her, but he turned off and discussed Milton.

Not until they had been going about together for nearly a week did he allude to Lizzy, and that was in connection with his sister's poems, which were of course a hundred times better than Lizzy's and not all harping on Death and Deverell.

Allingham had been to tea in Albany Street, played chess with Gabriel's father and looked over books of cuttings with the sisters. He thought Christina pretty but delicate-looking though they, none of them, seemed to notice it. He had been introduced to a cousin Teodorico with beady black eyes, and then he met Miss Sid again, more or less by accident. He ran into Gabriel and Hughes in Fleet Street and Gabriel said, walk to the Howitts' with them.

They drove to Albany Street, picked up William and Christina, and set out for Highgate. Gabriel, William and Christina were respectively twenty-six, twenty-five and twenty-four. William was already nearly bald and Gabriel wore a beard. Allingham, thirty, a man of the world, was the doyen of the party.

It was six miles to The Hermitage. They would stay on to supper and hoped with luck to catch the last bus home—or Miss Leigh-Smith might be there and give them a lift in her new carriage with india-rubber wheels. All except carriage folk in those days were fain to use the new omnibuses [1] that lumbered along the roads like rocking lilies in a storm, piloting " to

---

[1] . . . . some
With richest purple, some are blue
As skies that tempt the swallows back
. . . some barred with black
And yellow, like the April bees. . . .
CALVERLEY.

happy homes by Heath and Hill, by Park or Grove," the artistic and literary fraternity. Rossetti's little life was rounded by buses and Swinburne's, better off, by cabs.

Past the barracks, out of their own street by the York and Albany, Park Street, then as now the street of curios, and along the High Street of Camden Town that ran at the back of Number Thirty-eight, whose garden wall the boys had many a time shinned over to go to the play. After Mornington Crescent the road was bordered on both sides by houses with gardens and wicket gates as far as *Mother Red Cap*—Mother Damnable—painted on the sign dangling in the wind over the inn yard with its grey wooden benches shaped like old men's jaws. Then fields where cows were grazing in meadows, both sides of the road all along to Kentish Town, and it was good until they came to where the new road to Holloway forked off, turning westwards at St. John's Chapel in Green Street, low-lying, and at Carker's Lane the Fleet River that rises in the Hampstead hills (" and comes out by my place underground, poor thing!" Gabriel said), and crosses the road to lose itself in the watery meadows on the right. A few handsome houses on the one side and on the other farms and fields with cows looking like swollen mushrooms feeding, and the maid that milked them standing beside—a not too common sight nowadays.

Christina was hampered, like any mediæval lady in hennin and surcoat, by her five full-starched petticoats—the Pre-Raphaelite women refused to adopt the light, helpful, steel-frame that Eugénie had just brought in—and her flapping straw hat with strings that would come untied. At last they came to the three ponds lying in the hollow at the bottom of West Hill, belted by trees new-covered with keys of pale green, shining in the sunset glow. The sun was glinting on the diamonded panes of The Hermitage, what you could see of them for the ivy and wistaria, the creepers rooted in pots on the verandah climbing up to meet the verdure on the roof. And Mrs. Howitt and Anna Mary were sitting on the lawn with Professor de Morgan, Mr. Atkinson of Ambleside and a tall young lady who rose and sat down again as if weary when she missed the effusive greeting which Christina Rossetti, tired as she was, took care not to give her.

Though Anna Mary Howitt, subjugated, never took her eyes off her, between Lizzy and the sister of Gabriel waved all the trees of the forest of Broceliaunde and the waters of No Man's Land ran between. Always the poet had to think of this woman

73

in terms of romance—a Vivien, a Swan Maiden, a Banshee that Gabriel had bought or caught and carried home to bide miserably awhile among men. One day she would go " in a waff " back to her own people ! Gabriel would never be able to keep her, she was not really for him. . . . Would he care ? There was no knowing. No one knew.

5

It was over four years since Allingham had set eyes on the milliner's girl out of Cranbourn Alley, whom Rossetti's friends called grandiloquently " The Sid," and Rossetti, familiarly, " Guggums." (He had always been " Gug.") She had, he remembered, been rosy and slightly freckled. Some of the colour and all the freckles were gone now. She was terribly thin, her shoulders supported her brown braided, canezou jacket as if they had been two of the pegs that they hung the linen on to dry in the yard at home. If it had not been for her hair, bright, springing, vital as ever, he thought he would not have known her.

He could not remember ever having heard her speak and he did not, in the welter of literary and artistic conversation that always prevailed when the two Rossettis were present, hear her voice now, but he had a queer feeling that she might easily be talking and he not hear . . . a voice behind glass or under water, notes of queer stifled woe such as might rise from one of those patches of blood on Elfin Mere after the Maids had disappeared. . . .

The talk might have interested her, since, as he heard, she had recently taken up art. In that month of reaping, for painters, of the entire year's harvest now being prepared for the assessment of the Royal Academy and the verdict of the terrible Tutor of Art, Ruskin, no one in these circles talked of anything but prices and reviews, critics and editors, artists' hopes, and such moral impedimenta in their lives as in a Victorian age, might prevent the fulfilment of those hopes. A *crim. con.*, a running-away would easily dash a man's prospects.

Millais, returned from Scotland, with his thumbnail badly crushed, making a bridge of stones over the Finlass for Mrs. Ruskin to walk over, was supposed to be at work on his portrait of Ruskin for the R.A., but no one had seen him or it. Rossetti had sent nothing in. Holman Hunt was still abroad, but *The*

Light was ready and *The Awakened Conscience*, a subject slightly novel. But he would not be back to hear the critics on it.

Of the latter Allingham was already one and petted accordingly. Did he write that nice notice of Anna Mary's picture in the Portland Gallery? No, alas; but he had become a buyer and had paid George Price Boyce ten pounds for a small water-colour.

He did not tell them, but *he* had met Millais a night or two ago and had walked back to Gower Street with him to see the portrait, begun last year at Glenfinlas, of a thin, spare gentleman in a coat by Stultz—the one he had ordered to give his Edinburgh Lectures in—standing astride a small, rough, rock-bedded rivulet in the attitude of one just about to enter a drawing-room. . . . Cold, cold the blue tie, the grey suit, the gleams over the stream, the grey clouds at the back rolling over Ben Ledi. Allingham was no gossip but he had a touch of second sight, he noticed that people cut him short the moment he began to talk about Millais. Millais was in mischief! The picture was not going to get itself finished.

He asked Miss Siddal to take him a turn and show him Mrs. Howitt's flowers. He talked to her, told her what he fancied she would like to hear, about his friend Tennyson, the faery man who could see moonlight reflected in the eyes of a nightingale and hear the tiny shrieking bats in the garden at Montpelier Row, and who liked white things—white lilac—white peacocks. And about Ellen Britten, who had been with her at Mrs. Tozer's. He had met Ellen; she was a model too now. And then it was time to go and there was no Barbara to drive them home; and they were all to meet at The Princess's to see Miss Cushman on Friday.

They had missed the yellow bus from the Archway to Victoria and had to walk to *Mother Red Cap*, where Gabriel might pick up the one from Finsbury Park. Miss Sid walked between him and his brother. Allingham naturally offered his arm to Miss Christina, which she accepted. She seemed even more tired than the other girl. She told him what Doctor Wilkinson had said about Miss Siddal, as reported by Gabriel. It was her spine. She would be all right if she took care and went on with the codliver oil.

At The York and Albany they put her into her bus for Weymouth Street and Allingham parted with the Rossettis and went to his new lodgings in Queen Square. Gabriel had asked them all to tea in his studio in Chatham Place on the Friday of next week.

75

CHAPTER VIII

I

PEOPLE were so nice to Mr. Allingham that he felt pretty sure of getting a permanent job in London, and then, Good-bye Ballyshannon! He moved to very much better rooms at seventeen shillings a week, with the services of a maid. He could give suppers; fish, oysters, washed down with beer and tea and sherry-cobbler—dinners of cold beef, sausage and chops sent up on hot-water plates, coffee, tea, and jam roll (and marmalade for Munro).

This amiable, sympathetic and cultivated man who hobnobbed with established celebrities like Carlyle, Clough, Dickens and Thackeray and the interesting Pre-Raphaelite Brethren, and wrote a regular newsletter about them all once a week to Mr. and Mrs. Browning in Florence, was welcome everywhere. He would stroll in the morning into publishers' and editors' offices. He would lunch with the Smiths in Blandford Square or with the Tom Taylors at Eagle Lodge and take tea with the Carlyles in Cheyne Walk or with Tennyson in Lincoln's Inn Fields. He would pass through sale-rooms and picture exhibitions, dip into the churches of fashionable preachers or into the House when a debate was on. And he generally got seats for the Opera, where of course he took Gabriel or William. He went with them and " Miss Sid " to the play—balcony stalls—even to church, and to Gabriel's stiffish parties in Chatham Place—fruitless efforts to call a desert peace—inviting William and his sisters to meet the girl they were so afraid of his marrying, and others—George Boyce who did not like Miss Sid much and would much rather have met Annie Miller. They would all consume oysters and drink beer and sit by turns on the famous balcony that looked over the river. It was very " slow." After a while The Sid would fade quietly out of the room, leaving no particular void, and there would be a welcome closing up of the family ranks, for Gabriel really loved these people though he could not get them to be nice to his girl. And later the Rossettis would all walk away in a quiet party up Chancery Lane.

2

The river steamers "served" Blackfriars, and next day Allingham picked up the lovers at Chatham Place and they took boat to London Bridge, standing all the way because the steamer was crowded, staring up at St. Paul's with its fretwork of scaffolding as they passed, not altogether comfortably; watching the officer empowered to board all steamers and arrest for debt, recognisable only by the small silver key on his button-hole. And then by rail to Greenwich.

Women, thought Allingham, hate expeditions—the leaving their base, which may be their throne. All except his great and generous Barbara, who dressed for them properly and went out hatless, rain or shine, " in the sacred name of pigment." But Lizzy's kid gloves were soiled before they left the train, the braid on the hem of her long dress came unsewn as soon as they got out of the station and, by the time they reached the Park gates, her hair was really down and not merely arranged to look as if it were.

She had started tired; Gabriel bored. Allingham noted her absence of fellowship, of warmth in speech, her reticence of gesture as it were the setting in of some sort of ice-age in a woman. . . . Restless without being lively, fidgety without being alert, wilful without decision, draggled in mind and body. . . . He recalled with an effort the young girl he had seen for the first time in Mrs. Tozer's bonnet shop, eyelids then upraised that now drooped and, like the long stone slab of a tomb, hid the dull, dead, blue eyes. Or the next time, in the garden studio at Kew— taking off her bonnet with a modest but superb gesture, without patting her hair with a sidelong glance at the cracked studio glass as most girls would; sweeping up to the *estrade* like " Proud Maisie " she was posing for, fending off the tacit snubs of the Misses Maria and Margaretta Deverell. . . .

Rossetti wanted to see the sun set from the top of Observatory Hill. They would sit there awhile and then dine in one of the eating-houses by the Park gates or the Pier. Making the pace with his " slopperty walk," he kept well in front, trailing his umbrella in the sandy soil and humming " a *sotto voce* defiance of the universe," till they came to the platform with seats set, as in

77

a theatre in front of the view—marshes, houses and sky all of the same colour, blue grey, except, in the north, some mysterious, equidistant bars of a whiter white than water, more like iron at white heat.

The Blessed Damozel, breathing faintly, her upper lip raised in the known poise of pathos and her eyes gone to the back of her head, leaned over the iron bar of the railings and wished she were on earth having tea in one of the kiosks she had noticed long ago coming up the hill, when her spirit was younger. But Gabriel was pouring into her ears poetic accounts of what she was seeing before her—London, stretched out to the skyline, and—splaying out like a full-bellied snake, with the Isle of Dogs lying snared in its coils—the River that served it. Those mathematical bars on the north represented the great chain of Docks—West India, East India. . . . Where was the sea? She had never seen the sea! Rossetti would show it to her some day.

Allingham, who knew that women want their tea, persuaded Gabriel to let them go back into the town without trying to find the place where Brown's Aunt Cooper had lived, somewhere half-way down the hill.

Gabriel was annoyed and ceased to exercise his well-known charm. He wanted something more substantial than tea, but Allingham persuaded him to enter the first shop that came. Up wide wooden stairs, into a low-ceiled room where there was a window seat with geraniums behind it and a table with a clean cloth on it and a dusty cruet. They got beer and chops and Allingham read them his latest, the MS. of which he happened to have in his pocket, and Gabriel was so nice and flattering about it [1] that he won the poet to himself again.

At London Bridge Miss Sid was put into her bus for Weymouth Street. She was not one of those that kiss in the street, but Allingham fancied she was cross with Gabriel, about a girl called Annie Miller, of whom she had spoken to him once or twice. Miller was her name, but people said she had Italian blood in her. Her father was a carpenter in Justice Walk, between Lawrence Street and Church Street, just behind where Mr. Hunt lived. He had picked her up, much as Gabriel had Lizzy. Like Lizzy, Annie was respectable, and " good-hearted, with the makings of an excellent woman in her." Hunt had taught her to speak correctly and paid for her lessons in dancing and deportment. The idea, nebulous at first, of training her to be his

---

[1] He took no interest at all in the sea or ships, so it was very nice of him.

wife grew stronger; by the time he left for the East it was understood that he looked forward to finding Annie "finished" and fit to be Mrs. Hunt when he came back.

Mr. Hunt's seriousness rather bored Miss Miller, but she had been sensible enough—or her father for her—to accept his kindness and profit by it, especially the dancing. She lived near enough to Cremorne to have opportunities for frequent practice of the art with George Boyce and Frederic Stephens and others: many a time she and Gabriel would go to Highbury Barn and The Gun Tavern together.

The jolly Annie was merely a pawn in the game of checkmate which the best of friends will occasionally play with one another. Rossetti was getting back on Hunt—"He took my subject and I'm taking his model," he had said jauntily to Allingham.

3

Allingham was quite rude next day when he went to breakfast with his friend and found him in his bedroom doctoring himself— "You and your pills!" Miss Leigh-Smith and Miss Howitt were in the next room looking at Lizzy's portrait of herself. After breakfast they were all to go to Margaret Street to see Dyce's "window" in Mr. Hope's new church—then to Covent Garden for tulips.

Mr. Allingham thought he would consult Barbara about Miss Siddal, since she was by way of championing and befriending Woman. She had done nothing much as yet except set up a High School for Girls at sixpence a week, where witty Emily Davies taught and Marian Evans, assistant editor of *The Westminster Review*, as well as Barbara's Aunt Julia and pretty Bessie Parkes. But it was more a lark than anything else. The field in the fens near Girton was still under tillage, the Monster Petition not presented: the Women's Property Act, Divorce Law Reform and Votes for Women [1] still slumbered in the bosoms—in those days ladies had bosoms but no heads, to keep ideas in—of the so-called Fair Sex, stultified in what Barbara called their "culpable resignation to circumstances." The circumstances of this trio were easy; they made their sorties into

---

[1] "We shall get the Vote after I am dead and you will go to the Poll in your winding sheet," said Emily Davies, her elder, to Barbara Bodichon.

"This mad wicked folly on which my poor feeble sex is bent . . . the subject makes the Queen so furious that she cannot contain herself!"—Victoria R.

life from the shelter of the paternal roof and with the co-operation of their elders. Anna Mary's father had just shaken off Quakerism ; Bessie's was Joe Parkes of Birmingham, an active politician with Radical sympathies.[1] Barbara's father was blind.[2] Miss Leigh-Smith gave herself that licence in her relations with the other sex which women, chaperoned by family butlers and private broughams, could dare do under Victoria at the cost merely of being supposed eccentric. " A jolly fellow "—she flirted even " in a quite nice way." A Romola much too sensible to waste herself on a Tito like Gabriel Rossetti. Though she had never been to boarding school, she was not exempt from the cloistered girl's foible of romantic passion for members of her own sex, for Emily Davies and Miss Betham-Edwards and Mrs. Beecher Stowe and Anna Mary's rich friend Miss Coutts up the hill. There was also Dinah Mulock the novelist, and there had been Adelaide Anne Procter the poetess, mourned by Barbara and Bessie and Anna Mary like a lover. There was Charlotte Cushman with her deep contralto voice, called Captain Charlotte because of that and because she chose to play Romeo and Hamlet. And her more feminine sister Susan, whom a man had dared to desert, and Miss Eliza Cook, who dressed like a man down to her waist and had her hair cut short.[3]

But Bessie Parkes—" Bessie the Brick "—handsome, dashing and gay, dressed in the height of the fashion.

Anna Mary Howitt was the least impressive of the three, the only one with the true artistic temperament.[4]

4

Barbara Leigh-Smith liked Gabriel, but not this Pre-Raphaelitism which, on the face of it, reminded her, a would-be reformer

[1] Her mother a daughter of Joseph Priestley, the discoverer of oxygen.

[2] His domestic relations were unconventional and shocking to his brother-in-law. Florence was not as a child allowed to play with Barbara and Nanny. But Aunt Julia was fascinated by the beauty and cleverness of these two daughters of Uncle Benjamin, the pariah.—*Life of Florence Nightingale*, I. B. O'Malley.

[3] This style created in Society at this time as deep, if less costly, a scandal as the cropped locks of Joan of Arc, hidden by no hennin, which deeply shocking her judges, perhaps cost her her life ?

[4] She gave up painting because the great Critic of All said such severe things about her work, forcing her, so her mother said, " to withdraw from the practice of the fine arts," and adopt the other profession of marriage. Ruskin was never very kind to women beginners ; he nearly estopped Christina Rossetti from being a poetess.

of the status of her sex, of the mental starvation undergone by Woman in mediæval days; her disgustingly inferior position excepting during those few fleeting years when she is man's delight and may command him. Look, she said, at the faces of the women in the pictures these young fellows admired—the tight waists, the overloaded heads that must have ached so frequently, the lined foreheads, the pinched mouths, the sly slanting eyes, boding, biding, of the oppressed slave, of Lucrezia Borgia ever-lastingly brushing and sunning her golden hair—its abundance the sign of imbecility, Doctor Elliotson said, so much taken from her brains—perfectly aware of what her brothers were up to but powerless, or unwilling, to prevent them.

Chattels, these ladies, inured to death and horror, with iron nerves—if they possessed them at all. It is not so much the iron nerve as the sleeping one that avails the woman who never knows at any time of day if she may not be burned for a witch, have her lover's heart served up to her on a platter by a jealous husband, or her baby's brains dashed out on the castle stones by the other knight who has " downed " him.

Appearing to suffer from indigestion, looking too ill to be really pretty, Barbara had observed this Miss Siddall at The Hermitage. But she had never asked Mr. Rossetti to bring her to Blandford Square. She would now. The girl had nice manners, as good as Gabriel's. His were the result, she supposed, of his mother's training, and she had heard that the two governess sisters were very nice too.

The boys called her, among other sobriquets, " The Countess," but she did not, to Barbara's thinking, look in the least like one. Just a good, simple sort of person! Was there not some talk of Gabriel Rossetti's marrying her? That did not strike Miss Leigh-Smith as unsuitable. Artists painted where they loved and loved where they painted, and seldom married born ladies—not even Academicians. Look at Mrs. Redgrave and Mrs. Armitage and Mrs. Hart; listen to the " malaprops " of Mrs. Goodall and Mrs. Stacy Marks! As to Miss Siddall, she had heard something of noble ancestry on the father's side—tombs in a churchyard in the Midlands and armorial bearings sported; but the mother had been a housemaid, hadn't she? She did not know of Lizzy's occupying Gabriel's rooms while he was away in Newcastle, but if she had she would not have been shocked—Bohemians cannot afford to take this or that social lapse into account.

Allingham spoke long and passionately of Miss Siddal's life as present model and ex-milliner—and of how she had got ill in the exercise of both jobs, the long hours sitting in some constrained position for the one; the stuffy rooms, predisposing to phthisis, in the other. The hours at Mrs. Tozer's, so Ellen Britten had told Allingham, were terrific. In the Season the girls were often up all night. And artists had no mercy where a pose was concerned—Allingham told her the romantic story of the bath in Gower Street. "Too bad," Miss Leigh-Smith had said. Girls should be taught the rules of health; but it was actually contended—by men, probably, with their queer fetish of female delicacy—that "women should know as little as possible about that exceedingly delicate subject." [1]

Yes, she would certainly see Miss Siddall. She might go to her Cousin Florence's Home for the Care of Gentlewomen in Sickness in Upper Harley Street. Bessie would see about it.

Allingham felt pretty sure that Miss Sid would refuse to leave London with Annie Miller about; but he did not dare tell this to the Lady Bountiful of Blandford Square, for health meant more than hearts to her. With Miss Siddal's marital problem she would have dealt like the kind mistress who makes it her business to bring the recalcitrant sweetheart of a servant-girl to the point.

Nor could the relations of Rossetti and his model be fully discussed between a chaste Irishman and an emancipated Victorian maiden. Barbara knew of no particular reason why Gabriel should marry Lizzy unless he wanted to; if he did, why not? Did he actually owe her marriage? William Allingham thought so and attributed the girl's state of health largely to suspense and dread of another woman's taking her place. He had run into that Annie Miller yesterday when he went to Chatham Place for his sitting—which Gabriel had forgotten. They were eating chops and sausages. They made him go with them to Madame Tussaud's. Annie did not particularly want to go— Rossetti did. Leaden-footed, the confidant padded about with the buxom girl in the Chamber of Horrors while Gabriel, gloating on the effect of the calm, rosy, murderers' faces shining like turnip lanterns in the dimness, seemed unaffected by the dreary airs of death down here that made Allingham so uncomfortable. And

[1] We never do hear what exactly was the matter with Lizzy. Probably Doctor Wilkinson sent her out of the room while he made his report to Mrs. Brown, who was hardly capable of grasping its import and, if she had, less from reticence than modesty, would not have enlarged upon it.

Annie was dying to get upstairs to the Kings and Queens, to the lifelike old Quaker gentleman whom you jostle as you go by, the baby in the cradle and the lady in the glass case whose pneumatic bosom goes softly up and down under her laces. . . .

No harm in either of them! Gabriel was offhand, indifferent and absorbed : Annie, quiet, proper and sensible ; but he could not help thinking all the time of the lonely girl in Weymouth Street, and when they parted, Gabriel and Annie going in the direction of Piccadilly—to dance—he, in low spirits, fared home to his lodgings.

5

Things have a way of all coming at once. It had been Fine since the 1st and Very Fine since the 5th. The 13th of April turned out to be the finest day of all ; the day of Supreme Moments, of the pulling of the strings of shower-baths, affecting deeply the fortunes of Gabriel and Lizzy and of, perhaps, a greater than they. William Allingham called on several people, but no one was at home—neither Rossetti, with whom he had an appointment, not Routledge, the publisher of whom he had begged one. So he drifted where everyone in the set did drift when at a loose end, to The Hermitage, and Mary Howitt took him to the Gillies' to supper. They had all been discussing the health of Miss Siddall with Margaret Gillies and Doctor South-wood Smith and the "hanging off" of Gabriel. Allingham loved the villain in this piece and, though Miss Siddal's affairs were properly none of his, he found himself telling Anna what he had not quite liked to tell Barbara.

Walking down the hill from Hampstead, her arm tucked in his, his other arm holding her basket—passing in and out of alternate patches of light and dark that the shadows of delicately leaved, swaying boughs made over the road, glistening whitely with quartz ; agonised into dull blue here and there from the locked wheels of carts grinding in their slippers down the hill, he bade her notice this and the Pre-Raphaelite truth of Gabriel's description of just such a night, in the poem he had read aloud to them all the other day, and how, when the wind blew this way and that,

> All the leaf shadows at a breath
> Shrank in the road. . . .

(The rhyme, of course, was *Death*.) Just as the wind of the spirit will make portentous the shadows of our imaginings, distorting

83

them, magnifying them one minute and reducing them to nothing the next. How wonderful their dear Gabriel was! Why, when he could notice little things like that, was he so stupid and tactless with his women? Tiring them, chivying them, worrying their lives out. Neglecting, for a beautiful minx like Annie Miller, a woman quite as beautiful, and worth a hundred of her.

Anna Mary did not seem to have heard of Annie Miller. She questioned him. Then—he must not mention it to anybody else, but she really *must* tell him—Miss Siddal could not possibly mind *his* knowing—Gabriel had proposed, long ago and she had accepted him. The reason she had not announced the engagement was because of the opposition of her family. Lizzy's mother was most particular with her daughters and would not approve of Lizzy marrying an artist; they were always so improvident—to say nothing worse. Did he know that she was a Sidal of Hope? And her father descended from a family that went back to the fourteenth century and had been knights and had had a coat of arms? Anna Mary's father, who travelled all over the country doing those Annuals, writing up various places he went to, had been there and seen the names on the big tombs in the churchyard at the place where the family had lived in their heyday. He had had occasion to look up some papers about it in his capacity of antiquary.

6

Mr. Allingham went home conscious that he might have made mischief, but had forgotten about it next time he went to Chatham Place for a sitting. No one was there, but he waited and, presently, Gabriel and William came in together, tremendously excited about something that had happened yesterday. The ball was at Gabriel's feet and no one rejoiced more than his brother.

McCracken had sent *Dante drawing the Angel* to the great critic to look at, and Ruskin had written the painter " an incredible letter," was " his respectfully "—wanting to call—and yesterday he *had* called! " Seems in a mood to make my fortune! " Rossetti did not know it, but one of the Brethren, the one from whom he least deserved it, had been working for him. The P.R.B., criticising, teasing, lampooning, abusing [1] each other like

---

[1] Rossetti, in a lazy sort of temper, would actually call Millais " The Prince of Sneaks."

JOHN RUSKIN
From a photograph

pickpockets, strove when the good name or prosperity of a member of the band was concerned, to maintain complete solidarity. Hunt, meeting Ruskin in Florence on his way out to the Holy Land, was at pains to interest the great critic in the work of his dear Gabriel. He would have done it all the same even had he known of the visits to Chatham Place, the excursions, the suppers when her lieges drank out of complacent Annie's shoe. And one may set against this Rossetti's heartfelt congratulations on *The Light* in letters to all his friends, outdoing the very critics in its praise.

7

Ruskin had run in on his way back from King's Cross, where he had been seeing his young wife off on a visit to her parents in Scotland. He himself had just returned from abroad and had been obliged to sleep at Denmark Hill, as one of her letters told him that the bed was broken and must be mended before his return and, meanwhile, she would go home for a bit.[1]

John Hobbes, attending to the luggage—there was a good deal for the stay of a fortnight or so—did not realise that this was a supreme moment in the careers of these two persons. They did not kiss. There had been a wrangle—but there were often wrangles between them—and she had said cutting things, as usual. Mr. Ruskin was in a dream, as usual, and took no notice of them. Just as the train moved out of the station he took out his purse and tossed it into her lap—he wasn't sure if she would have enough for flies and porters at Perth. . . .

8

" My plans are made, and it would take a cleverer man than John Ruskin to upset them now ! "

This is what John Hobbes heard on that fourteenth day of April as he stood attentive at the door of the railway carriage, a sentence delivered with clear precision of utterance by Mrs. Ruskin. The two Johns, accustomed to her Scotch habit of dramatic over-emphasis, did not take much note of it at the time.

Yet it meant Doctors' Commons and a Jury of Matrons, a

[1] He was never to see her again except among the audience at his lectures, sitting beside her friend the wife of the President of the Royal Academy, crabbing him. She had Lady Eastlake's sympathy and that of the world in general. But not perhaps that of John Hobbes ! As valets will, he knew a lot.

parting and a re-marriage. All this was behind Patmore's babblement and Millais' distraction and failure to have the Ruskin portrait ready. She was going to get a divorce, so Jane Carlyle was telling everybody. When the case came on, Hobbes was out of England. His evidence might have helped John Ruskin had he indeed desired to be helped? But he was letting it all go.

At any rate, an action was raised by Euphemia Gray—or Grey—falsely called Ruskin: the marriage was declared null and void from the beginning by reason of the impotence of the said John Ruskin, by sentence of the Commissory Court of Surrey in the Diocese of Winchester.

9

John Ruskin was a Scotsman; Euphemia Gray was his cousin. Both of them legatees of the ferocities of the Covenant and with more than " something of the Shorter Catechist " in them. She came from a schoolroom full of gay growing girls at Bowerswell: the household at Denmark Hill was composed of four persons who never laughed. The master of the house, John James Ruskin [1] (of Ruskin, Telford and Domecq), with his queer arched eyebrows, his mouth with full curves like that of John Keats, had more of the artist in him than his wife or his son. The mistress, his cousin Margaret, whom he had married for love, with her narrow, peering, heavy-lidded eyes, ruined before their time with fine needlework, her forward-poking, impertinent mouth, was thirty-seven when her son was born, on a wooden bedstead which broke—beds had a way of breaking in this ménage—for her muscles were by then as rigid as her tenets. She held her child's finger in the flame of a candle " to remember him " not to tell lies, she whipped him with her slipper to save her own hand— " what for should she be hurt when *she* had done nothing wrong ? "

The boy never did lie, but he saw the flame of that candle in his mother's eyes until she died.

And after that and the death of another member of the family, Anne Strahan, who got in at the window and found the old Master, her father, hanging dead inside, and knew all about the ghosts of Bowerswell where he and she had lived, John was rudderless, except for the wooden concepts of morality these women had given him, wedged into his consciousness,

[1] He was delicate and always wore a truss.

adapted somehow to circumstances by his immense and cunning intelligence.

He was born under Aquarius;[1] Rossetti—one can give a pretty good guess—under Scorpio, with Herschel, the baleful star for artist-natures, in the ascendant. Between Ruskin who loved blue and Rossetti who loved red,[2] between the medusa and the salamander, the aquamarine and the alexandrite, the Scotchman and the Southron, the ascetic and the man of temperament who, with colour, had made himself a sort of soul (as Marion De Lorme with love, a virginity), gulfs for ever yawned. For to Rossetti " the colour of a picture is its physiognomy, the body of its life ! " But Ruskin's God could be rendered in stone. He seemed to forget that abbey walls were only a surface on which colour was laid and would have had little use for either a painted cathedral or a tinted statue. He loved Light *per se ;* concerned with the form of things and the way Light took them, fell on them, was abstracted from them—duly oppressed by the Shadow of the Cross that lay athwart the world. Rossetti, on the contrary, loved a rich, huttering gloom, such as savages know who cluster nightly round a camp fire, illumining but a little way along the low, woody arcades, fitfully shining on the boughs of the trees near by, making the twigs of the undergrowth shine like golden wire—a room full of furniture as opposed to the empty sheen of Alpine snows.

Both men were full generous. They had that in common. Rossetti out of *laisser aller* and caprice, while Ruskin was—we have it from himself—" nearly as just as it is possible for a man to be, in this world." Both were frank and subtle ; canny and unpractical at the same time. Than Ruskin's infolded nature, Rossetti's was infinitely less complicated, and Ruskin perhaps more simple because more highly educated than Rossetti. Artists are nearer the savage, to whom pictorial comes more naturally than literary, representation. They never cared for each other. Rossetti never troubled to read a line of Ruskin and, " Artists are very like pigs, so far as I know them," Ruskin wrote to Doctor Acland after his protégé had been more than usually trying.

[1] At half-past seven in the morning. The painter Varley cast his horoscope. The ages of 14, 18 and 21 were especially fatal to him. The Adèle Domecq disappointment filled one date.

[2] He was a Jacobite simply because the Hanoverians had taken not only the azure out of the Garter but the vermilion out of the Royal Standard.

CHAPTER IX

I

WILLIAM ROSSETTI did not set eyes on his brother's patron until November of this year, and then he only formed part of Ruskin's audience at a lecture. Miss Siddal's name had not been mentioned. Gabriel was afraid of putting forward too much at once and frightening away Ruskin, who really seemed to be far less disagreeable than he had been led to suppose. Though Hunt and Collins had read his books Rossetti had not, nor intended to do so. He regarded the poor Professor merely as a milch cow,[1] appointed by Providence to support and maintain the artist who was lucky enough to get hold of him, and a plaguey nuisance unless he was on your side.

The brothers had raced off to Islington to tell Hannay of Ruskin's call and promised beneficence and—it never rains in Bohemia but it pours—something was being done for Miss Siddal too. There had been a meeting at Poets' Corner and Miss Leigh-Smith had taken the girl home to lunch, where she happened to meet Doctor Wilkinson again, in a non-professional way. He wanted her to go and live awhile in Brompton where the air is good for consumptives; Barbara was firm for her Cousin Florence's place in the New Road. But Bessie Parkes, seeing Miss Siddal's fear of being shut up in London, suggested the seaside. She knew of some lodgings at Hastings both cheap and nice, high up on the hill where she would get plenty of air.

Mr. Allingham heard all this when he went to Chatham Place to sit for his portrait. Miss Siddal was to be rushed off to Hastings at once; Gabriel to take her down and return on Monday to dine with Ruskin at Denmark Hill and make the

---

[1] Ruskin's father, apart from maintaining him, was in the habit of placing fifteen hundred pounds a year at his son's disposal, besides buying him a Turner now and then, and dying reproached himself for not having bought him more.

John James Ruskin left a hundred and twenty thousand pounds, leaseholds and freeholds and pictures valued at ten thousand. Ninety-seven thousand pounds had been settled on Effie, on which she drew interest until her death. John Ruskin never thought of taking it away from her. Perhaps, as Howell said, he could not?

acquaintance of his father and mother. Young Mrs. Ruskin he would not see : the bed at Herne Hill was mended, but she was still away and her servants on board wages.

2

It seemed as if everything was going right. Barbara, Bessie and Anna Mary were " very thick " with Lizzy, Doctor Wilkinson " enraptured with the dear " and Ruskin prepared to worship her. Gabriel meant to take some of her drawings to Denmark Hill to show him. What she needed was encouragement ; she was so deprecating about her work that without it she would give up Art entirely—a thousand pities !

Then Annie Miller, healthy, vulgar and cheerful, sauntered in as if the whole place belonged to her. Gabriel turned her over to Allingham ; his mind was full of Ruskin and a little of Lizzy and he was off to the station to meet her and " Bessie the Brick," who was going with them as far as Hastings to look after the invalid as a man could not, starting again by slow train to get back to Robertsbridge for Scalands. Gabriel promised to meet Allingham on Monday at Southon's and they would chaff the Cordial Stunner as usual, and he would tell him all about Hastings and Denmark Hill.

3

Gabriel took a single for Lizzy and a return for himself, which cost one pound Second Class : he had borrowed the money from Allingham and a portmanteau from Aunt Charlotte. The two Cockneys in corner seats looked out of the paneless window all the way as the train sped through the smiling champaign. Gabriel knew the English country slightly, having been twice to the Scotts' in the North and once to Sevenoaks. But to Lizzy it was a revelation. The first weird flash of the sea, still, portentous, a sheet of white enamel spread before her eyes instead of the grey electro-plate of the river at home—the fresh smell. . . .

And, suddenly, there was the " little, bright, surf-breathing town " at their feet. And good, kind, pretty Bessie, who took her to her lodgings and put her to bed. That night Gabriel slept well and, from his window in East Parade, saw " the most wonderful of earthly sights," the sun rising over the sea.

Next day Doctor Hailes came in and saw her and gave Gabriel

the address of a chemist, Mr. Smith of George Street, whom Rossetti presently was calling his very good friend. The doctor was not sure that he would not move the patient soon to lodgings nearer the sea. High Street was apt to be hot at that time of year.

Number Five was a very old house, on the south side, with a garden sloping down to the stream—a trickle of water was all that was left of the great bight running inland between East and West Hill, navigable once for Roman triremes. The front of the house on the street was broad and low. It had a sloping roof of grey stone, out of all proportion in extent to the house face. A man walked about on it as if it were a garden, mending the stone slats. The rooms and the hall were papered the same, like a maid's faded cotton frock with the ghostly flowers of a hundred springs agone, meandering on a pale dun ground. On a flap shelf in the hall was a stack of empty medicine bottles—Mrs. Elphick's husband was an invalid and his room and hers were on the right as you went in, and he never came out of them. The staircase stopped at the next floor where the bedrooms were— two only—and access to it was through a door which was shut as a rule, for it led to the attic where no one slept now : it was haunted so badly in Mrs. Stanforth's time by an old man whom no one ever saw but whose footsteps followed one upstairs. Mrs. Stanforth had had to leave and all her tenants had done the same, Mrs. Elphick said, until she enclosed the staircase in " stoothing " and kept the door at the foot of it closed. It was only left undone now for the man who was mending the roof.

But the lady said she didn't in the least mind meeting a ghost.[1] Well then, there was another—a woman who haunted the lean-to wash-house or kitchen—it had been all three, but the people about here called it the Corpse Hole. It was said that the body of a woman had " rested " there one day preparatory to being taken away at night and cast into the bourne at the bottom of the garden, all a tangle of gnarled roots and Goya-like weeds sprouting out of dirty ash-heaps. No one went near if they could help it, for they had no idea what might be down there ! Anyway, a lot of old, queer, marked stones . . . graves, perhaps ? Gabriel said Roman altars, but he did not go to look. What had been the wash-house was now the larder, with the overflow from the earth closet draining into it under the floor. (The landlady always kept charcoal on the shelf to deaden the smell.)

[1] " *Même je le suis,*" she might have said, like the mysterious guest in the French ghost story, and vanished.

NUMBER 5 HIGH STREET, HASTINGS
From a photograph

Doctor Hailes said that these ghosts were all smugglers' tricks to cover the murder of an accomplice who knew too much, or to scare people from noticing what was going on. In all these coastal towns, since Napoleon first put England out of bounds, smuggling had been the staple industry and the staple pleasure too. Behind St. Clement's there were caves, excellent *caches* and the towns-people went there o' nights to dance by candle-light, and so covered their unlawful operations. The secret passage from the inn next door he had never seen—nobody ever had actually seen such a thing as a secret passage—but it was supposed to come out at Rockanore, a mile or so away.

Next day they had Mrs. Elphick in, and she told them of secret chambers and hollow walls and floors with movable boards where kegs and barrels reposed in rows within an inch of the officer's foot while he made his search. And there were double staircases in the smallest houses, steep, breakneck, like ladders twisted, and lofts with walls that let down so that you could sling a barrel into the room below. In one house she knew of there were pillars each side of the fireplace that were really cupboards—so that the master might take out a bottle of spirits when he could trust his guests—and extra doors for people who were "wanted" to get away by, all over the place. She had been to stay once in the house opposite and was shown into a bedroom, but, when she opened a cupboard door to hang up her cloak, she found a bed of nastur-tiums at her feet and a garden stretching all the way up the hill, so steep that the trees were trained on it as if it was an espalier, and anyone could pull himself up by the boughs and keep on lying on the ground until he got away. And the raised pave-ment opposite along as far as the Vicarage—underneath it was all cellars with doors you couldn't tell from the rest of it, where they took things straight off a cart as it passed slowly up the hill without stopping, for someone opened it from inside and took the barrels in.

Lizzy let herself laugh. Laughter did not suit her. But she was happy and, indeed, now that she had seen this, she would never, never go into a hospital, "with no means," as she put it, of "keeping herself alive." No, not even Miss Nightingale's. She settled down to water-colours—easier to manage in lodgings —she was not quite strong enough yet to begin her oil picture, her *magnum opus* it was to be. And Anna Mary was due at Scalands on Wednesday.

She and Gabriel took walks—never in the direction of St.

Leonards, then a-building—long stuccoed terraces and streets, scaffolding and dust, deadly for Lizzy—but westwards, about the fishermen's beach, dotted with net-huts and store-houses, high, black-tarred, gaunt, three-storied, built on the pebbles, at whose base old Nunky would sit in the sun weaving nets with a giant shuttle. His son, drowned in the lifeboat three years ago, had chalked his father's nickname on the black beams of the hut and it was never allowed to be washed out. And further on to Rockanore at the end of the old town, and up East Hill to see the incised stones. Gabriel, writing to Brown, noted things for him as a good Pre-Raphaelite should.

CHAPTER X

1

THAT Sunday in London was fine, remarkably fine, but Allingham was uneasy. He wished he had not betrayed Gabriel and Annie Miller to Anna Mary. He remembered the way her hand had closed on his arm after he had spoken. . . . She might have written and worried Miss Siddal about it? He called at Gower Street, but Millais was, of course, at church with his parents. Then he asked himself to lunch in Blandford Square; Miss Siddal was not mentioned; but Anna Mary, he heard, was going down to Hastings early in the week to *relieve* Bessie Parkes. So the poor thing was ill!

On Monday about five o'clock he found a note from Gabriel shoved in under his door, saying that he would have kept his appointment at Southon's only he had lunched with Ruskin late, after coming up, and felt very sick. He was going to his people's, and if Allingham liked to fetch him thence they might go on together to The Hermitage. He had told Ruskin all about " my pupil "—and " he yearneth."

2

Gabriel did not turn up. Nothing from him next day nor the day after. Allingham went for a walk and on his return found the wretch lying on the sofa, looking as like death as a person of his full habit could do, with a note in his hand received that morning from Anna Mary, dated Tuesday and bearing the Hastings postmark. It was quite a nice letter. Anna Mary was sure her dear Gabriel would see her point and not be cross with her, but she had left Miss Siddal in bed and was anxious about her. The night before, talking of friends in London she had been careful not to say much about Miss Miller, for she knew that poor Liz was rather worried about her because people kept meeting her in Gabriel's rooms, where they said she behaved as if all belonged to her, including the tenant of them. Anna Mary

93

thought that, considering, Gabriel ought to be more careful not to afford material for gossip. Artists and their models were *so* exposed to calumny. A little bird had told her—" You, Allingham ! " Gabriel said, " for you went with us to Madame Tussaud's that day, I remember ! "—how Lizzy's young man was seeing a great deal of Annie *outside* the studio, taking her to picture galleries and places of amusement—dances and so on. No harm but, as an engaged man, he ought not to give people the chance to say he was making love to someone else while his intended was away, ill.

The letter had made Gabriel so furious that he had had to lie down. Was there more in the Annie Miller business than any of them knew ? No ! Gabriel was not like that, but Allingham had never seen him so nearly moved like other people. He raged, he declaimed, but in his anger he was still the gentleman. There was no engagement whatever between him and Miss Siddal— no such luck ! Miss Siddal was his pupil and grateful to him for the pains he took with her. She had respect but no love for him. Far too ill, poor girl, to think of marrying, and he was far too poor. He would go straight to The Hermitage and explain.

Mr. Allingham's shirt was not clean enough for calls but he would walk with Gabriel as far as Tottenham Court Road. Waiting for the bus Gabriel began to think that he would write instead. Too delicate a matter to put in writing, Allingham said. If Gabriel would come back and wait while he changed his shirt he would go with him and take on the mother while Gabriel talked to Anna Mary and tried to remove the false impression which she (and probably Lizzy too, but he did not say this) had formed, before any more annoyance and perhaps pain came of it.

Mrs. Howitt had a cold and was fetched down from her bedroom. Shawled and shivering, she persisted in treating them like naughty boys. Of course Anna Mary shouldn't have written, and Gabriel shouldn't have shown a private letter : letters were not meant to be shown and she had never known any good come of showing them. Gabriel left and Allingham, as a dog that has got kicked in a game of skittles comes out from under the bench when all is over, remained behind for sympathy but got scolded for gossiping about the Miller. Better not to interfere between lovers—even if they weren't engaged. Every one knew that Gabriel had been wild about The Sid for years ! Yet she did not fancy that there would ever be a wedding. He was too much absorbed in his career, and anyhow he had not enough to keep

94

a wife on ; he was shrewd and business-like enough, for all he was so untidy and lazy.

At any rate, he did not bear malice. At a tea-party at Chatham Place next day Gabriel asked Allingham if he had any message for Lizzy, as he meant to run down to Hastings on Saturday and get one of her drawings to show Ruskin, with whom he was dining next week.

Allingham was going on purpose to have it out with Anna Mary, who might have left ; she was due at lunch on Sunday with the Leigh-Smiths, so the whole brunt of the discussion would fall on poor Miss Sid. But it was never any use arguing with Gabriel.

3

Allingham did not see Gabriel again for a month. But one Monday morning he met Miss Leigh-Smith in the Holborn omnibus and she mentioned that she had had a letter from Miss Parkes to say that Miss Siddal was " alarmingly ill." They had telegraphed to Gabriel and he was probably there by now.

Barbara might have told him more, but she had asked to be put down at Boston Street, where the bus stopped, and she got out. He thought she looked rather coldly upon him.

4

Yes, for the consequence which had been hanging in the stars ever since that moonlight walk and " My foolish disclosure," had come to pass. Anna Mary had " talked." She admitted it at Barbara's lunch on Sunday. Lizzy had come on so queer after Anna Mary left, that Gabriel, left willy-nilly in charge, had called in Doctor Hailes, who had sent up to Scalands to see if Miss Parkes would come and look after her, alone in lodgings with only a man to nurse her. She had a temperature, which had been set up by Gabriel's absolute and brutal denial, before Anna Mary, of any engagement between them.

Bessie was annoyed with Gabriel for making such a fuss about Anna Mary's letting out something that everybody knew. *Of course* Gabriel was engaged to Lizzy, and if he wasn't he ought to be, and she *had* written to Miss Leigh-Smith and told her all about it. Doctor Hailes would not allow the patient to see anyone all next day, and Gabriel had been well frightened and made

95

to feel ashamed of himself. He was allowed to see her late on Sunday evening, as he had to go up early next morning on account of his father—not so well—they had been anxious about him since his slight stroke on Easter Day. And there was the Ruskin dinner, which he must not miss. . . .

Though Lizzy wept more prettily than she laughed, Gabriel could bear anything but a woman's tears caused by himself and certainly no interference with his art! Art was more than women : women were cheap; he had no respect for them and would bear no reproaches from one of these chosen vessels of joy. But at that moment he said everything Liz wanted him to say, as he alone could say it, and soothed her. There was nothing else to do. She would have died.

He saw that it would be misery for both of them. He was bound to make her unhappy because his temperament demanded, and would have, something she could not give him, ever—something larger, more mutable, more vicious, even : his will to live, artistically speaking, would force him to see that he got it— *Bocca Baciata, The Kissed Mouth*, as opposed to the reticent croonings of the " meek unconscious dove," who would, of her nature, languidly, piously, for ever frustrate the artist's imperious " Now."

" What is it keeps me away from thy bower ? "

Why, any passing lure of sense and jollity, any woman who set not so much store by her virginity—a natural, healthy animal like Fanny or, at the opposite pole, the divine tomboy, Barbara. She, with her go, her fat, her resilience, would have been a better mate for this journeyman heart, that wanted little in the way of love-fellowship, but wanted it warm and generous, rich if not luscious. . . .

His life, as he could manage selfishly to live it, did not matter much : his work, and its pabulum, did. The senses and their gratification, painting and its practice, he would see to and prosecute with all his might. The rest might go and Lizzy with it.

This man was never seen to cry, not even when Deverell died. Sorrow, with him, needed fancied persecution and real drugs to exploit and bring it out.

5

The drawing-room at Denmark Hill, Rossetti told the fellows afterwards, made one feel as if one were in an aquarium. It was the awful translucency of everything. Water-colours, solemnly wedged in long coterminous rows, went all round the walls on a level with the line of sight: blue lakes and silver clouds by Turner, grey doves with sheeny necks by Hunt were met by prismatic refractions, from the middle of the room, of the crystals and minerals reposing on fleecy cotton wool in their glass sarcophagi. The host, doing the honours of his collection with a microscope in his hand that momentarily flashed contradictions, was rather like a mineral himself, so Gabriel thought. Those blue eyes of his seemed to focus things differently from other people's—with such capricious shiftings of angle, gleams of humour, flashes of wit: as it were, a spiteful saint; an anchorite who should also be a man of the world! The seer was too subtle for the artist; Gabriel was not really happy in his company; the whole *décor* of Denmark Hill made the latter long, somehow, to hide his own earthiness and pursue his more grovelling habit of thought amid the tolerant murks and warmer glows of Brown's house or Boyce's, full to the chin with curios, or his own place in Blackfriars, amid glooms kind to tired eyes, the dust and dirt that take off sharpnesses, the tatters that trim off angles, and the abraded corners of " old pieces " which break the line. He hated Mrs. Ruskin's pale lace curtains, her light brown rosewood drawing-room suite, her elegant armchairs where you could never hope to find a sovereign, as Hunt did once in his need, because they were too carefully dusted and gone over every morning.

He noticed when they went in to dinner that the portrait of young Mrs. Ruskin by Watts was gone and her bust by Marochetti covered up with an antimacassar. And that old Mrs. Ruskin looked pointedly away from that particular corner as she took her seat.

6

The guest was called away from dinner by a message: his father was very bad. Old Mr. Ruskin's farewell, " a look bordering on the tearful," [1] as he held up his glass after filling that of the

---

[1] He was " of a temperament peculiar to the British race who, under a calm, unruffled and cold manner, conceal an emotional and affectionate nature."—Jessica Sykes, in *Mark Alston.*

H 97

young man with Ruskin, Telford and Domecq's excellent sherry, saying old-fashionedly—" I drink to thee! " and young Mr. Ruskin's handshake—all finger-grip—were with him all the way home in the carriage which came round to take him to Albany Street.

It was only a little after seven and he took his turn to sit up with his father, relieving his mother, William and the girls. The Polidori aunts, close by in Park Village West, had been warned. Sitting there through the night-watches in a hard cane chair with not light enough to read by, he thought over the usual things that a recumbent, painfully breathing form lying prone beside one suggests ; defalcations and inattentions, trifling disobediences : the small irremediable magnified by the imminence of finality, like the light of the candle casting shadows deeper than the gloom it alleviates. Face to face, in fact, with the Eternal Verities : Ruskin, so lately filling the picture and, in a minor degree, Lizzy—both shunted for his father's hour !

A plump, short man—his eldest son had inherited his figure as well as the tendency to " old, atrocious boils " [1] and that other disease most easily incurred by the pure, the proscribed, the hunted man who knows not where to lay his head except on the bare ground or else in fœtid, lice and germ-infested caches ; one for whom ordinary measures of cleanliness and precautions against infection would be for months an unrealised dream, a mirage far beyond mere safety. Old Gabriele was of a gouty habit, an arrant snuff-taker, making odd gesticulations with his small hands tipped with bitten nails. Full of whimsies, he hated French women and loved English coal fires. His unique passion was Dante. It was the move from Frome that was killing him.

As he lay there, immobile, nearly blind, muttering low, he saw, he called on by name, he conversed happily with General Guglielmo Pepe, his associate in the original Carbonaro Ministry of thirty years ago ; he talked as if he were in a gold-hung Neapolitan palace instead of a small dark house near Regent's Park. Far back in Time, re-living his Glittering Hour. His son, sitting beside him attentive on a low chair, nursing Maria's cat, the child of Zoë, listened to the oft-told tale, that ended with the escape from Malta in an English gunboat. Of how he, Gabriele Rossetti of Vasto, the Improvisatore, the accepted Rhymer to the Extreme Group, had, by his " burning rhapsodies," persuaded a whole regi-

---

[1] His illness was actually an eruption " of the nature of carbuncle."

ment to desert from the other banner and raised his own country-side against the Austrian. How he and Pepe had penetrated to King Ferdinand in his bed; the Duchess of Floridia standing at the foot, and forced the quaking Bourbon to grant them a Charter. How somehow the quarrels of Pepe and Carrascosa had ruined all. And of the last great battle in the Pass of Monta-forte [1]—the breaking-up of the forces : the bloodstained trailing off into hiding, the gradual sneaking out of one's own country, an exile. . . .

And the bitter joke of it all was that Pepe and Carrascosa fought a duel to settle some personal score as soon as they were safe on English soil.

And when the ragged curtains of the dark, sheering off, showed the peep of a London day, there came the change. . . . The pale, shivering family, wife, four children, three sisters and Teodorico Pietrocola Rossetti, the cousin, peering with his beady black eyes, called in haste from Park Village, filled the little room. And plaintive, quiet Mrs. Rossetti read aloud the Italian translation of the Liturgy and the old patriot died slowly and quietly of old age . . . *marasmus*. . . .

He had been quoting Dante, calling on the names of bygone comrades. He had no word for the living.

> For here, where day still soothes my lifted face
> On thy bowed head, my father, fell the night.

Gabriel, stumbling down to breakfast about five on a chill, windy morning, thought very kindly of Lizzy, whom he might lose, like this, at any moment ! He wrote to Doctor Wilkinson, asking for an interview on Tuesday or any day before the funeral ; for as soon as that was over he meant to go down to Hastings and be very nice to her.

He had not now time for William Allingham ; his world had shifted—it was all Ruskin and Lizzy now—yet, to tell the truth, he rather resented the way Allingham forced his hand. The estrangement lasted until his new friend was barred to Gabriel by sudden illness (though the founts of benevolence were not stopped for that). By Saturday it was given out that Mr. Ruskin could neither see nor speak.

Gabriel got a letter from his patron to say he would be unable to see him or anybody before he left town. Mr. Rossetti perhaps had heard that Mr. Ruskin had had much upon his mind for the

---

[1] See " Fra Diavolo."

last few days—or he soon would hear. But he was leaving an order with a bookseller for a complete set of his published works to be sent to Mr. Rossetti and means to be back by August, when he hoped to see the drawings of " Mr. Rossetti's pupil."

And, by parcels delivery to Chatham Place, came a piece of opal—not a fine piece, but " Mr. Rossetti will like to let his eye rest on it." A magnifying glass was to be " used to its purple extremity." Beautiful, but Gabriel did not take it to Lizzy ; opals are supposed to be unlucky.

7

Painters were preparing for the Spring show. Allingham and Boyce went round to Gower Street to see some sketches Millais had managed to get ready for some minor exhibition. (He had missed the R.A.) They were all likenesses of Mrs. Ruskin. Mrs. R., *Waiting for the Last Word*, at a lattice. Mrs. R. saying to her young man, *Shall I see you To-morrow?*—in Millais's handwriting underneath. Mrs. R. accepting a man on the lawn in moonlight. Mrs. R. as a Seamstress, as a Ballet Girl and as a Peasant presenting *The Order of Release* to her man's jailer.

But the portrait of Professor Ruskin, which was to have been the picture of the year, was not finished—and by Saturday all the world knew why, and what had been on Mr. Ruskin's mind for the last few days. Unkind people said that it had been there since last November year. " I have made my plans——" She had given him a broad hint, then. The summons had come the very day Gabriel Rossetti had dined at Denmark Hill, and now the pillory was set up in the market-place for all who cared to throw rotten eggs at the most sensitive, the most retiring man in England.

Allingham, sauntering across Gray's Inn, was hailed by Thackeray out of a cab. He began with an inquiry as to his contributor's health—" You're not looking well, Mr. Allingham " —and on to the great case. At first disposed to be down on Millais ; " Thack " was easily pacified by Allingham, who took care to mention Johnny's kindness to young Deverell, sitting up with him all night. . . . " Bravo, young Everett ! " said the great man, clapping his hands and drove on.

Tennyson, in Stebbing's chambers, sat smoking like a furnace, discussing the Ruskins and Cayley's translation of *Dante*. Carlyle, over his breakfast pipe, considered the catastrophe inevitable and

MRS. JOHN RUSKIN
From a photograph

the less said about it the better.   Lizzy's Doctor Wilkinson and Professor De Morgan the Spiritualist spoke of nothing else for the whole of an evening, and William Allingham, escorting a famous medium to her bus, was snubbed for discussing " Mrs. Ruskin's husband " and " circumstances " which that lady coyly thought " needed not to be explained."

8

Ruskin's message was now invalidated.   People said and wrote that " the world was not going to be preached to by a mad *governess !* " Woolner declared loudly, " Ruskin is an unsafe guide for the *women* of England," and Mrs. Oliphant accused him of killing the Pre-Raphaelite Movement.[1] He became afraid of backing anybody and refused to write so much as a critique on Patmore's new book—" The circumstances of my own life unhappily render it impossible."   For the moment his services to artists came to consist in standing godfather to their children. At least his sponsoring would not compromise them with God !

Women condemned Mrs. Ruskin for not bearing her marital cross in silence.   Men, in view of her youth and extreme prettiness, the grounds of her complaint and the stories of her husband's domestic savagery, were down on him for taking a girl like that and burying her alive in a year of rain, " in this kind of house." [2]

Millais, their only permanent guest,[3] always said that the " wet " did it—" I do believe that in the Trossachs they have all the rain in Great Britain and a stock of their own into the bargain."   The weather got so on his nerves that the word *Rain* appears after the signature on all the little pencil sketches he did of Effie—sitting sewing, with digitalis in her hair—driving—fishing—in church—shaving her husband. . . .

She did complain a little to the young man of her husband's subordinating her to his terrible mother, and at Herne Hill, where she was mistress, treating her like a child, pinning a list of her misdemeanours on to her pincushion along with the housekeeping

---

[1] " Its dismemberment was connected in a spiteful manner with incidents in Mr. Ruskin's own career."—*Autobiography* of Mrs. Oliphant.

[2] So Ruskin describes it complacently to Furnivall, enclosing a pen picture :— " And a little garden eighteen feet long by ten wide, sloping down to the stream in front and up part of Ben Ledi at the back."

[3] His friend Holman Hunt was invited, but he did not go with him.   Might not the whole course of Ruskinian history have been altered if that gracious, kind and noble spirit had had a say in the beginning of it ?

money once a week. Being or pretending to be uxorious, pulling down her chignon in the drawing-room and enjoying her confusion when callers were announced. . . .

9

Did he love her, ever ? He said once, careless who heard him : " It would be better that she were broken on the wheel than come between me and John Millais ! "

Millais loved Ruskin as much as Ruskin loved Millais, and this love subsisted through life, long after the woman had come between them. Millais would never listen to a word against Ruskin,[1] and Ruskin's ridiculous art-petting of Millais gave colour to the theory, pretty universally held, that the husband had " asked for it," leaving his young wife alone for a week [2] while he went to lecture in Edinburgh. And there was another, graver accusation. He knew it and told his secretary, who wrote to him " soppily " to condole on his troubles, that " for you to adopt my principles might be prejudicial to all your prospects in life." And was at pains to refute Furnivall's hint, clothed in compliments—" Don't talk of my risking my reputation for young men. You need not think it great in me ! I do it for art."

He did not realise that, though the tale of his affliction roused and held the interest of a morbid and innocent girl, any accusation of immorality was likely to set her parents against him.[3]

The denizens of the farmyard crowed and cackled and " ploted " [4] the outsider. " An insolent capon," so one of the Positivists [5] declared in company of Holman Hunt, who never lied and who told him that the noun at least had no warrant.

[1] Ruskin is even said to have gone to the wedding—an impossibility, for they were married in the drawing-room at Bowerswell—and to have taken tea in Cromwell Place, so said Henry James. The tactless young husband sent on to Ruskin photographs of his and Effie's first-born, taking rooms for his wife, nurse and baby for the summer in the very manse where he had stayed with Mr. and Mrs. Ruskin in 1853.

[2] " Rooms contiguous." Mrs. E. M. Ward, who perhaps did not realise the exiguity of a Scotch bothie, said this to the authoress in 1924.

[3] Mrs. Latouche made inquiries, according to Mrs. Williams-Ellis (*Tragedy of John Ruskin*). It was said at the nullity trial that he had a defence ready. Holman Hunt tried to get him to plead. He would not. He did not choose to call *her*—but preferred, without a word of self-defence, to suffer public and private humiliation sooner than hold a woman who did not want him.

[4] To " plote " the goose is to pluck it.

[5] James Cotter Morrison.

CHAPTER XI

I

THE weather broke and on May Day, through the rain, all the smart folk fared to the Private View of the Royal Academy—Allingham as a critic! He had never met Mrs. Ruskin but he could have sworn that she was there. If so she had the grace to be dressed quietly—no crocus gown—a contrast to Miss Annie Miller, who, in red and blue like a P.R.B. painted window, was peacocking about in front of her portrait. She was the Queen of the artists' May, elected tacitly every year from some lady whose portrait adorned the walls. Her engagement was practically acknowledged and she had taken care not to forfeit her position as the "intended" of the painter of the picture whose subject was for the first time "the universal subject of discussion in these Islands, from one end to the other."

Of course the British Public was impressed by the picture, praising its choice of theme, its simplicity and "the lofty expression on the face of the Redeemer." But though the leaves, the panelled door, the lanthorn were all painted according to the canons of Pre-Raphaelitism, the *mat*-white foldless robe, like marble, like wood, without drawing, without handling, was plumb against them. Hunt's worst qualities were what endeared him to the Nation. No matter; one of the Brotherhood had managed to popularise the Movement and henceforth, as a Body, they were safe in the Abraham's bosom of the accredited picture mart of England and the brewers, merchant-princes, manufacturers, shipping agents, contractors and iron-masters flocked round, shocked, puzzled,[1] but solid for Hunt.

One of the Brethren, alas, could not keep his temper, or his pen, off the subject. Next night at Collins'—Munro, Stephens and Brown present—Rossetti, President, announced to "You fellows" that he was putting his design for *Found* into "The Portfolio" this

[1] "Such things are, but why paint them?" And "the general colour is so odd one can't quite tell what to make of it at first."—Miss Catherine Winkworth.

round, but was "haunted by certain consequences that might be shadowed forth in rapid action" and proceeded to read them one of his mirthless, undramatic little *saynètes* that they were in the habit of listening to patiently. It was called *Miching Mallecho—It Means Mischief.*

The first scene was laid in Robert Street, Adelphi, the chambers of good-natured Mike Halliday, Millais' great friend. Halliday announces that he has got "The Portfolio" at last from "that wretched Rossetti" and is glad to find, in spite of all their prophecies, that the fellow really has put in a design! Briefly, as President, he sketches the subject—a castaway crouching by the parapet of the bridge at early dawn, discovered by a lover of earlier days, who is pulling her hands away from her face to observe the ravages of her present life. He then sits down and ostentatiously addresses a letter to Millais—at Chatsworth—a dig at Millais' smart friends.

The second scene is laid at the Collins'[1] in Hanover Terrace. Slangy greetings and reiteration of the word "Stunning!" (the Brethren were already poking fun at themselves). And Millais, back from ducal *parages*, admits to being *rather* puzzled about "that design of Gabriel's," who seems to have lit upon the same subject as himself, about a woman and a market-gardener finding her in the street. Did he show it to Gabriel or didn't he? Anyway, he is now painting it. Halliday remarks that that will be a bore for Rossetti, but Millais retorts airily that old Gabriel would *never* have finished it! He knows of a brick wall (for which Gabriel is searching in vain), and "when my *Found* is done, 't will be the loveliest thing you ever saw in your life! Stunning!" The pet expletive goes off now and again like a popgun all round the room, a shield for some misgivings in the minds of the Brethren. (Rossetti was strong enough to dare to indicate this.)

The third scene takes place in the *Athenæum* office, with Mr. Hepworth Dixon dictating his review of the R.A. Exhibition. "Our readers will remember the striking originality of the artist's conception. . . . The editor's only objection is to a certain similarity of subject in two of the works exhibited. . . . We allude to Mr. Hunt's *Awakened Conscience* . . . Mr. Millais' *Found.* . . ."

So deeply was the idea of special injury done him by the stealing of his "notion" (as he conceived it to be) set in Rossetti's

[1] What a lot Wilkie must have known, and disregarded!

consciousness that he had told Ruskin about it, and using all the perspicuity and wisdom of which he was full when other people's affairs were concerned, Ruskin wrote at once (crossing out the *Mister* and begging Rossetti to do the same). "You feel it is not worth while to bring out *your* modern subject now he has done *his* first." He thinks *Found* a *dreadfully* difficult subject to carry out, but it will, it must, be done. . . .

He was really anxious that his protégé should drop this dreadful mediævalism, which he hated as much as would a man whose favourite songs were, *Comin' thro' the Rye* and *Katie's Letter* that he had young ladies sing to him by the hour, and who could bear to sit in his own dreadful drawing-room. Long ago he had owned to disliking the ugliness of Pre-Raphaelite faces—Millais' *Mary Virgin*, Hunt's *Viola* (for which Miss Siddall had sat) and Rossetti's *Lucrezia*, with her red hair and pink roses in it ! He detested, in spite of its moral subject, *Hesterna Rosa*—the gnome-like women sitting about on the floor (there were plenty of easy-chairs in his mother's house)—also *Paolo and Francesca*, floating through space in a cotton-wool snowstorm signifying the flames of Hell to which this sort of guilty person was generally consigned by Dante. But how could Rossetti and the man who burnt Goya and advised people—" for pure, all virtueless, stupid, deadly poison "—to read Victor Hugo and who nourished " a painful propensity for Longfellow," be at one ?

Ruskin's secret garden was in Philistia. The key of it hung always at his watch-chain and he was fond of gathering its flowers —say, calceolarias, fuchsias and nemophilas—and entertaining the fauna of it, such as Royal Academicians and holders of opinions contrary to his. He would ask the lion to lie down with the lamb— Rossetti to meet Clarkson Stanfield—begging the former on this occasion to be " not *too* Pre-Raphaelite," nor was he even afraid of the heavy-weight champion of the open-air school (who had lampooned *him* shockingly).[1] Anxious to propitiate him on his

---

[1] To the deuce with Ruskin
And his gas lamps seven !
We've the stones of Snowdon
And the lamps of Heaven.

Leave to Robert Browning
Beggars, fleas and vines ;
Leave to mournful Ruskin
Popish Apennines.

Charles Kingsley in a review of *The Seven Lamps of Architecture*.

friend's behalf on the morning of a day when Kingsley was lunching, he sent down a portfolio to Chatham Place for the artist to fill with drawings to show the " strepitous " clergyman. Not Lizzy's; he was afraid they might be too morbid for him. Nothing was to be put in that had " feeling in it," but, say, that drawing of Blackfriars Bridge, with which even Kingsley could hardly quarrel ?

2

Everyone realised that Rossetti had definitely succeeded the young Millais in Ruskin's affections. The Professor was now writing letters to that young man, describing himself and his character, his likes and dislikes, telling the worst of himself, recording his good points as lovers use, shyly flattering the other—" Among all the painters I know it seems to me that you, on the whole, have the greatest genius," also, as far as J. R. can make out, " are a very good sort of person." And, though J. R. owns to " no loves and no friendships," he tells Gabriel Rossetti all about that glove of Adèle's left in a drawer these eighteen years ago.

" The best friend I ever had," Rossetti said afterwards. Did he mean financially ? For quite soon Ruskin made him the proposition the rich are able to make, accepted faithfully, carried out for years, until the inherent flaw which sooner or later impaired all Rossetti's friendships—with men at any rate—brought it to an end.

The manifestations of Ruskin's generosity were connected with his own present complex. Gabriel was not " to let the idea slide " into his head that Ruskin was " doing things for him," for the British Workman, for anybody, in order to regain his place in public opinion. He is what he is, " and a good many people think I am very bad ! "

Managing him and his money box, Rossetti did pretty nearly what he liked with Ruskin during the good years he had him at beck and call. The elder man admitted that, in the company of the younger, he was " robbed of all initiative in thinking " : his mind could only " follow Rossetti's." He got back his Categorical Imperative when he had a pen in his hand. Then he became the imperious and sarcastic teacher and Rossetti the lazy and fractious schoolboy.

But, try as he would, Rossetti could not get Ruskin, who was doing the poor man real pecuniary damage, to accept Brown,[1] who had more passion in his little finger than Rossetti had in his whole body.

Ruskin could not bear Brown, his manner, his art which embodied the principles of the particular bias Brown saw life by. Disliking the morbidity inherent in mediævalism, the Professor fought it and its supposed concomitant, sensuality, in Rossetti, just as Eastlake was fighting it in the Royal Academy, while his wife did the same in the Press.

" Female horrors (their models) with thin bodies and sensual mouths, looking as if they were going to be hung, or dead and already decomposed," wrote " Corinne "[2] in her organ, *The Quarterly*. While her husband (" Little Eastlake," so he was called : she was " Lago Maggiore "), a less virulent but intensely disapproving Philistine, would slyly boast to his real intimates of having lately met a painter " deeply versed in all the literature of art, but absolutely uncontaminated by Ruskin."

Rossetti would soothe his fiery old teacher with farcical abuse of Ruskin. Ruskin was a sneak and only loved him, Rossetti, because he was one too ; and Ruskin only half liked Hunt because old Hunt was only half a sneak. Ruskin hated Brown and Woolner because they were straightforward—Woolner appallingly so. Ruskin used to adore Millais because Millais was the Prince of Sneaks. But now that Millais had sneaked away his wife Ruskin " was forced to hate him just for having a little too much of his favourite quality."[3] So Gabriel would run on, puzzling and disgusting Brown, who, simple and sweet, tough and testy, never knew what to make of this man who could poke fun at Ruskin and accept his kindness at the same time ; could exploit him—" That little transfer of pictures, how will he take it ? "— and laugh at him—" Old Ruskin wants a little Academy of his very own in every blessed manufacturing town, where he can rope in all the rising young men and dictate the laws of art to them to his heart's content."

He was to study landscape more—" scumble instead of stipple "—to make " careful studies of the whole, sacrificing all

---

[1] " *Don't* buy Madox Brown at present. Don't you see that his name never occurs in my books ? Do you think that would be if I could praise him ? He is an entirely worthy fellow, but pictures are pictures, and things that aren't—aren't."— Ruskin to Miss Heaton.

[2] Lady Eastlake.

[3] *Rossetti, his Life and Works*, Evelyn Waugh.

the detail " (*this* to a Pre-Raphaelite !). To exercise in light and shade, *or* colour, "in large grammatical abstractions," slowly and resolutely—" You can't make light and shade interesting in the same picture. Though nature can, *we* can't; we must sacrifice one or the other."

Mostly Gabriel did as he was told,[1] leaving "the pure greens" out of *The Nativity*—" Please do, or you will make me ill again ! " Endeavouring to get it to look " less like worsted work by Wednesday." Nor did he vocally resent hints as to the proper packing of drawings. He had scratched " the cheek of Lancelot " in sending it but, next time, he did put " a sheet of smoothest drawing paper " over the faces. For well he realised what a splendid business man his patron was, insisting, for instance, on his producing " small, easily saleable things "—it was much easier to find ten purchasers for a twenty-guinea picture than one for a two-hundred-and-fifty-pounder.

3

With the assistance of the rich Polidoris a plot of ground for old Gabriele was bought, close to the grave of Brown's first wife on the western side of Highgate Cemetery, by no means a favourite neighbourhood, haunted, and neglected. The grave under the aspen would hold seven ; and there, after he had been dead a week, the body of its first tenant was laid.

Wednesday, the 26th May, was a full day for his eldest son. Gabriel had asked for an appointment after the funeral with Doctor Wilkinson, saying he hoped to get down to Hastings that very night to attend to Miss Siddal, whose illness, still in the pathetic and not unbecoming stage, had provoked in him a recrudescence of affection. He had had a note about her from Miss Leigh-Smith, enclosing another from Bessie Parkes, which made him uneasy. She was rather bad. He designed a longish stay with her while awaiting Ruskin's return, and bade Allingham get Routledge to send the wood-blocks for the volume of ballads, which he had accepted a commission to illustrate, to Chatham Place, so that he could take them with him. He had already begun a sketch for one and must really set about them in earnest and some other " likely things to raise tin." He must resume his sittings when he came back, and meanwhile Gabriel was

---

[1] "You are a conceited monkey, thinking your pictures right when I tell you positively they are wrong."

leaving the field clear for him with *La Belle*. And Allingham was to tell Munro and Clough to write to him at 12, East Parade, Hastings.

He got down that night, armed with powders for Lizzy from Doctor Wilkinson and the blocks which had come in time for Lizzy to finish her drawing for *Clerk Saunders*. He didn't think her worse—rather better—judging from her appearance. He had taken a little walk with her and she did not seem fatigued. She *was* better : she admitted it herself and the glorious weather they were having would soon cure her. . . .

He was all kindness and thought for her—Would William send that shawl Aunt Charlotte had promised ?—" just the thing ! " He had taken some sort of line with his family and with himself.

The woman had taken her line too ; a stronger, firmer one than the man's. She did not want to be made to look silly again, or a repetition of the Anna Mary incident. A bit of an artist, she was a bit of an actress as well. Through her poetry she cleverly gave Gabriel to understand that her heart, such as it was, was buried in the grave with Deverell. " A startled thing . . . a bird with a broken wing. . . ." she could not give him the love she gave so long ago. Only

> . . . a sinking heart
> And weary eyes of pain,
> A faded mouth that cannot smile
> And may not laugh again.

Gabriel read her poetically garbed reproaches, marked and kept the poems but did not show them to Barbara Leigh-Smith. They were not very good—not nearly as good as her drawings.

CHAPTER XII

I

"IT is certain that my conviction gains very much as soon as another is found to share it." Barbara's Aunt Julia thought Lizzy's manners perfect and sanctioned her being asked to Scalands. "Several ladies here have called and been very attentive to Lizzy. Everyone adores the dear." She enjoyed it, Gabriel's pride in her, the sun of favour shining as well as the other luminous body—this was a glorious Spring. Her spirits improved, her worst symptoms abated and she began her drawing for *Clerk Saunders*. He had moved his traps to Mrs. Elphick's, who gave him a room in the haunted attic for less than eight shillings. "No one thinks it odd," he told his mother, "my going into Miss Siddal's room." [1] Miss Smith herself had said to the landlady that it would be most inadvisable for Miss Siddal to sit in a room without a fire.

Think it odd—why should they? An artist and his model! But he was beginning to care what his mother thought of his girl.

They *were* asked to stay at Scalands Gate. Lizzy was to have Anna Mary's room—full of china Christs hanging on ebony crosses and fonts for Holy Water: Anna Mary, brought up as a Quaker, was now as good as a Catholic.

Barbara's cottage was built on a hill over the village amid a sea of young birches, chestnuts, hornbeams and pines. From the windows one saw for miles over hills and dales; farmsteads and oast-houses with their tapering roofs and gilt vanes. She had built her cottage in simple style, as a protest against "Victorian worship of smugness and pretentious comfort." Here was comfort but no pretence. There was no hall. The front door opened straight on to the parlour and the staircase. Simple, like Lizzy's old home in Kent Place—but oh so different !

---

[1] "Having cribs in the same house," as he puts it somewhere else.

No marshes and no crawling, slimy river, but a peep at the sea from the window of one bedroom. The round table in the middle was spread for meals, and at dinner the door left open on to the garden permitted Lizzy to watch the birds picking up the crumbs she sprinkled for them on the step. In the kitchen adjoining, Henrietta Blackadder officiated alone, with her simple stews and innocent rice puddings. (Rossetti never got quite enough to eat here.) Miss Leigh-Smith had her own little room upstairs where there was a frieze running all round the top reproducing the Bayeux tapestry (Scalands was close to the place where the Battle of Hastings was fought) and a shelf covered with Algerian pottery and bookshelves below. There they sat in the evenings reading aloud, listening to the " dog music " from the kennels outside—pointers, beagles and retrievers, used for shooting by Barbara's brothers.

" It's wonderful at Scalands," said Emily Davies, who, bringing overworked School Teachers and Feminists, came down often to be " un-tired "—so Barbara put it to the painter, whose delicate model she had also undertaken to look after until he could be prevailed upon to shoulder the responsibility.

She and Bessie and Anna Mary had strong hopes of an engagement. His attitude to Lizzy was improving in proportion to her credit with them.[1] " Everyone here adores and reveres Lizzy," Gabriel said, and wrote, " She is lovelier than ever—but so weak." She managed to see the country riding about on a little mare. Down the hill into Robertsbridge, dismounting by the church garth and walking up by the hedge of southernwood to the old church, so spoilt inside that they would not go in. To Bodiam Castle, wandering by the moat where besiegers " sat down " with their catapults, under apple trees, creeping leaves and ivy in loads. And over the drawbridge into the Castle and up to the chamber to look out of the window on the stagnant water spread with a soft grey carpet of broad water-lily leaves. Through the hop-fields to Clive Vale Farm, which Anna Mary's people had once lent to Hunt when he was thinking of going out to his uncle in the Colonies to learn to keep sheep. There was the little table he had taken for a palette, with splashes of red, blue and green, and turpentine dried upon it. That did not particularly shock Lizzy, used to artists' ways by now. Then they wandered round the garden among the great red flowers, the little blue

[1] Had he married Barbara how different his life would have been ! It is possible that his fancy for her was one of the reasons for his delay in proposing.

flowers, not one of which could she name, but said they reminded her of the foregrounds of the pictures of Gabriel and his friends. She was observant, like these men, and would stand for hours by the lily pond in the kitchen garden under the old oak where the white owls lived, to watch the gold-fish, seen as if through a red blind under the murky water, and if she came too near they would sense her and dive, leaving a nameless stain as of blood and, presently, no more than a shy blur. . . .

"They always rise when the weather is thundery," the gardener said. It was now—the weather was breaking.

And at night they would go out to hunt glow-worms along the roots of the hedges, or sit in the red room and read aloud. Brother Ben, in from his own place and weary with husbandry, in his blue blouse with his dog Rough at his side, would be pretending to listen, rising sometimes suddenly to go out and eject a tenant. His was a largish property.

Well disposed to her friends as they were, conversation with Barbara's brothers was difficult for the two artists; and what must these good people have thought of the man, sauntering, trailing his umbrella that never left his hand, humming through his closed teeth nothing like a tune! And the woman, haggard, pale, hatless, with irises or what not wreathed in her hair. Did they pass discreetly on, when they came with their dogs, tramping through the preserves, and found the pair prone in the undergrowth, he lying on his back with one knee raised and his hands behind his head, while she plaited long grasses, making herself wreaths for her hair like Ophelia. Lying about was a habit Rossetti practised all his life—in the woods at Lymington with Allingham, in the wide field furrows at Kelmscott,[1] on the small sofa at Cheyne Walk—he was fat by then.

2

On these debateable borders of the year
Spring's foot half falters—

Barbara had worked it—and the electrical fluid spilled from the skies on the day of the thunderstorm. Gabriel Rossetti and Elizabeth Siddal were caught in the rain and took refuge in the dim, dark wood, by a little spring that welled up under a stone

---

[1] Between the acres of the rye
These pretty country folk would lie.
SHAKESPEARE.

half hidden by lush grass, that they knew of. There they cowered, shielded by the leafy screen which the arrowy death could not pierce unless God really wanted to find them. And, when it was quieter, making a cup of her fair white hand, she gave him to drink out of it, from the well . . . shyly, with the affectation of one who is aware that the moment has come, that she is making a man " athirst where other waters spring," taking him by her grace as she stooped, and the poise of her languid wrist that trembled. . . .

And she sang to him. They were both gay, like children on whom Doom lies.

He proposed [1]—to all intents and purposes—in

> . . . that hour my soul won strength
> For words whose silence wastes and kills,
> Dull raindrops smote us and at length
> Thundered the heat within the hills,

and ratified it that evening in her room among Anna Mary's Christian emblems. It still rained. Standing in front of the window that looked over the valley and the hill beyond, she was mistress of herself, playing gently with the white cotton blind tassel and tracing with her finger on the pane the progress of the shining drops that blurred the view, her eyes downcast, seeming to be interested in the pale green fields, helpless, prone under the driving sheets of rain. . . .

She did not believe he meant it even now, but she accepted him and they cut their monograms on the lintel of the window.[2]

3

At first Gabriel enjoyed being engaged, taking it as a cataclysm inevitable, a thing written. He wrote to Brown, " When I first met her I felt that my fate was defined." To Allingham he solemnly made over his interest in the Cordial Stunner ; " no chance for me any more."

And next day, when they returned to Hastings and Mrs. Elphick's

> . . . the memories of these things
> Like leaves through which a bird has flown
> Still vibrated with Love's warm wings
> Till I must take them all my own
> And paint this picture . . .

---

[1] He tells it himself in a poem written long before, pulled out and altered to fit her—*The Portrait*. [2] It is now the cook's room.

So he cleared away the whatnot with the china tea-things on it that stood in the window of the back room in Number Five, bought some tall pot-plants and put them in a row on the steps into the garden outside, to imitate the shade of the trees, and got her to stand up against them, " as in the wood that day," and made many a sketch of her " dear " face with outlandish flowers arranged in her " dear " hair and, in the evening, pen-and-ink designs for her new monogram (something with a dove in it, the bird she loved for Deverell's sake), as well as shots at illustrations to Allingham's poem and the blocks for Routledge. But he confessed to being lazy, writing to Allingham—" Poor Miss Siddal has done better than I have." He still owed Allingham for their fares down, but " be sure that I am really going to attend to that *petite affaire* of £ s. d. Meantime (light chaff in which Rossetti was always very heavy), *tenez vous bien !* " More references to the Cordial Stunner and a message to friends and enemies at home—" Remember me to Boyce and Munro and Clough and *forget* me to Coleman. . . ."

He now went about declaring that Lizzy was a genius, that those long tapering fingers of hers from which the blood seemed to have retreated, as in the first stages of the disease called pernicious anæmia, were those of an executant and that in her designs she fulfilled his desideratum, putting in " the fundamental brain-work that makes the difference in all art."

She was very very thin but yet desirable. The hair which had at first attracted him was still glossy, golden and upspringing as ever, the figure majestic in its length of limb, the noble shoulders sharp but unbowed, so that she raised the desire she was further than ever from consenting to crown, now that she had the excuse of invalidism. Courageous, uncomplaining, captain of her soul, she had the stoicism of one inured to varieties of hardship, as other, more sheltered, women are used to frequent, medically-imposed, changes of air. The changeling expression that—so the poet Allingham maintained—attested her fairy origin, held some of the unpleasant naïveté and super-imposed wisdom of the slum child, and evoked the mood of ruth that now and again comes over the artist, since Pity and Terror he must command or never know the full artist's passion.

She went back to High Street and Miss Leigh-Smith left for town, telling the girl that she would always find her room ready for her if she had a fancy to go there alone and be looked after by Henrietta Blackadder. The Triumvirate had lost interest in this queer pair whose engagement they had procured. It was now for the woman, who obviously wanted it most, to bring her man to the point of marriage.

Gabriel rather wished Lizzy would accept this invitation and let him go back to town. The spectacle of her ups and downs and the responsibility of tending such frail loveliness depressed him. " She is a sweet companion, cracking her little mirthless jokes. . . . But the constant sight of her varying state is much less pleasant."

There was something of Cellini about him as well as of Leonardo; of the cunning craftsman and the simple painter. Something too of Omar.[1] The Dream and the Business were never very far away from each other in his mind. If he married this sick woman he must give up Chatham Place. Wilkinson would certainly forbid their setting up there. . . .

He wanted to get home to begin *Found* while *The Awakened Conscience* was still on the walls of the Royal Academy, so that *his* " modern subject " could be compared with Hunt's. It would mean money, too. His means were still, as he put it, " small and fitful," and he paid Lizzy's rent and kept her, whom he had prevented from making money for herself by sitting to some other fellow. As for commissions—she wouldn't get much for the work she was doing, even if she ever finished it, so said his boding heart and business mind. She was going to be a permanent invalid and he would have to make enough money to support a wife and perhaps a brat . . . consumptives have children. No more Chinese inlaid cabinets or four-mark china for him ! . . .

His own sources of revenue were chancey. Aunt Charlotte was good at a pinch. There was McCracken, who adored him but had just asked him to accept thirty-five pounds instead of seventy-five for a water-colour, and of course Ruskin—but Ruskin might dry up ? Ruskin had not seen Lizzy, but Gabriel was sure that he would not admire her or the way she dressed.[2] He knew about her, of course. His letters from Switzerland usually ended with some such stiff, polite message as " I sincerely trust your best anticipations with respect to your pupil may be fulfilled."

[1] " *O take the cash and let the credit go.*"
[2] He liked the Dresden china shepherdess style of dressing—hoops, furbelows, fichus, and screaming crocus gowns.

Everyone knew what was happening to Ruskin, what made him crochety and, at best, absent-minded. Allingham wrote to tell Rossetti, who had already heard of it from Munro and Calder Campbell. He had even had a letter from Millais himself, telling him that he was going into the country, and one from Ruskin, so painfully before the public nowadays. Gabriel rather admired the man—" Seems to take his sell coolly ! "

The Scalands ladies were still away and the weather had turned. " It is very windy and rather slow here ! " He must see Allingham before he went back : he was just waiting until he could scrape together enough " tin " to leave " this stunning part of the world " and get back to town."

Miss Siddal, as soon as he was gone, went to Scalands. She wanted to stand again, to lie again, in the Silent Wood.

She was now more or less serene, as those who are definitely health-condemned, finding a quaint solace in the performance of one or two of the picturesque observances that may remain for them to do, making certain gestures of predilection, since nothing much mattered any more. She did not complain . . . but it was all nonsense this saying she was better : she was very ill.

She did not walk far, for Wilkinson had forbidden it. Just to look at the dogs in their wire pens, leaping, barking or standing up quietly like animals about to be vivisected, their stomachs like a brown mat flattened against the network ; or go the other way, to peer at the white owl sitting in the heart of the thornbush. But best she liked the wood near the house, with its " gellibirds," shouting cuckoos, blackbirds and thrushes, and nightingales warbling at dusk from the amber-tinted oak tree. And there was the other wood, farther away, where she and Gabriel had gone so often to sit in the great dark hall of the over-arching trees, a light roof keeping off rain and the heat of the sun alike. She would lie flat under the low boughs, nearly down to the ground in some places, with waving fern fronds to fan her, and for long hours would watch the movements of the underworld, the tiny restrained gestures of the small things, shiny, furry, feathered : creeping, pottering and flying low among and under the different kinds of darknesses, mossy, velvety and dun like the shadows and corners of the human body. Low-leafed boughs of the larch, like eyelashes, stirred now and then by the grey flash of a bird slowing down to take cover, like the prow of a boat beaching in the shallows of the shade. . . .

She lay so still that they were not afraid of her any more than she was afraid of them. She was not afraid of anything, not even of vipers whose bite deprives a man of his virility and makes a woman " silly " for life. Henrietta Blackadder objected to her bringing blackthorn and may into the house and even nightshade. Miss Siddall would actually handle the Dwale Bluth, as Mr. Brown called it, that would make her die if she so much as put her finger in her mouth afterwards. She gloated on the strange, weary pallor of this flower, the dull purple stem, the thin leaves veined like the hand of an octogenarian, faded like the moon, seen by daylight, which always made her think of a jealous woman. Nor did she feel disgust at the natural preying of creatures on each other. Near her would be the remains of an owl's meal, grey feathers glistered over with the kindly dews of night. She would think of herself as a dead savage, carried on a wicker bier to the woods by her kinsfolk and left to be parcelled out among the birds and the worms till there was nothing left of her but her bones.

Long day-dreams, with kind, courteous, natural death at the end !

She would get up and tidy herself and pick the white flowers of the celandine from the toes of her black shoes and go in, quickly passing the kitchen window, so thin that Henrietta Blackadder would hardly have time to see her as she went by— a " regular tallow candle." No wonder ! She ate scarcely anything.

And Gabriel Rossetti, healthy, full-blooded, cheer-loving, was back in town, breakfasting with Allingham, dancing with Annie Miller at the Gun Tavern, rowing with her and a friend to Pimlico to fetch Stephens in Lupus Street, and walking, all four, to Hungerford Bridge and by rail to Greenwich to attend the Fair. A wild, Teniers-like scene. Grown-up people rolling down One Tree Hill, little boys running about rubbing a wooden instrument with a toothed wheel down men's backs as they rushed past, to make them think their coats were torn. Kiss in the Ring, skirmishing with their own girls and others—Gabriel got some scratches. Then they would take the pretty ones to have a shrimp-tea in the little house at the Park Gates where he and Allingham had once led the austere and dreary Lizzy. And parted at Chancery Lane, each to his own place.

She got wind of one of these excursions and sent for him.

The weather had changed. In Hastings now there was dense fog and heat, "when sea and sky made one wall," and on the days when she was not so well he had to walk by himself on the cliffs baked dry as a bone, or below, on the beach smelling of fish, longing to get back to his own stinks at least—and perhaps to cheerful Annie? He would sit alone at the window, plumb on the street, of the parlour and listen to the Town Crier with his "O yes! O yes!" and wonder if it wouldn't be the easiest thing to put plagues and poems, skeletons and unfinished pictures into his sack and let him sell them all off without reserve.

She was no better. Miss Leigh-Smith again talked of her Home, which Lizzy would have none of. It would be the death of her to be shut within four walls to brood, with sick people all round her—and Death, perhaps—for Death occurs oftener in hospitals than outside. How if she should be puzzled by the disappearance of such a one and warned of the cause by the solemn looks of the officials or, confined to her room, hear the noise of a coffin knocking against the banisters, the shuffling feet of the bearers, and guess what it all meant!

Her wishes for once jumped with his and presently they were back in Chatham Place.

The papers were full of the state of the Thames, its wharves and bights,[1] so alarming that our legislators at Westminster had to have chloride of lime put on the window-sills of the Hall of their deliberations. Questions were being asked in the House. It was only a hundred years since the River of Dead Dogs had been covered over and a portion of it still festered to the sun. Nor are dirt and disorder in the home good for consumptives, and this fatal condition, the glory and the shame of Pre-Raphaelite ménages, was implicit in Number Fourteen. There was no witty Puck " to go before and sweep the dust behind the door." Nor would this Duke of Athens have engaged him. He hated to be cleaned up. Mrs. Madox Brown, born a country girl, did come in now and then and give " a hand's turn " with a broom,

---

[1] Edlington's Wharf, Lime Wharf, Mr. Hood's Iron Wharf, Randall's Wharf, St. Andrew's Wharf and then Puddle Dock, Sand Wharf, Hudson's Wharf leading up Bennett's Hill to the Cathedral. On the other side (west) Wood & Co.'s Wharf, Pig's Quay, Gas Light Co.'s Wharf, Dorset and St. Bride's Wharves, Stapleton's, Western Caves and the Grand Junction Water Works.

MRS. FORD MADOX BROWN AS CINDERELLA
From a drawing by Ford Madox Brown

Gabriel all the while begging her to desist sooner than risk the obliteration of landmarks. Her attitude was good—her husband drew her as she swept and called it *Cinderella*.

He was not well either. He got up to his work every morning feeling "so hopelessly beastly" and his work "so hopelessly beastly too." He took "physic" as he called it and such palliatives as Lizzy, out of her invalid's pharmacopœia, suggested, and found himself better but "confused," so that, in illustrating *The Maids of Elfin Mere*, he drew one of the ghosts spinning left-handed and had to do the drawing all over again.

He was looking up his translations of early Italian poets to see if there was any money in them, writing short stories,[1] asking William to find him some person to read him "some gospel for *Llandaff*,"[2] and went as far as Brown's in the broiling August sun to borrow costumes for *The Passover*.

And all the time various duns, that Mrs. Birrell did not choose to deal with—so sent them up! Benthall on the staircase opposite, agent for Mr. Duncan, kept on applying for the rent of the rooms, over-due and over-due, till Aunt Charlotte came to the rescue—"Pay D. G. Rossetti or Order. Twenty-five pounds. C. Polidori."

6

Sadness chastened him and the rueing that follows doctors' visits, the fall of the mind's barometer, coupled with the want of "tin" which drives men like Gabriel Rossetti to abound in ultra-recognition of wrongs and unreasonable assessments of blame. He seemed to see, in the stone-cold face of a mirror, Liz dying, a maid forlorn, in the Old Kent Road (which he actually fancied more unhealthy than Chatham Place), among alien enemies (as he chose to consider her own people). Hearing that Miss Leigh-Smith's health had broken down and that she was going abroad for it, he savagely wished that "there was Rome for my good pupil, whose life might matter a little!"[3] Why should lovely amateurs like Barbara have, through their unearned

---

[1] *St. Agnes of Intercession.* Not the sort of short story that pays which we write now.

[2] Seddon had succeeded in getting hold (for the benefit of the P.R.B.) of a Welsh M.P., Bruce, afterwards Lord Aberdare, who commissioned the altar-piece. It was he who later authorised and gave facilities for the opening by night of Lizzy's grave.

[3] *Rossetti, his Life and Works*, Evelyn Waugh.

wealth, the power of preserving the strength indispensable to the furtherance of the art they need not actually live by ? The constant bitterness of Brown and all the Pre-Raphaelites which had dictated their revolt against the state-subsidised " Muffs of Influence " surged up in him as he watched her putting touches in, scraping others out, quiet, unrebellious, sitting at her little easel placed on the table near the window. A great respect for her grew up in him. Sturdy in a way, yet so pathetic with those long loops of hair falling heavily, wearily, over hollow cheeks. Now and again with a patient adequate gesture she would put them aside with her long thin hand. Or too weak to get on with it at all, just sitting like a folded umbrella, in her own big chair. He could not but realise how bad she was ! The illness of a strapping wench like the other would give way to treatment, " whereas, perhaps," so he wrote, " *her* soul is never to bloom nor her bright hair to fade, but having hardly escaped from degradation and corruption, all that she might have been must sink out again unprofitably in that dark house where she was born." [1] He did not know where exactly or, if he had been told, he had forgotten, but it was in some slum or other on the Surrey side. . . .

His boding soul, aware of its insufficiency and lack of purpose, had actually come to envisage either Death for this poor creature or her inevitable return to influences from which he had rescued her full four years ago, with such a flourish of trumpets ! " From degradation and corruption ! " Strong words, such as poets use. He meant perhaps the degradation of illiteracy, the corruption of those who sit in darkness and gnashing of teeth and read the penny dreadfuls. Lizzy's Greenacre complex must have been in his mind. He had never forgotten about the fool-brother who had gone out and bought the murderer's knife " he did it with," according to advertisement, and shown it to the little child and made her a nervous subject for life ! The father seemed the best of them, but he was " sicklied o'er with the pale cast of thought," full of the dreadful sourness of those who go down into offices and litigate. A tall, thin-lipped man, so Lizzy described him, not in the least like a shopkeeper, after his day's work was over, sitting still, the black silk scarf he affected straying across his shoulder, nursing his fiddle, in " the dark house " of Gabriel's prepossession.

She had described it, the tiny parlour, the staircase, dis-

<hr>

[1] *Rossetti, his Life and Works*, Evelyn Waugh.

simulated, at the back, up to the next floor where the father and mother slept; and then higher, up to the room which she had shared with Lyddy, with the tiny grate that would not have held a fire even if her mother had allowed it. Sadic cruelty! Lyddy, who never really lay down in bed, but sat up to sleep: younger, not worn out as Lizzy was with nursing, yet morbid too, was perhaps also affected by the legend of the murderer who lived next door and by the hanging which they all attended. The executioner, according to custom, while the criminal was " dancing on nothing," had actually, in order to expedite matters, jumped on the victim's shoulders so that the rope broke and both executioner and criminal fell down into the trap.[1]

Browning, who lived then in Camberwell, had told him of how, coming away from the first night of *Strafford*, he had met the horrible people tramping by to Newgate to be ready, overnight, to witness the hanging. And even Macready had been nervous and would have liked to postpone the play because he was afraid that someone in the audience would shout " Greenacre! "

Well, he, her lover, had taken her away from the society of ghouls who could gloat over a hanging, out of the dark night of ignorance and imbecility and brought her here into his life, a lovely foundling, to paint from and lie with. . . .

And now she was too ill for either. " No man cares for my soul," she had said bitterly once, when he was making robust love to her as artists use when their model is pleasant to the touch as well as the eye. He was not troubling much about her salvation *then*! Now he suddenly chose to feel himself responsible for that. . . .

" I do not mean to make myself an exception, for how long have I known her and not thought of this till so late? "[2]

For many days, but not so many as the days of his neglect, " this subject," so he told Allingham, was " by far the nearest thing to my heart."

7

He had never loved her more than now that he was going about to betray her.

[1] The phrase has passed into dock language: it is a stock joke to say " greenacred " when a set of goods falls out of a sling, so violent an impression was produced on everyone by this particular execution.

[2] *Rossetti, his Life and Works*, Evelyn Waugh.

Some time ago, at Rossetti's suggestion, a club had been formed whose manifesto was "The Portfolio," which was sent round to the members for their contributions, lying at their houses for a week—"oft becalmed in the Port of Blackfriars." But this October Rossetti wrote to the President to say that it was his intention to contribute a sketch he had newly made for *Found*. Some time ago, he told them all, he had come across the very model for it—an old acquaintance, the wife of the ex-porter at Somerset House—a buxom beauty who used to throw nutshells at him in the old days as he passed under the arch to see Walter Deverell. He had run across the woman at Vauxhall one evening, and she, good Cockney soul, exclaiming "Lor! If it isn't Mr. Rizzetty!" had flung her arms round him in the friendly gloom, under the trees hung with pale-coloured lamps, lit only with the furtive flare of fireworks. He had loved it, for once, the careless frankness of the trull who can refuse a man nothing but has no particular interest in giving it—just "fond of a guinea" and not averse to delivering the goods. He did not quite know where he would get her to pose for him—hardly at Chatham Place, as he remembered her. She now lived somewhere in Wapping, with her husband. Old, and past work, Hughes had lost his job as porter and dispenser of artists' materials when, after Mr. Deverell's death, Sir Henry Cole had got the Head School of Design moved to South Kensington. Hughes was thoroughly unsatisfactory, but his wife bravely supported him by her toil.[1] She had been on the stage and was now by way of being a model—"Miss Fanny Cornforth" on her professional card. A handsome, full-bosomed girl, young but portly, even in the old days, when she used to stand in her blue print gown, arms akimbo, under the dark archway at Somerset House and chaff the students wanting to see young Walter Deverell, whispering to them that the cross old father was out and they could go straight in. Now, her still rounded face had something tragic about it. She had not "kept herself respectable," in Victorian parlance, and with her bonnet half off and hanging by its string, she did splendidly for *Rosabell*. She was so good-natured and obliging, sitting for hours in the cold and damp, that Gabriel made time to go and see her in her lodgings, somewhere down by the river. Lizzy had not seen her, nor Lizzy's watchdog Brown. Though he had taken a house here on purpose for the background of *Found*, he was painting it at Chiswick where he had

---

[1] "Fanny's incumbrance . . ." Rossetti to Watts, 1874.

FANNY HUGHES
From an oil painting by D. G. Rossetti

discovered an eligible wall,[1] dividing the churchyard from the Keightleys'[2] garden, that would do. He was sleeping at Mr. Keightley's and she at Weymouth Street. They had both had to get out of Chatham Place because of the cholera, which was frightfully bad.

[1] "Not too countrified to represent a city wall, some moss but no prodigality of grass, weeds, etc."

[2] Author of some books on Fairy Mythology, mystic poet and ardent spiritualist.

CHAPTER XIII

I

IN this year, 1854, exit William Allingham, fixed at his new post in New Ross and only over for very short visits, as a witness of events. Of The Sid's patient decline during the period that elapsed before Ruskin made his frenzied bid with Death for her life, one hears only from Brown, the faithful, the sturdy, the exaggerated in expression—Brown who loved her purely and without passion this side idolatry, calling her " a real artist, a woman without parallel for many a long year," Brown, who "smelt the mould above the rose," inspired Gabriel, intensely suggestible, to garner beauty before he lost it.

On the 8th of October he called in Chatham Place and saw Miss Sid, "looking thinner and more death-like and more beautiful and more ragged than ever." He meant " ragged " as the fringed mist wreaths that flee before the sun after a storm, torn edges of wind-buffeted cloud ; flesh *unhemmed* as it were, by the contours of health, except for that full neck without " drawing," straight from nook of ear to shoulder, constituting to some minds a defect, but a line adopted by Rossetti thenceforward, whomsoever the sitter.

2

" *And all my days are trances.*"

A creature of (bad) habit, Gabriel Rossetti hugged his hair shirt and complied with it ; the healthy animal side of his nature was being slowly starved out by the rigours she could not help. Living in a state of sleepy worry, his friends saw him strangely altered : " Life seems to play in him no longer, he still says good things, but so colourlessly and so hollowly." For the first time in his greedy, facile life he knew bitterness.

He had let her go back to live in Weymouth Street, and would turn out dispiritedly alone for the meal that " combines," so he said, " the sweets of an assignation " with a waitress they called " The Cordial Stunner." Her innocent favours he shared with William Allingham, who sent her valentines [1] and what not, from his banishment. Half-hearted back-chat from Rossetti—" She came in *on purpose* to see *me*, in a lilac walking costume. I am *certain* she does not regret *you* at all ! "

The waitress at Southon's was only a bluff. Now for Gabriel, as for Shakespeare, there was the Dark Lady. Fanny—whose real name was Sarah—was fair, but the adjective is less graphic than psychic. Bouncing, comfortable, all contour and no angles, the high spirits and high bosom of his old friend the nut-slinger of Somerset House were a welcome anti-climax to The Sid's haggardness, and corresponded to the more normal side of the temperament of this " great Italian trying to live in the Inferno of England," as described by Ruskin, who seems often to find apt phrases for matters his own idiosyncrasy never knew.

Using the occasional intercourse with *Jenny*—there could be no mistake about the guineas with her—as a bypass, his tenderness for the woman who now held for him scarcely any sexual appeal seemed to increase and flourish. He had ceased to live in the same house with her and called her by a more stilted name than " Guggums " ; [2] it was " Dear Dove Divine " : in his doggerel rhymes he identified her with the bird that combines meekness with a touch of the old-maidish acerbity. The very colours she wore suggested the sheen on the necks of her pets. He designed her a monogram to this effect and, in his letters, took to indicating her name by a hieroglyph representing a dove.

Had he made one for Fanny it might well have been a wombat.

3

Very soon, hard up for company and someone to sit up late with, he imposed himself on Brown in his new house in the Finchley Road. The excuse was *Found*, which Brown was always egging him on to finish.

He had " got in " the face of Rosabell : he had " met the right

---

[1] So now I give good-bye, *ma belle*,
And lose no great good by it.
You're fair, yet I can smile farewell
As you must shortly sigh it
To your bright, light, outer shell. . . .

[2] She was willing now, perversely, to call him Gug.

model for her the other day" (Why did not Brown then scent danger to his dear ?), but wanted models for the countryman, the cart and the calf. Brown must procure him a calf and, to do Pre-Raphaelite justice to his subject, he must live near his model.

A calf was got of the right age, restive and miserable. That was simple enough, but Brown was, as usual, terribly hard up and his house was too small for visitors. His wife was expecting her second child ; her sick fancies cost him something. She had had a month's longing to go to St. Albans, of all places, and he had indulged her. Emma, gravid : in his eyes " the most beautiful duck in existence," had enjoyed the trip, but dinner, night and breakfast at The Pea Hen had cost him one pound five with the tip.

But he went on working and starving : swaggering and even begging, painting meticulously, " finishing from corner to corner," spending a month on the bonnet-strings of the female emigrant and four on King Lear's carpet, paying his models handsomely, keeping open house, putting one of his last half-crowns into the collection " for the poor, cholera-parentless brats," begging of Seddon and Uncle Madox in order to maintain little Lucy in her high-class school at Greenwich and for the upkeep of Emma's mother, always in difficulties down there in St. Pancras—visiting pawnshops every three days or so with family plate, jewellery, rare engravings, *pâpier maché* ornaments and articles of clothing. Poor Emma's good Indian shawl was oftener with " My Uncle " or pinned round Dummy than on her back and only returned to her shoulders while she was sitting for *The Last of England*.

In one great bout of pawning, just before Gabriel came, he had raised eleven pounds. By the 24th of the same month it had dwindled to two and, five days later—" Money-box shows only £1 2s. 6d."

There was an inn opposite, but Gabriel preferred a room in Brown's house,[1] with its front door above the level of the pathway, up some steps and along a gravel walk bordered with white and purple candytuft, which little Cathy was forbidden to pick. The accommodation of Grove Cottage was scanty : parlour, kitchen and scullery on the ground floor and two bedrooms

---

[1] Five Socratean heads, all alike, were moulded on the first brick course, with which the builder had endeavoured to classicise his villa. The painter spent some time in hacking these off and so reducing the wall to a flat surface. They have been replaced since and now grin down as in the first weeks of Brown's tenancy.

above. A door with red glass panes gave access through a yard to a kitchen garden, sloping up the hill at the back, where Brown painted backgrounds and set up Dummy dressed in kingly robes (or his wife's shawl).

The guest arrived in the morning of the 1st of November but did not mean to sleep there that night, for Ruskin, who had been back in London since October, had at last asked him to dinner. So they inspected the calf, tethered opposite, and Gabriel went back to sleep at home—handy for Camberwell. Next day he returned and Brown started him on the calf. It " sat " so badly that Gabriel never got to work until half-past three, when he knocked off for dinner—at Brown's. His bed was on the sofa in the parlour and he wore a pair of Brown's trousers and Brown's great-coat ("which I want!"), while his host sat painting out of doors with a blanket off the bed round his loins. Gabriel was terribly heavy on the larder, the wardrobe, the colour-box and the purse and altogether contrived to " make the whole place miserable."

On the 27th of December Brown had only two-and-eightpence in hand. On the 30th he pawned his dress coat, waistcoat and necktie, Emma's silk cape and cameo brooch and the shawl for the dozenth time, giving his model two shillings out of the ten thus collected, and began a sad little poem—

> Ours are the nameless sorrows,
> The sudden and meaningless pain
> That lights on the new-sown laughter
> Like birds on the new-sown grain.

" Master Gabriel " (so Brown, when most outraged, would describe his friend) stayed nearly a couple of months. By the 31st the situation was horribly strained. Brown and his guest had sat up jawing as usual till five in the morning, Brown inconsequent as Rossetti was logical, arguing about suicide ; Gabriel standing out to do what he liked with his own body.[1] Rossetti had not yet touched his portrait of the calf, but talked to Emma of " several days yet " for the picture—euphemism for the same number of months. Then Brown told his guest that he must go—had he not noticed it ?—Mrs. Brown was within a week or two of her confinement, and a monthly nurse had to be housed. He might sleep at home or take a bed at The Queen's

---

[1] Brown took the Church's view as he, and Ruskin too, with a queer reservation, did eight years afterwards in the case of Lizzy.

Head? But Gabriel said that would be expensive. Nonsense, Brown said brutally; a bus fare one way would not break him: he might walk out from Blackfriars in the morning when he was fresh, and drive back home at night when he was tired out with work. Rossetti shouldn't think of doing anything of the kind!

" So "—and one can almost perceive the sob in Brown's voice, and observe the premonition—" he is gone—for the present!"

CHAPTER XIV

I

LIZZY nowadays worked in water-colour : oils tired her too much. Gabriel meant to see what could be done with some of her things, possibly through Ruskin, whom he met pretty regularly at the Working Men's College where he had taken a class to please him.[1] Ruskin was charming to him as ever but seemed in no hurry to make the acquaintance of his "pupil." He might have seen her ; in November of last year, he had nerved himself to face his public again and announced a lecture in the Architectural Museum in Castle Street, near Lizzy's old shop, addressed to workmen in the Decoration trade on Design and Colour. Gabriel charged brother William, in his capacity as journalist, to procure tickets for him and Lizzy and Mary Howitt as near the front row as possible.

Did the Professor take a hasty lecturer's glance over the row of stalls immediately below the rostrum and notice the triplet of oddish-looking people to which the one known face gave a clue ? Two ladies—Mary Howitt was dumpy and healthy and could not have been taken for the invalid he had heard so much of—were sitting by Rossetti's side and, very soon after this, he wrote to Professor Norton describing the sweetheart of Mr. Rossetti as "hopelessly mediæval-looking, more like a fifteenth-century missal than anything out of a fresco."

He was not ever in love with The Sid.[2] He was in love then, and always would be, with youth and health,[3] considering no female worth looking at after eighteen, hating what he called "grand faces" in women, caring only for "infinitely delicate

---

[1] His day, then, was Monday and remained Monday until after his wife's death, though his attendances grew more and more intermittent. This date is significant.
[2] It has been said.
[3] "The kind of painting *we* want in London is painting cheeks with colour." A lecture by Ruskin.

and soft ones." When he did see Lizzy, she was sickly and already past her bloom. He only wanted to look after her in order to set the mind of a great artist at ease and enable him to work with a free hand. And he fully believed in Gabriel's love for her and that she was at Death's door.

He had not been told all the ins and outs of it. He may have imagined that the girl was still living at home with her family, who naturally enough set their faces against an art education. Or—he was, after all, a man of the world—it may have occurred to him that the reason why Rossetti was not profuse in his invitations to Chatham Place was that the guest might meet Lizzy, bonnetless and in house shoes, and discover that she as often as not shared the flat with her lover.

Meantime Gabriel was working for an invitation for them both to go to Denmark Hill.

2

It came as the wind bloweth, and as suddenly. One morning in March Ruskin came to Chatham Place while she was out and bought every scrap of paper tinted by her. The showman was begged to name his own price and, realising the advantage of getting the drawings into Ruskin's hands, put them at what he considered a low one. But Ruskin declared that twenty-five pounds was too low, *even* for a *low* price, and insisted on paying at least thirty pounds for the lot, proposing to have them splendidly mounted and bound together in gold. Then he sat down and wrote to the young lady herself—an open letter—" promising further usefulness " as Gabriel, standing over him, noted. He ordered some more designs and Lizzy began them at once.

Brown got a letter from the delighted Gabriel at Finchley that night with all details. " Ruskin will have it that hers are better than mine—better almost than anyone's ! " Here he gave Brown a handle. " Just like Ruskin : the incarnation of exaggeration," so Brown wrote to Allingham, adding loyally, " Ruskin is perfectly right to admire them."

Another of Gabriel's happy letters had been written to Woolner, who was staying with the Great Unapproachable, as Tennyson already was called. Woolner told him about Rossetti's discovery of genius in the slums and he made Mrs. Tennyson write to Moxon to say that Mr. Tennyson wanted some of the illustrations to be entrusted to Miss Siddal. Moxon naturally wanted names, but Mrs. Tennyson was so interested that she offered to pay for the designs herself rather than not have them included.[1]

Gabriel and Lizzy quarrelled about a design of two nigger girls playing to two lovers. It had been " married," said she, to Mr. Allingham and now he had gone and sold it to Ruskin ! In a temper she dictated the letter Gabriel wrote to Allingham, to say that she was prepared to do him another and a better design as compensation.

The set was informed that Mr. Ruskin had not been introduced because she was an invalid whose movements were circumscribed by the weather. But, " some thoroughly fine day, Lizzy and I are to pay him our first visit together."

3

Ruskin's wife had left him in April : Millais would be marrying her in July, for ever lost to him who was still, in his critical capacity, inordinately praising his work. This generosity, however, was taken by the world as a sign of weakness. Behaving most decently, John Ruskin was compelled to play an unsympathetic part. It was harder to act than he thought, in the first flush of relief at having got rid of her, when he had almost cheerfully agreed to the third [2] of those propositions which her father, Mr. Gray, red-haired, speaking with a strong North-British accent, had laid before him.

He chose the worst for himself and tried to get away to Switzerland, where, under the blue and amid the snows with sunsets to tint them, he alone could find comfort. But he must see Miss Siddal and leave all tidy and self-supporting in that *ménage* before he left. On the 11th of April the

---

[1] The illustrations to the Moxon volume came to contain the work of members of such opposite schools as Horsley and Hunt ; Rossetti and Mulready—about whom Ruskin went nearly as mad as he did about Miss Siddal. She was only one of his charities. The worry about the books, the unruly contributors, especially Rossetti, is supposed to have killed Moxon. No example of Miss Siddal's work actually appears in it.

[2] (I) An accusation of infidelity against either party undefended. (II) Four years' refusal of cohabitation on either side to institute desertion undefended. (III) A decree of nullity in case of no defence from the party implicated.

He declared himself indifferent as to which of the other two was selected. He refused the first.

lovers were bidden to spend the day at Denmark Hill. The bus took them as far as the bottom of the hill; Lizzy was able to walk up. She was impressed, as Gabriel had been, by the importance of the house, by the actual time it took to get to the inner sanctum, along the solemn drive with the cedar stooping over it, by the solemn footman (*not* powdered) who opened the door, past the hovering maid and valet. She walked in like " the person of distinction calling on Dante " in the first drawing for which she had sat to Gabriel five—nearly six—years ago. Mr. Ruskin himself was standing in the hall to greet them. For a long moment her hand lay in his (" all finger grip "), and then in the father's, which had to be taken out of his pocket first. Led into the long, light drawing-room dancing with prismatic lights refracted from the pictures on the wall and the glass-covered cases sheltering minerals, she was motioned towards Mr. Ruskin's mother, at the far end of the room, whose welcome was gracious—unexpectedly so, to judge by the faces of her husband and son. Rising, with the effect of Royalty, she took the young girl upstairs to take off her bonnet. " My maid Anne," with appraising glance, relieved her of her cloak, and then Mrs. Ruskin led her to a window and showed her the view southwards, over the towers of Sir Joseph Paxton's palace, and indicated the whereabouts of the little river Effra, neither seen nor heard, at the bottom of the dell. She was next allowed to peep into Mr. John's study, where the table took up so much room that the rest of the floor was but a passage round it. There were no curtains to the window—he did not choose to keep the sun out. The room was tidier than any room Lizzy had ever seen; she much preferred it to Chatham Place.

After lunch she got very tired of lakes and waterfalls—Constance, Lucerne, Windermere, Thun and Schaffhausen: her host, not so much walking as hovering, taking pictures down and suddenly appearing at her elbow with them; so Mrs. Ruskin took her up to her own room on the western side of the house, darkish by day because of the big cedar on the front lawn, made her lie down, and had a talk with her.

" God be with thee ! " said the old father prettily when it was time to go, and the carriage came round to drop her at her own door, and take Rossetti on to Chatham Place.

Going home, she declared that she loved Mr. Ruskin's father but did not care for his mother ; she saw, through her calmness and serenity, all her innate cruelty, her arrant and enormous vanity. The son was kind, but she did not approve of the way he talked; his rather silly, perverse characterisation of people and things that didn't happen to suit him. And he *would* keep on dragging in religion, which made people feel shy, telling her that Prayer was often " long unanswered " and bragging about his own " great pieces of self-denial that all ended in catastrophe instead of victory." (Digs at his wife, she supposed.) She realised his absurd craze for youth—" Only the Young are happy "—but supposed he had had a lot to bear. . . .

She had made a good impression. Her behaviour was perfect : William, had he been there, would have agreed that it was not even " flighty." Her absence of affectation was pleasing to the old people and the economy of gesture that invalids, unconsciously husbanding their resources, practise. Mrs. Ruskin, who had seen a relation or two quietly die of " the decline," knew what it meant.

And Anne Strahan, as she was called, really a member of the family, approved of the " young person " Mr. Rosetti [1] was going to marry, so quiet and ladylike, " speaking so particular," her mouth never too widely open and handling her knife and fork quite nicely. She had not been told that Miss Siddal was a model and supposed her of a superior station to Mr. Rossetti, whom she classed with the other " artisses " that Mr. John was always bringing in to show them his pictures and keeping them, with his mother's consent, on to meals—geniuses who didn't know how to use their napkins and made noises while they ate. Anne, living in this house, knew what a genius was and waited on it with contempt.

To old John James—but he took care not to dilate on this point to his wife—Lizzy seemed the daughterling he would have liked to have had, to play with John when he was a child, and perhaps make him less unusual.

Young John was less impressed. He wrote to a friend on the other side of the world, where the gossip of London would be harmless by the time it had reached the breakfast-table. And even so he was guarded. He " found in her a perfectly gentle expression " and was sure that Rossetti " would not have given his soul to her if she had not been perfectly gentle and good."

He respected her for her probity in business dealings, her diffidence in accepting favours—so unlike her man !—and stub-

---

[1] So Ruskin always called him and spelt his name, then, as all his friends did.

bornness in sheer refusal of them, and he always, in his letters to Rossetti, sent her his *reverent* love. (The adjective was carefully chosen.) But she represented but one of his many charities. He had other young-lady-irons in the fire; there was one in America who was taking up landscape to please him and a rich one in Yorkshire who was buying up Turners on his advice. The difference between her and his other protégées was that she had something in her. He told her so.

" The plain hard fact is that you have genius."

4

The very next day he came to Chatham Place, bringing in his hand, with his mother's best regards to Miss Siddal, a packet of Ivory Bone Dust, well known as a powerful restorative and not easy to get, since it is only kept by shops where they sell goods made of elephants' tusks, paper-knives, napkin rings, hair brushes, and so on. The formula accompanied the packet.[1] Then (" No joke ! " in the words of the astonished Gabriel) he made to her sweetheart, as representing her, a certain proposition, suggesting two equally magnificent alternatives for her acceptance. One, that he should from that day forward purchase all her work, paying for the drawings one by one as he received them, selling them to her advantage, if possible, at a higher rate and, if they gained more, the difference to be of course hers : if not, he would keep them himself and be glad to do so.

Or, that he should pay her a round hundred-and-fifty a year for all she did ?

Would Mr. Rossetti look in on him at Denmark Hill, say that afternoon, and tell him which of the propositions suited Miss Siddal best and to which she would agree ? He was off. . . .

Gabriel, speaking at the door, promised to see her at once. And Ruskin, going downstairs, bade him not forget the packet of Bone Dust—he had observed him absently putting it aside— as Mrs. Ruskin was anxious that Miss Siddal should begin on it immediately.

[1] To one pound of dust add two quarts of water, boil gently for eight hours and let it stand all night to get cold. Carefully remove the jelly without disturbing the sediment (if the jelly is not firm it is because it did not continue boiling and must be boiled again), put the jelly into a clean stewpan to warm, add six ounces of loaf sugar, two teaspoonfuls of brandy, one wineglassful of sherry and the juice of one lemon. Strain through a jelly-bag into a pan, then strain again through another jelly-bag into moulds. Stand to get cool. The flavouring may be varied.

Gabriel sent a note, to William at the Board of Trade, giving the good news; telling him that naturally, the moment Ruskin had gone he had rushed out " to call " upon The Dove (using the familiar hieroglyph) and " had found her out." Probably gone to the Browns' and irrecoverable for the next few hours. He must see her in the evening, for he had promised to go to Ruskin in the afternoon. He had had an exhausting day and it was not over yet. For he had an idea that his Lizzy, in her queer dislike of being beholden to anyone, would jib at even Ruskin's patronage. She was, however, to be " severely coerced if necessary."

The *clou* of the note to William is that he intends to bring her to tea the day after to-morrow. William is to prepare the ladies in Albany Street for the introduction of a prospective daughter-in-law. The formal expressions " *call upon her* " and " *found her out* " are part of a plan to make these women feel that she is going to be a family asset and no mistake about it ! And also to establish domicile ! She has her own rooms and lives in them and he calls upon her there and finds her " out calling " too, like any other independent lady of no fixed occupation.

She *was* coerced. He saw her that night and had a talk with her. Her own feeling was against Ruskin's first plan for the very reasons which made Gabriel prefer it. She foresaw, as Ruskin did, that there might be " goodish intervals " when she could not work and might run short of money. Both she and Gabriel knew that Ruskin would not allow that, so that they two would get the best of the bargain. But be sure that Ruskin realised the punctilio of this girl of the people, and thought the more of her.

Little excited notelets fled on the wings of the post from Gabriel to William and to Brown. Over, the long winter of his discontent ! Lizzy would be all right now that the Ruskins had taken her in hand, treating her as a personage : not a model but a great artist who painted even better than Rossetti did. Gabriel's megrims left him, like the headaches of Millais, who was just about to be wedded to Mrs. Ruskin and " perfectly aghast " at his own happiness. Now, with two of the P.R.B., all was merry as a marriage bell. " I love her and I love everybody and feel happier than I have felt for a long while." But as usual disposed to shift his burdens on to other people's shoulders— " Would you have leisure," he wrote to Brown (who had perhaps less leisure than any man in the world), " to go with Guggums to a colourman's and help her to buy all necessary tools ? " He suggested Roberson's, " the only eligible demons for oil-paints," but he cannot take her there himself as he has got " a feud with them " (euphemism for an unpaid bill). Brown will see that she is not overcharged, as she would be if she went alone. And—he is still on tenterhooks as to the attitude of Albany Street —" Lizzy will take tea, and *perhaps* dinner, at my mother's to-morrow."

Brown obeyed. Next day he was obliged to go to the City to raise money on the Wharf to pay his rent, got it with much difficulty and then fetched Miss Sid. They were all three to meet when the shopping was over at The Pantheon for dinner. But when Lizzy's things were chosen and ordered to be sent to Weymouth Street (where she wondered how she was going to manage oils because of the smell of them and the size of her room) they could not find Gabriel. " Of course not," said Brown, and they had to wait. He did turn up and they dined and then on to tea in Albany Street. Miss Siddal was presented to Mrs. Rossetti and Miss Maria ; Miss Christina she had already met. Miss Christina was dying to meet Ruskin and Gabriel said grandly that Lizzy must bring her to Denmark Hill one day soon, before Ruskin went to Switzerland—everyone knew he was anxious to flee away before the date of——. But such details must not be mentioned before Mrs. Rossetti.

The tea-party was stiff. William was away and Christina never raised her eyes from her needlework, though Miss Sid bravely took no notice and devoted herself to her future mother-in-law, who seemed fairly pleased with her. But Gabriel was glad when it was time for him to " escort " Miss Siddal home.

Then, astonishingly, Mrs. Rossetti asked Brown if he would not sleep there—William's bed was vacant—and he soon found out why. She wanted to talk with him. The two sisters went to bed so that Gabriel's mother and his best friend could sit up late into the night talking about Lizzy, of whom one can be sure that Brown admitted nothing that was not favourable.

Mrs. Rossetti confided to him that her eldest daughter was fairly well disposed to Miss Siddal : her younger daughter less so. Both had their doubts as to the young woman's orthodoxy. Would Mr. Brown kindly take an opportunity of reassuring them on that point and herself on some others ? Had he seen any of her people ? She supposed them to be respectable, though tradesmen. Gabriel had a story about a pedigree and would

136

have it that they were of as good or better extraction than the Rossettis—but how could that be? The Della Guardias of Vasto! Miss Siddal had not mentioned any of her relations to-day, nay, she had rather pointedly avoided the subject. How many were they in family? Had he seen any member of it? Two or three brothers, Brown believed, and two sisters: he had once seen Lydia—" Lyddy " as they called her—of whom Lizzy was very fond. There was another one. . . . The old lady did not mark Brown's pause and her questions began again. Did Gabriel ever go to see them? She gathered not. It was understood, was it not, that these shopkeepers disapproved of their daughter marrying an artist? Absurd! Artists' models, it was well known, had no status whatever and had to sit to everyone that paid them, for any part that might be required.

Thus did Gabriel's mother dismiss Miss Siddal's claims to social eligibility.

5

On Sunday Rossetti and Miss Siddal came out, " per bus," to Finchley and stayed the day and spent the night at the Browns'. Gabriel, in his new carefulness for her reputation, took a room at the Queen's Head. They had brought with them the packet of Ivory Dust for Mrs. Brown to cook, mistrusting the capacities of Mrs. Birrell in a matter so complicated. They sat up only till two o'clock, and by that time the Browns had heard all about it.

The night before Brown had been having mushrooms for his tea and thinking of Death, " a very natural consummation," so it seemed to him at the ripe age of thirty-four. His Emma had a little trick of running away (taking baby) to her mother's, to be fetched back with promises of reform. He was terribly hard-up. Emma, distracted by the approaching cataclysm of childbirth, had been keeping house ever so much worse than usual. And the lease of this beastly but cheap " crib " was up and they must move in August!

He now thought of going out to India, where, it was said, there were fortunes to be made. But the very person who suggested it dissuaded him, saying that he was not the man to make one.

The mental anguish suffered by this Titan—duly registered in his diary (he was a good one to complain)—did not prevent him

137

from paying the deepest attention to Gabriel telling of how the Ruskins were all " delighted with Lizzy," old John James calling her " a most noble, glorious creature," and declaring that " by her look and manner she might have been born a countess." Rossetti had then trotted out the father's story of a lost pedigree to show justification for this remark. And in a talk he had with Mrs. Ruskin after they had come out of the bedroom and Mr. Ruskin was showing Lizzy his pet missal, the old lady, " who was known to have much medical knowledge," had cheered him. Yes, her son also had been threatened with consumption. Open-air sketching had cured him. In Mrs. Ruskin's opinion the illness of Miss Siddal was principally weakness. She needed, of course, the greatest care if she was to recover. . . .

How on Earth, Emma said, was the poor thing going to get that, living with Rossetti, who had the digestion of an ostrich, eating at all sorts of odd hours, travelling backwards and forwards between Chatham Place and Weymouth Street at all times of the day and night and in any sort of weather ? People in her state ought never even to be out after sundown : the damage was now more deep-seated than either Gabriel or Mrs. Ruskin knew. Why, the old lady had only seen the girl once, dressed up, pleased and excited at the novelty of the visit : what should she know ?

Brown did not hint at all this to Gabriel, who, even if he took a warning to heart, would not observe it for more than a day. God send Mrs. Ruskin to be right ! At any rate, something was being done. Ruskin had talked of his pet Wales—a place called Pont y Monach, near Aberystwyth. . . . But Rossetti did not think that Miss Siddal would agree to Wales—nor did he intend her to do so.

Meanwhile she should be kept quiet and her thoughts continually occupied. She might work a little—indeed she ought to be made to draw sometimes " in a dull way from dull things," but not wear herself out with " fancies." The Professor made her promise to do her best to break off " those disagreeable ghostly connections of hers," by which he meant the whole chain of morbid notions, the sad death of her first sweetheart and that more indurated early one of her handshake with a murderer.[1] The Professor saw her, perhaps, as she was, avid of sensation—of many things—death-smitten persons snatch at all they can of the life they are soon to leave—and constitutionally unable to support

[1] She had of course told Mrs. Ruskin of this.

138

it when they get their desire—"You inventive people pay dearly for your powers," he told her. Selfish and self-sacrificing, sweet or bad-tempered, according to her daily chart of health, one never knew how she would take things; and it needed all his tact to move her even a little one way or another, by compliments and emotional appeals and such like.

Meantime, when the weather improved—it was a cold spring —why should she not come sometimes and walk in the garden at Denmark Hill? She did not seem to care about that but liked the specially selected luncheon-parties he gave for her. Once it seemed unavoidable that she should meet Robert Browning and young Frederic Leighton, "if Ruskin couldn't manage to put them off to another day." They would be rather too noisy, Browning especially, for Ida—as he now called her.

6

About this time Gabriel had a psychic experience—rare with him, so matter of fact, so sensible! Sitting up late writing to William Allingham he was, to his surprise, *told* loudly (by whom?) that it was three o'clock and—"lo, it was horridly light!" and happened to be "the very morning on which he first woke up, or fell a-dreaming, or began to be, or was transported for life, or whatever it is" twenty-seven years ago. Though he looked more he behaved like the boy he was and resented interference. They were all managing him too much, even telling him how and what to paint. Ruskin wanted him to drop *Found*, "a subject of a pathetic, exciting nature," with which a man like Rossetti should not concern himself just now but wait until his mentality was better adjusted "to touch the higher chords without effort," devoting himself for the present to "drawing pretty faces and things involving little thought and no pathos at all."

He had obeyed,[1] but now they were interfering in his affairs of the heart too.

The fellows all were!

"Why does he not marry her?" Brown had entered the question in his diary the moment he was told of Mr. Ruskin's proposition. Ruskin put it more delicately, asking Gabriel if he had any plans "respecting Miss Siddal" which he was prevented by "lack of income" from carrying out, and what would be the

[1] "Gabriel has laid aside *Found* and now paints in water-colour," so says William in a note to Scott, the picture's godfather: sure to be annoyed!

certain income which would enable him to do so? His own feeling was that it would be best for them to be married, and then Rossetti could afford her " the complete care and protection " which Victorian conventions would not allow him to give to any but his wedded wife. As paymaster, he agreed to Jersey for a week or so, and then—" If she would only make up her mind to take you! " the young couple could go quietly to Vevey for the summer.

The backwardness was assumed to be on the lady's side, though the Professor saw well enough, through the prismatic glasses of Heaven's blue with which he surveyed this muddy world, that, to Rossetti, full-blooded, voluptuous, this delicate creature without ostensible appetites could not seriously, physically appeal; and even sensed the derivative, or derivatives, which he would presently, if he had not already done so, offer himself. So diplomatic, however, was Ruskin that Rossetti believed him guiltless of all intention of swaying his judgment and supposed himself,[1] throughout negotiations, a cunning Odysseus playing with a blind Polyphemus.

7

Suddenly something had to be done at once. She got very ill and let herself be persuaded. " The wizard is Ruskin, of course," Rossetti wrote. But she had not written him the little signed promise he had begged for—just four words—" I will be good " —and go exactly where he thought suitable, though she did not say no to his finding her a nice quiet place, not too dull, " where she could pass the time with some pleasure to herself." He had her leave to write to his doctor friend at Oxford.

8

Incidents such as had promoted the lifelong friendship between Acland and Ruskin were of frequent occurrence in the most snobbish of Colleges.[2] Long, long ago, when both were under-

[1] He was no judge of character. Later he announced, speaking to George Meredith of someone, that he " could not get on with men who were not men of the world " ! What about Watts and Hall Caine?

[2] Dr. Gaisford of Christ Church was perhaps responsible for the tone of the College of which he was Head; being a stickler for aristocratic privileges he would never, on principle, let a servitor, however admirable, rise to the rank of student; so that Christ Church was easily the paradise of Noble Tufts, who paid dear for their exclusiveness, dining alone at the High Table and their dinner costing them twelve shillings as against seven for pretty much the same food eaten " below the salt."

graduates, young Henry Acland was crossing Tom Quad and noticed a noble lord riding a freshman round and round it, as the time-honoured custom was. Acland much admired the good-humour with which this particular freshman took it and realised that John Ruskin, four years younger than he, was already a man of the world and a citizen of it, though he had never been to a public school. The son of a wine merchant, whose mother made him ridiculous and vulnerable to practical joking by insisting on accompanying him to Alma Mater and keeping house for him there. She was always present at the Wines he gave—but the paternal sherry was especially good!

Henry Acland was now forty. There was a Mrs. Acland and a quiverful of children. He was the busiest man in Oxford.[1] No respectable person in the county thought of dying without him and he would often drive seventy miles a day to reach a death-bed in time. His fellow-doctors gave him six years more to live, at the rate he was going, putting a bit of meat into his mouth with one hand and scribbling something with the other at the side of his plate, always going somewhere and on to somewhere else, and a crowd lying in wait to ask him questions.

The importation of Rossetti's lady friend, as a man's sweet-heart was then innocently called, into their midst was another job for Mrs. Acland, like reading aloud to chimney-sweeps and running Sunday Evenings for undergraduates—"Music and Quiet Talk from eight till eleven." Hers to keep the patient quiet and amused while the doctor had her under observation and prove the London one, who had diagnosed one side of her lungs seriously affected, to be wrong—and save her, and Rossetti's art. For Ruskin, sending specimens of her work, told him (by permission) all about the hindrance to the artist's progress involved in the illness of this young girl to whom he was so deeply attached, and his own fear that the matter would soon be "sealed in death." He wanted Acland to examine her and direct her how to look after herself, a task at which she seemed singularly incompetent; and then, if he agreed with Ruskin that change of scene alone could save her, ascertain where she should be sent. She was still too ill to be moved for a few days yet; he would let Acland know when to begin looking for rooms. She would be able to pay two pounds a week.

[1] Lee Reader to Christ Church, Physician to the Radclyffe Infirmary and to a Royal Prince, Regius Professor, Curator to a Museum or two and owning the largest practice in the county.

Lizzy was honest enough to realise that he who pays the piper has a right to call the tune; but there was a good chance of her refusing to go anywhere at all. She desired to go to Jersey. But Ruskin dreaded the passage for her—he wanted her somewhere in England—but "the doctor will certainly let you see a little sea if you tell him that you like it." There would be rocks, and heather too, in Devonshire as well as in the Channel Islands. The point was that she should be seen first by Acland. She should be quite quiet in her own digs and see no one unless she wanted to. Mrs. Acland might trespass on her time for a quarter of an hour, but she would *not* bring her children (Rossetti had infected poor Lizzy with his horror of the young). The doctor would only want her to put her tongue out once and let him feel her pulse . . . that was all.

Ruskin had taken on himself to engage a room for a week at one pound,[1] which was what she could pay. Would she pack her things and go at slight notice, for every day was of importance? Could she get one of her sisters to go with her on Monday, when he believed the rooms would be ready? Would she please excuse his pressing her in this way? And he was hers most respectfully and, in a pregnant postscript "If one of your sisters can't, Rossetti says he will take charge of you to Oxford."

Neither sister was available—or even told!

[1] To Acland he had said two pounds a week for a fortnight.

142

CHAPTER XV

I

" MISS SIDDAL is at Oxford, where Ruskin's friends pay her all sorts of attention." So William Rossetti to Allingham.

It was her last excursion out of the dowdy night of Bohemia into the day of well-lit rooms, clear, clean windows, cheerful wallpapers and modern furniture, a world whence dust was banished and objects of *virtu* relegated to their proper place in a museum. She moved as an equal among well-groomed, well-behaved men, and women elegant and sophisticated. She became acquainted with the famous " Oxford manner," the expression in the voice, the gesture, the behaviour of people to whom Conduct was three-fourths of life ; their " every thought a mental reservation." [1]

It was her glittering hour ; she did not make the most of it. Too ill, perhaps, and it was a cold summer ! Her lover had taken her down, beautifully dressed for travelling, and was proud of her before porters. Her room was in George Street, where she could be left in peace as she had stipulated, but she was to be free of the Aclands' house in Broad Street at all hours of the day and, if she had occasion to stay out after dark, the doctor would escort her home himself. Gabriel stopped on a couple of nights and was asked to go down again for the laying of the first stone of the new Museum. He did not accept " because of the expense." But he laid the seed of a job for himself and his friends. " I am asked by the architect to do some designing for the Museum and probably shall."

After he left, Mrs. Acland did her best to keep the doctor's pretty patient amused with a minimum of excitement. She took her to some of the Lee Lectures where everyone, when the lecture was over, sat at little tables furnished with miniature railroads on which ran microscopes, illustrating the lecture or,

[1] Robert Ross, *Masques and Faces.*

143

alternatively, with cups of coffee—an idea of the doctor's. There were the teas to the chimney-sweeps, after which Mrs. Acland and Miss Cardwell usually read aloud. Lizzy did not read, her voice was not good enough. But she made herself useful on the Evenings for Undergraduates, for she liked youths and, with two exceptions, did not care for the older men to whom she was introduced—Ruskin's tutor Osborne Gordon, with his donnish insolence, queer, mocking face and half-closed inscrutable eyes, or Dr. Pattison, who came from her part of the country,[1] because he sneered so. She did not admire Wynter, who appeared to carry his head on a charger like John the Baptist, or Venables, whose features had suggested to Hunt those of Christ in *The Light*. She got on well enough with Mr. Dodgson, shy and precise : in the words of a German professor of whom she had never heard,[2] a " grown-up child," like another man she came to be very fond of, Algernon Swinburne, just now being prepared for Oxford in his North-country home. " Lewis Carroll " sketched Gabriel[3] for her when he came down, and made her and the chimney-sweeps laugh and the undergraduates thaw ; but she was too old for *him*. Another of her friends was " The Common Object," Ruskin's friend, Mr. Wood, who was Bible Clerk at Merton and pricked attendances at Chapel and dined on remnants from the High Table, going about alone and dressing so shabbily that he came to have a nickname out of his own book.[4]

The Aclands, to please Ruskin, introduced her to their friends " in the most exclusive quarters." Probably she shook hands with Prince Leopold. The great ladies of Oxford, to oblige their dear doctor, called or left cards upon the favourite model of the man whose art Ruskin was gradually making the fashion. Oxford drawing-rooms, beginning with Dr. Acland's own, began to show signs of P.R.B. culture. Ruskin spoke of Miss Siddal's own work in the same breath as that of Turner, Watts and Millais. Mrs. Ffoulkes, wife of the Principal of Jesus, a professed Jacobite whose mother, Lady Isabella Lumsden, had hidden the Pretender under her hoop and made white cockades for him when he held his Court in Edinburgh, sent for Miss Siddal to her house in St. Giles' and insisted on a rehearsal of the pedigree, which she did not absolutely pooh-pooh. Hunt's " perfect lady," the wife of Dr. Combe, Superintendent of the University Press,

---

[1] Hauxwell.   [2] Novalis.   [3] Where is that sketch now ?
[4] *Common Objects of the Country-side*, by J. G. Wood.

ELEANOR ELIZABETH SIDDALL
From a drawing by D. G. Rossetti

had kindly fetched Miss Siddal out to Abingdon to spend the day, but the conversation, connected with Hunt and Millais (not Deverell, whom Mrs. Combe also had known), was not particularly acceptable to Miss Siddal. She had to listen all over again to the record of P.R.B. determination to paint from the real thing. Well she knew it—the cold bath that had nearly killed her! Mrs. Combe had been told that Miss Siddal's father, a " local auctioneer," had brought an action against the young painter claiming fifty pounds for the injury to his daughter's health, but that Millais had settled the matter by paying the doctor's bill and that she herself had admitted that she was none the worse for the chill. Nothing of the kind.[1] Her father had never brought any action, he was *not* an auctioneer, he had never lived in Oxford. She had a relation an auctioneer, but he lived in Sheffield. That was probably how the mistake arose. She was perfectly polite, but her voice took on its slight sibilant hiss. What *would* have interested her was Millais' letters about Walter Deverell's illness and death, that Mrs. Combe did not think of showing to her guest. Lizzy could not get her to take the slightest interest in the subject. Walter had died in Millais' arms, indifferent to those of Gabriel. But now, Lizzy did not wonder at that.

She was happiest with the Puseys, and from them " got religion," which served her to die with.

2

This man (whose life's tragedy was consumption too) and his sisters were the persons she saw most of during her stay. There is a freemasonry between those suffering from the same disability; their complexes reach out one to the other; their lot is ameliorated where there is no priority in suffering or invidious comparisons to be made between persons languishing in a common hell.

Edward Bouverie Pusey, like herself, was an aristocrat; his father the Honourable Philip Bouverie Pusey, his mother a Harborough. Their son was a broken-hearted man who had

---

[1] Yet the *Ophelia* legend seems to bear the stamp of truth at any rate. Allingham thought so! In a letter written from Ireland about McCracken, the artistic ship-packer of Belfast and his complaint: " He says he is ruined by his purchase of *Ophelia*; surely he did not lose by it? Now he goes throwing cold water on her who had too much."

loved at eighteen, married at twenty-eight, and lost at thirty-nine. His wife had died of the disease of the age; she too came of a family all of whom suffered more or less from " a chest affection." She had borne him five daughters and a son. Little Lucy and Harriet and Eleanor died in the same year they were born. Elizabeth and Charlotte, respectively Mrs. Luxmoore and Mrs. Cotton, survived. Until they were old enough to keep house for him, his mother, though she had a house of her own in Grosvenor Square, managed the large house in Christ Church —as much of it as the widower could be persuaded to use. The drawing-room—his wife had died there and it could not be used. The bedroom he could never be persuaded to re-enter, or the garden.[1] The study had been re-papered: it hurt him to see, covered, the paper *she* had chosen. . . .

The Pusey ladies received Miss Siddal's return call most graciously and one of the sisters took a fancy to her. Lady Lucy, who drank green tea and dressed in the old-fashioned style,[2] amused Miss Siddal very much by alluding to her son as Ed'ard, and saying " ooman " for woman and " t'other." Lady Lucy liked little Miss Siddal quite well and would complain of Ed'ard to the sympathetic, well-bred girl, saying that neither she nor Charlotte could ever get him to dress himself properly. Certainly he was untidy; his necktie always limp and his face suggesting the use of a blunt razor. The long mouth set in whiskers all round and under the chin reminded Lizzy of a ploughshare lying in high grass, but his eyes were fine and he would have been a personable man had he not been so slovenly.

He talked to the young stranger of his dead wife, recognising in the one, perhaps, the taint which had killed the other. " To save her I would have given up anything, gone anywhere. . . . But God's will be done ! " And, getting up stiffly, showed the young girl a part of the wall in the corner of the room where he had secretly, as a prisoner files away his bars, scraped off the new paper, to disclose a bit of the old that *she* had known.

He had no small-talk, but with him, Miss Siddal seemed to have plenty. Whenever she went to call on Miss Pusey, he would get her alone and ask her embarrassing questions about her spiritual convictions, but so sweetly and decently that she could not resent it. Miss Pusey told her that all women looked

---

[1] The smell of verbena always affected him because he had offered Miss Barker a sprig of it when he proposed in the garden of Fairford Place.

[2] She affected that and is said to have maintained the last sedan chair in London.

upon Edward as a Father Confessor and came immense distances in flies, getting themselves set down at his door, for interviews, and some of them he persuaded to go to Clewer. He now, since procreation had turned out so ill for him, advocated the excellence of the state of virginity. He did not even realise that Miss Siddal was an engaged woman.

She liked his sermons in the Cathedral, to which the undergraduates flocked, sometimes walking there with him across the quad, past the terrace with its flight of steps and border wall of grey, Cornish granite. She knew why he kept his eyes on the pavement : his wife lay buried in the nave of the building to which they were going and he had followed her body to its last rest there. He would never forget the blear shroud over her coffin, floating in the wind, and even now, durst not look up lest a vision of that hour came before him. It was an effort to go to church at all that day and, no sooner had he preached than, as the hymn began, he seemed to drop down in the pulpit, out of sight, nor could she expect to see him again that day.

3

In the beginning of June Miss Pusey took her down to Clevedon, in Somersetshire, a new watering-place, a mile from the sea. No pier, no parade, on the west marshy, on the south and east hilly and beautiful; with the usual views. From Cadbury Camp you could see the Mendips and the mountains of Glamorganshire. She could sit on the shore and look westwards across the Bristol Channel to Penarth (where is now the wilderness of masts and funnels of Barry Dockyard). The water is hardly brackish, but it looks like sea, and shallow, with verdure nearly down to the water's edge, so that the landscape with its fairy colours, its vivid but poisonous yellows and greens, reminded her of a picture of Gabriel's she liked—*Two Women at the Well.*

She managed to " keep herself alive " in the usual way, going out to sea in a boat now and then, until Midsummer Day, when Rossetti came from London to fetch her back, taking a room at the inn for a few days. He was bored, perturbed and restless, so that one day he got up at six in the morning, for the first and last time in his life, too early even to go to breakfast with Miss Siddal, as he told William Allingham in a letter written in the hotel parlour to pass the time till she came down. Liz was now,

147

he said, able to take long excursions on donkeyback to a certain ditch where she could dig up golden flags for the balcony at Chatham Place. The donkey boy, said Gabriel, had asked if there were *lions* in the place she came from, for he was sure she came from very far away, much farther than he could see! "There's your fairy for you!" (He did not tell Allingham that the local people called her "outlandish.")

She herself was not communicative about her time in Oxford, neither then nor ever. She said that everyone was very kind, even trying to get her to settle there. Perhaps everyone meant Miss Pusey? But nothing and no one, she said, would induce her to do that.

Ruskin, reading between the lines, felt it necessary to write to Acland later to say that, "however that wilful girl may have behaved," her heart was in the right place. That she was not ungrateful, he was sure, but "sick and sickly headstrong." . . .

What was it she did or did not do there which made it incumbent on her sponsor to apologise for her? "Sorry for what you tell me about Oxford." Sins of omission rather than sins of commission? The Warden of New, a great swell, asked her to his own house to show her a blackbeetle painted by Albrecht Dürer, intending to fetch up a real one as his wont was, from the kitchen to compare with it. But she never went! That sort of thing. Perhaps it was her way of dressing? Nothing like bad manners or dereliction in her devoirs to the Aclands at any rate. Before she left she made them accept a little drawing, representing a church among the mountains, "a strange and somewhat weird arrangement of colour!" so Oxford, in the main, thought. But Miss Sarah Angelina Acland said that her father was very glad to have it and considered it a most remarkable piece of work, marvelling much that a girl "brought up within a street or two of The Elephant and Castle," should have selected such a subject and have been able to execute it from pure imagination. A Cockney, Miss Siddal had never been in the country before, so far as she knew. . . .

Perhaps her *laches* was nothing worse than disobedience to Dr. Acland's orders, but Ruskin's diatribes have a very special bitterness. "These geniuses are all alike!" He had known five of them, Turner and Watts and Millais and Rossetti—"and now this girl!"

There is no clue to this outburst. The doctor declares that Miss Siddal was "a kindly, gentle person," not beautiful but "known to everybody as Rossetti's favourite model." [1]   But he did not, obviously, "take" to her.   To Ruskin he wrote rather stiffly that it "had been a great pleasure to him to be of service to Miss Siddal."   In another letter he gave Ruskin his diagnosis—the result of the one grudging examination which Miss Siddal had promised to permit and had permitted—embodying his own private observations of her habit as she lived.   His verdict, given coldly and as it were without interest, was fairly favourable ; the young lady's lungs were not fatally affected.   She had no "really inarrestable, infixed disease" even, as yet.

The cause of it all was "power long pent up" (in the Old Kent Road, perhaps) "and now over-taxed."   There was nothing else for it ; she must cease work and be absolutely idle for the present. Just what the other two doctors, Wilkinson and Hailes of Hastings, had said, and she had taken absolutely no notice, but worked on, spurred by her artist's vanity and Ruskin's encouragement.   In these last few fevered months she, so conscientious, so honourable, was trying to make good ! . . .

Mr. Ruskin must not force on this clever pupil of his any more, but concentrate on getting her out of England—away from Rossetti—for the winter, if he wanted to preserve her life.

But those who had known her during these five years that she had been going about with Rossetti and had sampled her strange, wild obstinacy, never believed that the Professor would get his way unless, indeed, her equally strong sense of decency prompted her that she owed him obedience in return for kindness.   And she was as anxious as anyone to avoid all appearance of pauperisation, and was working herself to the bone—so near the surface already—in order to procure at least some of the money to defray her travelling expenses and get some of her own way as to destination.

Her wintering in all sorts of places was spoken of.   Algiers—but she feared earthquakes, in Africa !   Switzerland—but she loathed Switzerland, its pink sunsets and eternal snows : she was a Cockney with a Cockney's ideals.   Paris was what she wanted (and got—using all the determinative power of quiet persons)—Paris with its Boulevards to wander up and down, its Rue de la Paix like Regent Street, only better, and the Great Exhibition.

[1] So Sir Henry's biographer.

CHAPTER XVI

I

"*I WAS born to conceive what I cannot execute, to recommend what I cannot obtain and mourn over what I cannot save.*"

This had been Ruskin's cry of incompetence in the case of Effie, the young girl whom he took young in order to train as a wife. In the case of Lizzy, a less intimate charity, he had recommended what he could not procure from this obstinate personality—the adoption of a given scheme of salvage.

It was his own evil hour.

On the 31st of May William Rossetti wrote to William Allingham that Millais was immediately about to marry Mrs. Ruskin—that it was no secret, everybody knew it, and Ruskin knew that they did and had not been able to settle down at all, although so far back as April he had written, " the worst of it for me has long been past," in a letter to Lizzy herself, the wooden woman whom he trusted because he so respected her. He knew " how difficult it was to be brave " when one was ill. Himself, on this very day of writing, " could have sat down and cried heartily."

He went down to Tunbridge Wells, where lived a relation, William Richardson, unsympathetic in a soothing way. He dropped *Modern Painters*, though he kept his engagement—at God knows what cost, for he had no means of ascertaining whether Effie and Lady Eastlake might not think fit and proper to again form part of the audience—to give the Third Lecture, addressed to Workmen in the Decorative Trades, of the course which he had begun. But he did no more public speaking for three years after that, giving his father's and mother's Puritanical dislike for this form of activity (both his parents considered lecturing little better than play-acting) as an excuse.

By June he was too ill to examine Rossetti's poems " properly ": by July he could neither see nor speak. This month John Everett Millais married Euphemia Chalmers Gray, daughter of

George Gray, Esquire, Writer, Perth, in the drawing-room at Bowerswell, where John Ruskin, six years ago, had stood at her side to be married.

The notice of the wedding somehow got itself in among the Deaths in *The Leader*.

" Ruskin is in the country, unwell." So Rossetti to Allingham. But the absent benefactor was still mindful of his protégé and was sending " a Stunner called Waterford " to call on the painter that very afternoon. " There, Sir ! "

2

Miss Siddal was sleeping alone all through this hot midsummer in Chatham Place. Gabriel, desperately afraid of the cholera still hanging about, had taken a bedroom at the Queen's Head nearly opposite Brown's, and was working by day in The Hermitage [1] studio which Mr. and Mrs. Howitt as usual had given him leave to use while they were away.

And it was here, according to his old friend Scott, that he denied her before men.

Scott, who had passed through the more terrible forms of the cholera epidemic in Newcastle—working with little Swinburne on death-carts and in hospitals—to cure himself of the consequent " fit of the dismals," came up to town. He called on Rossetti in Chatham Place but " found him away and Miss Siddal in bed." So Mrs. Birrell—giving Mr. Scott ideas. . . . Mr. Rizzetty was at Hampstead—he would find him at the Queen's Hotel or The Hermitage, she didn't know which.

He walked over to The Hermitage that evening and rang the house bell. Informed that Mr. and Mrs. Howitt were away he inquired for Mr. Rossetti. The maid, without troubling to go with him, pointed out a building at the bottom of the garden to which access was gained by a flight of rustic steps leading to the studio, where she said Mr. Rossetti was.

Mr. Scott's experience [2] and his deductions therefrom are best given in Mr. Scott's own words :—

[1] The Hermitage was doomed : a row of villas were to be erected on its site and, anyway, according to Miss Smith and Miss Coutts, it would have been insanitary to go on living there because of the projected extension of Highgate Cemetery down the hill, for the houses at the bottom would get all the graveyard drainage. They were all fighting it and the Howitts had taken a house farther up the hill.

[2] It led to a storm of vituperation from the champion of Miss Siddal, vocal and able to use the medium of the Press. " The New Terror " in the *Fortnightly*

"I found myself in the romantic dusk of the apartment face to face with Rossetti and a lady whom I did not recognise, and could scarcely see. He did not introduce her; she rose to go. I made a little bow, which she did not acknowledge; and she left. This was Miss Siddal. Why he did not introduce me to her I cannot say. Perhaps the maid should have called him instead of allowing me to invade the studio without warning; she may have even done it for a lark; for myself, I had not yet heard of such a person as Miss Siddal." (He must have.) "Perhaps Rossetti was already beginning to revise his intention of marriage; an even way of life the most unlikely possible to suit his late development."[1]

A more probable explanation of Rossetti's failure to introduce his sweetheart to his friend is forthcoming. The "Great Italian" doing his best to behave in "the Inferno of England" had to consider England's prejudices, and the most rampant of them all at that time were the almost purdah-like arrangements for the claustration of women.

Scott was an arrant gossip. The lateness of the hour, the need for chaperonage would never enter the head of a Bohemian, but what would Mrs. Ruskin in Camberwell and Mrs. Acland in Oxford, who had chaperoned Miss Siddal so carefully while she was there, think of her being caught sitting all alone with her young man in the dark, in the greenhouse—let us call it—of a house in Hampstead while the mistress of it was out of town? He probably hoped that Scott, who had never set eyes on Lizzy, would suppose the female with him to be a model whom one need not, as a rule, introduce. He had just given her the chance to slip quietly out—which she had taken.

It is possible that Gabriel did not even know what Scott knew,

and "The Poison of the Parasite" which appeared in the *Athenæum* (without its provocative title and with some of the strongest epithets left out) were penned in the days when the publishing of personal memoirs after Death was a new terror.

> The infinitely little ghosts
>   Of sprats deceased on unknown coasts,
> And many a long putrescent prawn
>   Preserved unfit for human victuals.
>
> Prince! Lord of flies and rhymester's spawn
>   That scarce deserves a strong man's spittle.
> Beelzebub, thou hast in pawn
>   Less than the infinitely little.

[1] *Autobiography* of W. B. Scott.

that the perverse creature was at the moment choosing to occupy his bed in Chatham Place, and that the housekeeper had betrayed her. Scott was dead against her from that moment.

"*She began to think herself a genius too and did small, quaint, quasi-poetical imitations of his works. . . . And then, her health not being good, by Ruskin's assistance she went to Mentone.*"

She was to stop in Paris one night passing through. Rossetti, writing to Brown to inform him of the final plan, gave her a longer term there, feeling sure she would take it. But she "*must* try to get to the south before the cold sets in."

A drawing which he had on the stocks would, Rossetti estimated, bring in about ten or fifteen pounds, which was for Guggums. But he owed (?) her twenty pounds already, and when the *Lancelot* was finished, twelve pounds had to go for the rent of Chatham Place where he was not even, for the moment, sleeping. All the same, she must have ten pounds clear in hand before she left London, to set " her dear mind at ease about her finances " and " save dangerous transmissions." So, " under the circs," will Brown oblige with a loan of ten or fifteen pounds which Gabriel does not doubt he will be able to pay back in a few weeks ? Indeed Brown may absolutely depend on it ; the sum destined for Gug would go to him automatically. And he is painting " her dear face " for *Guenevere*.

A good deal of lip-service ; it connoted a certain shameful sense of relief ? Brown *thought* that Gabriel *knew* he was going to get on better, with Lizzy away.

Brown did oblige ; he had now the wherewithal. Rossetti and others had made the " dangerous discovery " that he now owned a cheque-book and that his cheques were honoured all right. So one day in June, when Emma, worn out by privation and child-bearing, had " begun the day by quarrelling " and again run away as far as St. Paul's Terrace to her mother's, taking Cathy and the baby with her, Brown was able to seal the reconciliation with a bracelet of " gold mosaic," as a result of Rossetti's and the fellows', waylaying old White the picture-dealer, catching him boozed at a Promenade Concert and forcing him to pop in at Brown's and buy the little *Brent* for forty pounds, and then another picture for a hundred-and-twenty.

Gabriel called on the Brownings in Dorset Street—they were on the wing for the South, all the delicate women were being sent off to avoid what came to be known as the Crimean Winter—so as to be able to give Lizzy a letter to them, later on, in Florence, if she went there. He was rewarded by an appreciative slap on the back from " robustious Robert," who quoted to him some of " that 'ere *Blessed Damozel* " of his and invited him to come and hear Tennyson read on one of two successive days at his house. Gabriel himself began to itch for Paris, where the Brownings would be till Christmas. . . .

Lizzy was not well enough to travel alone : a chaperon-escort must be procured so that he could run over to see her—and have a look at the Exhibition. He thought of a relation of his own on his mother's side—his only English quartering, a Pierce, married to a sharp and busy solicitor, who had his office not far from Chatham Place and often joined Gabriel for the meal which he so detested taking alone. Mrs. Kincaid was a matronly sort of person of forty and upwards. She was brought by arrangement to tea in Chatham Place to make Miss Siddal's acquaintance. Lizzy took a dislike to him at once—to his wife, unfortunately, not till later.

Ruskin was due home but contrived not to set foot on British soil until Lizzy was well off it. He came back two days after she had gone. Of all the protégés, Gabriel and Lizzy (yet in his bitterness he was never unjust to *her*) were the most unsatisfactory and came very near to breaking the heart of the man whose mind and thought fell, like crystals, into certain mathematical patterns. His own magnetism made no way with one or the other. He could never laugh at them, and when Gabriel permitted himself to send growling letters, reacted unpleasantly. And his long talks with the sturdy Carlyle were disturbing the Protestantism which was sanity's sheet-anchor for the weaker man.

According to that quiet, subtle observer, Gabriel's brother, it was now that the first taint of morbidity (as he calls it) showed itself in Ruskin, coinciding with the change in his religious belief. Burying his head in a tuft of grass " on a battlefield [1] wet with blood," he would lie and hear as in a shell the sound of the sea, " the cry of the earth about him continually." He saw ghosts. He took to reading novels, valuing them " because of the unknown

[1] In the Vaudois.

growth of souls, in and through any form of misery and servitude; there is an infinity of what men should be told."

4

Old Mrs. Rossetti was at Hastings, William abroad and Maggie at Muntham, so there need be no family good-byes. Brown did ask Christina to call and bid God-speed to her future sister-in-law—crossing the Channel was a serious event in those days—and she professed herself willing—" But I do not encourage her to," Gabriel said.

Miss Siddall's own family . . . but *she* did not encourage that. She was savagely determined not to inflict her family on him, as a counter to his backwardness in making her known to his. This was the ground of some of their worst quarrels, taken with the denial of their engagement, which had made her so ill last year, and the allowing her to slink out of the studio at The Hermitage without being introduced to his greatest friend.

However, there was no quarrelling in these last days—she was so pleased and excited about her first trip to the Continent. She had always before her pale eyes the mirage of Paris; through Paris only did she feel able to envisage the prescribed push southwards. On the Friday night before she left England she actually consented to take him to her home.

A bus to The Elephant and a walk southwards along the country roads of her childhood—now, because of the new building rage that had set in in South London a few years after she was born, considerably built over, most of the Hatches closed and the greenness of the spinneys gone—till they came to The Bricklayers' Arms. Then, for Gabriel, it began to be *terra incognita*. Past The Swan with its appropriate sign and The World Turned Upside Down, with its " watering " for horses, the trough and the bit of green gravel in front. When they came to the Asylum for the Blind, where sat the horribly mutilated man to whom Gabriel tossed a penny, and had passed the two turnings on the opposite side, Thomas Street and John Street, they were in the very heart of her complex and, sure enough, she began to talk of it.

Mr. Greenacre was an immensely tall man dressed like a farmer, " fish-faced " Annie always said, with a big slopperty mouth and very bright eyes, but Lizzy could remember nothing but the feel of his hand—clammy ! Annie had actually been with her mother to his shop—he was a grocer and sold tea, mixed with sloes the people said, sweets and a kind of special rock called Amalgamated Candy, made of cloves, cinnamon, lemon and peppermint. Somewhere quite near was Carpenter's Buildings,[1] the very place in which Hannah Brown had been murdered a week before her wedding-day to this man. He was wealthy, they said, landlord of Number Eight and three other cottages in Jane Place, two tenements in Carpenter's Place and eight in Bowyer Lane. But, although he was rich, he did it all for the sake of the woman's savings. Though she was only a laundress living in one room with her mangle, she had four hundred pounds and jewellery[2] which fetched a hundred. Greenacre made her sell it to buy her trousseau and she went to Carpenter's Place (where he lived with another woman and her child), to be married thence. She was murdered there instead.

Wilkinson had said that it was good for Lizzy to talk about this, and the temperamental washerwoman and her epileptic murderer interested Gabriel, and the circumstances, squalid and romantic, in which the murder was committed—on the night when snow fell continuously for five days and five nights and the whole of England was covered by a white cloak under which ill deeds can be done as conveniently as in a dark one. As the poor girl murmured of her obsession, he *felt* the soft flakes on his forehead : saw the fresh red bloodstains on the snow, the murderer padding along on his balled shoes of silence, heard his heavy, labouring breath that created a bloody aureole of mist about him as he disposed of portions of the body here and there, the legs in the osier bed at Cold Harbour, the trunk in the Lock Fields, and the head, that had caught in every weir between Stepney and Paddington by its matted hair, with its helpless, shapeless mouth that never now could say " I will "—this head had the absurdest peregrinations. Wrapped in a bag, it was under his arm as he called on Hannah Brown's landlady to say there would be no wedding—" indefinitely postponed." Getting into the Camberwell bus he had betrayed the murderer's addled inconsequence, and nearly fainted when the conductor asked for the fare—" Sixpence a head ! "

She had made Gabriel read the descriptions of Hannah Brown, forty, high-chested, with large thin hands and a split ear whence a fellow-servant had once wrenched an earring ;

---

[1] Renamed.
[2] Probably stolen. She had been housemaid to Lord Woodhouse in Norfolk.

silly and vain, killed in a smart pea-green dress, some of her wedding finery. " A strange-tempered woman," said her landlady, volunteering an account of Hannah's physical conformation which led to identification and, the woman said, distressed Hannah so much—" For trees that don't bud, don't bear fruit ! "

Pretty Sarah Gale loved him and had to be given morphia in her cell so that she should not hear the yells of execration that greeted his appearance outside Newgate. She heard and fainted. She was not allowed to see him after he was dead. He left her his spectacles.

An interesting degenerate—Greenacre; a bit of an actor, staging the usual remorse and half-feigned terror of retribution. He attended service a few days after the deed and, coming out of the cold into the warm Chapel and seeing the candles flaming in the misty damp with their light concentrated round about the altar, cried out from his pew—" My God ! Hell's on fire ! " [1] falling straightway " into a stupor." Nobody suspected him of having much more than ordinary on his conscience and they were used to epileptic subjects in those days.

When they came to Number Eight, Lizzy, telling Gabriel to sit down, went to the foot of the stairs and called. Gabriel chose to nourish an indefinable yet delightful feeling that they were all the time being watched—that someone was there besides the canary that hung in the window fidgeting in its cage, neatly peeling its seed. . . . Then Lizzy came back and, in the twilight, her hair seemed to go white and she looked like a ghost herself, sitting squeezed up in her father's armchair, still and self-contained, not even starting when there was the noise of a key in the lock. He was sorry when Lyddy walked in and said, without listening to their explanations about the back door, that They had all gone to the play and would not come out till the end, unless mother got one of her faints. No, she had never had any letter ; but she would make them some tea at once.

While she was in the kitchen Lizzy rose and, from the whatnot near the corner where he kept his fiddle, took out her father's music-book, handsomely bound in leather and engraved with his name and his Arms—three birds and the word " Honour." From the wall she lifted down a heavy china plaque, showing the family coat of arms, per bend and gules and an eagle displayed. This family, she explained, with whom the Siddalls

[1] The man had been an actor. " I think the devil will not have me damned lest the oil that is in me should set hell on fire." Falstaff in *The Merry Wives*.

had intermarried, dated from a Knight of Beely in Henry III's time, a much older family. The head of that family again was the Duke of Rutland. Then, out of a drawer in a Flemish cabinet (that Rossetti meant to have some day) she produced a piece of brownish parchment purporting to be a document granting the Freedom—whatever that might mean?—of the City of Sheffield to Christopher Siddall in 1792. Also the marriage certificate of Charles Crookes Siddall and Elizabeth Elenor Evans, married by banns in the Parish Church of Hornsey in the year one thousand eight hundred and twenty-four.

Gabriel forbade Lyddy to light the lamp, and they three sat together in the gloaming until it was time to go back. He enjoyed the quiet, the neutrality of the surroundings, the presence of a few " good " things such as the Flemish cabinet and the one or two nice bits of pewter that, beautifully polished, hung on the walls and shone in the temperate gloom. He was pleased, so he wrote to Brown, to find Lizzy's "native crib" so comfortable.

Just before they left a girl came in, unexpected by Lizzy he could see, and perhaps by Lyddy? Tall, dark, shy and yet sophisticated looking, with a queer permanent frown. Her hair was dyed and scented; the carmine of her lips aided by art, she made the other two girls look immature and faded. . . .

" My sister—known as Tump ! " Lizzy introduced her.

CHAPTER XVII

I

THE Kincaids dined in Chatham Place on the Saturday night and Mrs. Kincaid slept there, so as to be in good time for the early start at seven.

On a cold rimy morning in September the two women drove to the docks to take steamer for Havre. Lizzy had, thanks to Brown, forty pounds in hand which must take her, when she had rested, to the South and must last her till the first of November, when she would receive another forty from Rossetti, who meant to work like the devil. He did not begin that day, full of that peculiar thwarted feeling which sets in for the one who is left behind in the emptied room, with the brown paper strewn about and the mark of the cabman's dirty boots on the stairs. Mr. McLennan of Inverness, calling, found him on his back, waving his legs about in the air and " Mon-Dieuing ! " McLennan disapproved and set it down against him.

Later, Gabriel roused himself and did a good action. Getting hold of Browning he took him to see Brown, who was grateful and called him " Gabby," as he always did when pleased with him—though his fifteen pounds was still in abeyance and he knew " Gabby " was in funds just now—for Ruskin had sold *Rachel and Leah* (for which Rossetti had not dared to ask him more than twenty-six pounds) to Miss Heaton for forty. The twenty-six would have more than covered Brown's loan. " At this rate he will soon get rich—perhaps even pay what he owes ? " Brown complained, with the clumsy sarcasm of the large-minded. He disapproved of the immoral arrangement between Ruskin and Rossetti and Miss Siddal—Ruskin acting as dealer for both as well as subsidising them. This relation between the artist and patron was debilitating to the moral fibre of Rossetti, already sufficiently relaxed. And she, Brown thought, was beginning to exhibit some of the off-handedness of the pensioned, willing to take all she could from Ruskin without the exchange of obedience.

"*Tell Ida she is to go South immediately. . . . Paris will kill her or ruin her, like Sir Dean Paul's bank.*[1] *I cannot have you going to Paris or near Ida at all until you have finished Miss Heaton's drawing.*"

Ruskin had only approved Miss Siddal's stopping more than one night in Paris in order that she should, as she had promised, go and make friends with the Brownings. "What the devil else was she to go there for except for that?" Well, she must stay on in Paris if she chose, but he would be d——d if he would help Rossetti to cross the Channel till she was safely got off to the South. He attempted to play on Rossetti's presupposed jealousy of him and other men—"Positively, if *you* go to Paris, *I* will!" And kept them rather short of money and was unhelpful about the mode of sending it. Rossetti had better ask at some of the money-lenders' in Leicester Square. *He* always did it through his bank but he didn't choose "to be heard of" as sending to Paris in the matter. Neither would he bother Browning. Rossetti knows B. well enough and must write himself, "and that's flat." Relenting, he admits to being "ill-tempered." "You are such a very odd creature and that's a fact!" Poor fellow, he may want some money for himself, but "I am inconvenienced for the moment."

Rossetti did want some for himself—his fare to Paris—but he didn't like being "poor-fellowed" and the idea of Ruskin pretending to be hard up! He did not in the least mind being called an "odd creature"—of course he must so appear to a "fiddle-faddle" like J. R., just now "mighty poorly," prone to feverish nights, going early to bed on toast and water and physic.

Lizzy knew she was being naughty, but intended to remain so. She had written to Ruskin suggesting that he should drop the payment of her allowance now that her ill-health and absence from England prevented her giving a due equivalent. He brushed this aside—she and Rossetti were a couple of —— Words seemed to have failed him; still, he would go on "thinking for them both."

And Rossetti would go on taking Ruskin's money and his own way when the time came. He was not going to let the Exhibition close without his seeing it. He would run over presently with Munro or Scott. . . .

[1] A very notable failure of the time. The felons were deported to Cayenne.

He was banking on a drawing Ruskin had commissioned for Miss Heaton and on another for Miss Bell. For, from the North—hard-bitten, rough-hewn, intense—came the liveliest patronage of their art that could be looked for by the Pre-Raphaelites. Miss Heaton of Bingley near Leeds, the daughter of one of the enterprising and go-ahead purveyors of ugliness there : Miss Bell of Winnington near Liverpool, where she had founded a school for the daughters of the Captains of Industry, forced to live and rear up their families, like a landscape painter, alongside of his " subject "—these two ladies, through Ruskin, who commanded both, were Rossetti's best buyers at this time. Of Miss Bell, brilliant and clever, powerful and masterful, Ruskin was the all-round hero—" no subject in the world too high or too low for him to deal with." His to arrange for their local anæsthetic, telling them when and where to buy these oblongs and squares of captured colour and stabilised light, holding up before their sad, smoke-bleared eyes, like Perseus, the shield-mirror in which they might envisage the Gorgon's Head and survive in a land fouled by the disjecta, clouded by the smoke of its fires, soured by the acrid steam of its blasting and welding.

Full of ruth at the sight of the amenities of their famous beauty spots, desecrated by their own hands, these Masters of Mines and Factories were being persuaded by Ruskin and other æsthetic Jeremiahs crying in the wilderness of slag, to make themselves at least Houses Beautiful in its midst, giving Beauty, which they had sacrificed to utility, a refuge within four walls covered with representations of what lay outside no longer. Ruskin, abetting this thwarted instinct for romance, had recommended strongly the work of Rossetti and his sweetheart. Her aspect was by now familiar to Miss Bell and Miss Heaton, as Princess Sabra watching St. George kill the dragon—playing the harp in *Dante's Dream*—gathering buttercups as Matilda, weeping as Guenevere at the tomb of King Arthur. Alas, they never knew when they bought a picture if they would be allowed to keep it, for Ruskin served them as a man of his generation *would* serve innocent ladies who ventured on the manly sport of picture-buying, "making" the price for this or that gem, arbitrarily forcing exchanges. . . .[1]

[1] Miss Heaton had ordered a *Beatrice* of Rossetti, but Ruskin wanted it for himself or someone else and made her, instead, take a *Paolo and Francesca*, or a water-colour replica of *Rachel and Leah*.

"*You won't go to Paris, I am sure, when you know that I, seriously, don't think it right*," wrote the Professor to Gabriel.

Well, but in November, when Lizzy had been gone some six weeks, she wrote to Gabriel to tell him to come and bring her some money. She could not leave, actually, for want of funds. Then Gabriel showed that he could work at that pinch and began a fresh picture in three compartments, sat up all night and finished it in a week. It was so perfectly beautiful that Ruskin came, saw, was conquered and acquired it from the artist for thirty-five pounds—down. Letting Miss Heaton and her requirements slide he sent Gabriel off to Paris with his blessing to release Lizzy and The Incubus out of the hands of creditors— "They will have more debts than they say; people are always afraid to say all at once."

And he was to pack her off to Nice as soon as possible.

4

The debts were not so very serious, arrears for the rooms in the hotel and clothes for Lizzy. She had found that she could not wear the creations of Miss Minchin, the dressmaker recommended by Mr. Benthall on the same floor as theirs in Chatham Place. She had ordered herself a couple of dresses in the fashion, desiring to discontinue Pre-Raphaelite gowns in Paris, just now when the new steel petticoat that gave circumference without weight, brought over from America, was favoured by fashion, *i.e.* the Empress, who was about to produce an heir to the dynasty.

Gabriel found Lizzy well: high, the barometer of her hair, upspringing and glorious as of old. She made the most of her recovered looks so as to justify her determination to stop on. The hot dry air suited her, like the sweet champagne that was served with her meals. She had taught herself some French, and when they stood to watch the laying of the new boulevards, the old walls razed to the ground (Baron Haussmann had promised Napoleon that there should be no more barricades), she would repeat, as children in England *Peter Piper*, the topical French equivalent : "*Le mur murant Paris, s'en va en murmurant*," complaining because it had been there for a quarter of a century and now must go. But she was, Britishly, down on the French character. The conceit of them and their incessant jabbering !—

"Do they think they are saying something?" she would ask. And so proud of their Glass Palace, imitated from ours, because it had a transept so many *mètres* higher! Prices ran cheaper than in the London one, entrance a franc, and the days were different. In London Fridays and Saturdays were the expensive days, and it was not open on Sundays at all. Here Friday was the only expensive day—and Sunday the cheapest—a few centimes. The two women could not afford to buy, but stared at The Regent and the *Étoile du Nord* and were perfectly happy wandering in and out the glittering cases, in the sections of *Bijouterie et Cristalleries*, of *Dentelles et Broderies*, of *Soies et Soieries*, of *Vêtements, Modes et Fantaisies*. But when Gabriel came, they only managed to drag him there one afternoon, and he and Munro hurried them past the beastly diadems by Bapst, the awful bracelets, rivulets and necklaces of Dumas and Paillard: turning a blind eye on the *vitrines* of Watte and Dufour of Belgium, of Backe and Krug of Germany, absolutely disdaining the English exhibits of Messrs. Hunt and Roskill and their terrible mourning jewellery made of *chêne fossile noire*—that is to say, Jet. Munro and he paused a moment to consider the work of a would-be Pre-Raphaelite, John Hancock, the boyhood's friend of both, an *épergne* figuring some knights killing each other—to put on a dinner-table! He seemed to like best, and so did she, the French *or ciselé*—chased gold—which he was pleased to compare with Lizzy's hair, saying that he would make hair like hers the rage in London. He gave Munro, whom he had run up against in the Louvre, the impression that he was frightfully in love with The Sid.[1]

5

He had got to Paris on the 8th of November. The Exhibition closed by decree on the 15th. Rossetti and Munro saw Lizzy and her companion off by rail to Nice, with money in hand. Away, altogether, only a week and now he was back in London, telling the fellows all about it. Yes, he had seen Napoleon driving with the Empress in an open carriage although he had just been shot at for the second time. No one could say he was a coward, although Hugo called him *Le Petit* and he looked like a clammy

[1] "Rossetti every day with his sweetheart E. S., of whom he is more foolishly fond than ever. Great affection is always so to the looker-on, I suppose. Well, well!" Munro to Hill.

pork butcher. Eugénie at his side, pale but blazing in gold and colour, like a bell-flower bent her proud neck, saluting with her indefinable air of deprecation, " as if entreating you to believe that she was *obliged* to be Empress ! " so Mrs. Browning said. And they had seen her rival, The Castiglione, by accident. Stunners both ! The Castiglione was the vainest woman in the world—Gabriel quoted one of her speeches, the right sort of speech for a Stunner to make :—" *Je suis et m'en contente, ne voulant être ni par les autres ni pour les autres.*" A spy and a thorough tomboy—to dissimulate her job perhaps—climbing so that everyone could see her, to hear the chimes at midnight, with the Director of *Beaux Arts*, on the roof of the old Louvre that he was rebuilding, making the join between it and the Tuileries that was later to save Eugénie's life. By the way, old Nieuwerkerke was behaving as if the whole place was his own, giving pictures away wherewith to trim the walls of St. Cloud as if they were pieces of furniture. " *L'Impératrice demande encore des tableaux.*" Turning the public out of the galleries and giving parties there, murdering masterpieces, he and Godefroi, always drunk, with his precious *sauce à refaire*, a black mixture like mud of which the recipe was scrapings of varnish, lots of dust and spirits of wine applied with a swab. The hands of *Marie de Medicis* were now gone. For Rubens Ruskin did not so much care, or for Claude whom Nieuwerkerke and his henchmen were now " restoring to the truth," making him clear and silvery instead of hot and highly coloured as he really was ; but what of the Veronese ? Rossetti privately did not care for the Veronese, but they had cleaned *The Marriage in Cana* quite thin.

6

By the 2nd of December Mrs. Kincaid and Lizzy were in Nice, at the *Hôtel des Princes*. Miss Siddal had kept her room and eaten her Christmas dinner upstairs, " plum pudding and all very *good*—very *good* indeed and an honour to the country ! " She has a bad boil of which she cannot get rid—but she tells Gabriel that it is on account of hotel bores that they want to move into lodgings.

She had been made self-conscious by her association with Gabriel Rossetti and his friends. Clever and receptive, she had been taking it all in, and some of it wrong. Her letters—even William noticed it—constantly betray the note of facetiousness that is the refuge of the artistically and educationally destitute, handed the whole bag of letters to play and form sentences with. She indulged freely in the chaffing manner of which William complained—one of the reasons why she and Christina, so just, so elegant, so simple of phrase, could never get on. Here is her first letter, written about three weeks after her arrival in Nice. She had not been allowed to retain her passport. It had been taken charge of by the police [1] and she was put through some irksome precautions. First she had to borrow it for half an hour and, presenting herself at the office, let them have a look at her and gave them a sample of her handwriting to compare with the passport. If the two signatures should be considered to vary it would mean that she was pretending to be someone else, and be as good as a death warrant! They would at once take it into their silly foreign heads that she was a murderess escaping from justice or was, at any rate, a thief. But *she* would be let off hard labour because of her thinness! . . . And so it goes on—the would-be funniness. She would have to stand in front of the *grille* while the man behind it, like a mutton chop sticking to a gridiron (he is " Mutton Chop " to the end of the interview), stands looking " as much like doom as over-done mutton *can* look, fizzing French," not one word of which can she understand. Back to the police station where the Two Cocked Hats hand over the enclosure reluctantly. . . .

The letter ends on a note of doubt—" *But* believe me, Yours most affectionately. . . ."

Frivolous yet passionate, with the desire of the dove to brood alone—" First-class, one can get to the end of the world, but one can never be let alone or left at rest "—all this is part of her complex, connected with those wilful seclusions of hers in Chatham Place, " alone, withouten any company " [2] or sound, except the river noises, the sleepy, heavy sucking of the water at the base of the pillars of the bridge, the flapping wash, slowly dying away, of the barges that went past, or the bells of the purlmen plying in their little boats, up and down and in and out of the big lighters, selling bad beer in the small hours of the morning to the weary foredone workers who, heated and drugged, must needs send for more—much more.

[1] A precaution natural enough, considering the state of politics at the time, the whole of the Genoese littoral honeycombed with spies and political agents. Nice was Nizza then, and part of the Kingdom of Piedmont.
[2] Chaucer.

Gabriel sent the letter on to Ruskin. He evidently thought it funny, in a Jan van Hunksish sort of way. Ruskin returned it saying that it was excellent and all "too true, poor thing!" and that he had often boiled over himself about the ridiculous passport system of the Continent. He wanted to get her up into his "pet" Alps. She really must manage it as soon as the Spring came.

7

She was still away and Gabriel Mon-Dieuing, murmuring her name as he sat at his easel—little Cathy heard him—"Guggums! Guggums!" (surely the ugliest name "Love ever wearied of?"), full of commissions, making red hair the fashion as he had promised Lizzy to do, was battening on Brown in his new house in Fortess Terrace, too expensive for Brown and too big, though there was a new baby coming in December. Brown's important work had had to be laid aside for want of patronage and he was doing pot-boilers and journeyman's work of sorts. His guest took him out now and then to dine off a lobster or to the play to see some Stunner or other—Madame Ristori or Miss Herbert—and introduced dealers, full of specious promises. Old White hinted at "a speedy fortune in two years more for Mr. Brown, when Mr. Brown would command the highest prices and be in a position to give him (White) a ' pic ' now and then for remembrance." Brown's sardonic entry is—"Amen, I say." [1]

Gabriel at last sends Mr. Plint of Liverpool, who almost commissions *Work*, but says he will "write" and, going out of the studio, is struck with one of Gabriel's sketches for Moxon's *Tennyson* and offers forty guineas on the nail for a water-colour on the subject.

The apportioning of the Llandaff decorations was a perpetual grievance. Brown had been consulted as to the possibility of Rossetti's undertaking the altarpiece. Not that he grudged Rossetti the work, but, still—"Seddon needn't have asked me my opinion!"

Gabriel was dressing better and talked of buying a watch and had managed to send Lizzy fifty-five pounds since she left—but no sign as yet of Brown's loan! As Brown had cynically foretold,

[1] As a matter of fact, *Work* had to be set aside while *The Stages of Cruelty*, for which little Cathy was sitting at the moment, remained unsold for thirty-five years.

he was getting on better without her. The hatchet-face was filling out : he looked "handsome and a gentleman" and behaved as if his hosts were made of money. He would stop in bed till ten or eleven, then he would breakfast, leisurely, alone, translating sonnets beside his plate or teasing little Cathy, making faces at her through the red glass pane of the door into the garden, or chasing her till she fell, dressed as children were then, into a bed of nettles. He hated children.

It was frightfully cold and England was at war. Brown and his wife were pleased to think that Lizzy was missing the influenza epidemic, and Gabriel was glad he had refused to go to Wales. A friend of his, down at Abergele, had said in a letter that he had caught in his hand a live woodcock which, with its long bill, could not get into a cranny to keep itself warm. Nobody in Fortess Terrace thought very much about the men crouching down in those deeper crannies outside Sebastopol, but made up a good fire and sat over it. One night, as they basked, some-one inside saw a spark fall; someone outside rang the bell— the chimney proved to be on fire. Emma Brown tried salt and a wet blanket; but Brown put down his pipe and went what he called "right at it"—up through the trap-door in the roof and, walking gingerly on the slates of the high house, stuffed another good blanket down the chimney. Shouts from Gabriel down below to say the remedy had been efficacious. Meantime the painter had not been idle, and had carefully raked all the live coals out of the grate and spread them over the new Kidderminster, of claret-colour powdered with chocolate and *fleurs-de-lis*. But Mrs. Brown forgave him and the larger holes soon had chairs and tables arranged over them.

8

Mary Howitt, who kept William Allingham informed of his London friends' doings, as well as those of Aspasia her cat, told him all about Gabriel's new Stunner, the beautiful Miss Herbert, and how he never missed one of her first nights and even went again and took his friends. No danger to Lizzy; Miss H. was far too great a swell to look at an artist. She stayed with the aristocracy when "resting" and never accepted presents of any kind. Mary did not believe that Rossetti had ever seen her off the stage, but she must have come expensive in tickets !

Another Stunner, Lady Waterford, was also too high up to

affect Lizzy. But Gabriel was always about with Annie Miller, painting the girl by day and taking her to Highbury Barn by night, where she made good use of the dancing lessons Hunt was paying for. Anna Mary wondered what Mr. Hunt had said about it when he got home, invalided, from Syria, where Mike Halliday had had to go all the way to fetch him.

Either Mr. Hunt didn't know about Annie and Gabriel (and Boyce, too—there was safety in numbers) or he didn't mind, for on his return from abroad he stayed with Gabriel in Chatham Place until he could get back into his old rooms in Claverton Street. Yet he was besotted on Annie. Halliday and Martineau, who roomed with him, found him a thorough nuisance. She would call in, "looking most syren-like," to ask about something or other, saying she couldn't stay, just when they were sitting down to dinner, and Hunt would jump up and keep them waiting while he put her on a boat to go home to Chelsea. . . .

What wonder that Lizzy, out there, was getting restless and talked of coming home! Money difficulties were put forward, but it was less a question of funds than either Ruskin or Rossetti supposed. The latter actually wanted to borrow from one of the Yorkshire patronesses, but Ruskin put a stopper on that. He would ask his own Miss Heaton to lend Rossetti twenty-five "in a way that would leave it quite within her power to refuse comfortably," and if she did refuse, he would supply the money. Rossetti should have thirty pounds at once, anyway. No, he wasn't at all put out. He just wanted Ida, for her own sake—*he* wasn't going anywhere near her—to stay abroad. If she would only get out of Nice! But, if she did really want to come home—instead of stopping to see "some Alps and gentians," she just must.

His appeal seems to have stayed her. She faintly suggested the Dauphiné. No, nothing but Alps would satisfy Ruskin. He had only allowed for the South of France in the first place because he didn't know her well enough to know what she would or wouldn't like—"that time when she chose Paris instead of Normandy," in his despite. Well, he is sick of it! If she will agree to Switzerland like a good girl, let her write and say so. "It is no use my stirring myself up if her mind is made up to come home."

9

In the Spring, she returned to England, no better. Her physician noticed "a continuous decline in vital force" from now onward. Henceforward she was always ill and, less patient of pain and discomfort, adopted the new panacea from which Mrs. Browning, a grander, more reasonable woman, had refrained, though she congratulated her generation on its availableness : " What a wonderful thing these new inhalations seem to be ! "

Lizzy was, of course, forbidden to sleep near the river, so the rooms in Weymouth Street had to be kept on. Nowadays Gabriel had to paint her reclining in the big armchair that was moved there from Chatham Place, her head deep sunk in a pillow placed at the back, the long fingers of one hand laid under her chin—like Mrs. Browning's " spirit hand " propping hers. Her hair in these pictures is always spread out as if it were a peacock-feather fan, in flat languid loops, like water flowing away, water of pale gold—still the most vital thing about her, perhaps draining away the rest of her life. Old Mrs. Ruskin had always said that it ought to be cut off because of the weight and the effort of growing taken from her reserve of strength. And the very tending and dressing of it were tiring for an invalid.

10

And Gabriel had found a new and deeply stimulating environment—something that, as it were, oxygenated his blood while she was away. He had founded a School of his own : at least revived the Pre-Raphaelite impetus with the new blood of William Morris and Edward Jones.

PART II

CHAPTER XVIII

I

EARLY in January of this year, 1856, Rossetti had written to Allingham of his meeting with a certain youthful Jones who designed " Holbeinesque fancies not a few," one of the " nicest fellows in Dreamland," and his friend Morris, also a denizen of that region.

By " Dreamland " the practical Rossetti meant the magazine run by these two young men and their set, in which an appreciative notice of his own illustration to Allingham's *Maids of Elfin Mere* had appeared. The comparatively moneyed Morris financed this venture : his father had died leaving him the care of a mother and two sisters and enough [1] to do it on, including a house and garden at Walthamstow.

There were no cheap reprints of the classics in those days ; if you wanted a book you must buy it, and Morris, the plutocrat who could afford to lose three hundred pounds on a magazine— a year of *The Oxford and Cambridge* cost him that—provided literary food for his friends ; Shakespeare and Malory for Jones : Tennyson [2] for Morris, novels for everybody. *Aurora Leigh*, *Guy Livingstone* and the works of Miss Charlotte Mary Yonge, to whom Lady Eastlake conceded the power of passion [3] she would not allow to the other, great, Charlotte.

---

[1] Copper, in 1848, was worth £160 a ton. In 1844 veins were discovered near Tavistock. Capital of 1,024 shares of £1 each. Of these Morris' father held 272. Within six months the shares were changing hands in the market at £800 each. Mr. Morris' holding rose for a while to the value of two hundred thousand pounds.— *Life of William Morris*, by J. W. Mackail.

[2] Tennyson, with his ghostly memory and magic of phrasing, his " gleams across the dreary moorland " and his idle tears that the Portuguese call *saudades*, i.e. rueing, of which Howell talked so much.

[3] *The Heir of Redclyffe*, " like a deep blue Italian sky with a rich, gorgeous Italian sunset."—*New Quarterly*. " Beast as she is," said Jones of Lady E., " she is no fool." Miss Yonge was almost a Pre-Raphaelite through her intense close visualisation of mediæval times ; for instance, *Leonard the Lion Heart*, *The Chaplet of Pearls*, *The Dove in the Eagle's Nest*.

WILLIAM MORRIS
From a photograph

One does not associate the Oxford Movement with the Pre-Raphaelite one or Sir Guy de Morville with Sir Palomydes.[1] But had it not been for *The Heir* and his knightly proclivities, coupled with the visit of Morris and Jones to a certain picture gallery, the revival [2] of the Movement might not have taken place.

Some years before a handful of young men who had never heard of the P.R.B., but were full of ideas and fun, sat about the floor and the window-sills in a small room in Oxford and talked incessantly of the formation of an Order or Brotherhood. Sir Galahad was to be the patron and the whole thing was instigated by young Mr. Edward Coley Jones, of Exeter, whose Celtic imagination had been fired—or chilled—by the sight, in boyhood, of a Cistercian Monastery in full working order, eight miles from his home in the heart of Charnwood Forest.[3]

This order was not to be purely monachal—wives, " if there should be any," were to be " associated together." A sort of Abbey of Thelema : a foundation of clerical and lay workers established in the heart of London where, nowadays, there was most to be done. The Good Knight of Walthamstow began by helping in the slums of Marylebone, lifting bodies into the cholera carts. He always went ahead violently with anything, like the Heir of Redclyffe giving up hunting because it interfered with his reading : trying to make girls interested in good men, not bad ones—" blessed damozels," such as Amy in *The Heir* : not Flora Bellasys in *Guy Livingstone.*

Both as good as gold—yet, " the low sun gives the colour," and to Gabriel Rossetti, the practical, the material, the earth-bound, who visited in Dreamland, but assuredly did not live there altogether, these lads gravitated. When Ruskin's Edinburgh

---

[1] The Great Unkissed, with whom in after days, of all Arthur's knights, Morris humbly associated himself.

[2] The third and last fytte and flicker was in the late '70's, when young Wilde " went down " from Alma Mater, came up to London and settled in Salisbury Street with a few Delft plates and peacocks' feathers, picked up the ageing Burne-Jones on his robust shoulders and carried him into the popular repute he had merited so long.

[3] Like the dominant in music this pious hope and wish appears in his letters for years after he had taken up painting ; and once, when the plan was seriously menaced, he desired to go into the army and get killed. See Appendix for Charnwood.

May 1855, ". . . Am afraid that our monastery will come to naught. Smith has changed his views to extreme latitudinarianism, Morris has gone questionable on doctrinal points. . . ." Somebody else, called Ted, was " too Catholic to be ordained."

Lectures came to be published they bought the book, read what he said about the P.R.B. and, next time they went down, walked over to Tottenham to see the collection, mainly of Turners— but including a Hunt, a Millais and a Rossetti—enshrined in the gallery Mr. Windus,[1] of Godfrey's Cordial, had built for it. After they had seen these pictures they elected Rossetti their king.

And in the Long Vacation they went to France to see Cathedrals and got their Pauline revelation, for which Jones had been prepared by the day at Godstow. They arrived at Beauvais on a Saturday, limping, footsore, despondent. Next morning they attended High Mass and knew, once for all, the way they were to go. Suddenly made aware of the gaiety, the headiness, the sacred glory of Colour that, while Line represents duty and religion, stands for the pleasures of the life which men share with one another till Death parts them, and that poor old Ruskin,[2] so pale and watery and friendless, had missed. Unused, unwonted nerves in them were played and wrought upon by the sight of the pied banners, oscillating, upborne by infants in red and white procession, the gold rays from the pyx—that so affected Joan of Arc [3]—falling dim and dun on tessellated floors and the embossed embroideries of copes and chasubles. Add to this the noise that is Colour's concomitant, sonorous organ peals and blare of trombones that made the incense-laden air to rock and tremble and the colours to shake before their eyes—red and blue, the " choosing cloths of Heaven—and Hell." [4]

And afterwards, when all was quiet, by the river-side in England, Jones[5] chose "Heaven's colour," the quiet flame of blue that was the dragon-fly, hovering, poised over the glinting water . . . long enough for him to have painted it.

" Stay, thou art fair ! " This moment lost them, as it were,

[1] Everyone went there though they never saw Mr. Windus. His taste was exquisite and all the artists sat at his feet. Ruskin drove his Effie over and poor Brown walked all the way from Finchley. Windus was rich and spent the money he made on the Cordial and his contract for all the mail coaches in England, on buying Turners, with which he never parted, for he was not a dealer and gave himself tremendous moral airs. After the Ruskin-Millais affair, he would not even allow Millais to make a sketch of his own picture for reproduction.

[2] Said his master Turner, dying—" The Sun is God, my dear ! "

[3] The processions of small angels, as she may have seen them, dancing in the beam from the pyx at Notre Dame des Victoires, where they dance still on fine Sundays.

[4] " One of these cloths is Heaven and one is Hell;
Now choose one cloth for ever, which they be."
The Defence of Guenevere.

[5] See *King Cophetua* and *Margot.*

172

to Holy Orders. The idea of droning cold phrases in the plain white churches of non-Catholic countries became hateful to them both for evermore. " Save me from that ! " said Jones, deeply, truly religious, albeit without white scapular and black gown, " for I have looked beyond the veil."

On the quay at Havre that very night they made up their minds that they would not be parsons and gently broke it, Morris to his mother and Jones to his aunt, on their return.

It was an awful thing to do, then. Art, which came to be a gilt-edged security, was then a very great adventure and fathers and mothers, with neat curacies in their eyes and a bishopric to follow, when informed that a son wanted to take up painting, felt much as if he had proposed to follow the players or run away to sea. But Jones' father, who was a carver and gilder by trade, played up and started his son as an artist, while Morris, for want of a better job, articled himself for instruction in English Gothic, to the perpetrator of " Phil and Jim," [1] a charming man whose boast, however, was that he had restored nearly every church in England and would already have begun on Magdalen only, luckily, funds were not available. But the desecration of St. Albans was being perpetrated and Morris, faithful servant, helped it on.

2

Soon it was the Bissextile, the year when it never rained— " blue sky from Christmas to Christmas "—and " London streets glittering like the golden ones of Zion," while to Jones it was " always morning and the air sweet and full of bells." One recognises the faintly hysterical touch that went along with his real shrewdness and competence. For Jones was now more than " the man who wrote to Ruskin and got an answer by return " ! He was the man who had lessons from Rossetti and was allowed to enter his studio freely : while Rossetti, who notoriously hated being watched, would merely nod and go on painting. It was " so nice when he loved someone, for they need to be in no doubt about it." [2] False premises, dear Mr. Jones ! Of those who were useful and whose society promised him amenity he was *fond*, petting them, " tempering " them, now and again applying the rules of his own hard, ferocious, unrelenting spirit to their backslidings and recalcitrances. For he was a leader born, sharing with Napoleon the advantages of the bilio-lymphatic

[1] George Edmund Street. [2] *Memorials*, by Lady Burne-Jones.

temperament—" 'Tis the hidden fire that wins me my battles ! "
Master, like Napoleon, of the direct statement, he dominated
people's nerves by his short, unreiterated directions and
commands, nor blurred significance with repetition.

This sinner the young men took for their saint and, lacking
the earnest Hunt and the frivolous Millais, the Pre-Raphaelite
Brotherhood was born anew.

3

Rossetti had persuaded them both to leave the beaten track
that leads to ease and a competence, for the thornier ways of
Art.[1] " Rossetti says "—most of Jones' sentences began in that
way now—" that I ought to paint and shall be able." So Jones
would do his best.

Morris in Street's office all day and at a Life School at night
was worked to death. But it was worth it. Rossetti called
them his Dears ! (So, imitatively, Jones was to call men he
liked for the rest of his life.) And he praised them to people,
saying that they were wonders of their kind—" Jones especially ! "
He did not take to Morris though he praised him perfunctorily,[2]
Morris who adored him, the blood-red ray in the spectrum of
his life—serving him by word and deed, buying his drawings,
composing legends[3] for them ; mystic jingles, little rhyme and
less reason, flying wrack of confused thought, spindrift of
romance, all about queer patient people without dimension or
repoussé, like the scene on which they are made to move—rushy
floors of enchanted castles, set in orchards reddening to the sea,
in a country which is no man's land except he dream. There
was Alicia who wore a scarlet gown " when the sword went out
to sea." Why on Earth, or in Dreamland, did she ? Some
subtle, far-flung, far-fetched curse ? And " Fair Yolande of the
flowers," walking with her maidens on the rain-washed leads
of her castle near the sea—they are all built near the sea in
Dreamland—

> No one walks there now,
> Except in the white moonlight
> The white ghosts walk in a row.

---

[1] " Morris and Jones have now settled in London," D. G. R. wrote to Allingham.
" I have persuaded Morris to give up architecture and start painting." His mother
never forgave him for it—she blamed it on Jones.

[2] " You would think him one of the finest little fellows alive, with a touch of the
incoherent, but a real man."

[3] " Morris has written a stunning poem to my Blue Closet picture."

Or that " blue " parlour, in some other haunted place, where

> Alice the Queen and Louise the Queen,
> Two damozels wearing purple and green,

are given leave

> Every year on Christmas Eve
> To sing in the Closet Blue one song
> *Laudate Pueri.*

So great, so modest withal, pleased with the approval of mere workmen,[1] of children, of animals . . . yet Gabriel Rossetti vastly preferred the society of Jones. Morris was too original, too independent for the king-man, who was really made uncomfortable by the other's violent simplicities, his " scorn of scorn, hate of hate, love of love," his rudeness, his lack of humour and subtlety except of the animal kind. There was nothing affected or stagey about Morris ; he just took life as he found it (in the mediæval chronicles) crude and cruel—with patience and piety, while Jones, holding quite as grim a view of life, invested the sadness with all sorts of quips and cranks and adorable babyishness. As subservient to Rossetti as Morris, he was more clinging, affecting to go about on leading-strings, hardly able in the end to get married, so he said, without Rossetti.

Rossetti rather encouraged the notion of getting married, hoping thus to break the spell which he himself wielded over him and which meant, at least, responsibility. He had to be careful lest he was accused of robbing these youths of their April. Jones was his *Liebling* as Deverell [2] had been, and he wrote to the boy ever so humbly—" I know I must be fonder of you than you possibly can be of me. Anyway, I am far fonder of you than anybody, and you, I know, are fonder of me. . . ." Then, ashamed of his sentimentality and pulling himself up with a jerk—" This letter begins to read rather flabby. . . ." [3]

4

Soon Jones did get engaged and, by the 15th of February, Gabriel moped so that he even missed Mrs. Birrell's ginger cat

[1] Of one of his own books, nearly stillborn, he said proudly, " The men at the Works think a lot of it."

[2] See Jarno-Jenssen's *Kunstler-Monographien.*

[3] What we should call " soppy " nowadays. Everybody said " fond " for " loving " in those days, even sweethearts ; it was an elegant sort of periphrasis for that gross word " love."

which Lizzy fed and so brought about the place. He would sit daubing away in the dusk until he heard the click of the lamp-lighter's rod, setting agoing the "two seedy flames" of the standard by the gate, definitely proclaiming nightfall, when he would get up and spend an hour—so he told her—looking for his hat and stick before he could go out to get some dinner. He wrote her a Valentine—"Come back, dear Liz . . ." He missed the woman, if only to deal with duns and undesirables whom, from her shop training, she spotted at once and treated with a firm hand, and to wind up the clock, which had run down all the time she was away.

On her return she attended to these things, choosing now, however, to sleep and spend most of her time in Weymouth Street. How could she sleep at Gabriel's place as of old, for any night the fellows might come in at any time and stay well into the next morning? And, in the daytime, they were all in and out constantly; Hunt, whom she disliked because he had once snubbed her about some technical point, and the two adoring boys, to whom she was merely the betrothed of the Master, who, for reasons into which they did not venture to pry, deferred the announcement of his engagement to her. They did not admire The Sid. Morris, the more indifferent of the two, by way of kowtowing to Gabriel, made one of his jingles about her, founded on a North-country custom of rack-rent of which Howell had told him :—

> There was a lady lived in a hall,
> Large in the eyes and slim and tall.
> And ever she sang, against the noon,
> *Two Red Roses across the Moon.*

Gabriel would go to see her in Weymouth Street whenever he could spare time from his work, his friends and his amusements; and that was not very often. When Lizzy got tired of being alone she just put herself into a bus and went to the Browns' to tea and sleep, if a bed was not handy, on the sofa or the hearthrug. She could sleep anywhere. Gabriel objected to her seeing so much of Emma Brown, partly because she was silly and saw ghosts and put Lizzy up to being discontented with him, Gabriel—which she did *not*, Brown denied it. Poor Miss Siddall (characteristically Brown and his wife always refused to dock the last *l*—"Gabriel's wretched swagger") complained enough already of Gabriel's wasteful goings on and needed no

176

extra working up. Gabriel, on her account, was always exceedingly rude to Mrs. Brown, who found " his brutish conduct " difficult to overlook. One day he had come along, thinking to find Liz at their house—it was after a quarrel they had had the night before. He had missed her, and went without saying good-bye to Mrs. Brown, who did not resent it. But Brown wrote on Wednesday and demanded an apology, which he did not get till Sunday if at all, for Gabriel and Lizzy simply came to supper, shook hands, said nothing about it and ate heartily.

Brown was very useful, running errands and seeing people for Gabriel, procuring calves, lending costumes, being surety for borrowed " tin." Yet Gabriel never thought of " going without " himself, or of lending My Uncle some of the fine things he purchased when in funds ! Brown had, on several occasions, pawned the family silver, his studs and the clothes off his wife's back sooner than borrow for himself. These were the " goings on " that drove Lizzy frantic and made her spiteful. The nobility of Brown's nature forbade complaint or retaliation—but he permitted himself to write it down, using his own forcible coloration and quickening of the diapason in the chronicling of what he called " scenes of the strangest physical and moral confusion combined with reckless extravagance " in the ménage which Rossetti hesitated to invite Lizzy to share. This senseless, causeless hanging back was what maddened Brown, on her behalf.

CHAPTER XIX

I

FIGHTING had stopped in January, and Peace which mattered a good deal to people—other than artists—was declared officially in May; there were to be illuminations, which would delight artists as well. Allingham was invited by Munro to stop with him and Miss Munro in Belgrave Place till Boyce's old rooms in Buckingham Street could be secured for him. Boyce was an artist now.

There were still some illuminations left round about the Mall and Buckingham Palace when Allingham arrived and, in the evening, he and the Munros paraded the Mall arm in arm, among the noisy, guffawing crowd in front of the Palace, under the glare of the fireworks. At ten they went home, sent the lady to bed and began to tell tales.

Gabriel and Lizzy first! Munro told him all about Paris and how fond of Lizzy Gabriel seemed to be. Over, then, the reign of Annie Miller! Annie's new beau was Boyce. Did Hunt mind? He had objected, as her self-constituted guardian, to Gabriel's flirtation with her last year. Boyce had had to ask leave to paint Annie but Gabriel just took her. Hunt either didn't guess or refused to wrestle for her. But Munro had seen a very stiff letter from Hunt to Boyce, " feeling bound to acquaint him with the fact " that he only permitted it on the understanding that she was to be looked upon as Hunt's own " protégée " and that he considered himself responsible for her future, " as far as other artists might affect it." Supposing another artist should wander into the studio while Annie was there and make overtures to her? Boyce was to say that Mr. Hunt was very particular about her and never allowed her to sit to anyone but himself and a few personal friends.

So Mr. Hunt had found out that Annie was a bit of a minx! (Allingham hated Annie for making Miss Sid so unhappy.)

ELIZABETH ELEANOR SIDDALL
From a drawing by D. G. Rossetti

Not until Sunday morning did Allingham find Gabriel at home—in his shirt-sleeves, showing Tom Taylor *Dante's Dream*, about which, though polite, Taylor, a good-hearted Philistine, seemed more than doubtful. He was a very powerful man on the Press. He departed full of cheer, and the two old friends called on Boyce in his new chambers in Great Russell Street. Then Gabriel offered to take Allingham straight to The Sid's rooms, but insisted on going round to see the house where he was born, in a blind-alley with a stonemason's yard and a thicket of trees at the end of it. Standing on the cracked flags on the other side, Gabriel, waving his arms like a foreigner, had pointed out " the room where I painted my first picture ! " Then in another cab to a pawnbroker's in Wardour Street, where there was a " bit " he coveted. At long last they came to a tall house in Weymouth Street, where it ran into Great Portland Street, with a garden at the back and in it a plane tree whose top was level with Miss Siddal's windows. She herself, looking frail and thin in her black silk dress, was feebly setting about the stretching of a piece of Whatman's for a water-colour drawing illustrating a ballad—ladies sitting on a stretch of yellow sand in full dress, their hooped petticoats ballooning in the stormy weather, waiting for their lords who had sailed long ago to fetch " the King's Daughter from Norroway " home.

Rossetti, in his deep, grave voice, flowing on like a still stream under tree shadows, recited to them the ballad which they all knew by heart.[1] Then he took the job of mounting out of Lizzy's hands, wetting the nice clean sheet of paper, laying it face downwards on the table and the board on it—and calling for the paste which a devoted lodger on the first floor had prepared on her fire for Lizzy and now brought up. He then turned up the edges of the paper all round the board, pasted it down and put it back on the table with a piece of soft paper over it to prevent the dust settling. Then he bade her put on her hat and come

---

[1] Lang, lang may the ladies sit
With their fans intil their hands
Before they see Sir Patrick Spens
Come sailing up the strand.

Half owre, half owre to Aberdour
'Tis fifty fathoms deep,
And there lies gude Sir Patrick Spens
With the Scots lords at his feet.

out with them until the paste was dry and the paper, contracting, had made a fair white even surface to paint on. She assumed a black mantelet and, her bonnet carefully adjusted on the loose masses of her hair, walked with her sweetheart and Mr. Allingham out into the sunny calm of the June morning. They took a cab to Red Lion Square, setting Miss Sid down just before they turned in, as she desired. She had never set foot in that house [1] since the death of Walter Deverell.

A firm of feather-dressers had taken the whole of it on from Mr. North Cox, he of the queer stipulation which had annoyed Miss Siddal. Entering the dusty, empty suite, windless though one of the windows and all the doors were open, brushing a place on the pane with their handkerchiefs, they looked down on the square garden with its marigolds and lilies and thorn bushes and low trees. Three sets of tenants, Gabriel pointed out, had had these rooms since he and Deverell rented them, but "so pale and watery and colourless" as not to leave a trace of their presence, while the address of a model written in pencil on a wall was as fresh as on the day Walter wrote it. Lizzy had always said that the house was haunted and that when she was posing there, dumb and numb on the *estrade*, those two hateful sisters of Walter's, coming in to see what they called "the mad Pre-Raphaelites," and giggling, singing and taking off their crinolines, would dress up, Maria as Viola and Margaretta as Olivia, and run upstairs with their trains over their arms, cheered on by young Spenser Deverell, to see if they could frighten or impress the other lodgers. They would come down again, saying they had been frightened themselves, pretending to be faint, for they had felt people brushing past them all the way up, and on a certain landing by the old powdering closet a finger had positively been laid on Maria's shoulder. . . .

It would just do for Jones and Morris, who were moving. Gabriel persuaded the Fauconniers to accept them as tenants at the old rate of twenty shillings a week for the first floor—three rooms, a bedroom behind and another, really a powdering closet. But there was that rarity, a North Light, and they could cut the little window higher to admit more of it. Morris, who had taken to designing furniture,[2] had made some chairs and a settle [3] which would go in the studio nicely.

[1] Still existing.   [2] The germ idea of The Shop.
[3] It had three painted shutters over the seat, a ladder to the parapet round it at the top, and a door above that leading on to the roof for minstrels to sing in at

180

Dust was not easily thrown in the eyes of William Allingham. Dreamy, mystic, withdrawn, he was more a man of the world than either Rossetti or Brown, and quiet reflection on the London scene in the emptiness of his Irish home, endowed his vision with shrewd and prophetic clarity. He regarded Lizzy's refusal to enter the door of Number Seventeen merely as a wile to bring her man to the point. She was using Walter, who couldn't contradict her, to inspire the notion that Gabriel had taken her away from a man who would have married her if he had lived (and perhaps that was the reason he had died?), fomenting, for reasons of her own, the remorse which Gabriel undoubtedly felt. . . .

But Allingham knew that, beyond a first spurt of excitement on her romantic discovery, the lad had not loved her—not enough to hurt. There had been an inclination to a cousin, a Miss Hogarth, which was noted by others. And then—King Death had intervened.

He did not think that Lizzy knew much about a woman Gabriel's friends called Fanny—though her name was Sarah— whom he had even heard of in Ireland, and, as Hunt was still going to marry Miss Miller, Gabriel's sweetheart seemed to be troubling no more about her than she did about Miss Herbert, whom Gabriel never saw, or spoke to, off the stage, though he went nearly every night to see her act.

Allingham talked to Tennyson about Gabriel, but Tennyson was not in sympathy with him and his life; he himself, though a poet, had always managed to " avoid the drop into Bohemia." He was building himself a summer house at Farringford, " in the broad, anti-Pre-Raphaelite fashion," and owned himself shocked by Morris' Republican ideas. Through Woolner, he knew about Rossetti's engagement to a " milliner's apprentice " and also of the unfortunate connection with " some woman at Wapping," which stopped the way to its fulfilment. He granted Rossetti a great artist, in spite of his " commonness," and admitted that the time of the greatest sexual excitement for boys—and

Christmas. Burne-Jones painted the scene from the *Nibelungen Lied* on the inside of one shutter ; Rossetti the *Salutation of Beatrice* outside one of the doors.

men—*can* be also that of the greatest spiritual life; that the two voices can speak to the same ears and Purity and " the other thing" exist side by side in the same nature, " both to merge at last into the sorrowless Eternity." Only he *must* have *The Gleam*.[1] That, Gabriel had no more, since the days he went about with the boys on the model hunts, each with " a glory on his face as of one who feels a light in his hair, feeling faint in sunsets and at the sight of stately persons," [2] and finding " freedom from corruption, pride and disease " in the spirit of Pre-Raphaelite brotherhood.

William Allingham left London this time with the impression that Gabriel was fond and proud of The Sid : at any rate, he was quite " good " with her. He could afford to be, with his splendid secret mistress: his sensuality placated, helping, not interfering, with his art. That so carefully warded virginity of Lizzy's, whose denial used to agitate and make him ill, was a fetich he did not want now. His feeling for her was just the remnant of an adolescent's sick fancies, born of his reading, echo of the ballad refrains of Keats and Poe and the great Italian. She was no longer *La Belle Dame sans Merci*, Annabel Lee, Psyche or Beatrice. Even Dante admitted that after his holy passion for that lady he went through a phase of earthly love. She was Poor Lizzy now, and a sick woman at that ! There it was !

5

But the disciples murmured. The engagement had now lasted for nearly seven years—they had been going about together constantly for that space of time. They knew she slept at Chatham Place and they were puzzled—some of them shocked, especially Holy Hunt. To Heaven was raised the parrot cry— " Why does he not marry her ? " The question was even put by bluff Robert Browning who knew them both so little ; Ruskin, more deeply versed in the incompatibilities of men and women through his own experiences and sequestration for ever from the joys of love, asked no such question. He had attended and was

---

[1] There on the border
Of boundless Ocean,
And all but in Heaven
Hovers The Gleam.
TENNYSON.

[2] From D. G. Rossetti's printed story in *The Germ*.

attending, so far as he was able, to what he conceived to be the real crux of the matter and reason of the man's recalcitrance —the woman's ill-health continuing and likely to continue, as far as one could see. Hers was the disease of the age and a present nightmare to everyone. Full well he knew his Gabriel, so different from " glorious Browning "—noble and strong enough to carry his invalid, literally and metaphorically. Gabriel's place was not and never could be, at the pillow of an invalid. Like most artists, he recoiled from shouldering responsibilities other than artistic ones and would, when the creative mood was on, have more regard for the susceptibilities of a nicely stretched bit of paper than the racked nerves of a human being. He did not easily endure the tempers, the peevishness of the poor drugged thing, come back no better for her cure, good to paint but bereft for ever by illness of the magnetism which makes the woman sexually interesting.

Not "waters engulphing or fires that devour," not " earth heaped against " him, not Fanny and the other Stunners only, but " death in the air," an atmosphere so paralysing to Lizzy's healthy, full-blooded lover that he would lie awake, shivering, in bed at Chatham Place, or get up to sit in his nightshirt at the big window from which he could see the trees in the Temple "seeming to wave their heads" at him in vain protest, and hear the clocks of St. Bride's and St. Botolph's striking the Hour of The Bower, driving all Time into one resounding clash of doom so that he could not tell if it was " this day, to-morrow, at eve or at noon. . . ."

And "Fettered Love, motionless, can but remember." A natural, selfish, sensual man, he abode much with Fanny, the tame, the eager, the abundantly phosphorised. . . .

6

Yet, for the son of Lavinia, the brother of Maria and Christina, procrastination was not a cloak for desertion and the breaking of promises. He had engaged himself to Elizabeth Eleanor Siddal, and he meant to marry her and face her father and mother one of these days. But, sexually spited, baulked by her long resistance, she would have to take him without any of the sweet fruits of love—she would be just an ailing wife, like Tennyson's, to keep house for him and to paint from. Marriage projects from time to time assumed cohesion, as a tuft of cloud that capricious wind-currents play with, gains form and once more dissipates in the field of Heaven. She came near or nearish to her heart's desire that autumn. Brown, hard at work on a paying commission by day, was painting a portrait of William Rossetti for love, by lamplight, and sat at it from eight to twelve every night. William had fixed that hour because he really must be home early for his long day at the Board of Trade. Then Gabriel came in and said that if William could wait five minutes while he told Brown something they might go back together. William, who knew his brother's five minutes, curled up on the sofa and dozed on and off till three in the morning while Gabriel discussed marrying Guggums and wintering in Algeria. This was in October.

Algeria materialised into Bath. By December the tenth Gabriel and Lizzy, " better than when last in London and not quite so thin," were at Mrs. Greene's, Number Seventeen, Orange Grove, living " in a mud bath " and reading *Aurora Leigh*, " a novel *à la* Jane Eyre, a little tainted by George Sand," and *Wuthering Heights*, " a fiend of a book, an incredible monster, the action laid in Hell, only, it seems, places and people have English names there." And he is " really ashamed " to plague William so, but could he spare ten pounds for a fortnight?

Yet he was making money—" lots and lots of commissions," says Brown (cheerful, himself " over the bar at last "), in a letter to Allingham. Little Lydia, on her return from a visit to Bath, reports Gabriel—not the invalid—as being wheeled about in a Bath chair, wagging his head from side to side, his tongue lolling out, to the great scandal of passers-by. Happyish, perverse. . . .

CHAPTER XX

I

BY the end of the year it was current gossip that the marriage was off. There was a Portuguese, a friend of William's who had sat to Millais and was now sitting to Gabriel. A frightfully good-looking fellow, like a Velasquez, with a voice of gold. He seemed to get hold of everybody. This man Howell was for some reason trying to put Gabriel off the girl and marriage generally, forcing him to envisage the sacrifices of personal comfort he would be called upon to make, the curtailment of petty liberties, the expenditure on other than pleasures—there might even be children, but Howell did not think that likely by the look of her!—to be incurred in the performance of this gesture which his world was stupidly calling on a great artist to make.

Jones and Morris were active in a new scheme which, to a certain extent, embodied the old idea of a Thelema. Hunt was to be asked to join, in spite of that little trouble about Annie Miller. Gabriel was quite agreeable to living in the same house with him and her if they ever married; Hunt was such a secretive " cuss " that no one knew when that would be.

And no one, except perhaps Jones, wondered how The Sid would like it. Did she even know about the scheme? He could not ask, for no one ever quite spoke his mind to Gabriel.

It was to be a " sort of joint establishment or College composed of various artists " where they could write and paint together, the strands of their various marital engagements being plaited tidily in a skein. They had been looking over houses. Jones, who always fancied Kensington,[1] discovered one to let called Cedar Villa and told Gabriel about it.

On their return from Bath Gabriel had made Lizzy give up her rooms in Weymouth Street and had taken lodgings for her

---

[1] In the end he took Selby House, Hammersmith, at a hundred guineas, to be near Howell.

in Hampstead. She was no longer independent, having relinquished Ruskin's allowance because she was too ill to earn it.

She liked Spring Cottage,[1] with its big garden all round except on the side next the lane running down to South End. It was nearer, across the fields, than Chatham Place, to the Browns', who had now come to represent nearly all she had in the way of friends. Mary Howitt was annoyed with her for not keeping Gabriel up to the mark to which she and Bessie Parkes had helped to push him years ago at Hastings and had lately, she fancied, made the move to the new house an excuse for not seeing so much of her. The two others, it would seem, had merely taken her up out of pity and respect for Gabriel and his art.

Lizzy had less of her sister's company. Lydia Siddall had engaged herself to a young fellow called Joseph Wheeler—on the staff of the *Daily Telegraph*. He was a little younger than Lydia and very much in love. He had run across her by accident, very much in the way Gabriel had met her sister. Walking along the Roman Road and looking into a shop-window he had noticed a beautiful girl reaching up for something required by a customer—a good figure never looks so well as when the arm is raised showing the lovely line from elbow to waist (Lyddy did not wear stays). It was a string of candles of which, with her long reach, she could just manage to get hold. Though Aunt Lucy Day kept a shop, like the Siddalls, she had known better days. There was a title in her husband's family and her son would have been a Sir if everyone got their rights in this world.

Lydia was emancipated to a certain degree by her engagement. It was now Mr. Wheeler's business, not her father's, to look after her, so she was able to take her young man to see her sister in Weymouth Street and Hampstead—both quite good addresses. Gabriel, who happened to be there one day, asked her to come to his studio and sit for her arms which were unusually fine. Lyddy agreed but did not tell her mother, who might have stopped relenting to Lizzy, as she was just beginning to do, if she had known. Presently Mrs. Siddall was actually persuaded to meet her future son-in-law. She disapproved less of his profession now that he was decorating a Cathedral for the son of Lord Aberdare. But one thing she

---

[1] Two or three minutes' walk from Keats' house, absorbed now in a block, but *their* sitting room and bedroom over it, with leaded panes in the windows, remains as it was.

would not do—let the painter and his friends have anything to do with her fourth daughter, far too young " to be in the company of such unruly men " as Mr. Rossetti and his friends.

Gabriel, on his side, pretended to be afraid of the handsome, cold and stately matron, with the floods of gold and greying hair which she let down on the slightest provocation of comment and admiration; and refused to spill any of his well-known magnetism on her.

2

It was after dark one night and the lamps had been lit in the street outside and the candles inside, and the firelight was dancing on the diamond panes of the tiny window at the back. Quite a party was gathered in Lizzy's sitting room. Her mother and sister, who had been there all day, and James Siddall and Mr. Wheeler, come to escort the two women home. Mrs. Siddall and Lyddy were just going up to the bedroom to wrap up for the succession of bus rides that would take them back to town when Mr. Brown walked in. He had had his tea. He seemed taken aback at finding company there, suggesting that he had wanted to see Lizzy alone, which irritated Gabriel, always jealous of Brown's influence over his sweetheart. And he *would* keep talking of Cedar Villa, discussing the position of the rooms and their assignment to the five persons who were to occupy them—two married couples to begin with and one bachelor. Of the two best bedrooms Georgy had picked out the one she preferred for herself and Ned, and did so hope the other couple wouldn't want it. Mr. Hunt, being the elder, would naturally have first choice. All this did not much interest Lizzy's people, for Lizzy was not mentioned, and abruptly, Mrs. Siddall made a move. Lizzy took the ladies upstairs while James and Joseph Wheeler sat mum and the conversation flagged between Brown and Gabriel. When the women came down again Brown had slipped away.

Then, like a concealed fire, Lizzy burst out in one of her new white rages that were so pathetic because, artists both, Lizzy knew that Gabriel knew how ugly her voice was when she raised it at all. Nothing would induce her to have anything to do with a scheme which involved her living in the same house with Mr. Hunt. She did not object to Mr. Morris and Mr. Jones hardly counted. But Mr. Hunt she hated. Yes, Gabriel *had* spoken of it; but she had thought of a range of studios with a bedroom and kitchen behind, such as they were beginning to build now, for each couple. Gabriel, who could not have got into a rage if he had tried and whose voice would, in any case, have remained beautiful, pointed out that Brown did not seem to be including *them* in his scheme at all! Everyone knew that dear old Brown did get dates and numbers wrong; he had meant three couples, of course. Then why had Gabriel not corrected Brown at the time? What would James and Lyddy and her mother think? Then Gabriel, gently—" Did they know, because she had always been so particular with him not to mention their engagement before anyone without her permission—not even her mother." Her mother knew perfectly well, and Lyddy and of course Mr. Wheeler too, that she was engaged. Did he suppose that they would condescend to come there to tea with his mistress? She would go straight to Aunt Day's in Barnsbury to-morrow morning, where Lyddy would give her half her bed.

She had worked herself up to a temperature. He rang for the servant and asked her to see to Miss Siddal. After her gibes he could not stay or even offer to sleep on the sofa. She would be all right when she got to bed and he would be back to-morrow. He kissed her, put on his hat and walked all the way home to Chatham Place, to clear his mind a little. She had made him thoroughly miserable and herself ill. He felt these wretched quarrels in his spirit while she proved them on her body. Which was worse? He meant to have it out with Brown next day. So did she.

In the stillness of the morning—but the Browns would be up —she passed down the hill (almost a watercourse with the melting snows of three days ago), walking, lagging, sometimes running in feverish spurts. Leaving the village at the bottom, she struck across the winter fields into a world of black and white, picking out the darkling, hardly discernible footpaths that ran in a westerly direction, crossing the Fleet River by the little bridge just above Carker's Lane, so that she contrived to come in at the unfinished end of the new terrace with its arched middle façade, large inscribed with the date of building (so that all men could see) in which Brown's new house was. Stumbling over brickbats covered with snow, slipping where the footpath was still frozen, she reached the knocker and almost fell down on the doorstep. Brown was in the studio, palette in hand, too absorbed in " a bit " to notice the signs of a temperature in his visitor or he would as usual have made her lie down on the hearthrug and, covering her with a rug, let her tell him all about it. Not a bit of it! With an unusual amount of gesture, from her, she stood over him, raving against Gabriel, hissing accusations and letting her voice go—Brown was not her lover, only her admirer. She did not listen to anything he said and he had a letter in his pocket, just received from Gabriel by messenger, and was conning it in his mind as she ran on—simply murdering herself. . . .

Brown knew that Gabriel was as much upset as she could have wished! In the letter his phrases came ill-turned, uncouth; her anger last night had made him " more unhappy than anything else in the world could do." She had seemed so embittered and estranged when they parted that he feared it might be the end of all things between them! She had said she was going away—God knows where—and all because of this scheme for a joint household which Brown knew, or must understand, was utterly dependent on her wishes. He would drop it if there was the slightest chance of its affecting her happiness. He had had no idea of the violence of her dislike to Hunt : he should have thought that the objection had a right to be more on his own side. Hunt had not actually been acting a friend's part to him—or to Lizzy—lately, but he had hoped that the " feeling would fade out " when once he and Lizzy were married and their union beyond the power of mischief-making to break up. She *did* know all about the Thelema scheme : he had, of course, talked it over with her many times, and the only reason last night why he hadn't at once stopped Brown and cleared up the mystery of the " two or three married couples " was because she got so cross whenever he mentioned their engagement, and he did not know how she would take his mentioning it before Mrs. Siddal.

Brown must be the arbiter. Disingenuous, all three of them. Brown, because of his zeal for Lizzy and acting on a pious motive, had, as Gabriel suspected, relied on their consciousness of his own well-known muddle-headedness—hadn't he been scolded for it a hundred times?—and had purposely created the confusion in order to see if Gabriel or Lizzy herself would rise to it?

Gabriel had countered him by remaining mum.

Lizzy, fighting for her life, as she saw it, was disingenuous too. She had really only the slightest of grudges against Hunt ; because he had once snubbed her about a picture, and for not taking more notice of her generally. It was Annie Miller she despised, hated and detested, and here was Gabriel calmly arranging to have the girl live in the same house with them ! Yes, she would let Brown take her home and she would lie down, and that evening she would see Gabriel, hear him out and bid him good-bye for ever . . . go to Aunt Day's or her mother's or back to Weymouth Street where they loved her—anywhere—out of the world !

She did not go away. She could not. She refused to eat. She could not. Brown sent his wife a telegram bidding her return at once from Hastings, where she was recovering from the birth of little Arthur, to take charge of Miss Sid—"dread-fully ill." In the evening Gabriel came, armed with an explanatory letter that Brown had sent him by messenger, but Mrs. Brown, just come in, would not let him show it. She didn't want the poor girl excited and any more mischief made. She ordered Gabriel out and bade him stay away until Miss Sid could stand him : she might have to take her back with her to Fortess Terrace so as to nurse her properly and feed little Arthur too, but, for the present, she stayed there all day and was fetched at night, while the girl brought the baby to her twice a day. Feeding was the thing for Miss Sid too, only, if she ate, she suffered so much pain that she wilfully refused all nourishment except beef-tea. She *was* taken to the Browns' in the end, to see if change of food would do her any good, but no, on Sunday Brown set down in his diary : " She is, I fear, dying." And that Gabriel, alone in Chatham Place, was so wretched all day that he could not leave him !

Gabriel abased himself plentifully before Brown, preserving, however, his mediæval, pasha-like attitude towards women, professing himself unable to " feel any anger with her now." (What for ? Brown would interiorly rumble.) " Only pain at the sight of her sufferings." And then : " What to do I know not." (Why, behave better ; leave off plaguing her and give her her heart's desire.) Brown felt inclined to say this out loud, only Gabriel was so down, his proud crest so abased. . . .

3

The rift did not close. Gabriel was occupying himself, Brown was glad to see, with his Monday Classes at the Working Men's College, their monthly meetings in Titchfield Street where, by

ANNIE MILLER
From a drawing by G. P. Boyce

paying threepence, the men could hear addresses and eat thick bread-and-butter, interesting himself in the Seddon Memorial Fund, attending with Brown the committee meetings that were being held at various houses, the teas at Ruskin's where the host was so absorbed in his own funny love affair that he hardly asked after Lizzy.

At dinner in Red Lion Square one night someone met Gabriel, looking handsome but fagged and weak, saying very little. This was accounted for by someone else who said it was no wonder, since the lady he was engaged to was in a consumption. Could a man whose sweetheart was smitten with the dread disease be gay?

4

Presently she got a little better and he was allowed to see her, and realised with the humility of one well in health, who had by his robust thoughtlessness brought about a cataclysm of this sort in another, that she was being kind and patient with him—" far more than he deserved." He admitted as much to Brown, and Brown let Lizzy know that Gabriel was ashamed of himself. But she had not seemed to take any interest in the fact and passed over Gabriel's promise not to see Annie again—or Hunt either. Too ill to care.

5

Gabriel had, at any rate, been behaving worse than Hunt knew. On the face of it he had been committing the unpardonable sin among artists, that of stealing Hunt's model under cover of Boyce, to whom Hunt had given her leave to pose, on condition that Boyce pledged himself not to pass her on to any brother brush. It was the common talk of the studios that Annie pretended to be sitting to Boyce and was all the while playing truant from him with Rossetti, who had flung himself on Boyce's mercy, making out that he wanted her for a particular picture. It was really to take her to Cremorne. Several of them had seen her there with Gabriel, and more than once. All poor Boyce knew of their intimacy was Rossetti's visiting-card stuck on the *estrade* while he was out and scrawled on it, in pencil, one of the imperious mandates that none of his friends and toadies could afford to gainsay or neglect! How could Boyce help obliging him? And it happened again and again. Then he received a letter from Hunt who had come to know of it, and it was a jag in their friendship, unhealed, until Hunt quite found Annie out, and wrote a long, considered letter announcing that Miss Miller could now sit to whom she liked and that he washed his hands of her.

Brother William was quite decent about it, Lizzy said, treating her like a sister-in-law, finding means to convey to her his own

> *Turn over*
>
> *Mr. D. G. Rossetti.*
>
> *14. Chatham Place. Blackfriars Bridge.*

> *Dear Boyce. Annie & I have come with 1000 apologies, but really she must — Do let her — sit to me tomorrow, and probably for some Days to come. Pray pardon*

impression of the matter, but standing up for Hunt—"wholly blameless in the matter"—and declaring Gabriel to be "*properly* but not *gravely* censurable."

Not gravely! Thus the brother, holding the scales evenly,[1]

---

[1] I remember an instance of the Spartan impartiality of William Rossetti, even where his own affairs were concerned. His wife had inherited some family silver with a crest on it and displayed it on her dinner-table when there was company. He insisted on her keeping these items in a cupboard, for, if she wanted to go on using them, her husband *must* send in a return, in his capacity of Income Tax Commissioner.

GEORGE PRICE BOYCE
From a photograph

although one dear to him was concerned. And this is what Lizzy really thought about it.[1]

She must fly—anyhow, anywhere, as far as possible from Gabriel and his minions. Her sister took her for a hydropathic cure, to a quiet little village in the Derbyshire hills, now a famous Spa where, as advertised, " the cold winds spend their violence on the huge eminences that environ it, but merely sweep the valley " and " even winter is shorn of its terrors and its very frosts are imbued with an exhilarating temperament." There " water, cliffs and baths are more carbonised than anywhere in the kingdom " and the waters, " slightly tepid in taste," drunk freely, are especially beneficial in cases of consumption and nervous diseases. They chose a Temperance Hotel, Mrs. Cartlidge's, Lime Tree View, which the Wheelers of Bamford had recommended, and left her there to take the waters or not as she liked. She never touched them. It was a rest she had wanted and a respite from the feverish life with Gabriel in London.

She did not propose to pay any visits yet : she must be able to produce her young man when she left cards on Mrs. Gilchrist of Cartlidge Hall and Mrs. Middleton of Hope—two of the high-up ones. There were plenty more distant connections. A Cartledge-Eyre of Owlbrooke had married with a Greaves of Rowlee near Hope—or was it William Greaves of Twothornfield in Edale ? Gabriel had got the pedigree. He loved it. The family had come down in the world, but its ancient wealth and consequence were patent. One of the eccentric Miss Greaves had left the Siddalls a lot of money, so James, who had seen the papers proving it, always said, but everything had got mislaid,

[1] We can tell, for Gabriel, though he buried his own poems, kept hers.

> O God ! forgive me that I merged
> My life into a dream of love !
> Will tears of anguish never wash
> The poison from my blood ?
>
> . . . . . .
>
> Love floated on the mists of morn
> And rested on the sunset's rays ;
> He calmed the thunder of the storm
> And lighted all my ways.
>
> . . . . . .
>
> Oh Heaven help my foolish heart
> Which heeded not the passing time
> That dragged my idol from its place
> And shattered all its shrine !

O

by way of a traitorous certain John Sanderson of Sheffield, and her father was always wasting money in trying to get the better of him.

She was leaving Hope for an excursion with Gabriel when she should have forgiven him and let him come to her.

Meanwhile, still, sad and suspicious, she wandered about, in the woods under the cliffs and along the banks of the Derwent on its pebbly bed, avoiding the set Zigzag Walks which invalids slowly scaled to attain to the Heights of Abraham or the Hill of Masson, and went round by ways she had discovered for herself : through Harp Edge Field and The Plantation and on to Cromford, taking the stone wicket by the last cottage of the upper wood, till she came to a lonely, coldish place near the Toll Bar Corner, right under the lee of a great cliff, and stopped long to rest in a dell among masses of fern and lichenous rock and the deep shade of elder trees and the young grass growing under like a scanty beard, the greenest, wickedest-looking grass she had ever seen, probably full of snakes, that she was not afraid of. It reminded her of Scalands Gate. As the weather got warmer she would be at her old tricks, lying in the long grass here in northern Derbyshire as she had done in Sussex, amusing herself by scribbling—Gabriel in his letters encouraged her to offer herself this outlet; it was the recipe of his master, Hugo, for the alleviation of real or fancied sorrow :—

> *Laissez tout-ce-qui tremble*
> *Chanter.*

He was right, for the verses which she posted to him began to show a less terrible mental oscillation than they had done.[1] They suggested more the sobbing sleep of a child that has been affronted by its elders, half-pacified, half-angry still. . . .

> Slow days have passed that make a year,
> Slow hours that make a day,
> Since I could take my first dear love,
> And kiss him the old way :
> Yet the green leaves touch me on the cheek,
> Dear Christ, this month of May.
>
> .   .   .   .   .   .
>
> The river ever running down
> Between its grassy bed,
> The voices of a thousand birds
> That clang above my head,
> Shall bring me to a sadder dream
> When this sad dream is dead.

A silence falls upon my heart,
  And hushes all its pain.
I stretch my hands in the long grass,
  And fall to sleep again,
There to lie empty of all love,
  Like beaten corn of grain.

Calmer :—

Oh, never weep for love that's dead,
  Since love is seldom true,
But changes his fashion from blue to red,
  From brightest red to blue,
And love was born to an early death
  And is so seldom true.

. . . . . .

Sweet, never weep for what cannot be,
  For this God has not given :
If the merest dream of love were true,
  Then, Sweet, we should be in heaven ;
And this is only earth, my dear,
  Where true love is not given.

Resigned and bitter :—

O silent wood, I enter thee
With a heart so full of misery—
For all the voices from the trees
And the ferns that cling about my knees.

. . . . . .

Can God bring back the day when we two stood
Beneath the clinging trees in that dark wood ?

And God did, in a way. . . .

---

[1] Ope not thy lips, thou foolish one,
    Nor turn to me thy face.
  The blasts of Heaven shall strike me down
    Ere I will give thee grace.

. . . . . .

And turn away thy false dark eyes
  Nor gaze into my face :
Great love I bore thee ; now great hate
  Sits grimly in its place.

CHAPTER XXI

I

IN town, where best he liked to be, keeping fairly healthy in spite of the smell of the river, the needs of man's sexual existence accomplished without recourse to the female's harassing necessity of legal sanctions : in Lizzy's absence, working (his friends were all agreed on this point and even honest Brown conceded it) far better, Gabriel Rossetti looked over his sweetheart's verses with the impartiality of a critic tinged with the remorse of a human being who knows that, by his own behaviour, he has been the occasion of the wail in them. He took note with a view to the effect on the reader, apart from himself who knew all the circumstances, of the literary liberties she took—the permutations of time and place—the substitution of Gabriel Rossetti, absent and unkind, for Walter Deverell, loving and dead, the silly shots at himself.

Knowing full well what he was doing to her—and she to him—he made allowances for the passion, thwarted, thrown back on itself, immanent in one relegated by illness to the backwaters of Life and Love—

> How can it, ah, how can Love's eye see true
> That is so worn with watching and with tears ?

But he fancied that a milder, quieter mood was setting in, signs of a comfortable cynicism. *" For this is only earth, my dear."* Complaisance with the changing fashion of love, some recognition of the worthlessness of fair words ! Surely the poems held reminiscence of past ease—joy of which this author might again be susceptible ? *" Can God bring back the day when we two stood, Beneath the clinging trees "*—in that dark wood at Scalands when their engagement was but young. Perhaps God could ? He must take time soon to go to Matlock, see her and remind her of what happened in Scalands Wood and walk in the other dells that she would show him, and take her to Haddon and

Hope and the Shivering Mountain which had so inflamed his imagination when she told him about it long ago. But, meanwhile, his days were very full.

2

For, alack, when she was relenting towards him with the canny deliberation that women will use towards their men, trusting Love to let them rave awhile—maybe a long while—corresponding in their minds to the harm which has been wrought them, the female playing with the redoubtable male sex-urge of which she knows so little and most of it wrong, denying the need that can in him be so easily satisfied outside the " golden girdling bar " which circumscribes her, all was lost. While The Sid, relying on her looks (for she was still beautiful enough) and the queer half-magical power she possessed over him, was paltering over issues positively vital to her, the discs of the kaleidoscope had fallen together into another pattern and the Thelema scheme was partially realised. " We shall have our monastery, Crom. There is a good chance of its being founded," Jones had written to Price years ago. " I know it will, some day."

In Oxford.

The members of the old Order of Sir Galahad who had " gone down " were in the habit of putting themselves into slow Parliamentary trains—they were poor—to visit the men of their time who were still " up." Fulford and Crom Price regularly, Jones and Morris intermittently, absented themselves awhile from felicity (the hours with Gabriel) so that they might experience an old thrill; a bout of single-stick with Maclaren for the sake of Morris' figure and then out to his place at Summerstown, so that Jones might get a background for his first picture (*The Blessed Damozel*): evenings with beautiful Faulkner, now Mathematical Lecturer to the University, in his panelled rooms, tea and toast from nine onwards. They would turn a table in Pembroke with Fulford and smoke a churchwarden with Dixon, who had wanted to be an artist but was so poor that he was obliged to take Orders. (The daring " blokes " who had embraced art as a profession were the envy of those who had drifted into safe places in the University.)

Morris and Jones had never rested until they got Gabriel down and introduced him to Oxford as " the greatest man in Europe." He took his place at once and became easily king—

197

nothing else would have served him. This man, built all on grand lines even to his vices, without vanity, pettiness or pretension—except to reign—this charmer with no obvious weapon of conquest except his voice and his serviceable memory, without the steady ingraining of University culture acquired in the course of many terms by those who had led him there, found himself thoroughly at home by virtue of his academic grounding, his natal Latin civilisation and the foreign *aplomb* with which he was able to counter the terrible Oxford manner. He feared neither Don nor Devil, not Liddell the magnificent, nor slender and elegant Acland, nor even crusty Pattison, asking with his well-known insufferability if Mr. Rossetti would have *all men* painters and no other occupation for the rest of mankind ? The other answered promptly, Yes. Quite soon everyone came to accept Rossetti at his own valuation, from the brilliant Faulkner down to the Irish architect, Benjamin Woodward, " the stillest creature that ever breathed, out of an oyster." [1]

Riding and single-stick did not appeal to Rossetti and Maclaren's gymnasium knew him not. There seemed then but slight chance of his ever growing fat and bandy, as Morris threatened to do. He never walked but he liked being rowed, and Faulkner, a great oarsman, liked rowing him. It was terribly hot, the summer of Klinkenfues' comet,[2] with " its draggled tail like a sad turkey." [3] In these days the river was the only comfortable place. Rossetti did not, could not row, but he could sit letting his beautiful hand trail in the water composing and declaiming sonnets while they rowed and sweated.

> Water, for anguish of the solstice :—nay,
> But dip the vessel slowly—nay, but lean
> And hark how at its verge the wave sighs in
> Reluctant. Hush ! Beyond all depth away
> The heat lies silent at the brink of day.

Nay but he was never so happy in his life again, not even much later when he had occasion to write *Nuptial Sleep*.

Faulkner took them wherever they liked, upstream towards

---

[1] This " Thirteenth-century Gothic man," as they called him, was responsible for the New Crown Insurance Office, just opposite Chatham Place. He had won in the battle between that style and the Palladian and his design for the new Oxford Museum had been accepted—a momentous decision for the three friends whose praises had been duly sung to him at Wallingford by Ruskin, Acland and Scott.

[2] People were afraid it would collide with the earth and made their wills in consequence.

[3] C. Bowles.

the "far-off, other end of Thames" or towards Town where, luckily, they had a *pied-à-terre*. For when Allingham came, he wanted to be taken to a certain village within a few miles of London. When they got there, however, it was discovered that between them they had not enough to pay for beds at the inn and they decided to walk the six remaining miles to Holborn, where Red Lion Mary, summoned at once, produced extra mattresses—Rossetti naturally would not, at all costs to others, go to sleep by himself in Chatham Place—and next morning Jones got up early, took his easel out into the square and began to paint the lilies, just blowing, for *The Blessed*. So he really could not bring himself to obey Rossetti's orders to accompany him to Oxford and hear about a proposal Woodward wanted to make them . . . something good! But he thought he might possibly manage it for the last Sunday in that month, if that would do. This business, as it happened, affected the mere disposition of Jones' time for many months to come, while it altered the course of Morris' whole life. And, after all, Jones had to make time to run down for the day, to Leyton. His *Blessed Damozel* had to wait.

Under a cherry tree in Mrs. Morris' garden the three friends sat the whole day, talking over Woodward's offer. The ten bays above the gallery in the new Debating Room at Oxford were to be filled with paintings and, all-powerful for the moment, he had nominated his friends. The artists were to give their work for nothing but live free. The Union would pay their lodging and travelling expenses and the cost of scaffolding and painting materials. The work all to be done under the direction of Rossetti; the executants selected by him, one for each bay, say ten artists in all. Rossetti meant to invite Prinsep, because he liked going to Little Holland House, and Spencer Stanhope and Hungerford Pollen and Hughes, and dear old Brown, of course. He himself would undertake two of the bays—possibly three. There was the roof above to be covered with a simple floriated design—"Suit *me*!" said modest Morris. Faulkner, too, might be useful at that. He was not bad at mathematical patterns. The subjects, said Gabriel, were all to be taken from the *Morte d'Arthur* and done in tempera, a medium he knew nothing about as yet but would soon find out. The application of colour to architecture was a novel idea—Woodward's own.

All right. Rossetti, who had never read a line of Malory,

made himself conversant with that work. Jones gave up his *Blessed Damozel* and Morris put off his visit to the Manchester Exhibition. Brown, sounded, could do nothing. He had one of the frescoes for Wallington commissioned, and the exhibition of Pre-Raphaelite paintings he had got up in Russell Place at a cost of forty pounds was slow in its returns, and little Arthur, whom Emma had neglected at a critical period because of The Sid, was ailing. But he would run down and look at them now and then. For Lizzy's journey to Matlock Gabriel still owed him money, but Brown forbore to dun him till August, when Gabriel, disgusted at himself for " forcing you to ask for it after all your kindness," paid something back.[1]

3

There began for the Three something in the nature of a continuous picnic, a Summer School that lasted well into the winter. Morris went down first and took rooms in The High for himself and Jones ; Rossetti came and settled down with his two pupils to paint little grey Oxford in that primary colour which the Brotherhood so much affected.

They were by way of having no canons but those of art, playing ducks and drakes with Life, but taking these other matters with deep seriousness. They were full of magnanimity and otherworldliness : " Don't let anyone persuade you that you are a fool for not looking after your own interests—God doesn't call such people fools ! " So the youthful Jones. But they neglected those of the Corporation that employed them, wasting both its time and its paints without compunction. " Oh, that's nothing ! " Rossetti said, carelessly upsetting a whole pot of lapis lazuli—" we often do that." And writing to ask to have sent him by bearer " a crumb of violet-carmine "—a guinea's worth, say, which was never used. And Morris hurtling a fifteenth-century folio at the head of a workman, missing his thick head but taking a panel out of the door ! They all knew no more of tempera than Rossetti did of wood-engraving. The paint would not lie ; the walls were not even ; between the bays occurred certain ridges over which you had to train a face, if it happened to come there, like a creeper. There were windows

---

[1] Rossetti was at least disinterested ; Munro told Birkbeck Hill that had he given to small saleable pictures the time he had given to his large ones for the Union, he could have made a thousand guineas.

in these bays that made anything painted on the wall invisible; so they were whitened to tone the light, and Morris thought it funny to cover the surface with wombats! Amateurs were roped in. Faulkner would make arabesques and lozenges when required, while Price would stipple in the black lines. They perhaps knew as much about it as the others.[1]

The expenses of " our Oxford labour of love," as defrayed *by* Oxford, were heavy, but at least the artists did not spend money on models but sat to each other. Morris was good for Sir Tristram or Sir Launcelot, in real armour made by a little smith near the castle, and Jones, with his long, straight, colourless hair and his pale blue eyes, for any sort of " woeful wight, alone and palely loitering." Prinsep, only nineteen and weighing sixteen stone, did for kings, while Price, for priests, would stand for hours in a dalmatic. For lovely and absent women they made shift with Johnson's housemaid or one of the College bedmakers. Rossetti did Lizzy as Guenevere, from memory.

4

Deliberately, seriously and extravagantly undertaken, the work could not be said to march on apace, but those were glorious days for the jolly three, " living Malory " for months in this little walled town of low houses of grey and yellow stone, pebble-dashed, interspersed with palaces; pacing the narrow streets where every day clattered along, under over-arching gables, cavalcades of gracious Youth (knights, so you may imagine them) passing through the city gates out into the green, pied meadows beyond the ramparts, where lists might be set and tournaments held and men could " sweive and strain " till blood flaked the buttercups. Everybody rode in Oxford, and the caterers for this amusement—ostlers and livery stable keepers—whom they liked to call squires and *palfreniers*—abounded. There was nothing else to do but row and ride and study. In the evenings, back in their digs, Gabriel would read aloud to Jones, sedulous, narrow-chested, bending over his pen-and-ink drawing, while Morris cooked fish or toasted bread and buttered it on Mr. Johnson's nicely varnished table.

[1] William Michael Rossetti, January 18th, 1858, to Allingham: " The things there (at Oxford) are very new, curious and with a ruddy bloom of health and pluck about them. Gabriel's very beautiful, both in expression and colour. Jones' next and to some extent more; exactly the right kind of thing. Val's promises real power."

They were so happy at home that they could hardly bear to accept the hospitalities of Oxford or stand even the very slight amount of formality required at Dr. Acland's table. As for Mrs. Liddell's invitations to Christ Church, they found it necessary to break camp and rush up to town sooner than attend Lorina's dinners. Their dress-clothes were non-existent or unsuitable. Rossetti, day in, night out, wore the plum-coloured coat he was still wearing in the Haunted Glen at Penkill ten years later, and Top's only two white ties were making a loop in his window to hold his brushes, drying. But he amiably would wash the so expensive blue paint from his hair, prepare an apple-pie bed for one or other of his friends, doff his workman's blouse and endure what he called the " ridiculous arrangement of one coat with no back and another with no front " to repair to a gathering at the Rose of Sharon's—Acland, in whose favour they made an exception.

CHAPTER XXII

I

MISS SIDDAL now wrote from Number Seven, Durham Road, Sheffield, where she was staying with some cousins of hers in order to attend the School of Art there on Wednesdays and Saturdays.

It was the last splash, the last lark, the last independent gesture of her life—except one.

The Ibbitts, in whose house she was living so as to be near the School, were relations, descended from one Anna Siddal, who had married twice : first a man called Hodskin (her son by him happened to be the auctioneer with whom that tiresome Mrs. Combe of Oxford had chosen to confound Lizzy's father) and, secondly, a Sheffield man, William Ibbitt. Anna's children therefore were not Lizzy's first, but her second cousins—or cousins-german—she did not know which !

Miss Sarah Ann Ibbitt was a teacher of music and drawing, while her brother was musical. Quite humble, Gabriel believed. The young man worked in an organ factory : his sister went out to give lessons. This set of her relations did not interest Gabriel as much as the ones at Hope. She was keeping Hope to take him to if ever he could tear himself away from Oxford and come and see her.

A girl she met at the Ibbitts', Annie Drury, had got her taken into the school, informally. She was not a registered pupil. The Head Master had liked the look of her. She had hesitated, thinking of cross Mr. Deverell—but Mr. Young-Mitchell was charming. For the rest, it was rather like Somerset House, of which she had caught glimpses on her way in and out to sit to Walter, though women were admitted on Wednesdays and Saturdays. But not into " The Life." She almost immediately got into " The Figures "—that is to say, " The Antique." And on other days she and Annie went, accompanied by young Mr. Ibbitt when he could get a day or an afternoon off from the works, to places of interest in the neighbourhood, by rail or omnibus or "Shank's Mare," as Miss Ibbitt called it. Lizzy could always walk with the best of them. They did Haddon and Hathersage and the Peak Country, going as everyone did, down the Blue John Mine, and Mr. Ibbitt, as everyone did, bought his young lady a Blue John ring of amethystine fluor. Another time it was Eldon Hole, a chasm a hundred and twenty feet across with a silly little railing over it, and she frightened them by pretending to totter. And Mam Tor, the mountain of shale and sandstone in alternate stratification, Willie said, so soft and friable that it fell out in particles and the whole hill seemed to shake. Once they were within a mile and a half of Hope and got a nice view of it on a little hill between the Noe river and the Bradwell Water where it lay and of the church where her ancestors lay entombed.

Willie Ibbitt was at her feet, and Mr. Young-Mitchell was supposed to admire her. So did the two assistant masters, Godfrey Sykes and Charles Green, in a less discreet fashion, while her fellow-students, Hugh Stannus, Stirling Howard, and Ferguson Branson, M.D., and four Henrys—Lomas, Colman, Hems and Gamble—ran about and fetched things and sharpened pencils for her.

Then the girl students soon set about to make it unpleasant for the favoured one, hitting on what was to them her weakest point—her outlandish style of dressing. For this year all the women were enlarging their circumferences in some way or another.

The girl students would have it that Miss Siddal acted from motives of economy—proper crinolines [1] were dear and always getting out of order—the steels poked out and stuck through the stuff and, even if you made out the necessary contour with petticoats, the washing of eight or more came expensive. A certain amount of fullness Lizzy wore as a concession to the mode,

---

[1] In 1854 the crinoline appeared in Paris. Four narrow steels, each covered with tape, were run into a calico slip. The steel nearest the waist was to be four nails from it and one and three-quarters in length : the remaining three only two and a half yards in length and one at six nails distance from the upper steel, while the other two had to be each two nails distance from the second steel. None must meet in front by a quarter of a yard, except the one nearest the waist. The flounce of the skirt was generally from fifteen to seventeen inches deep.

Even Mrs. Browning confessed to a weakness for the new style and bought a crinoline. It was nice and cool for Italy and, besides, Robert insisted on her dressing like other people.

but she managed that beautifully and passed serenely about among the easels without upsetting them or asking that room should be made for her. The girls made caricatures of the simple outline she presented and left them about for her to find. But it was Mr. Young-Mitchell who happened to pick one up. Realising the spite that drove the clever pencil, his black eyes flashing, he mounted the *estrade* and said this sort of thing must be put a stop to. So she triumphed, for they were nearly all in love with him and afraid of incurring his ire.

She could do as she liked with him or any of the masters. Foreign travel had given her a certain *aplomb* : consequence and the uplift of the spirit that goes with it suited her looks and the " Comet Summer " was good for her complaint. " Prettier now, in a more usual way." [1] Gabriel liked getting her cheerful letters. It was nice to know that the restless spirit for whose fate he was considered responsible was more or less assuaged. She had found " something to keep herself alive with " (her own phrase), something safer than going down to the sea in boats at Hastings or over-walking herself as she had done at Clevedon. In her art he had long since ceased to take interest, now that the silly girl had given up the Ruskin subsidy.

And more and more he was coming to appreciate the society of men : which he had hankered after ever since the break-up of the P.R.B. Morris and Jones suited him better than Hunt, Woolner and even Deverell. They, too, were content—more than content. They had their Thelema now, without the help of some fellows who had discussed it with them when they were undergrads. The present members of the Pembroke set were worldly, permitting themselves to make fun of *The Heir*, bored by these three who always insisted on discussing paintings which they had never seen and did not care to see. Their club was the *Old Mortality*, and their organ *Undergraduate Papers*, edited by Edwin Hatch, " a pompous emptyheaded fellow," and Nichol, " a handsome Scotchman." And one evening Hatch brought to them in Orange Street a little fellow, five feet four-and-a-half inches in height, with a pouting mouth like a fledgeling's, set in a white face, red hair like Lizzy's and the same long, thin fingers. Rather ridiculous, wearing large full trousers which fell over his feet, shod in little low shoes which he crossed and recrossed as he stood and wearing a coat that allowed for his dreadful sloping shoulders.

[1] So said one of Gabriel's " lady friends."

He was a Swinburne of Capheaton, a family which boasted descent from the five who were " there before the Conquest," an aristocrat with republican leanings : as a lad in Paris he had refused to take off his hat to Louis Napoleon. His father, a sailor, seldom at home, had married an Ashburnham. Algernon was their first child, born all but dead and not expected to live more than an hour, with a right hand so weak that he wrote pot-hooks and hangers all his life ; nervous—starting as if he were hit when spoken to suddenly ; fanciful, seeing his own face in a mirror he would smash it, thinking that someone was laughing at him. But, withal, the pluck of the devil and the most beautiful manners of his time.

In his high-pitched Northumbrian sing-song he read them *Queen Yseult*, just composed for *Undergraduate Papers*, right through, with tremendous zest and earnestness. Impossible to bore those three, inured to all the wilful *longueurs* of poets ! Morris, twiddling his watch-chain, incapable of jealousy but not favourably impressed by the personality of the little author, declared that it was far better than his own *Dying Blanche*.[1] Jones would have it that the boy was going to be greater than Shelley, Tennyson or Wordsworth. Thus encouraged, young Algernon—they were already " Gab " and " Top " to him—read his other " piece " about Rosamond, Queen of the Gepidæ, and Morris vowed that this was better than *Sir Peter Harpdon's End*, which *he* had just finished. He then read them his *Helen of Troy*, and Swinburne followed with some of *Chastelard*, on which he was now engaged.

From this day onward there was a fourth every night in George Street, and the noses of the two Old Mortality men were completely put out of joint. Hatch, leaving England to take up a lucrative professorship shortly after this, wrote a pathetic farewell letter [2] to Swinburne. He might never see him again . . . perhaps it would be as well if he did not. . . . " I shall never forget how I loved you once, but I feel that the chain that bound us is somewhere snapped asunder."

By Rossetti, of course—healthy-minded, when all was said and done.

[1] Early consigned to the flames.
[2] A marginal interpolation in Swinburne's handwriting on the letter, preserved—
" For the matter of that, rot ! . . . No golden band between us at all."

What did happen in Oxford? As Algernon Swinburne read
out that night from his own Marian play—

> When I was fashioned first and given such life
> As goes with a sad end. . . .

"Would it not have been——" so the Master who, in the
course of his duty, had looked into Swinburne's room and found
the boy lying on his bed " reading French novels and——" said
at Tennyson's dinner-table—" would it not have been better "—
hesitating—" if he had not lived to reach the writing stage at
all ? "

Tennyson always laid the leading astray of him whom he called
the " *puny youth—big lyre* " down to Rossetti, and told Jones so.
Rossetti indignantly repudiated the accusation in a letter to
Tennyson—" You remember what I told you in a cab." Tennyson did not remember what Rossetti had told him in a cab. He
had no patience with that kind of thing.

Who or what did corrupt the little man ? Himself seems to
imply that these—compared with him—hearty young ruffians
sophisticated him, with his polite allusion to " those past days in
Oxford when you fellows might have respected my young adol-
escence. . . . I don't say that you did. . . ." Friendly chaff,
sexual vanity, callous indifference ? He was proud of his dereliction and played with it, as children will lave their pretty hands
in the gutter.

> The morning sun beneath the stars that fled
>   With twilight through the moonless morning air,
> . . . the hopes that triumphed and fell dead,
>   The sweet swift eyes and songs of hours that were,
> These may'st thou not give back for ever. . . .
> But flowers thou may'st, and winds and hours of ease,
>   And all its April to the world thou may'st
> Give back, and half my April back to me.

It was, perhaps, as he said, only half his April, as it were, only
half a reproach . . . one does not know ? Inexpressibly sad,
like the memory of a slight or a blow implicit in a good dog's
eyes. And as an accusation it loses half its force when we know
that it was Swinburne who extended to Rossetti " the loan of

De Sude (as Rossetti innocently spells it), the most immoral book in the whole world." [1]

It was not lent him by Milnes. Milnes' mantle—or "utter absence of mantle" [2]—will not do to cover the "importation of the Marquis." Swinburne had a copy of *Justine* at Eton.

4

From his mother, the Lady Jane, brought up and educated in Florence, speaking French and Italian like English, he may have inherited, together with the red hair of the Ashburnhams, the morbidity that was the Janus face of her prudery. Lady Jane's boy was not allowed to read Byron or even Shakespeare except in Mr. Bowdler's edition.

Murder will out—so will the *macabre*. There are unplumbed wells of Freudian suggestion here and in young Algernon's family history. Who knows the tragic secret connected with the house at Niton where he was born—at any rate lived as a child?

---

[1] *Justine et Juliette*, by the Marquis de Sade, a name unmentionable, unwritable in those days. So Allingham, who was present at Tennyson's dinner, supposed. But even Heads of Colleges were not such Dryasdusts as they may have looked and were up to what might be going on that night in the last house by the Bridge—Merriot's, in the 'seventies.

[2] *Vide* Tennyson.

CHAPTER XXIII

I

ABOUT the great Manchester Exhibition, opened by the Queen and Prince Albert in May of this year, there was a conspiracy of silence among right-thinking but needy artists. Their best buyers, the great steel, coal and shipping magnates of the North, were more or less responsible for its ineptitudes. So painters came never to mention the Exhibition, except to inquire about trains to go there and seize the opportunity of seeing some of the really fine examples borrowed from the Continental Galleries. The works were arranged chronologically, beginning with Giotto and Van Dyck and ending with the last Pre-Raphaelite flicker in the canvases of Millais and young Leighton, who was rivalling him. Brown's Liverpool Prize picture, for which he had received thirty-five guineas, hung on the ceiling, where Christ washed Peter's feet for all men (with eyes in the tops of their heads) to see. Ruskin, who was there for three days in July lecturing—mindful of the souls of his audience of operatives who should be given bread instead of stones if he could manage it—sent some Turners— *Laugharne*, *Eggleston*, *Troy* and *Virginia Water*.

In the end everybody seemed to have been in Manchester some time that summer, except Gabriel Rossetti, and there is no record of his ever having set foot in the town.

His Lizzy did. A special grant was made by the Manchester Committee for the use of schools, and one September morning a hundred and fifty people left Sheffield by special train, among whom was Miss Elizabeth Siddal, strong and lively, her hair and complexion as bright as ever, taking an active part in the excursion programme and using her influence with the Head to get places for several of her friends who could, by no stretch of the imagination, be called Art Students—the Ibbitts and her sister Lydia, who had come over from Bamford, and a Mrs. Button. But Charley Green attended to it.

They started at 8.30 and were timed to return at 5.30. It

was a wet day and the rain came in at the windows, so all the way to Manchester, Miss Siddal wore a cloak over the new dress she and Miss Ibbitt had finished, sitting up late the night before, in order to shield it, as they came near Manchester, from the "blacks" dreaded of ladies, that drove in from its thousands of smoking chimneys.

When they got out, ladies in crinolines and gents in white ties, and all passed into the long matchboarding corridor that led from the station to the Exhibition, the school party got a shock. Though Miss Siddal was wearing the fashionable bonnet, nearly dropping off behind, drab in colour but with a fascinating pink lining to frame the face, they quite expected to see, when she took off her waterproof, the plain falling folds of the dress "without bombast" they had made fun of. But no! Since the episode of the caricature she had been determined to show them that, though she preferred simplicity in dressing, she had not lived in Paris a year for nothing. She could wear the crinoline better than most people, for in height she excelled, while the other girls as a rule were dumpy, with wide hips from which the round cage of folds depended, so that the width at the waist of the dress corresponded to that at the hem. Lizzy's dove-coloured silk gown was looped over a crinoline in the fashionable manner like theirs, but her narrow hips made all the difference : her "Tower of Malakof" swayed gracefully. Her skirt was of stuff, worn, according to the newest fashion, with a silk *casaque*, or jacket, and with her figure, her white face and her hair—when artlessly, as her manner was, she had taken her bonnet off and let it show—she made a sensation. So Miss Drury, who was pleased for her friend and shared her triumphs, has recorded. And young Mr. Ibbitt became quite particular in his attentions, proud of passing with the lovely, fashionable Miss on his arm, in and out of the great pillars wreathed with shawls and hung with carpets, past the crystal fountain in the middle, thirty feet high and the statue of the Amazon on horseback with a life-size stuffed tiger fastened on by its claws to the horse's neck in front, almost the first thing you saw on entering. And you had to go round one side to see her face and the other to see that of the horse, transfixed in terror so that you expected to hear him scream. And on into the French Section, where there was a tree with mechanical birds that chirped hopping about from branch to branch, and one that tried to eat a beetle—rather a failure this, for it never quite got its head down.

Lizzy led Annie Drury away from these horrible staring things into the quieter picture galleries; they looked out for Mr. Ruskin's Turners, so that Lizzy could tell him whom Lizzy considered she had perhaps rather neglected, that she had seen them when she got back to town. A tall young man stooping to see them better, got into conversation with her and Annie. He introduced himself as a friend of Mr. Ruskin's and of Millais', to whom he too had sat—Charles Howell. He said he had seen her at the Rossettis'—he had not. That he was obliging Mr. Ruskin by looking in to see how the Turners were getting on— that was true. Mr. Ruskin had feared, since the opening day, that they might suffer, since they were put where they were totally unprotected from the sun. " And they have ! " he said. " Look, the rose-colour has all gone out of the sunset since one last saw it at his house ! "

He said there were plenty of fakes there—he could tell one anywhere : his father was a copyist in Portugal. She did not take to him, he was too *outré*-looking, like an actor. But it would stimulate Willie Ibbitt, and she let Mr. Howell take her to see the Triumphal Arch at Trafford and the panorama of chimneys in full blast at Kearsall, two thousand at least, and their smoke staining the skies, which might have been blue.

The Arch, so the guide-book said, was Italian in style, thirty-three feet wide and forty-eight feet high from soffit—he explained what that was—to base, a light stone-colour with maroon cloth draped over it in festoons and gold tassels at the corners. Feathers covered the keystone of the Arch, while from it drooped gracefully garlands of flowers attached to the entablature and side arches. A frieze in Arabesque style, turreted at the top, supported pot-plants lent by the Royal Botanical Society of Manchester. A bust of the Queen, again flanked by pot-plants, was posed majestically behind what looked like ropes of red sausages. They laughed at it together. Standing there by the side of the man who, next to Morris, was to become the cleverest art decorator of his time, she discovered that she also had taste. She told him that she was engaged to Mr. Rossetti.

On the way home Willie Ibbitt proposed and she communicated the fact of her engagement to him also, and he said she was a young sly-boots.

Gabriel, getting Jones to open his letters for him and in most cases reply to them, found time to run up to Matlock soon after this, where, to be sure, The Sid was back to receive him. He had heard something of her Manchester triumphs as well as of Ruskin's vexation over the baked drawings, from this very cheeky Howell, whom he often met in Albany Street.

He put up, with her, at Mrs. Cartlidge's and, when it was wet, they stayed at home and made portraits of anyone who would give them a sitting. Gabriel did a good head of an old lady, Mrs. Wetherall, and one of Mrs. Cartlidge's son, an artist too. When it was fine they made the regular excursions—to Chatsworth, Haddon and The Peak. It was nicer for " Guggums " than going about with Willie Ibbitt, for, although " Gug " did not know the place-names or buy you fluor brooches or paperknives, he made far more interesting and romantic the places that happened to interest him. He said that the entrance into The Peak Cavern was like the beginning of an awful dream— the little sad, white rope-maker's cottage, on which the sun never shone and the rain never fell, set against the cowering roof and descent of the pit, the posts for packthread and twine, sharp, white and blear against the hollow blackness, the shrill cries of the cordwainers and the hum of the wheels rising up from where the cave led, diminuendo, into depths where perhaps

> Alph, the sacred river ran
> Through caverns measureless to man
> Down to a sunless sea.

And the Shivering Mountain—he *would* not call it Mam Tor— like a couchant beast shuddering with nervousness, over Eldon Hole, whence its fate was to come ! And he was tremendously intrigued by the Ebbing and Flowing Well, just a seeming shallow pool lined with stones as if to form a trough for cattle, but in which a miracle accomplished itself, for every now and then a rush of water poured in when you least expected it, filling it to the depth of four feet or so and then ceasing as it came. . . .

One day they went to Castleton, for Hope, and looked across to the spire of St. Peter's-by-the-Roadside, the church holding, they believed, the tombs and entablatures of her ancestry. They walked through the valley, where there were Sheep Trials going on, and stopped to watch and rest before climbing the hill up to the village. Hope Hall, someone told them, was now a public-house, so they walked straight into the garth of the little stone church (Perpendicular so she told him, who did not know anything of terms of architecture) with its chambered porch and clerestoried nave and broach spire, with a clock and six bells—rebuilt, all, but in the fourteenth century.[1] Some Greaves relations were buried in the chancel whose entablatures she made him look at, and then, out into the graveyard under the sycamores and lime trees to sit, in the high moorland air, on the tomb of an ancestor, one Jacobus Sidall—the proper way to spell *her* name ; why had Gabriel insisted on taking out the *l* and leaving in the *d* ? And there was the tomb of one Anna de Grant de Hope, who was married here in the seventeenth century and brought into the world a Christopher, ill-starred, who married an heiress, Rachel Greaves of Hathersage, but fell into misfortune. Ruined by the failure of the flax industry, he was forced to declare himself bankrupt and died of a broken heart, to be buried, away from here, in Sheffield, where he sang in the Cathedral. That was where Father got his music and fiddling. Gabriel, who could write beautifully about music, really hated it, and she herself did not care about it much. The Greaves were of better blood even than the Sidalls, descending from a Knight of Beeley in the eleventh century—perhaps if they went to Beeley they might find out some more about her people ? He fancied they had originally come from Manchester—Slade Hall —something Scott or Mr. Howitt had told him. . . .

She left a card on Mrs. Middleton. Both the old Miss Greaves of Hope Hall, who used to drive about in a landau, smoking clay pipes (a legend which amused and intrigued Gabriel vastly), were now dead. It was one of them who had left that money to Lizzy's father, which he had been jockeyed out of by the lawyers. But he had now got all the evidence collected and was going to the Courts about it one day soon—unless Clara carried out her threat to burn the lot so as to put an end to his worrying about it.[2]

3

It looked just now, for Lizzy, more like marriage than it had ever done before. Her lovely colour and renewed health, the attentions of Mr. Young-Mitchell, those of William Ibbitt and

[1] Restored hopelessly in 1880.   [2] She did.

Charley Green swayed Gabriel towards a desire for closer communion with her, only attainable in one way.

But he could not marry her without money to support her and keep up the boundless extravagance by which his soul, more than his body, lived. Ruskin was not much good to him now, desperately disliking his present set of friends, especially Morris. He would have it that the *period* madness, in which Morris encouraged them, was safe to dish the P.R.B., once so far on the road to success, with their splendid catchword of a name and their new attractive style; but lately they had been weakening, practically giving up the game, " leaving the opposite party (*i.e.* the R.A.) most untoward advantages." Ruskin always had a leaning towards this " opposite party," by way of Turner. He refused to help the P.R.B. with America, where an Exhibition was being got up, including specimens of British Art, " with a certain bias " towards a movement that, now that it was nearly dead, had become rather widely known. " No, I have no knowledge of America," he answered curtly, " although " (thinking of Norton) " I have some very good friends there." Yes, Rossetti would hate him for refusing to help, but " I do not choose." A business man, he knew full well that mediævalism would not, in the long run, go down in America and considered that the drawings Rossetti was sending across would " put an end to any idea of his reputation ever beginning there ! " [1]

" Yours, in *im*perfect sympathy," so he signed the letter.

As punishment, perhaps, he was not allowed even to see his Ida's drawings before they were despatched to New York, where they were, as Ruskin prophesied, laughed at. He might have saved her from that ! But not the rest. For though he kept running down to Oxford to " see what They were doing," he was so out of their counsels, that he was not even told what was happening to her who was his special care.

[1] William Rossetti had been engaged as secretary for England by Captain Ruxton, who was arranging the British Section with Gambart.

MISS LOUISE HERBERT (MRS. CRABBE)
From a photograph

CHAPTER XXIV

I

*O*XONIAS, *Oxoniœ, Primo D.G.R. fecit,* under a drawing of Miss Jane Burden, of Oxford, done in this year, does not seem to mean anything but Rossetti's enthusiasm for, and celebration of, her native town. But it implies the ascension of a new star—that is to say, a new model—in his horizon and the declension of both Miss Herbert and Miss Siddal. There was never room for more than one (model) in Rossetti's heart.

Janey was only a model to him in this, the beginning.

The Union paintings and the Llandaff triptych, conceived though not begun, kept him running backwards and forwards between Oxford and London. Then news came of a benefit performance at Oxford in which Miss Herbert was to appear. Ruskin, who had procured him the commission, had signified his desire that "her beautiful face" should be seen in it. (Like Rossetti, he had never seen the lady except across the footlights.) Word was passed and a box at the Theatre Royal was taken. Rossetti would be down in time for the performance, while Allingham, who was staying with him in London, must go down in the morning and get himself a room, easy enough just then, for Term had not begun. He arrived about noon. Jones, and Faulkner whom he did not know but admired, met him at the station and took him to the King's Head in Holywell. They ordered their beer and sat to drink it on the balcony overlooking the inn yard and Burden's famous Livery Stables. The sun was shining, it was very hot.

What happened while they sat there, reminded Allingham of the Model Hunts of the Prime. They all knew—for the Prince was vocal of his needs—that Gabriel, eager to secure Ruskin's advance on the second bay which he had undertaken to do, must get the Guenevere done and out of the way. His sister had kindly sat, but her face was not suitable so he was doing it from memory of Lizzy away in Matlock (quiet and tolerably happy by all accounts).

Gabriel and his need was always in his friends' minds. They saw a tall girl, bareheaded, her black burnished hair shining beetle-wise in the strong sunlight, crossing the inn yard in front of them, carrying a jug of beer very carefully—and herself like a goddess. Jones exclaimed, "The very thing for Gabriel!" She must be procured for the Master at once, and it fell to one of them to do it as long, long ago poor dead Deverell had got hold of Elizabeth Eleanor Siddall for his friend.

But that very evening, when they all met in the box at the Theatre, there the girl was, with another, in the stalls immediately below them! They pointed her out to Gabriel, who was making a sketch of Miss Herbert which he meant to twist into a scroll and throw at her feet in lieu of a bouquet when she came forward to take her call. The others were to do the same. He looked down and agreed that the young woman's hair was magnificent—though not the right colour for him (he was apt to depreciate their finds at first).

Faulkner had been at pains to find out her name and where she lived. Her father kept the best riding horses in Oxford and his daughters rode them : even the most difficult ones. People said that Miss Jane Burden, although she was more than usually tall, managed her horse beautifully—as well as a circus rider. One of the two, Faulkner did not know which it was, was a bedmaker in College.

They all agreed that she did not look English. Her hair, though not her height, her skin of a beautiful clear olive, her full lips were, to Faulkner, suggestive of Semitic origin. Allingham said that her surname was probably a variant of Burton—one of the true gipsy patronymics. More like an Ionian Greek, Jones considered! Well, God knows what strain—the English were such a mixed race—but surely a most wonderful creature, Allingham said, and no one contradicted him. And a perfect model for Guenevere, vice The Sid, away, ill.

It would be all right about sitting, Faulkner thought, if the young lady herself was approached in the right way.

2

No, her father had no objection to Miss Jane's sitting for her face. He told the young ambassadors that she had educated

MISS JANE BURDEN
From a photograph

herself and was a great reader, probably of the kind of poem they liked to illustrate. Faulkner had had a word or two with herself, and had found her kind and complaisant, with beautiful, dull, speedwell-blue eyes. Jones thought them finer than The Sid's light grey ones, which bulged a little. She was tall, taller than Lizzy. Both women had the long, columnar neck now so much admired by Gabriel.

Apt to scent disloyalty to The Sid, Brown was pleased to observe Gabriel's apparent want of interest in the afternoon's work of Jones, Faulkner and Allingham. He said nothing. Nor did Morris, but he hardly took his eyes off Miss Burden and, during the second *entr'acte*, went and stood with his arms on the red plush ledge of the box, talking to Prinsep, but seeing her well through the back of his head, for, in the train next day, he wrote a poem describing her with accuracy.

At a quarter to ten Brown and he started by the London & North-Western, with cheap return tickets—ten and six—for Manchester, where Dixon was going to put them up.

But Morris missed the train coming back and stayed on with Dixon, visiting the Exhibition for the carved ivories, that was all. He returned to the house, to paint an apposite little water-colour—the only one he ever did—of *The Soldan's Daughter in the Palace of Glass* and to write *Praise of my Lady*.

There it all is, her healthy pallor, her brow—" o'ershadowed much by bows of hair "—the slow, deliberate movements of her slim body, " like knight's pennon or slim tree. Set gently waving by the wind," that delighted him,[1] and her long hands, where along the wrist, " the veins crept languidly," her great sad violet eyes, her full lips, pale but " made to kiss," a trifle discontented

Waiting for something, not for me.

The modesty of him, " choking, growing faint " to watch the ways of a maid with a man! And was the man, Rossetti, even then?[2]

3

Let us hear what the women, fundamentally no judges of beauty, have to say about the looks of the daughter of " the

[1] Quiet, just letting it work, in a delicate woman the deadliest and most certain form of attraction for a burly man.

[2] So said Miss Ionides.

palefrenier "[1]   Granting the young lady's eyes fine, Mrs. Boyce would have it that her complexion was coarse, her lips thick and niggerish : that she did not hold herself well and her hands and feet were too large. Developed perhaps overmuch by equestrian exercise so severe as to have been almost professional, it would seem ? One lady told another lady[2] that Miss B. had for certain been in a circus, for no one, except a trained performer, could manage her steed as she could. " Extremely well educated *by herself*," said another, " but made no use of her knowledge because she hardly ever spoke—too timid ! "

And too tall. Every one of them came to resent her noble inches. " She makes us all look like pygmies beside her," little Mrs. Bell Scott complained.[3]

Next day, in Johnson's rooms in George Street, where he and Jones had moved because the men coming up wanted their rooms (there was nowhere for Morris to sleep, so when he came back from Manchester he would have to find himself other digs), Dante Gabriel Rossetti made his first sketch of her. Miss Elizabeth Burden came along too, just to reconnoitre : perhaps what she saw pleased her, or perhaps Miss Jane preferred to sit alone, but, as a fact, she was never again chaperoned, except by numbers.

For this, the first sitting, the obliging young lady did not have to assume one of the costumes run up by Red Lion Mary, but just sat in an easy attitude so that the painter could get the hang of her, keeping on her own everyday dress. It was a light print, nearly white with much washing. At the neck was a muslin collarette with a tiny bow of the same, tied with floating ends, which showed her long full throat, with almost an Adam's Apple. The white dress made her skin look brown and her hair nearly black. She looked like a schoolgirl, and probably felt like one.

[1] Boyce thus prettily indicated the social position of Miss Jane Burden to his proud French wife (a De Soubeyran), in whose eyes Morris himself was merely " a great, noisy, repugnant individual."

[2] Mrs. Hain Friswell.

[3] Indeed, her height and that of Miss Siddall when, after their respective marriages, they became fast friends and chose to dress more or less alike, set the measure for the second flight of Pre-Raphaelite ladies—and models—for they all had to work just as if they weren't married. Mrs. Rossetti was sitting to her husband on the day she died. Mrs. Morris, who thoroughly disliked mediævalism in dress and furniture, although she consented to embroider birds and beasts in crewels, later, when they were house-hunting, told a friend that she would " just as soon have a *brand-new* house if one could have been found."

Some few days later, when Morris returned, Rossetti convened all the fellows to come and have a go at her. He had dressed her up as Queen Guenevere in one of the property dresses, a rich brocade gown patterned with a design of pomegranates set in diagonal chequers. The black sleeves of velvet ended in upturned cuffs, the bodice, tight-fitting, was buttoned down to the navel, then broke into heavy hampering folds about the feet. She was standing beside a tumbled bed, with a little dog lying among the folds of the sheet, close by the chest that served this Queen as a dressing-table, with a bit of white napery over it and a mirror propped up : a plate of apples and a book of Hours. He had invented a good way for her to wear her hands : languidly making the two ends of a girdle approach, so as to clasp it.

There were four of them in the room with their easels drawn up close below the *estrade* : Rossetti, Prinsep, Hughes and Morris. She did not seem to mind how many people profited by the sight of her beauty. Then Gabriel went out for a moment to show Patmore (who had come down to see the work so as to write about it for the Press [1]) the quickest way to the Union, and Morris, who had been scrawling something with a piece of white chalk at the back of his canvas, passed it up to the model when she asked nicely if she might see what they had been making of her. (While Gabriel was in the room she had not ventured.)

" *I cannot paint you but I love you !* " was what Morris had written. She read, and quietly handed the canvas back with the others and he dusted it all off.

Business superseded the Dream for a time at least. Things were going ill for them, in both hemispheres. There was a panic on the American money market so that, instead of the four sources of returns which the interchange on the Exhibitions between New York and Philadelphia would have yielded, the promoters of the stunt would have to fall back on one alone. Money, at the time of writing, was not to be had ; Ruxton could

---

[1] " Sweet, bright and pure as a cloud at sunrise, so brilliant as to make the walls look like the margin of an illustrated manuscript." *Saturday Review*, December 26th, 1857.

hardly get a sovereign changed. They did not hear this until the Exhibition had been open for a fortnight.

And here in Oxford they were "particularly in a muddle."

The members of the Committee were beginning to think that they had been rather rushed into the scheme by Woodward of the angel face. He had let them begin without obtaining sanction. Charles Bowen, the treasurer, admitted irregularity, but spoke so well for his friends that they were only admonished and bidden to use despatch.

The roof across which Morris had been straddling daily for months, spilling paint-pots on defenceless heads, did get itself done by the end of November. First to begin, first to finish : he did nothing by halves in any walk of life or art, letting a thing slide with the same energy with which he had taken it up.[1] Such a subservience as his to Rossetti never was—out of the *Morte d'Arthur*—the surprising services, the impossible mediæval renunciations he made and performed in full consciousness of where they might lead him, submitting his very life and career to the arbitrament of "that hard intellectual force against which few were able to make a stand." To expostulations on this head he had only one short, sharp, schoolboy answer : "Yes, I have got beyond that. I want to imitate Gabriel as much as I can."

He was not one of those whom women love. Like the paladins of whom he wrote—his own Sir Peter Harpdon, simple, clumsy, forthcoming and downright, he did not interest the opposite sex. Pure, as *The Heir*,[2] or modest as poor Palomydes, resigned never to feel

> . . . her warm arms round his neck
> The hot love tears burn deep like spots of lead.

Ever this good knight's complex was the sense of inferiority, the conviction of his unsuccess with women [3] and corresponding failure in Art. Sex-mute but not sex-blind, with an insight that

---

[1] They got to call him at Oxford "Mad Morris." "He used to put his head against a wall and bang it for fun," said the great Pauline (Dr. Walker of St. Paul's School) to me.

[2] When Sir Guy de Morville proposes to Amabel in the back drawing-room at her father's house, there is not such a thing as a closed door. Nay, there is not a lover's kiss in the whole book !

[3] See title of his subject for the wall painting, *How Sir Palomydes loved La Belle Iseult with exceeding great love out of measure and she loved not him again but rather Sir Tristram.*

Stendhal might have envied, a more than hint of the doom of every one of us helpless creatures walking in "this half-sleep, half-strife, that men call living," he knew, like little Swinburne, all the peripatetics of the passion he was unable to inspire. With his uncanny insight, not with his mortal eyes, he now came to visualise the plight of another Pilgrim of Love whom really he did not much like, in the vulgar health-resort which had been chosen for her, surrounded by paralytics and *fausses malades* in bath-chairs, sipping the sour salt waters at the spring or moving slowly among engineered walks of asphalt ; like the others she would be taking her cure but not submitting to it ; restless, yearning, conscious of change and disturbance in the very centres of her life :—

> I cannot stay here all alone
>   Or meet their happy faces here.
>
> A little while and I am gone. . . .

He " saw " The Sid, in a place he did not know, which had never been described to him, in her chosen dell with the old trees whose roots were " fleet," but saved, there under the lea of the cliff, from being uprooted and thrown down, as she too was protected from the gale, lying amid the long grass, kissing it or passing it through her teeth to make a thin, sharp noise. Or on the floor of the wood, as of a Moorish palace, with its arabesque of newly-dropped catkins, coiling in crescent shapes, and the dead leaves lying about like the bellies of speckled toads ! She might have her knees drawn up in Rossetti's favourite attitude of hers, that spring at Scalands four years ago. Morris set her in Joyous Gard in the midst of his favourite orchards down by the sea—the red of apples and the blue of waves—languishing and singing in the form of an incantation—

> Gold Wings across the sea,
> Gold light from tree to tree,
> Gold hair beside my knee,
> I pray thee come to me,
>   Gold Wings !
>
> Gold Wings, the short night slips.
> I pray thee, kiss my lips,
> Gold Wings across the sea.
>
> Gold Wings across the sea,
> Moonlight from tree to tree,
> O sweet knight, come to me.

> Are not my blue eyes sweet?
> Is it not time to meet
> Gold wings across the sea? [1]

Blue eyes, yes, but dark is the fashion now and poor Jehane du Castel-Beau must face it. She could not. The call becomes more imperative—

> Summer cometh to an end
> Undern cometh after noon,
> Golden Wings will be here soon.
> What if I some token send?

She sent it, a doctor's letter; she had got ill.

[1] *Defence of Guenevere*, W. Morris.

CHAPTER XXV

I

"NOVEMBER 14th, 1857," Rossetti unfortunately called away through Miss Siddal's illness at Matlock.

This entry in the diary of Cormell Price is corroborated by an awe-stricken letter, written about this date, by Jones' sweetheart to a girl friend in Birmingham. "Miss Siddal dreadfully ill again."

Rossetti went to her at once and did not return.[1]

Just then a letter came to William from America slinging another stone at the poor defenceless creature, fit to crush her vanity if she had any. Stillman wrote : "We are a sensitive people on some points," and, while admitting that the P.R.B. had "saved the Exhibition as far as oils were concerned," he suggests that the secretary for England should have realised that "the eccentricities of the Pre-Raphaelite School were new to us" and have left out of his selection, among others, *Clerk Saunders* and *The London Magdalen*,[2] "which have their values to the initiated, but to us, generally, are childish and trifling."

Gabriel backed up "my pupil" to Norton. "All I can say is, if they don't like *Clerk Saunders*, they're wrong." By this time she was too seriously ill to be worried by strictures on her art.

Who had told her about Gabriel's new model? Probably Gabriel himself.

She knew the usual run of Oxford belles, the Miss Prices, the Miss Puseys, Faulkner's sisters and Miss Sarah Angelina Acland, all dressed by Miss Boxall. As for Miss Herbert—"My Lady Audley," everyone knew, would not look at a mere artist : she liked lords. And once, in the earlier days at Fortess Terrace, Lizzy had acquired a new garment as the price of her tolerance of Gabriel's inaccessible stage love.[3]

---

[1] He sent a message to Allingham, "Terribly ill, but better now"—that I am here !

[2] Her version of *Found*.

[3] "Gabriel has bought The Sid a superb Indian opera cloak, costing three guineas, and they are for The Princess's, to sport her and it next Saturday."—Diary of F. M. B.

Gabriel had left Oxford in a hurry and the linchpin fell out of the axle of the Union paintings. After March of this year not a brush was laid to the walls by anyone of the original lot, though notices of the work's progress appeared in papers from time to time. For the next two years, indeed, the committee was negotiating with Mr. Rossetti, away, nurse-tending. Steady old Top, left behind in Oxford, could be approached and called upon to render some kind of report,[1] but very soon there was nothing to report on. Scott went down to Oxford, borrowed a ladder and peered about. Only the head of Tristram peeped over the *chevaux de frise* of sunflowers in Morris' attempt to render the subject of his own particular complex;[2] the gorgeous purples and blues of Jones glimmered on faintly, while Rossetti's " Launcelot and the Queen " had utterly disappeared, so that no one could say which of the painter's loves Guenevere was meant to resemble.[3]

" The greatest fiasco ever made by a parcel of men of genius," Scott said. For a long time afterwards, in Academic circles, the phrase " I have come to my Oxford Union " signified down-and-outness in money and credit. The boyish failure of *The Germ* seventeen years ago was transcended by grown men. For the second time the Round Table was dissolved, and this time sister Christina refrained from making sonnets on the subject. They had behaved too badly. Ruskin made it an excuse for seeing less of his friend. People knew why. He did protest too much to William : " But I have a sincere regard for you and your brother and sister—just as much as ever—and I am heartily sorry to see so little of you." The sense of change was over them all and the " sick, sure knowledge that things would never be the same." But at Christmas they did rouse themselves and give a party—their usual party—rather like one of the Mad

[1] He thought there was " some good " in the designs of Pollen and Stanhope if they had been finished, and he protested against the proposal to cover the whole thing with a coat of whitewash, though he had not objected to that as far as his own painting—" ludicrous in some ways "—was concerned. He did the roof over again for them.

[2] *Sir Galahad receiving the San Grail.* " Unfinished," records William dryly.

[3] Certainly not Miss Herbert who, in the end, was put out of the Triptych in favour of Miss Burden.

Hatter's—" Beer and squalor at all hours and a Stunner or two to sing."

The Stunners convened, whoever they were, sang. There was plenty of beer for all and the other thing, but the merriment did not ring true. Gabriel, the recognised cynosure, was " going to hook it to-morrow," presumably to Matlock. Brown was, as usual, gloomy, and more so because his Emma was ill, and Jones because, though his sweetheart was all right, he was too poor to marry her and too ill, so that Mrs. Prinsep—" Aunt Sara "—called on Georgy at her mother's home and asked if she might carry her sweetheart off to Holland House, where he stopped, off and on, for nearly a year. Morris, mostly at Oxford in the society of his old schoolfellows " Crom " Price and Charley Faulkner, regained some of his old casualness, though his engagement to Miss Burden languished, off and on, for nearly a year. But he put his poems together for publication and his Janey sat to his friend for several heads—to illustrate the volume. But it was never illustrated.

3

And, now that it was all over, their " twitterings at dawn " were being collected. Back numbers of *The Germ* were rare and already sought after. Dixon, the favoured cork-cutter, got one from William Allingham as a New Year's gift. Rossetti, who was counted the leader of " the three lettered race," skilfully maintained his legend, refusing absolutely to exhibit in public, so that on his account, little, short-lived, private exhibitions had to be set up, as nearly as possible fulfilling the old P.R.B. ideal of a picture gallery—a room " hung with pictures, decked with flowers,[1] enlivened with music," to which the critics [2] had to go and grumble and vent their spleen on the smaller fry. Madox Brown, who did all the work and got all the kicks, had started in Russell Place, Bloomsbury, what people styled and still style, the

[1] Another piece of " Pre-Raphaelite eccentricity."

[2] " The Brotherhood has taught us at least to be exact, that everything is still unpainted and that there is no finality in art." The same critic is pleased to observe in the " thoughtful " pictures of Mr. Rossetti (other artists have suffered from their pictures being " sicklied over with the pale cast of thought ") that their eccentricities, errors and wilful aberrations were fast modifying and softening. (See Millais', " Hunt too much tamed ! ") But the critic who saw so far into the tortuous Pre-Raphaelite heart, ascribed to the brush of Rossetti poor Brown's masterpiece, *The Last of England*.

Pre-Raphaelite Exhibition. And then there was the Hogarth Club,[1] " that afflictive phenomenon," as Carlyle called it, which met only once, but to which *Bocca Baciata*, counted, so far, the master's finest realistic work, was then drawing crowds. The whole thing, otherwise, was regarded as ridiculous.

Of Ruskin, the arch-critic, the heart was woe and the temper caustic.[2] He was really upset about Lizzy—he could not bear to see the portrait of her rival queening it there !

[1] " Club not small enough to be friendly and not large enough to be important, a room to which nobody sends things and Friday night meetings to which nobody cares to go. Funerals are performed in the shop below through which one passes." The club, Seventeen Piccadilly and, later, Six Waterloo Place, started in 1856. After holding one Exhibition it was dissolved in 1861 and became the Burlington Fine Arts Club. Exhibitors—Boyce, Hughes, Alfred Hunt, Holman Hunt, Burne-Jones, Leighton, Morris, Prinsep, Watts, Windus, Stanhope, Woolner, Woodward, Stephens, Wallis, Mulready, Brown, Inchbold, G. E. Street, Dyce, Cox and Edward Lear. Millais could not join it because he was unable to be in the same club with Ruskin.

[2] He wrote to Alfred Hunt that he had no patience with these Pre-Raphaelite absurdities and that the thing would not answer unless the P.R.B. sent their best work instead of the sweepings of their studios.

CHAPTER XXVI

I

"MISS SIDDALL continues dreadfully out of health," says Oxford, through the mouths of Price and Birkbeck Hill. And, writes Brown in his diary, "Gabriel so unhappy again." "Frightfully fagged and weak and his face-ache so bad as to be almost an illness," Allingham tells the Brownings in his news-letter to them away in Florence. Ruskin details the symptoms to Professor Norton in America: "Gabriel glooms much and is restless and *dulls*[1] himself, wants and wants and I can't amuse him."

Gabriel was vacillating between London, Matlock and Oxford, visiting American fortune-tellers in Bond Street and generally encouraging his natal Dante complex, talking in numbers and the numbers generally nines. Lizzy was working it from Matlock.[2] Nine was *molto amico* to her. Yes, Dante was nearly nine years old when he first saw Beatrice: she was about the same age. An interval of nine years elapsed between this meeting and her denial of his salutation, at the ninth hour of the ninth day. It was nearly nine years since Gabriel had engaged himself to Lizzy. *La gloriosa donna della mia mente* died on the ninth day of June. Lizzy had now nothing of Beatrice but her paleness. She was old too, by women's calendar.

Dante, for some reason or other, consonant with his devotion to Beatrice, feigned a passion for another *donna gentile, bella, giovanna e savia*[3]—the last word would never do for Fanny, the

[1] Anticipatory of the final difficulties, the nightmare of Watts and Hall Caine. Ruskin seems to be hinting at the sort of palliative for neuralgia with which Lizzy brought her Gabriel acquainted.

[2] "Superstition and some pressure from her—light and imperceptible."—*Letters of Birkbeck Hill.*

[3] "No claim of breeding or education or intellect could be made," says William Rossetti, "by Mrs. Hughes." During a discussion on "the burning mountain," as she called Vesuvius, at "Mr. Rizzetty's" she suggested that they ought to put it out by digging at the root. "They have tried," said William, obliged to be civil to her, by the tenure of his brotherhood.

blacksmith's daughter of Essex, out of whose mouth with its row of pearly teeth issued the broadest Cockney. Well, well, the lilies and languors of virtue have always flourished near the roses and raptures of vice, and in the parterre of Red Lion Square florets meet for the hair of Jones' *Blessed Damozel* stood stately, along with ranker, less ethereal blooms.

One day, just after Gabriel had returned from visiting the pale invalid at Matlock and there was a chance of finding him at Number Seventeen, where he was known to paint with Jones every now and then, Brown, who wanted to ask him something about the Working Men's College, called there and found him and Jones with Fanny.

He entered it in his diary, for, at sight of the " beautiful blonde woman " against a background of marigolds which her colouring could well stand up to, he felt that strange aura of misfortune which, although he had met Fanny before, had never visited him so strongly as to-day. The picture was commissioned by Boyce and to be called *Bocca Baciata*.[1]

" A most beautiful head, such a superb thing, so awfully lovely ! . . ." All these superlatives earned by one woman's face ! Arthur Hughes, seeing the picture, wrote off to Allingham to come over quick and see it, for he fully expected that Boyce would have " kissed the dear thing's lips away " before the other could get across the Irish Channel.

Those lips, and the rest, were now for Gabriel only. At least she was faithful. Scott about this time wrote off, to Howell : " A woman of these parts has got Gabriel and will keep him till his death." Naturally Scott hated Fanny, as he hated all Gabriel's intimates, and she disliked him, the dark hairy man from the North who suddenly went bald. Her criticisms would burst out as the door closed behind him : " Oh my, Mr. Scott ! 'E 'as changed ! 'E ain't got a hyebrow or a hyelash—not an 'air on 'is 'ead ! "

They laughed at her and she pouted beautifully ; that was the worst—or the best—of the witch ; " Well, I know I don't say hit right."

[1] " Bocca Baciata " (The Kissed Mouth), a phrase from the *Decameron*. Exhibited at the Hogarth in 1860. Boyce never parted with it. It hung on the left-hand side of the mantelpiece at Glebe House. I often asked who the fair girl with the brown-red hair set in a cluster of marigolds was and was answered with a certain reserve. For Hunt, who like Gabriel, had known her of old, Fanny was just " the large-throated, disagreeable woman Gabriel painted so much."

Brown's wife was ailing, his child dying, he was desperately poor but he was still thinking of other people. The Sid must come back to cope with Fanny. Morris' approaching marriage with Miss Burden was announced, but that of Georgy to Jones still hung fire. They had been engaged for nearly three years, but Jones was patient. "Domesticity is nice," he admitted, but, in his opinion, a man who had any sort of special work to do in the world was better without a mate.[1] He still wanted to copy Gabriel in everything, even in deferred happiness. The Macdonalds had moved to Manchester, but Brown, the kind busy-body, persuaded the young girl's parents to lend her to them in London for an indefinite period. There was a revival of the Thelema scheme and Georgy again looked over houses. But Morris declared that he and Janey meant to have a house all to themselves and began treating for land to build it on out Greenwich way. Morris loved a flat country and its quiet, unassuming sadness. Rossetti was to help to design furniture for him, painting a press [2] with Youths and Loves, and a picture on one of the doors of the Red House. Already in Red Lion Square two girls were stitching away (one of them their best Stunner [3] who had just got off with her life) at some tapestry Morris had designed himself, "queer birds and trees on a greenish-purply ground." So Allingham told Browning in his news-letter.

"Trees, Press and Tapistry greatly conceived indeed!" so Browning wrote back. And later, on the receipt of *The Defence of Guenevere*—" Morris' admirable poems—the only new poems, to my mind, since there's no telling when."

But the volume fell stillborn from the press : the Laureate's version of the story (with one good line in it) overshadowed that of Morris, as a dashing dahlia a low-lying pot-herb. Morris

---

[1] So his nephew wrote much later.

> " White hands cling to the bridle rein,
> Red lips tarnish the scabbarded steel.
> He travels fastest who travels alone."

But Georgy helped him.

[2] A young man in a mantle on a gold ground betwixt the sun and moon. Said Birkbeck Hill, " What could one put in such a press ? "

[3] Madeline Smith, living in a London boarding-house very miserably since her acquittal, for her mother had treated her with great unkindness, not allowing her so much as to come into the drawing-room when callers were there. She married one of Morris' men.

luckily had the bank balance Allingham spoke of; and the "Towers of Topsy" soon rose, not at Greenwich but in the Valley of the Darenth, and Morris and Miss Burden were married [1] by Canon Dixon that April in the little old church of St. Michael's at Oxford. Faulkner was best man—Jones was there but not Rossetti. Then a six weeks' tour in Belgium, Paris and the Rhine. The house was not ready for them, so when they came back, they took furnished rooms in Great Ormond Street. It was not all Gabriel's fault, for he had set to work on his doors and finished them in a week—for Janey, it seems, he could spur himself. And Georgy Macdonald went there to call upon the bride whom she had not yet seen. "Never shall I forget it!" She was smitten with an admiration that was only surpassed by that which afterwards possessed her for Lizzy.

3

Rossetti never wrote to him now; but as autumn slid into winter, Allingham found himself on the old road to Blackfriars and shaking hands with his dear Gabriel " as if nothing were "—Gabriel's way when he was in fault—and spending three delightful hours with him in the studio, smoking away as of old. William and Arthur Hughes were there too, as it were, playing hide-and-seek among the canvases, for Rossetti had begun the big compartment of the triptych depicting the Infant Saviour on the knees of the Madonna—for which Miss Herbert had given one sitting [2] —being adored by Shepherds and a King. Most of the pictures were religious, with a dash of Socialism,[3] perhaps attributable to the idiosyncrasies of Rossetti's chief buyers, Colonel Gillum (introduced by Browning), who ran a Boys' Home, and Mr. Plint, a Nonconformist penetrated with the teachings of Canon Kingsley, of whose envisagement of artists and their uses in the world, all who attended his lectures were aware.[4]

[1] A Mrs. Hain Friswell says " the man was a heathen "; married in his own drawing-room and " by a ceremony of a curious character " which he afterwards had painted on a wall.

[2] It is Mrs. Morris now.

[3] " My dear Sir . . . could you introduce *both* Carlyle and Kingsley, and change one of the four *fashionable* young ladies into a *quiet, earnest, holy*-looking one, with a book or two and tracts? I want *this* put in, for I am much interested in *this* work myself, and know those who are." Plint to Rossetti.

[4] " Aristocracies of mere birth decay and give place to aristocracies of mere wealth and then again to aristocracies of genius, which are really aristocracies of the

MRS. WILLIAM MORRIS
From a photograph

There was a Christ head done from Jones, commissioned by a dealer who was beginning to see that there was money in Gabriel, and, what Allingham liked much better, the *Mary in the House of John*, an illustration, cynical in all seriousness, of the cruelty and futility of the Crucifixion. He had painted the Virgin and St. Anne, just two bereaved old women in their house on the wall of Jerusalem, looking out of the window, Mary parting with one hand the blue curtain so as to see in the fading light the outline of the Hill where, many years ago, her life and her hope went down, with the headstrong gesture of her Son.

Gabriel had tidied up his room—or someone had done it for him. His pictures were hung on nails instead of forming an indistinguishable part of the sagging stack of canvases and portfolios under the window-ledge. His personal appearance was neater, though, with a bad figure, he could never have looked as smart as William, always considered " a marvellous swell."

" Dear old buffers, both ! " Hughes and Allingham agreed as they walked away—William " pursuing his serene and gracious way as usual," Gabriel settling down and the triptych " awfully jolly ! " So Hughes.

To the Brownings, always eager for news of this family, Allingham wrote : " The Rossettis I saw, all well and going on as usual."

He knew they were *not* going on as usual and Gabriel most certainly not well and much altered.

4

In December, Hunt had returned from the East—illish but famous. Tales of his artistic exploits and dangers run made their way home and Annie Miller, " sitting " all over the place now, smiled her smug smile. Hunt had been living through the winter on the shores of the Dead Sea, all alone, with an Arab and a goat. He was the only Christian to penetrate into the Mosque of Omar. He had nearly been assassinated. He had only just missed being elected a member of the Royal Academy [1]

---

merest scribblers and sprouters." Charles Kingsley at Crewe in a lecture in 1871. But he wrote of " mountains, silver veined with rills, cataracts of white cotton thread zigzagging down every rock-face." His bark was worse than his scribble.

[1] He had " tied " in voting with a great friend of his, but no relation, another Pre-Raphaelite artist of the same surname—Alfred Hunt. Neither was then elected or even came near it again.

and he was going to snub them properly. His picture was ready and he intended to show it all by himself. He took Hook's house on Campden Hill, with a high tower from which he could paint sunsets, and was settling up with Annie. He did not intend to marry her now.

" You remember Miss Miller, doubtless ? She has been sitting again to Rossetti and myself." So wrote Boyce to Allingham. She had " gone professional " as a result of Rossetti's fulsome encouragement, abandoning her home at Chelsea and the lectures that Hunt was paying for—emancipating herself thoroughly. She now lived in Augusta Place, near Clapham Road. Hunt wrestled with her for the soul that professional modelhood might endanger but, according to all accounts, her " determination to go on sitting was entirely her own " and could not be shaken. Hunt was upset : he had not yet met the beautiful woman who made Miss Miller's defalcation a matter of no moment to him.

William Rossetti, the best brother a man ever had, admits that *his* was " properly, but not deeply, censurable in this matter." [1]

5

By the end of next year Brown was so hard up that when little Arthur [2] died after three days' illness he had to borrow the money to bury him. Woolner, who had been lucky enough to secure a Llandaff commission too, but was not so favoured in the matter of advances as Rossetti, declared himself to be earning exactly fourpence a day. Jones, prudent, dared not marry—with the contingency of a family to keep.

And " A Happy Christmas to you all ! " was Gabriel's pious wish from Paris at that date. For the " Head of the Pre-Raphaelite School in England " had had to cross the water to escape the complimentary duns of the season.

There was no particular reason for him to be hard up. Though Art does not, so to speak, pay, his did pretty well. He had at least four steady buyers, Colonel Gillum—who was paying him a

[1] Grant Allen saw " the making of a novel in the whole affair," but he never wrote it. Annie Miller is the one Pre-Raphaelite heroine who has, perhaps out of consideration for these two great men, been " kept dark," and references to her in P.R.B. memoirs are scanty, though in the 'sixties and 'seventies her name was on every tongue.

[2] Lizzy always had that baby on her conscience. Taken up and carried out at night to Hampstead and laid on the sofa while its mother ministered to her in her extremity, it had not had a chance.

regular sum per quarter as advance on work in hand—Messrs. Leatheart of Newcastle and Rae of Birkenhead and the Misses Bell and Heaton. Miss Baring had just commissioned *The Magdalen at the Door of Simon the Pharisee* [1] in pen-and-ink, for fifty pounds. Lady Trevelyan of Wallington was coming forward for *Mary in the House of John*, when it should be finished. Plint had given him forty-two pounds for the pen-and-ink drawing of *Hamlet and Ophelia*, for which Howell had sat, and thirty-one for a little water-colour of *Guenevere*. Of this, in oils, the price would have been three hundred and sixty-seven pounds. For a water-colour portrait of Miss Macdonald as *My Lady Greensleeves* (as they sometimes called Jones' Stunner) he got a hundred and five pounds. And Mr. Leatheart, at Scott's suggestion, had re-commissioned the illusive and accursed *Found* for three hundred and sixty-seven pounds. [2]

But the sheet-anchor of his monetary position was now the triptych which, so his brother asserted, " might be going " to bring him in four hundred pounds. [3] He would keep fiddling with sections of it, hesitating to begin the centre compartment, which, singly, was to bring two hundred pounds, continually bothering Seddon for advances, " feeling sure that it would not be finished for some time to come. . . ."

Taking it all round, he was in a better position to marry now than he was ever likely to be again. The bar to their union on Lizzy's side had gone in the person of the old man, her father. [4] Before his death he had come down a little. He admired Rossetti's poetry, of which Liz had sent him specimens now and then, and he used to read it aloud o' nights to the family circle, sandwiched in between large tracts of Dickens. But he would never have consented to a Sudel or Sidel of Hope marrying a man who was not even an Esquire (as *he* was, if we all got our rights), one of the cheap-boozing, hard-drinking, out-at-elbow, knocker-wrenching crew, with not so much as a spare shirt to their backs

[1] Sala, in Brompton Square, had a photograph, signed. Rossetti had, says G. S., two models for it, one an actress and the rest was done from a typically Pre-Raphaelite model (whatever that might mean to Sala ?).

[2] It had at first seemed necessary that Rossetti should go to Newcastle to secure this splendid commission, but, as Mr. Leatheart was good enough to settle for the sum, he disappointed Mr. and Mrs. Scott and from William, who had been going to pay his fare, borrowed a " few pounds for home use."

[3] " He didn't take less and possibly got more," says William.

[4] There is no photograph extant of Mrs. Siddall. One, as a young girl, the husband carried about with him and when he died it was put in his coffin.

or a whole pair of shoes between them, so he understood. "A business man" (thus he set himself down) in those days regarded an artist much as a Don an undergraduate.[1]

As a social gloss to the unconscionable protraction of the engagement Lizzy had given countenance to the idea of her father's unwillingness to part with her so disadvantageously. But that tale would not work now: Charles Crookes Siddall had died of gastritis, at the age of fifty-nine in July, and was buried in Victoria Old Cemetery at Hackney. Gabriel Rossetti had nominally been engaged to his daughter for the last nine years.

The Cabbalistic number again!

6

Gabriel began to astound his circle by talking of settling down, so seriously that brother William, flustered out of his usual discretion, felt the need of a confidant and bethought him of Scott, the friend of his boyhood, witness of perhaps his one and only recorded escapade—and that was political![2]

He got hold of Scott and asked him if he was aware that Gabriel was intending to take this important step pretty soon? No, it was news to Scott, always professing himself to be surprised at nothing. From the date of that dark evening in The Hermitage, when Gabriel, not trusting his old friend, had neglected to introduce his girl to him, there dated, in Scott's mind, Gabriel's revision of any project of marriage. Oh, he was probably fond of her still, but she had been his Stunner too long: there were others: it was Annie and Fanny and God knows who

[1] Miss Ethel Newcome threw over her cousin Clive for the Marquis of Farintosh, not only because she was worldly but because she knew that, after marriage, her society must inevitably consist of Fred Bayham and his like, while Clive fell back on the pretty daughter of his landlady. Nor were Mr. Rossetti's own friends entirely free from these notions, while discriminating between the general and the particular. Birkbeck Hill liked to go about with the artists, but this is how he wrote to his sweetheart about artistic society: "Faulkner, Morris—poet and artist—and myself rowed three or four miles down the river to play skittles in a low tavern, five games, and drank two quarts of cider on Saturday afternoon, when all the low people were about. Think of that!"

[2] Once, when the two boys were staying with the Scotts, they attended a Methodist Revival Meeting on the Town Moor—Brother Speedman eloquently speaking. Young William exhibited the revolutionary bias he never abandoned (even when he became a Civil servant), interrupted the meeting and was reprimanded.

else ? It had been Barbara once, with the " tin " and the hair. Gabriel seemed always to go mad over women's hair and coloration.

Mr. Scott sat with William, while Gabriel was away at Matlock, William delicately mending the fire when it didn't need it, in a studio filled with what Scott was pleased to call examples of his brother's " late development." He got William to agree with him that Gabriel had, in process of years, become " more susceptible to influences which might prevent " him settling down into an even way of life. Yet, he pleaded for his brother. Gabriel neither smoked, betted, gambled nor drank. And, as for his unpunctuality, the irregular hours he kept, hardly ever going to bed until three or four in the morning, the frowst of his " digs "—never a window open, all the latches stuck, the stream of boon companions lurching in at any minute, for he was a man much in request, every hour bespoke—Miss Siddall was an artist herself and used to Gabriel's ways ! so Scott, sharply. He knew all about that, their keeping house together every now and then in Chatham Place so that she never until lately had been able to let her family know exactly where she was to be looked for or written to at any given moment.

CHAPTER XXVII

I

SO said they and so thought they, and meanwhile she would be sitting, poor Burd Alane, in the window of her sitting-room on the ground floor of the Hastings lodging, in her usual, forlorn, nervous attitude, one hand clasping the elbow of the other arm, of which the wide upper sleeve of striped brown and black silk disclosed the black velvet under-sleeve, tight to the wrist. The gesture seemed somehow to hold her together, in a world that was slipping away. By herself nearly all day, except for the kind landlady running in every now and then to have a look at her lodger and a " How are you to-day, Miss ? " and then—the sad, stiff, seaside door closed carefully against the wind, ballooning under the carpet. . . .

Number Twelve Beach Houses—a stone near the door said 1700—was a very old structure indeed, modernised. A pagoda-like series of bow windows reaching to the very top had been thrown out and stone steps—eight—led up to the front door. The low-ceiled rooms were papered with bunches of poppies and daisies, like a child's tossed bouquet, the window continually lashed with spray when the wind was at the back of the incoming tide, and always the smell of fish, trailed, gutted, packed and tossed into crates for London before her eyes. . . .

She seemed to herself full as repulsive—sick, sick continually, a thing of disgust—deserving of avoidance by all.

At last Mr. Chatfield had the sense to look up the address on the letters he occasionally took to the post, always the same, except for one or two addressed to a Mrs. Wheeler at Barnsbury. Mrs. Chatfield knew that her boarder was supposed to be engaged to a Mr. Rossetti and she wrote—Miss Siddal said she might—to say that the lady desired to see him and bid him Good-bye before she died.

It was not the first time this had happened to Gabriel. He

236

was hard at work—by way of beginning the centre compartment of the triptych. . . . But Gold Hair had sent for Gold Wings, and he went !

<h2 style="text-align:center">2</h2>

She was not crying Wolf ! It was desperately true. He wrote to his mother on arrival—" She is dying daily and more than once a day," lying prone after one of these gastric spasms as if she would never " lift that golden head again." Gabriel arranged to stay down to nurse her, as was proper. He refused Emma Brown's offer to come and perform this office, saying that he fancied Liz preferred being alone with him, and that the sight was really far too painful for anybody else—outside the family—to bear. Then he settled down, as it were, to his pious task with a kind of exaltation, like Swinburne's lover tending his leprous mistress,

> Changed with disease, her body sweet,
> The body of love wherein she abode,

but owned that it was almost too much for him, who had never offered or been called upon to nurse anyone before—the squalor and intimate services of illness, the sounds—convulsive *hoquets*, gurgles and reachings, heavings and contractings of the riven body of a love lying there and all conscious of its degradation. . . .

> I pray you, let me be at peace.
> Get hence, make room for me to die.

Almost any woman, not only a princess, would say that. Of it all, Gabriel, a Latin, was able to give his mother details in language of an almost epic frankness. He had never known anything like it—the obliteration of personal vanity in pain—" that kind of pain which one can never remember at its full." It made him feel as if he himself were " living in a vault." He would rise from his chair at her bedside when she did get to sleep and pace backwards and forwards between their rooms, looking from the window on the front on fine days, past the Fish Market and the boats, to " where the sea ends, in a sad blueness beyond rhyme." And at night, from his own window at the back, he would watch the townspeople dancing by candle-light before the mouths of the Smugglers' Caves behind St. Clement's Church, where he must take her the moment she was able to get up, for she was at any rate to die a married woman. But she

237

must not die. If he were to lose her now he would go mad; so he told William, who had written nicely and of whose affection he owned never before to have stood in such need. He had been to a stationer's and ordered, to please her, notepaper stamped with her future initials (a gesture counted unlucky). And on Friday the 13th of April, he announced their marriage as likely to take place in a few days and he might be coming up for half a day to get some money he had left in a drawer at home. . . .

"I have hardly deserved that Lizzy should still consent to it, but she has done so." [1] (Perhaps she had just been able to wag, in confirmation, that lovely head, supine on the pillow.) And he trusted that he might still have " time to prove his thankfulness to her " and they would go straight to Chatham Place. There would be no wedding trip—he had too much work on hand.

But, by the 17th of the month, she was dreadfully ill again. Gabriel told them she had been as bad before in many respects but not in all respects at once, as now. The weather was against her : she was always affected by it. When it was fine she was able to take beef-tea and jelly without bringing them up again, but now she could not even keep a glass of water down and, if it could not be stopped, she would die of starvation and exhaustion.

Mindful of his promise, on which she was now too weak to insist, he was endeavouring to secure a special licence, for even if she recovered sufficiently to go through the ceremony it would be bad for her to enter a cold church. But a special licence meant delay, so he trusted to God he might be able to use the ordinary one he had in his pocket, for, if he could not, " there would be so much to grieve over and . . . to reproach myself with, that I do not know how it might end with me." [2] Threatening suicide—selfish even in his best moments !

His mother was evidently aware of these things with which he had to reproach himself and blamed, though she had not prevented them. Maybe, stern and undeceiving of self, a Roman matron if ever there was one, she was aware that she and Maria and Christina had cause for self-condemnation too.

---

[1] *Family Letters*, William Rossetti.   [2] *Ibid.*

3

Allingham, in his usual news-letter, told the Brownings all the town news about the Lords and the Paper Duty, Home the Spiritualist, the London Riflemen—how all public resorts were dotted with blue, grey and green uniforms and reviews of about twenty-five thousand of them in the Park—" And now to smaller matters. Gabriel Rossetti was married three weeks ago to Miss Siddal, whom you have heard of—once a model—with a talent for drawing and long very sickly, as she still is, I am sorry to say. They are supposed to be in Paris. . . . Rossetti's manner of working is not altered."

Trust a loving woman's will-power working to an end! On the 22nd day of May Gabriel had written to his mother from Hastings to say that there had been an improvement, sudden, unaccountable! She had got out of bed, dressed and come downstairs to the sitting-room; and ate—not much—without having to bring it all up again as soon as she had swallowed it. Next day he had got Mr. Nightingale to marry them.

Dante Gabriel Rossetti, Artist. Bachelor. Son of Gabriele Rossetti of Vasto, to Elizabeth Eleanor Siddall,[1] daughter of Charles Siddall, Optician, both of full age. Witnesses, Alfred and Jane Chatfield. Elizabeth Eleanor's signature, like a cockroach scrawling over the tiny oblong indicated for signature, suggests her weakness, while the second " l " in the letters of her name is hardly made out at all. But it served. She was married so, by the skin of her teeth.

Love, like Greek fire over a cold altar, played about the heads of these persons, both of them making do with an old spent impetus, the one anxious to placate his God by offering amends for procrastination, the other in feverish haste to cheat Death, but drawing down, Heaven knows what form of vengeance for her withdrawal, in the past, from Nature's simple purposes until it was almost too late. A dreary couple: she, temporarily invigorated by the long-desired consummation, little more—he, mildly pleased with pleasing her! Everything was to be done as she wanted, and Paris was the place where she sometimes felt well. So Paris it was to be, and this very afternoon they would try to get to Folkestone.

Gabriel wrote a few letters while Mrs. Chatfield prepared her

[1] Perhaps she wanted to be on the safe side. The wilful alteration he had made in her name would not, maybe, have stood in law.

for the journey. To Brown he said, " I can't really give you any good news of her health, but we must hope for the best." It was just possible they might get as far as Folkestone without a relapse. To William, business; he sketched an announcement of the marriage, for *The Times*—" If the governor's birthplace is wrong, please alter." And he begged William to see about letting the studio for a bit, as he was not likely to want to use it for some time to come except for a day or two now and then. What about some painter of his acquaintance who would not mind the owner dropping in for an hour or two now and again ? He had settled in his own mind that Chatham Place would not suit Lizzy, though she would be certain to clamour to go back there at once if she survived the honeymoon ! A locum tenens was the best way to stop her.[1]

They reached Boulogne that day with only the usual concomitants—she was used to being sick—and put up with some friends of Mr. Ruskin's, the Maenzas,[2] in the Grande Rue, leading straight up from the Port to the real Boulogne, the walled and bastioned city at the top of the hill which she was never to climb. In the mornings they walked about the Port. Madame Maenza told her that Monsieur Ruskin used to go out, from here, mackerel fishing, off Hastings, at five o'clock in the morning, about the time Mrs. Rossetti was living in that town. In the afternoons they took proper little drives along the coast, to Wimille and St. Marquis, and along the St. Omer Road. There were not then any villas to break the grey, flat line of the sea-shore, from which England even on the very finest days never looked as nice as Boulogne from England. They were only French châteaus, like English country houses, and one of them was to let, with a garden from which Rossetti could get any amount of backgrounds. He proposed to get rid of Chatham Place in its favour. She did not care about it, and when she had recovered from the crossing and was safe in Paris, which agreed with her—" as it always does "— Gabriel waived the château—" The Boulogne scheme is given up, I believe."

---

[1] William, on May 23rd, thinks he can " comfortably " let it to Allingham, an old friend of Gabriel's, and writes to adumbrate the scheme. If Allingham cares to write he will find that he can " comfortably " place the rooms at his disposal. Allingham did not take them. The Rossettis themselves came there straight from Paris.

[2] Madame Maenza was the old lady in whom Ruskin long took an interest, so that Howell, his factotum, was several times sent to Boulogne to relieve her necessities.

The Hôtel Meurice was expensive, and after a week they moved to lodgings in the Rue de Rivoli—the less favoured end—where the landlady was an Englishwoman called Houston. They settled down and began some work, painting, sitting and reading aloud to each other. Rossetti had friends in Paris but made no effort to look them up. They were reading Boswell, and he painted *Doctor Johnson and The Ladies of the Town* sitting at the Cheshire Cheese, and *How They Met Themselves*, an illustration of the old German superstition of the *Döppelganger*, he and Lizzy meeting their doubles in an enchanted wood and, half swooning, brought suddenly face to face with their own painful dual personalities.

She began a little water-colour called *The Woeful Victory*, for she had got Gabriel and all that it meant !

4

The meeting with the Joneses did not come off. They had been married on a Saturday in June and went to Chester on their way to join the Rossettis in Paris. But on Sunday morning Jones was speechless with a cold on his chest ; the journey to France had to be given up. His letters are coloured deep with disappointment. He sends his love—" I wish it was such stuff as Indian carpets for her to walk on "—to Lizzy, whom, in Chatham Place, he had never noticed. But now, he " hoped she'd stand him . . . he'd do anything to be agreeable and so would Georgy." He signs his name in a new way which he hopes Gabriel will notice—his Aunt Keturah's married name hyphened with the other, which he was just beginning to use. A married artist must neglect no opportunity of fixing his name on people's memory.

The bottom was knocked out of Paris by the secession of the Burne-Joneses and Rossetti said it was time he went home and got to work on *Found* :—" There is so much money in the picture if only I could get it finished ! " And Lizzy was anxious to see again the Hampstead doctor, Crellin, the only one who had ever done her any good. They were both tired of " dragging about," having become aware by now of the subtly fatiguing quality of the Paris air and their feet blistered by the stone pavements that seemed, in the heat, to rise up and hit you. Hunting about in the old *quartiers*, Gabriel had bought her some lovely necklaces and a couple of dogs—one called Punch. (" What fun ! You'll buy horses next ! " Jones chaffed.)   But they had spent all their money !   Just as they left the platform of the Gare du Nord they got hold of an English paper and saw the account of the death of a friend—bankrupt [1]—and the dreadful position of his starving wife and children.   Lizzy was wearing, to carry them, all the beautiful things Rossetti had bought her.   God's Pre-Raphaelite children : they were both full of immediate, picturesque benevolence and, on arrival at Charing Cross, stopped their cab at a pawnbroker's where Lizzy lifted the necklaces straight off her neck for Gabriel to sell, and they took the proceeds to Mrs. Brough at her lodgings in the Borough before going on to Chatham Place.

5

On their return the newly-married pair learned—through Mrs. Letitia Scott, who had been to see her there—that his sister and her sister-in-law had become an Associate of St. Mary Magdalene's Home at Highgate (for Fallen Women) and wore the habit.[2]   There was no word of this from the family to Gabriel, no letter from any member of it, and for all the desolate bride could tell the wedding day might have been taken as one of mourning in Albany Street—perhaps Maria went twice to church that day ?   None of his mother's answers—if there were any—to Gabriel's letters from Hastings announcing his marriage are extant.   Perhaps " Old Antique " did not answer them. More probably she wrote what was adequate, for she was a courtly sort of old woman.   Lizzy had hoped to find a particular welcome for herself from Gabriel's mother on her arrival at Chatham Place as a bride.   Gabriel knew better.   Though his mother had shown sympathy, listening to his agonised accounts of what was happening at Hastings, it was only because she did not want him to go mad on account of the crime he had only just escaped committing.   A soul, through his *laches*, dying impenitent, unas-

---

[1] Robert Brough, a Bohemian of the first water, was author of some strong anti-social ballads.   Rossetti was never tired of quoting one from his burlesque of *Medea*, about " Lord Tom-Noddy, the son of an earl," and petted accordingly :—

A full-blown colonel at twenty-one
Is Lord Fitzdottrell's only son.

Brough was bankrupt in 1858.   There had been a Benefit for him at Drury Lane in July of this year, in which Miss Herbert had taken part.

[2] " A simple, elegant black gown with hanging sleeves and a muslin cap with a lace edging and veil, very becoming to her."   So Mrs. Scott, who went to call and found her walking about the grounds with a bishop.

CHRISTINA ROSSETTI
From a photograph

soilsied by any rites, for his sweetheart was, they had always known, deeply, subtly irreligious. "Old Antique" was thankful that in marrying, she had let him have a formal service of some sort. Kind-hearted Gabriel! Too good for Lizzy, as every mother's son is too good for the girl he wants—or feels he ought—to marry.

Nor are Miss Rossetti's impressions of her new relation anywhere adumbrated, either in letter, verse or speech. Christina was a great lady. William was equally punctilious in his estimate and his dealings with his plaguey sister-in-law. The pensive, polarised philosopher, full of fairly good intentions towards her, was disconcerted by the determined *noli tangere* of the mind which Lizzy practised with regard to him and nearly everybody. She had, he averred, a way of turning off the conversation, just when he fancied he was getting forrarder, casting what he called " a dry light on the subject," leaving it exactly as it was so far as her own point of view was concerned, giving " dusty answers," paying out mere lightsome chaff. . . . Flighty! That was the word. One never knew where to have her. That this manœuvreing for position was sub-intentional there is not the slightest doubt. The fay *par excellence!* William's adjective for her explains, really, everything.

But, honest, William did not dismiss her as a nobody. He knew better. The woman who could interest Swinburne could not have been a fool, since mere beauty had no lure for him.

And Christina had not understood. It was too near : Lizzy's long agony was at once too personal and its early symptoms too puzzling and recondite. In the Home on the Hill she escaped them and could consider the sorrows and trials of yellow canaries, furry wombats and dormice. As far as human beings were concerned she had more sympathy with the Marian Erles of this world than with prim and prudent maidens who insist on the ring, and being received into their lover's family before consenting to crown his flame.

So, deliberately, it would seem, Lavinia, Maria and Christina chose to leave this soul duly to perish, because it would not accord itself in any way to their mould. None of the women of her husband's family were about when Lizzy broke up and, except for her own sister, young and inevitably preoccupied with her own affairs, she lived and died, an exile of the heart.

CHAPTER XXVIII

I

THIS was the first blow dealt, the first hint of what was to come. The daughter of Heth, married into an alien tribe, fending for herself and reinforced by weakness, created a legend wherewithal to arm herself against the slings and arrows of her new kin. Mrs. Scott, on a visit to town that summer while her husband was in Ayrshire, sunning himself in the rays of his Egeria's [1] calm and considered affection, wrote to tell him the London news and the names of the people who had come to dinner that night in Aubrey Road. There was, she said, Mrs. William Morris, tall and stately, " looking un-English," dining in her bonnet because she had to catch a train back home that night; Mrs. Edward Jones, " a little thing " singing French songs after dinner " in a high, wild voice, quite novel and charming," while her young husband, " looking like a schoolboy " in spite of his yellow beard, turned over the leaves for her. But to Mrs. Scott's evident chagrin, the new Mrs. Rossetti " is invisible to everyone . . . has not yet been seen in the house of his mother."

No, not ever or hardly ever. She had been a good girl, withholding herself, like any Victorian maiden to whom " the orange-blossom is the fox's brush of married life." [2] The fay had been at pains to constitute herself the respectable daughter and sister-in-law, accepting the usual obligations of conventionality and lip-service. . . . And all she got was—a waste-paper basket [3] a year later !

2

And Chatham Place did not do. She got ill again and went back to the Hampstead cottage. Thence they could look over

---

[1] Miss Alice Boyd. [2] *Plain or Ringlets*, Cuthbert Bede.
[3] " Please thank Christina for her paper-box, which will come in very useful."
D. G. R. to his mother, January 1861.

houses—there or at Highgate. She seemed able to exist on these heights only. Gabriel came to her every day, returning to his own rooms to sleep.

She had not yet been introduced to Ned Jones' wife. The tale of her beauty, the bulletins from Matlock the year before had, for Georgy, made Gabriel's new wife into a legendary personage, a Melusine, a Tiphaïne out of the old French legends that Ned and she read up for subjects; her excitement was intense when came the day appointed for the meeting by the Wombats' Lair in the Zoo. The Browns were going too. And while Gabriel was rattling his stick between the bars, trying to poke up the owls into a vulgar fury, little Mrs. Jones gloated on the slender elegant figure of Mrs. Rossetti, the details of her bonnet—not so ugly and pokesome as most—of her dress made in the fashion, but with tiny differences that a woman would notice at once. For most men except Gabriel this Stunner had no particular sexual appeal; but the girl who had, after her first interview with another Stunner, Jane Burden, gone home and literally dreamed of her in the night, prepared for Gabriel's by the fulsome praise of his disciples, her zeal sharpened by the delays and difficulties of meeting, found her " as beautiful as in imagination—poor thing ! "

The use of that tender, popular phrase of commiseration, the hint of some unformulated ill that might lie in wait for sov'ran, yet vulnerable, beauty betrayed the thought that leaped to the little woman's mind as she followed the tall one upstairs into the bedroom with its latticed window and tiny panes that made it rather dark to see to do one's hair. Mrs. Rossetti could never have known that difficulty ; she just waved her hand at the bed, where Georgy was to lay her bonnet, and took hers off without looking into the glass. Ringlets had been lately exchanged by Fashion for bandeaux—hair was, just now, often confined in gold silk nets—but Lizzy wore neither. The resilient loops and bows which her bonnet had imprisoned leaped out unruffled and, without the aid of brush or comb, lay in ordered disorder on each side of her face, like the folded wings of the Cherubim singing in their quires, saluting each other in the morning, as in young Millais' design for a Gothic window which Ruskin had once shown her.[1]

[1] At Glenfinlas he and Ruskin went " pitching into architecture " and made designs for church windows on grocers' paper from the village shop. Ruskin used this one of Millais' at his Edinburgh Lectures.

And Georgy always declared that she then and there, once and for all, got a sense of the romance and tragedy that were mingled in the life-web of these two. For them already Love had folded his wings, ever so gently, decently and in order, without vulgar fuss and flutter. Though their desperate quarrels had not begun, Love's amenity was for ever foregone between the man and the woman, who, as soon as they got downstairs again, allowed Gabriel to produce and show with pride, her sinister drawing, done in Paris, *The Woeful Victory.*

The daughter of the Methodist Minister, whose foregathering in childhood had been confined to certain worthy and calculable types, whose reading had been carefully regulated—she and her sisters were not allowed to read even Shakespeare—had never seen anything like this wonderful creature, weary and wayward, with her slight artificiality of manner, her rather upsetting mixture of humour and tenderness, of melancholy alternating with excitement—not to call it flightiness. Georgy Jones, like William Rossetti, felt some strain in association with one whose values were so utterly different. All the time she was conscious of variations in the soul's barometer of her companion, as a fly might sense a thunderstorm far away. Shrewdly she noticed that Mrs. Rossetti seemed to calm down when her husband sat beside her on the sofa and took her hand and called her "Guggums"—and then, even the silly little hiss went out of her voice.

Her complexion never altered—a rose-leaf with the light shining through. Fays never did show when they were ill, neither did they really ever die, still they could not live just anywhere, but made conditions. . . . Perhaps this one had her Saturday nights when she chose to be invisible, like Melusine? [1] . . .

[1] Melusine, the famous ghost of the House of Lusignan, the daughter of a King condemned by a witch whom she had offended, on one day in seven to be a snake from the waist downwards, with a tail, grey and sky-blue mixed with white, until she should meet a man who would marry her on the condition that he never looked on her on a Saturday. Count Raymond of Lusignan broke his promise, peeped, and lost her for ever. He died a hermit on Monserrat and Melusine still haunts the castle when a Lusignan is about to die. And there was Dame Tiphaïne, the fairy-wife of the Connétable Du Guesclin, *bonne et sage* and an expert astronomer.

Rossetti was anxious to placate Christina in Lizzy's favour, so another day they all visited the Maze at Hampton Court, for him to get his illustration to Christina's *Prince's Progress*, but, when they got there, for some reason, he refused to go into the Maze at all—said he was afraid of getting lost!—and just took the plan from the Guide Book.

And later, Miss Siddal condescended to go to see Georgy at her home and they started the illustrations for the book of Fairy Tales they were bringing out together—Georgy had learned, at Mr. Brown's classes, to engrave on wood very nicely. Lizzy would bring her sewing and use Georgy's wonderful sewing-machine that Mr. Watts had given her as a wedding present :—" A little thing that makes dresses and buys the stuff and almost pays for it "—so Ned chaffed them, as he chaffed Georgy's sister Louie,[1] pretty, short-sighted and a tremendous flirt ; he swore he always could tell, even at a distance, if she was talking to a man or a woman, by the shape of her shoulders. Lizzy wanted Georgy to know her sister, so she and Georgy met Louie and went to see Lyddy in Barbara Street, a turning out of the Roman road opposite Pentonville Prison yard, where you could see the prisoners exercising—and other excursions if Liz was well enough ; one never knew beforehand. . . .

Mrs. Ned had heard from Emma Brown, loosely, the opinion of the doctor to whom Lizzy had let herself be taken some years ago. He had diagnosed her complaint then as consumption of the lungs. She had heard Lizzy's brother-in-law talk of curvature. Now, after seeing Lizzy herself, she was inclined to agree with dear Dr. Acland, who had once had the patient under observation for a whole fortnight—as far as the wilful girl would let him (she had been very naughty at Oxford : Ned had seen Dr. Acland's letter to Ruskin). Acland had considered the lungs to be only very slightly affected : the prime cause of ill health, in his opinion, was " mental power long pent up and lately over-taxed."

He evidently thought Lizzy clever, with a lot in her, and, as for " over-taxing," Georgy had had every opportunity of observing Gabriel's effect on her own Ned, who had had to flee from him to the ward of the Prinseps for nearly a year, and poor old Morris, whom he had stimulated almost to death in the forcing-house of his godhead.

[1] Afterwards Mrs. Baldwin, the mother of a Prime Minister.

Georgy thought that all Miss Siddal really wanted was a good rest. Had she only fallen in with Barbara Leigh-Smith's plans for her some years ago and gone into the Sanatorium in Euston Road she might have been well to-day, instead of posing as the " frail wretch " of Gabriel's sonnet, whose " spirit rends while his body endures "—till it can no longer. Georgy, indeed, felt the cold aura of doom, mingling with her percipience of a greater romance than she had ever been permitted to read on the printed page, much less watch in the making.

CHAPTER XXIX

I

JOHN RUSKIN had been abroad most of the summer in the company of the New Englander whom he had met in Gambart's Gallery and had made a friend of, with the fatal facility of great men for choosing companions who have power to hurt them. Stillman, "blond, refined," six foot three in height, nourished in infancy on the salted breasts of pigeons (surely an appropriate food for the caustic critic he afterwards became), started as an artist and sat at the feet of Ruskin till they quarrelled because the Professor set him to draw pigstyes and he criticised the Professor and his work.[1]

Ruskin had had a little too much of Stillman; that was why, on his return from Salève, he drove to Chatham Place to pay his respects to the newly-made bride and experience again the never-to-be-forgotten charm of the soft, southern voice of her husband.

But Mrs. Birrell's servant, trained to exhibit a lack of reciprocity with regard to duns, shook her earrings, could not or would not give the Rossettis' address at Hampstead, and Mr. Ruskin left, after half an hour spent in looking over the handsome book presented to Gabriel " by a lady-friend," [2] in which, for the last few years, the painter had taken to sticking drawings of his wife, adding to or taking out as love or duns dictated.

Now, the Professor (or Fessie) had fallen in love too, and with a little girl, not yet of marriageable age. The moment he began to draw, he saw " only her hair and lips, lovelier than all the clouds . . . and man's forehead, grander than all the rocks." And he had just written a book to please her. Her mother was beautiful too—" the ablest and best woman I have ever known." The scene was now set for a tragedy, far worse than that of Effie

[1] " Ruskin had not yet learned the true method of painting." W. J. Stillman in 1870.
[2] Lady Dalrymple, Prinsep's sister.

Millais, who had let her new John send the other John a photograph of their first baby and whom he was to visit in her new and splendid house in Cromwell Road. (These three behaved beautifully and in the most modern manner.) Ruskin did not tell his friends about Rosie when at last he got hold of their address and called on them in Spring Cottage, but even as he entered the room, the woman saw that his heart was gone. She inclined her head and long neck a little and impressed a kiss " full and queenly kind," on the lips of this man—" so ugly—the sun says so ! " (He had just been photographed.) Mrs. Rossetti made him feel that somebody cared for him a little and that she was " a woman in ten thousand." He never forgot it : she meant him not to. After all, he had been very kind to her and had tried to give her a lift with her painting that would never be any good now ; she had done nothing worth looking at since three years ago. She needed all her strength and virtue to produce her child properly that she might die without the reproach of barrenness.

She did not seem, in the twilight of the lattice window of Spring Cottage, to have lost her looks or even her colour. He thought he had saved his Gothic Cathedral after all !

She was sitting for her portrait—it was to be called *Regina Cordium* (Queen of Hearts). Ruskin told Gabriel to go on painting while he told them all about Switzerland and how, the first thing when he got home, his mother had gone and fallen downstairs, breaking her thigh-bone. " All her own fault ! " her son said in his queer way, that would have been sarcastic, if it had not been so full of amenity, as of the Angel Gabriel possessed of a sense of humour. " She will wear such abominably high shoes ; they turn round and make her slip." And now she had to keep her leg up and be waited on by Anne, whom she considered at times to be " fairly possessed by the devil," and was bearing the confinement to her room pretty well, with the help of the worst possible evangelical theology, which he read to her, himself, by the hour. . . .

He had no ear for music and Lizzy's rather flat, affected laughter did not dismay him. She told him of their efforts to get a house of their own up this way ; Chatham Place was too expensive to keep on merely as a studio. There was one in Church Lane with a garden stretching down the hill towards London, worth (Gabriel said) at least two hundred a year to him in backgrounds. And he was drilling—what did Mr. Ruskin think of that ?—with the Artists' Corps in the waste ground behind the Royal Academy. Ruskin capped it by telling them about the boxing lessons taken from the great Tom Sayers, whom he had once asked to supper at the Working Men's College, sending down some of his father's cases of wine, but the wretch had not turned up !

As for money—as he showed Ruskin out—Gabriel said that Wondrous Plint was still being wondrous and had expressed himself willing to pay in advance for several things. That was what they were living on now. They intended to keep the *Regina Cordium* for themselves, as it was going to be as nearly a faithful portrait of Lizzy as he could make it and he would not sell it for gold !

2

The baby went wrong, and Lyddy took Lizzy to the sea to recover, much against her will. She was all the while dying to get back to London. She did not trust Gabriel, now, away from her.

He did not want her back. In her pride she realised this and dropped the notion, " just now, when he had so many things to upset him," telling him instead, like a good little girl, that she was better and had actually " gained flesh within the last few days." But he is to know that she is still in constant pain and cannot sleep for fear of another illness like the last. (One feels the sage young Lydia holding her pen.) He is not to be anxious about her : she would not " fail to let him know in time." Or Lyddy will. And, after all, it is better for her to be in Brighton with Lyddy than all by herself in the Hampstead lodgings.

As for their contemplated move she really does not know what to advise. It would be all right if the rooms in Chatham Place could be kept on but she cannot see where the money is to come from just now and that, she supposes, " will settle the matter."

Gabriel seems to have written to his old friend Dr. Marshall, now grown a tremendous swell, about her, but Marshall was out of town. Lizzy, or Lyddy, had been sure he would be, at this particular time of the year and she liked Dr. Crellin well enough. He understood her.

She enquires stiffly about " the fate " of a particular picture which he had on the stocks when she went away but supposes that it is going—or gone—*somewhere* this week? Perhaps he will let her know where? And not go on worrying himself about it " as there is no real cause for doing so."

For herself, she would be glad if he would send her down her water-colours " as I am quite destitute of all means of keeping myself alive." She had managed that for the first few days in " the usual way," going out in a boat—boasting of her famous immunity he knew of—" What do you say to my not being sick in the very roughest weather? "

Money she can do without until Thursday and, after Thursday, she and Lyddy can manage to make do with three pounds a week, including rent.

And she is his affectionate ——. (One wonders if ever, even before marriage, she signed herself otherwise?)

The Angel had folded his wings with a vengeance. The patient formality of her letters at this time—contrasting with the fervour of her verse—betrays the state of their communion, and explains to some extent the writer's failure to inspire those of her husband's blood with affection, or even liking. Fay, indeed! Something bewitched and hindered: Little Bridget warped by seven years of ghostly converse. . . .

True, she was, at the time of writing, deeply soured and annoyed. She had wanted " the little house in the lane " badly and Gabriel, while finding money for any sort of extravagance in jewellery for her or *bibelots* for himself, had let it slip for want of the thirty pounds which the landlord, doubtful of the solvency of one of the painter class (perhaps in communication with Mr. Duncan, the freely caricatured landlord of Chatham Place?), had insisted should be paid over before giving possession. The longish period of uncertainty had harassed her and given her neuralgia and that was why her sister had taken her to Brighton. (Hastings and Old Nunky were now impossible: she had a pronounced " scunner " against the place where she had married and so nearly died.)

And Gabriel had sold her portrait.[1]

---

[1] " Its first purchaser," William Rossetti, commenting on this letter, says cautiously, " may have been John Miller of Liverpool." Gabriel, he presumed, " would rather have kept it for himself." In the sale after her death it was removed from the auction under some arrangement. Mr. Ruskin at one time had it.

The money problem in September was pressing as usual, and more than usual. Gabriel was under heavy obligations which he resented, while profiting by them. He was thrall to two gentlemen who valued his art enough to keep the artist while he worked off his commitments. The position left loopholes for evasion.

Colonel Gillum and Mr. Plint were collectors : Mr. Gambart was a dealer, introduced to Rossetti by Ruskin, the noble sheepdog of whose rounding up Rossetti was still afraid. Ruskin had met Ernest Gambart with Rosa Bonheur at Glenfinlas in his terrible year, had honestly liked the little, thin, energetic Frenchman but not Mademoiselle Rosa.[1] Gambart was always in and out of Chatham Place and one day he saw *Bocca Baciata*, which Rossetti had borrowed from Boyce to " do something to." Falling in love with it he offered Rossetti his own price. But of course Boyce wouldn't sell. So Rossetti tried to put the dealer off with *Burd Alane*, a drawing not " married to anyone else," but Gambart would not give enough for it, so Rossetti agreed to finish another picture, that was lying about, " for better wages."

Marshall of Leeds fell on that one and carried it away under his arm, so in a day or two, Gabriel tells Brown that he believes he will accept whatever Gambart likes to offer for the other. He is aware that this sub-dealing will play the devil with his honour ; for he cannot possibly, if he undertakes a picture for Gambart, get on with the one he owes Colonel Gillum " without actual ruination," unless the plan which he submits strikes his adviser as a feasible way out of it. He has a pen-and-ink *Cassandra* nearly finished—he might persuade Gillum to take that, instead of the *Hamlet*, for which payment had already been made. Not that he quite likes infringing Gillum's compact —and, *ought* he to sell *Cassandra* for so little ? Might he not ask an extra ten pounds ? He does not forget that Gillum's " quarter day " falls at the end of the month. If the deal does come off it will enable him to devote a little clear time to " poor, dear Plint." [2]

Later in the month he wrote to Aunt Charlotte—who still kept a soft corner in her heart and a loose purse-string for her

---

[1] Had Ruskin, perhaps, heard Rosa's criticism of him ? That he saw Nature with " little eyes, *tout-à-fait comme un oiseau*," and shade always as purple—" yes, red and blue."

[2] *Rossetti and his Work*, Evelyn Waugh.

pet nephew—that his wife was returning from the seaside, *he trusted*, that very night. Pathetically presupposing, as usual, that his family was interested, he wished much that he could give " better news of her." . . . He had no news, nor knew, indeed, if she would arrive that night at all.

Now, Lizzy's elusiveness was for her husband too. She had told him, dryly, that she was better and promised that she would manage not to suffer to the same extent from sudden and violent fits of illness as she had done. She would take things in time and so prevent them. With the help—under medical advice, of course (Dr. Gull was a friend of John Tupper's), " of laudanum (or some other opiate) and stimulants in alternation"—she had settled down to a drugged peace, of whose provenance he was perfectly cognisant, with her man, who had long since learned the power of obstinacy that may exist side by side with so much sweetness. He did not stop her doing anything she wanted to do, but allowed her to cope in her own way with " the continual decline in vital force " that was going on in her.

Love flies out of the window when illness, *i.e.* ugly circumstance, comes in at the door ! Who shall say that, when Gabriel heard her bragging to the maid of the amount of "laudnum " she could take, it did not set him ever so little against her : that the memory of that time at Hastings when, for over a month, the revolting phenomenon of illness was in his ears and before his eyes, was not again " more than he could bear " and led to the counter-drugging he now began to practise ?

He managed to be " good " to her. He answers kind enquiries about her in the style of a devoted and appreciative painter-husband. " Yes, indeed, my wife does draw still." He hopes that she is going to do better than ever now, " with her real genius—none of your make-believe "—if only she could add precision in carrying it out, " but that needs health and even the strength to work is rarely accorded to her."

4

The nostalgia of having a whole house to themselves somewhere, or shared with somebody nice like the Joneses or the Gilchrists, was present but not overpowering. Leaving the cottage in November they decided to winter in Chatham Place, till they could settle in " more suburban quarters." They took Mr. John Holt's rooms—suddenly—on the second floor of Number

Thirteen, in addition to Number Fourteen, and were allowed to open a door of communication between the two. Yet if he could find "a nice place elsewhere," they would leave the river and he "hoped that would be before long." He did *not* hope so; he adored Chatham Place, "so quaint and characteristic."

"Nothing but the conviction that these rooms are not good for my wife's health would induce me to move." [1] She knew this conviction would not really weigh and settled in with her own rather stagey resignation. He made a last attempt to get hold of his mother, writing to tell her all about these new arrangements, hoping that before long they might have the pleasure of her company in Chatham Place. Nothing, he said, would give him greater pleasure as nothing, indeed, gave him more pain than the present state of things, amounting practically to an estrangement. If only his mother would believe how much it made him suffer and how earnestly he wanted it all put right!

Mrs. Rossetti faintly proposed that he should bring Lizzy to Albany Street, but Lizzy refused. There had been a bad quarrel and a night on Brown's hearthrug—"There, you've killed this baby too!" He had to write to his mother to say that just now his wife was too ill to be given the letter and that he must wait until she was stronger. His mother sent him another portrait of his father which he himself had painted long ago—his first picture after *Mary Virgin!* So that was that.

And now hardly any of the Albany Street people except William—who sets it meetly down that he went to Chatham Place "not exactly often, but not rarely"—passed through the door, once grimy and repellant, now painted a nice, clear spring green, that gave admittance to Mr. and Mrs. Rossetti's bower, refurbished and decorated, as far as possible, like the Morrises' at Upton. And all the pretty things Mr. Rossetti had collected in his bachelor days, and huddled together in corners for lack of space, were now spread out. For the fireplace he had used some very old, blue glazed Dutch tiles representing subjects out of Scripture. The studio was wainscoted with green and had a design of sprouting trees all round on the wallpaper. No pictures, only the portrait of Browning on the mantelpiece and, under it, the cast, from life, of Keats. The drawing-room was hung round entirely with Mrs. Rossetti's water-colours of "poetic subjects." And he had lately acquired several yards of gorgeous old Utrecht velvet for curtains and to cover settees. It was too heavy for

[1] Letter to Norton, *Ruskin, Rossetti and Pre-Raphaelitism.*

255

Mrs. Rossetti in her present state to manipulate; she had to get someone to come in and make them up under her direction. Red Lion Mary was company but when the velvet was used up, Lizzy was much alone. Lyddy and Georgy were a long bus ride away. Mrs. Brown was at Ramsgate, recovering after her illness, and Gabriel was not sorry, for he did not consider Emma good for Lizzy, though she was the oldest friend she had.[1] Gabriel did not really dislike Emma Brown, but thought her silly and untruthful though, for the matter of that, all women were except Lizzy (he chalked that up to her), and too fond of talking about ghosts. One kindly ghost, Emma always told them, used to come into her room at Church Norton when her mother was away and rock the cradle. But Georgy Jones was all right and good Bessie and he wished that Barbara Bodichon too, with

> her cheerful spirit
> That never needed a stick to stir it,

as Emily Faithful used to say, had been available. Or even Isabel Frith, the Philistine R.A.'s wife, who yet had a dream she never told and kept her room for one day every year, but managed to be cheerful and gay for the other three hundred and sixty-four.

5

Impossible to like Gabriel's present cronies—acrid Meredith, whose wife had just left him, or quiet Gilchrist or dull Hughes, while Mr. Ruskin had begun to bore her. But that winter an old Oxford friend of Gabriel's, whom she had met as an undergraduate, brilliantly clever (though Meredith didn't think so [2]), but who had, alas, gone down without taking a degree and returned to the bosom of his family, turned up again. His stalwart grandfather, the friend of Mirabeau, had died suddenly and with

[1] They were not related, as Mrs. Scott thought, though both their mothers were Welsh. Little Annie, Elizabeth and Lydia used to be taken to see Mrs. Hill at St. Paul's Terrace and to play in the garden when they lived at King's Cross, in among the part that was now being cleared away like "other hideous eyesores" and "atrocious little streets" (*Illustrated London News* of this date) to make room for the Underground. Later, Mrs. Brown was never at home to anyone on Fridays, when she paid her weekly visit to her mother, and to Mr. Gandy.

[2] "He is not subtle and I don't see any internal centre from which springs anything he does. He might possibly make a great name, but I doubt if there is anything solid." But Jones thought him greater than Shelley or Tennyson or Wordsworth. Rossetti, as only second to Morris, considering Morris "the greatest literary identity of our time and superior to Swinburne in execution."

Cousin Jack, who had succeeded to the Northumberland estates, he did not get on. He had settled in Fitzroy Street, among the bars and stews of the New Road,[1] on four hundred a year, alternately staying in Newcastle with Scott, with the Ashburnhams at Battle, and with his own people in the Isle of Wight.

The Old Mortality crowd had taught Algernon Swinburne to drink and he went on drinking until he had destroyed the coats of his stomach. But, as yet, his health was not affected [2] except for a queer nervous twitching which his enemies called St. Vitus' Dance, and his face was like a rose-leaf under the lee of a sunflower, and he was universally and invariably courteous and debonair, as befitted one of ancient lineage and no churl. But he was missing the chaste airs of his old home, the intake of the breath and scent of the moors, the power of stretching his puny limbs for hours along the stones cut with runes, sunk in the long grasses that wave in the salt North wind, watching the pink legs of the heron, listening to the sly ripple of the Font and the Pont at his elbow, baby rivers fringed with bog myrtle and the androgynous sundew, half-leaf, half-flower. He could no longer get his rides on Boldon Sands, where the horses of the sea toss their ragged manes to affront the moors, or lie mother-naked on the sands watching the bright green undertone of the tenth wave as it reels and falls behind the Stag Rock at Bamborough. All, all foregone—health too! Withdrawn now from

> Greenland and redland,
> Moorside and headland,

he was wilting in the shades of " The Phoenix " and " The Green Man " and his pink cheeks growing muddied in the clammy airs of Marylebone.

6

Both Lizzy and he were red-haired, both mined by diseases of the digestion, both poets and both of ancient lineage. He was the grandson of the sixth baronet, of Capheaton in Northumberland, whose ancestor had been knighted by the Second Charles for loyalty to the First. His forbears had " ballad names out of long ago," Dacres of the North, Herons of Chipchase, Thorn-

[1] Euston.
[2] The " ineffable gusto and blaze of the unfettered Swinburne," that Mr. Gosse speaks of, were still there.

tons of Netherwitton—and there was, too, the mysterious foreign connection by which the youth set such store, the Grimaldis of the Côte d'Azur of whom the Marquis de Sade was a scion, all sounding soft on the ear of the Victorian romantic that Lizzy was.

The common disgrace of their hair was a bond, for, in those days, that shade entailed a certain mild degree of persecution, for was not the betrayer of Our Lord a red-headed Jew called Iscariot? Once a year, in Algernon's part of the world, the villagers turn out to stone the squirrels, bringing in so many head of " nasty Judases," and Fanny, the North-country woman on whom Lizzy had hardly set eyes since she passed under the archway of Somerset House on her way to sit to Walter Deverell, called her the " Cyprus Cat," while to Swinburne she alluded as " The Freak."

7

Most sincerely Swinburne admired the " noble lady " whose *preux chevalier* he was to be all his life long.[1] " A wonderful as well as a most lovable creature, so brilliant and appreciative a woman—quick to hear and keen to enjoy." And her looks, perhaps too queer to attract amateurs of a less qualified type of beauty, delighted him. She was his Félise—without the cattishness and with the eyes. Epithets and their multiplication gave him no trouble, his verse runs over with descriptions of the eyes of Elizabeth Eleanor—" the greenest of things blue, the bluest of things grey," like " colours in the sea,"—" green as green flames," blue-grey like skies—" eyes coloured like the water-flower and deeper than the green sea's glass," and so on.

It did him good to know her.[2] She was the only woman in his life—ever. And it is odd that he, so violent, so emphatic, so really cold-blooded, should be anyone's hope and joy as he was hers. Her carpet knight—her page who kept his lady so well and so long amused; how could Gabriel be jealous, though his new friend Hardman would have it that the young fellow was strongly sensual. The husband risked it and left her for hours alone with young Algernon while he sought more virile and congenial

---

[1] " I shall always be sorrowfully glad and proud to remember her regard for me."

[2] He did not have his first epileptic fit until the year after she died.

companions, returning often to find the two where he had left them, in the balcony room, looking out on the eternally ambulant river scene, or across to the Sunny Hills and the blue beyond the smoke. Or Lizzy would be lying back in her own chair under the window, being read aloud to in that soothing Northumbrian voice from her pet Tennyson, with whom she shared a love of white lilac, white peacocks and liked to be called Ida after his Princess. Swinburne indulged her in what Rossetti called "wishi-washi," and then gave her a turn of Beaumont and Fletcher, skipping freely. She "rippled with appreciative laughter," and thought it better than Shakespeare. He was aware that for Victorians, indecency is sanctified by the process of time, but he had to be careful about "The golden book of spirit and sense"[1] or even things of his own with rather less of the latter quality. Nor did he trouble her with his political skit called *La Fille du Policeman*.[2]

But when the *châtelaine* had retired to the solarium, as they termed Number Thirteen, consecrated more or less to her, Meredith would tell the story of "the desire of the pure printer for the fig-leaf" and little Swinburne, mildly drunk, and shedding superfluous garments freely, would dance or oblige Gabriel and the other men, with "*La Fille*" complete, or wild excerpts from the works of his own distinguished ancestor, "that complete acme and apostle of perfection" the Marquis de Sade. *Justine* was a difficult book to get hold of in those days ; he assured them all that he did not possess a copy[3] but must rely on his memory. The adventures of *Justine* (*and Juliette*) were too much even for the ferro-concrete sensibilities of the complete man of the world that Hardman was ; "as fond of good sound bawdy as anyone." But he confessed to being "altogether bowled over by the Marquis."

Her husband was less afraid of shocking Mrs. Rossetti than was the young Swinburne. Looking, all three of them, out of the south window across to the other side, Gabriel would style his wife affectionately "Countess of Puddledock" or "Baroness of the Stews," after Mrs. Martha Jacobson the procuress, granted these titles and many others of an impossible nature, by the Merry Monarch. He would stretch out his forefinger and apostrophise

[1] Thus he characterised *Mademoiselle de Maupin*.
[2] The sub-title of this work, finished later, *Ce qui peut se passer dans un cab-safety*, is indicative of the bawdy that the little gentleman spared the lady.
[3] They all knew better. But perhaps he was afraid to lend it ?

the great Diocesan church of the district, spouting the lewd
rhyme—

> Blessed Saint Saviour !
> For his naughty behaviour
> That dwelt not far from the stews.

Christina would have blanched with horror, but who lived
with her brother must have a stomach for the unrefinements of
humanity. " In Charlotte Street where I was born," he told
Algernon, " every other house was a disorderly one." And all
about the stews on Bankside with their funny names and signs—
The Cardinal's Hat, The Castle, The Bell, and Paris Garden
opposite the end of the bridge, where Count Robert of Paris
once had his own house, that afterwards the butchers of London
bought for the dumping of entrails and garbage, and where the
bull and bear baitings were held. Rossetti was firm that it was
the smell as well as the colour of blood that so stirred mediæval
hearts—even that gentlemanly one of Philip Sidney's—like the
sound of a trumpet. This noisy, blood-red sub-essence of
cruelty was what Shakespeare wrote his plays on, and it went
with Elizabethan loveliness, like lewdness, the rap of the bear,
the guttering fang of the dog, the burning of heretics, and the
stags brought down in front of the chair of the Maiden Queen at
her famous huntings.

And then Algernon's family carried him off to spend the winter
on the " frowsy fringes of a blue land," as he was pleased to
describe the Riviera, playing about with his sisters and pretty
Mrs. Gaskell on the shores of that " tideless, dolorous, Midland
sea " ; and Lizzy lost her harmless, necessary cicisbeo.

CHAPTER XXX

I

TORPID—the great Pre-Raphaelite word for weariness and ineptitude—getting fat in spite of the drilling; Rossetti—in the opinion of Stillman "one of the men most dependent on company that I have ever known" and getting it anywhere he could—was busy making new friends to fill gaps in his visiting list. Brown, just now rather useless—" seedy, poor old chap, gout and many other diseases falling thick upon him "—Jones and Morris very much married, Munro going to be, Allingham in Ireland, Boyce at Brighton, ill, and Howell,[1] the best fun of them all, now, for the one disinterested action of his life, in hiding in Portugal.

A more worldly set was enjoying the hospitalities of Chatham Place nowadays : collectors like Murray Marks and Anderson Rose, the solicitor who was forming a collection of China and old pewter in Arundel Street, and Spencer doing the same with books : there were Doctors Liveing and Cameron as well as Sandys and the young Greek Ionides, who introduced him to the American painter Whistler (of much avail to him a year later), Meredith and his crony Hardman, gay, Catholic and very appreciative of " the celebrated Pre-Raphaelite painter at his meridian—a jolly fellow, going to him again on Friday." At Chatham Place Mr. Rossetti would receive them and say that Mrs. Rossetti had gone to bed—" *perchance to sleep !* "—with the help of her new solatium.

He was trying to be a good husband, though indeed the accepted etymology of the word denoted something [2] he never could have been. But he was perhaps never nearer the norm than in these months of matrimonial crux. The usual thing was happening : nature as ever was shielding the race. In January he

---

[1] Charles Augustus Howell, led away by patriotism and Orsini, had assisted in the bomb-throwing.

[2] Hus Band = the Keeper of the House, Anglo-Saxon.

wrote, "in confidence, for such things are best waited for quietly," to tell his mother that Lizzy was pretty well, for her, and that they were "in expectation of a little accident which has befallen Topsy and Mrs. T. who have both become *parients*." Theirs, however, would not be born (if at all) for another two or three months.

This was why Lizzy would not let Mr. Ruskin see her, but stayed within her bower when he called at Chatham Place. The stupid man thought she really might have put on a dressing-gown and run in for a minute, sooner than not greet him. He commented on it all while he was about it and told them both home truths, Gabriel—"in little things habitually selfish," thinking only of what he liked and didn't like to do, instead of doing what would be kind. "But you can't make yourselves like me, and if you tried, you would only succeed in liking me less." Or perhaps they both liked him better than he supposed they did? Dying to be assured of it! He owned to having no power in general of believing that anyone cared for him. He fully admitted his lack of sympathy with so much (Mediævalism?) that they appreciated—"and so I lose hold of you!"

It was true enough. Ruskin's power over the younger man *was* waning, diminished by the contempt inevitably experienced by the people who actually make things, for those whose job it is to criticise and pull them to pieces.

And for the poor Professor everything was changed now, going wrong, "and so fast wrong!" People should "lie on a stone bed and eat black bread, but they should never have their hearts broken!" The little girl he was in love with had been forbidden to work, compose, write letters or use her head in any way, but might draw "as that does not use her brain! It is a different Rosie every month now!" [1] In public life, having "blown up the world that called itself Art," [2] he had managed to get the Press of this intelligent country against him.[3] Labouring under

[1] "Rosie seems but half herself, as if partly dreaming, some obscure excitement of the brain causing occasional loss of consciousness . . . nothing to do with any regard she may have for me. . . . Her affection takes the form of a desire to please me more than any want for herself, either of my letters or of my company." She was, of course, growing up, but kept a child by her parents. She died when she was twenty-five.

[2] ". . . and left it in an impossible posture, uncertain whether upon its feet or upon its head and conscious that there was no continuing on the bygone terms."—Carlyle.

[3] "We don't look upon Ruskin as an impostor, only as a humbug."—*Illustrated London News.*

a very strong inferiority complex—" poor moth me ! "—he was everlastingly trying to assert himself to his friends and got so far as to tell Rossetti that he didn't choose to have anything to do with him " until you recognise my superiority as I do yours."

Tactless, he dared to patronise Christina, who had allowed her brother to forward him copies of her poems for him to read. [1]

2

Bonnets were worn " a trifle large, more in front from the top than before "—a subtle change, becoming to drawn faces. Cambrai and lama lace was in, and cheaper than Chantilly, useful for kind, dissimulating mantelets. But Mrs. Rossetti, who would have known well enough how to adapt Fashion to her condition, refused to go out. She had a horror of any such presentation of the personal grotesque as had made her stay at Hastings a remembered nightmare. Gabriel had to go without her to the christening of little Jane Alice Morris in the last days of January.

He went down with some of the fellows, Marshall, Brown and Swinburne, who was just back from the Continent and had not yet called on Lizzy. Janey was going to put them all up somehow, in the fearless old Pre-Raphaelite fashion. The Joneses were already there—Georgy to help the delicate Janey in preparing for such a large party. It was given to show the new house and the new baby [2] to as many of the old P.R.B. as could be got together and to the members of the new firm [3] which had been constituted, as it were, on its ashes, to fight Mr. Perkins' aniline dyes and nurse the silk trade, nearly killed by Cobden's Bill of three years ago, since when no lady's gown had been able to " stand alone." Premises had been acquired in Queen's Square,

[1] " Your sister should exercise herself in the severest commonplace until she can write what the public like. *Then*, if she puts in her observation and passion, *all* will become precious. But she *must* have the form first." " Most senseless ! " commented Rossetti, " and I think I told him something of the sort in my answer."

[2] " It was a wonder she survived ; there were so many muddles before she was born."—Chariclea Ionides.

[3] The firm, founded in 1860, consisted actually, like the P.R.B., of seven—Rossetti, Morris, Brown, Jones, Faulkner, Philip Webb and Peter Paul Marshall. Faulkner wrote to William concerning the first and only prospectus issued of Morris, Marshall, Faulkner & Co., 8 Red Lion Square, Holborn. Fine Art Workmen in Painting, Carving, Furniture and the Metals. " A very desirable thing," Scotus says, who had not been asked to be a member—and he did so like his fingers in every pie—" a very desirable thing, Fine Art Workmen ! But isn't the list of partner a tremendous lark ! "

over a working jeweller's shop, with a large ball-room built out at the back which could be used as a show-room. Morris had already been offered eight thousand by a prominent firm of upholsterers [1] if he would give it up and work for them only.

They all went over the house and laughed to hear of the criticisms of Mr. Morris' neighbour, who went about telling everybody that these Morrises had been married in their own drawing-room and gave parties on Sundays. The innovations interested this lady vastly—the walls unpapered, hung instead with embroidered cloths—so dust-making! Not a carpet anywhere but little islets of Persian rug in " surrounds " of paint. Red brick hoods over all the fireplaces and brass dogs. The absence of mirrors—Mr. Morris happened to hate them—puzzled Mrs. Friswell. She thought that the windows of the hall need not have been cut so high and the roof raised so dreadfully steep, but she granted the chimneys " charming," and even Janey's gowns, made of a strong diagonally ribbed blue [2] material, warranted never to wear out, suitable either for dresses or for curtains. She would only change for supper to one of silk in the same colour; [3] the products of Leek were nearly all, so far, blue or red.

Back from Leek that night was the host, tired and hot, sitting at the head of his home-made T-shaped table—in a draught, for he preferred it—looking magnificent (the upper part of his body was better than the lower); his hands stained to the elbow with the woad he handled all day and every day, those eyes of his, with the filmed observant look of an eagle, seeing everything. He would be shocking people on purpose to see what they could stand, offering them " pig's flesh " when he meant ham, and fish " with a pudding in its innards " when it was stuffed—asking his guests when they left the table if they were " full " ? One saw how he had come to fret and estrange his wife by his fidgettiness and want of *apropos*.

An inarticulate, disconcerting creature, she was to-night more silent than ever. Gabriel too; Georgy, his neighbour at supper, noticed that he drank the health of Baby in water, confining his

---

[1] Was it Hellbronner's where, for very long afterwards, the P.R.B. ladies used to get their expensive dress-lengths of brocade that "lasted"?

[2] Wrongly dubbed by Mrs. Friswell "peacock-blue."

[3] Dyeing was, for them, a tremendous speculation. "*Kiss me, love, for who knoweth?*" Morris would quote as he saw twenty pounds of raw green silk go into the vat, hoping to come out blue.

repast to raisins, which he munched " in a royal manner," helping himself from the dish in front of him before the proper time and, with scant, strained and elaborate courtesy, flinging a word now and then to the little woman at his side.

Later that evening Georgy went with Janey to look at the beds " strewn about the drawing-room " for the men. To Swinburne, on account of his diminutive stature, they had allotted the sofa.

3

Lizzy mostly chose to stay at home during these " gestes." She had gone longer than ever before and they had strong hopes. But in these piteous months of *malaise* and ungainliness, while Woman " carries the angel of death under her girdle," [1] she would not " sit " much—which gave Fanny her chance. Gabriel did not object to his mate's appearance, any more than the proud burgess in the Flemish picture may have done; but Lizzy, to use the phrase in other than its slang value, knew she was nothing if not picturesque. She still let him draw her sometimes, sitting back in her big arm-chair propped up with a cushion, her head sunk in the hollow made by its weight, her hair dressed elaborately, lifted from her brows, spread like gold lace on the pillow. But that was not enough. . . . In pique, letting slide the three pictures for which Mr. Plint had already paid, he had pulled out *Found*. Mr. Leatheart had now commissioned it. Since McCracken's order lapsed, he had been careful to hide it, perhaps from obscure tribal notions of concealment, perhaps to ward off chaff from those yet alive who had presided at the flourish of its inception. He had re-christened it *The Drover*. To Lizzy he said, " This means good money," to pacify her for its revival, involving the original model.

For Fanny's hair, equally abundant, was less red and more truly golden than hers. And Fanny, of the curiously tragic countenance, stoutish though shapely, comfortable, without angles, strong as a horse, could sit for hours without getting tired. Fanny could chatter and amuse, or hold her tongue when she was told to do so, could cook things with onions—Gabriel often went, Lizzy was sure, all the way to Wapping to enjoy her savoury stews. Of Fanny, Lizzy was positively unable to tolerate the mention although, to all his friends, she was grown a gorgeous commonplace.

[1] *Flower, Fruit and Thorn Pieces*, Jean Paul Friedrich Richter.

She came every day to sit, not only for the castaway crouching under the lee of the bridge-head, but for ladies, classical,[1] Roman, mediæval, mythological—for Cassandra, Delia, Lucrezia, Lilith, Blancheflor and Fair Rosamond.

It was obvious that poor Mrs. Gabriel moped—she saw so very few people. Mrs. Ned, of course, but Mrs. Ned was busy—she had married a delicate man and they were moving to rooms opposite the Museum, roomier than Great Ormond Street in view of a coming event. And Lizzy's sister, whom Gabriel liked and could always do with, was about to be married. Algernon Swinburne was back in town, living in Newman Street, but he was a man, and worse, a boy. She only had her pets, that Gabriel jeered at. . . .

Ladies were by way of keeping birds in those days, not Alsatians. Pale canaries moped in a hundred cages in Pimlico, larks attempted to soar in Wood Street, parrots and macaws shrieked and croaked everywhere. Mrs. Rossetti preferred doves, that filled the rooms with their soothing senseless croo-crooing. Wicker cages hung on nails at every window in her part of the chambers—there was a bullfinch too!

Looking up at the cages, rising, busying herself to feed the little things every now and then, she would return to the particular stool she affected, in the middle of the room, to brood over wrongs real and fancied. . . . Real, her loneliness, her outlandishness, the dreadful solidarity of Gabriel's family who regarded her, she well knew, as little more than an ailing, incompetent interloper. Their fertility in devising, contrasted with her own paucity of production, annoyed and hurt her. William was engaged on a translation of *The Inferno* and would come to, or after, tea, bringing sheaves of manuscript of his own for discussion. Gabriel was " pushing on " with his translations from Italian poetry and William was helping him to collate the section relating to Dante, whom William knew all about. Their mother was attending to the " literals "—she was stronger in the Italian language and its locutions than either of them. The manuscript had been sent round to some of Gabriel's friends, Allingham, Gilchrist and Ruskin—the latter was going to pay a hundred pounds towards publication. Christina's volume of poems was forward, and as she put them together, correcting, naming them, Gabriel looked

[1] One can ascertain pretty well the pictures for which Mrs. Hughes sat—they were the ones that patient William, at his brotherly task of executorship in Cheyne Walk, missed and could not, " for practical purposes, trace."

266

over and, with the unerring eye of the great critic he was, picked out the best, *When I was Dead my Spirit Turned*, and desired that it should be renamed *At Home.* William and Christina in return read Gabriel's. To William's "Isn't *The Portrait* rather spoon-meat?" he agreed, but disregarded Christina's grammatical corrections.[1]

"Thanks about the *ye*, but I am afraid I don't think it matters much."

4

"It may have been," to use William's cautious phrase, "about this time" that Gabriel finished and handed to Ruskin for his approbation something much nearer to his heart than the poems of Guido Cavalcanti and Ciullo d'Alcamo. They were his own, collected since youth, in a little book covered with old, already faded, green silk.[2] Ever since November he had been working on them, "furbishing up enough for a volume," he said in a letter to a brother poet. And "I really believe I shall print the thing!"

Presently his friends in London were bidden to come and hear him read the poems aloud, one by one as they got "furbished up" until all, or nearly all of them—certainly Swinburne with his marvellous memory—had got them off by heart.

These privileged persons heard recited in that soft cajoling voice, *The Blessed Damozel*, *The Witch* (as he first called *Sister Helen*), *The Last Confession*, inspired by Italian patriotism, *The Card Dealer*, *The Song of the Bower*, *Beauty and The Bird* (or *The Bullfinch*), one of the cycle of birdcage poems commanded by the Misses Deverell, *Placata Venere* (afterwards called *Nuptial Sleep*)—so says William?—*The Burden of Nineveh* and *The Portrait*, *Love's Nocturne* and *Jenny*. To absent ones like Allingham he posted them and then, ashamed to be nervous, "but indeed a belated MS. frightens me," frantically reclaimed them. To Ruskin he sent *The Portrait*, *Love's Nocturne* and *Jenny*, asking him to send on one or all to Thackeray for *The Cornhill*. A thorough man of business, he designed this first mild journalistic appearance as a *ballon d'essai*. Ruskin, fastening on *The Portrait* and *Love's*

---

[1] She said that he had used the nominative case when it should have been the objective *you*.

[2] I have seen two of these dear-bought leaves, livid, nearly black, like the head of an Egyptian mummy, indescribably *macabre* and horrible-looking. The boards and the silk have, of course, perished.

Nocturne for *The Cornhill*, was very funny about *Jenny*, refusing to send it on on account of its " too great boldness for the common reader." [1] Besides, he added, "fail" does *not* rhyme with " *Bell* " nor " Jenny " with " guinea."—(Didn't the poor dear Professor know that the name can be and is pronounced Jinny ?). " The throwing of gold into a girl's hair is disorderly—the lover is altogether a disorderly person." He did not want to seem prim and did not " mean to say that an entirely right-minded person never kept a mistress," but sent the more ladylike *Nocturne* to " Thack "—who took no notice of it.

Her husband came to be so utterly absorbed in this book that he hardly replied when Lizzy spoke to him or noticed when she entered the room : when he did, he let her see that her restlessness and the unwieldiness of her body disturbed and displeased him.

And by him just now her fundamental ideas of equity were being most deeply outraged in many a way. The girl who had had the heart to put by Mr. Ruskin's subsidy the moment she found herself unable to deliver the goods with regularity, who placed probity before art, could not bear to see her husband cheating his employers, *i.e.* his buyers. It seemed to her that he was in honour bound to supply the work for which he had already been paid, before taking up fresh commissions. The *Llandaff* altar-piece was positively due before the end of August. For all sorts of other work Mr. Plint had paid him on account and he had spent already the six hundred and eighty-two pounds, yet she could hear him telling people that he " felt himself bound to do *Found* " for Mr. Leatheart (who, wise man, had *not* paid ahead), so that he could " devote himself properly to Plint's pictures." Putting the cart before the horse : that was dishonest. She had no patience with Gabriel's theory that dealers should consider themselves honoured by being permitted to help great men to live ; she knew also that she and Gabriel could live less extravagantly. There was no need for so much entertaining. Gabriel seized on the slightest excuse for a party and parties meant *her* disappearance from the scene. That was nothing : she did not want to see sottish men like ——! All day and every day, urgent letters went by Croucher, the family handy-man, or Green the frame-maker, or Red Lion Mary, to friends, to his mother's. Linton wanted to meet William, so would William arrange to come in one evening " and I'll ask two or three men besides " ? . . .

[1] One sees what he thought of the magazine public of that day.

Two or three ! More like twenty. And the parties had taken to costing so much more ; for that Mr. Hardman had taught Gabriel to give proper—or improper—supper parties, beginning at the unearthly hour of half-past eleven, champagne cup and punch after and cigars in the drawing-room. Howell, who came from Oporto, knew all about wine—where to get it—and had introduced a friend of his, Mr. Keeling, a wine merchant. . . . Gabriel never drank too much, but one night he came to her after they had all gone, and they had a worse quarrel than usual and she told him she was certain the child was dead in her body.

She frightened him well and he let a kind, warm-hearted woman [1] whom he had lately come to love and trust much, see it. "My great anxiety about my wife lasts still." . . . All, he assured Mrs. Gilchrist, was being done for the best : he had confidence in Dr. Hutchinson and had taken care, moreover, to get another opinion from Dr. Babington. Her nurse, recommended by his mother, who lived in Arlington Street near their old home, was an old North-country woman, full of character, all of it good and her conversation so fascinating ! Mrs. Jones at once engaged her for her own affair, to come off at the end of the year.

Faced by this new crisis, Lizzy herself was calm and sensible, not in the least down-hearted, which the doctor agreed was the greatest of assets. She was writing poetry. " And we can only hope for a happy termination "—Rossetti, paterfamilias for the only time in his life, writes. . . .

5

It was not to be. Legitimate paternity at least, was denied him. By May Day " there was illness and anxiety in Chatham Place," says Mrs. Jones, who managed to get regular news about her friend from Red Lion Mary, who " sewed " for them both. Thus she learned on Friday early that, in the night, Mrs. Rossetti had been confined. And then she heard from Gabriel. "Our fears were correct in one respect, the child was still-born." " But," he added, " she herself is so far the most important that I can feel nothing but thankfulness." To his mother he imparted the tidings in stiffer fashion—" and she is doing pretty well, I trust." To another friend he wrote, " She fares, as yet, thank God, better than we ventured to hope." Anxiety of course there still was

[1] Anne Gilchrist, with her beautiful, speaking face, her eyes full, dark and liquid, vivacious, full of heart-stirring enthusiasms, never lanquid, fidgety or out of temper. A copious talker. She was the same age as Mrs. Rossetti.

and, pathetically enough in view of the family attitude, he begs his mother not to " encourage people to call just yet—excepting yourselves, of course." No indication whatever of this intention was exhibited by Albany Street; no such thing as a mother trod, in felt slippers, dealing sympathy, the muted halls of Chatham Place—except in the young wife's poetry.

AT LAST

O mother, open the window wide
　And let the daylight in;
The hills grow darker to my sight,
　And thoughts begin to swim.

And, mother dear, take my young son
　(Since I was born of thee),
And care for all his little ways,
　And nurse him on thy knee.

．　．　．　．　．　．　．　．　．

And, mother dear, when the sun has set,
　And the pale church grass waves,
Then carry me through the dim twilight
　And hide me among the graves.

It was a girl. Emma Brown thought that, though Gabriel desired a son badly, the child, had it lived, would have made an immense difference to them both. Extreme melancholia overcame the mother. She had taken much joy in preparing the usual layette and cradle, swathed and wreathed with lace and ribbon, and now she would sit alone for hours on her low stool in the middle of the River Room rocking it, ready and empty. When the Joneses, her first visitors, came they found her so and, as they entered and Ned was about to close the door, she cried out in a wild sort of voice, " Hush, Ned! You'll wake it! " Jones, who did not adore her so whole-heartedly as Georgy but only loved her because she was his dear Gabriel's wife, suspected her of a certain amount of histrionics: he had been shown the poem. A later form of her mania was a desire to hide away all traces of what might have been, to hand everything useful over to Georgy for *her* approaching necessity. Gabriel, letting superstition get the better of sense, wrote to Georgy telling her he had heard that his wife was thinking of sending her a " certain small wardrobe—but don't let her, please! It looks such a bad omen for us."

" Us " still! For he meant to try again, and her quick recuperation and renewed beauty revived his ancient passion for her.

But she chose to consider that the mishap was all his fault. Elegant again, soft, beautiful as never before, she was soon fit to see women visitors and often Mr. Swinburne. In that flighty way of hers which she did not now trouble to control, she complained of her husband and gave the young man to understand that, if it had not been for Gabriel, the child would have been alive now. Algernon, through his mother's warding, innocent [1] more than most, of the mysteries of gestation and parturition, excessive, inconsequent, full of violent and grotesque imaginings, may have conceived that his Lady had been made the victim of some fearful Elizabethan malfeasance or other, and, talking as usual wittily, bitingly and at random, to astonish people, made mischief for Rossetti at one of Milnes' smoking parties and vastly amused the host, in his red robe and cap almost like a cardinal's. Rossetti, informed by Brown at secondhand of what had passed, only laughed to hear that " procuring abortions " was to him, Rossetti, " an every-day amusement." Forced by Brown and even Jones to take some steps, he expostulated mildly with Algernon, who cried and took the matter so much to heart that Rossetti, generous as ever, did not press the point. But it was another nail in Lizzy's coffin.

Algernon was probably tipsy when he said it : half a glass of wine was enough to upset him. His increasing propensity distracted Mrs. Rossetti, who knew well enough what drink led to and, thinking as all nice women will, that she could cure him, took him in hand until Brown actually got quite anxious and Gabriel, to tease Brown, pretended to be jealous.

Algernon came every day for her to lecture and mother him and she, when he attended their parties, used to pin a bit of paper with his address on to his great-coat, inside the collar, so that, should he be too overcome to give it properly, the cabman would know where to deposit him.

For they were entertaining tremendously. Invitations, lively and informal, ran, " Come, we have hung up our Japanese brooms, etc." Countesses rolled in their carriages to Blackfriars to see the Pre-Raphaelites in their habitat—the Ladies Waterford, and Trevelyan, and Bath, all eager to break new ground and meet the

---

[1] Swinburne, when *Poems and Ballads* was withdrawn in the first week, was admitted, even by some of his reviewers, to be " not virtuous enough to know what they (his poems) meant or vicious enough to explain them."

exponents of the cult they admired and whose pictures they bought. A good sprinkling of Philistines like Hardman and Anderson Rose; journalists like Hepworth Dixon and Joseph Knight; among authors, Westland Marston and his daughters. Patmore and a wife, Meredith with his handsome head, Edward Lear, round and funny; Martineau, Halliday, chattering Tebbs and Mrs. Tebbs who was their dead friend Seddon's beautiful sister. There would be Sandys, Mark Anthony and his daughters; Peter Paul Marshall and his wife Gussy, the daughter of jolly old John Miller of Liverpool, the picture buyer; "Val" with a head like a broom and the heart of a —— (*vide* Rossetti's Limerick), and Inchbold, a dangerous guest because he always wanted a bed [1] and never went away; Hungerford Pollen, Munro, Hughes and Faulkner and a couple of Christina's admirers, Cayley and John Brett [2] ("*No, thank you, John*"). There would be Morris and his wife, of course, and the Joneses. Not Stephens; not asked, he had just married Mrs. Charles and had said Lizzy was "freckled." Holman Hunt was away. Excepting Georgy there were not many of Lizzy's particular friends. Emma Brown was at the sea and Bessie Parkes and Barbara Bodichon were abroad. But Mary Howitt brought her shy husband, Alaric "Attila" Watts, and sat with him in a corner taking notes for her diary that would have rejoiced a daily paper of to-day.

"On Friday evening, June 20th, 1861, we went to a great Pre-Raphaelite crush. Their pictures covered the walls and their sketch-books the tables. The uncrinolined women, with their wild hair which was very beautiful, their picturesque dresses and rich colourings, looked like figures out of some Pre-Raphaelite picture.

"It was very curious. I think of it now like some hot struggling dream in which the gorgeous and fantastic forms moved slowly about. They seemed all so young and kindred to each other that I felt out of place, though I admired them all, and really enjoyed looking over Dante Rossetti's huge sketch-book." [3]

---

[1] There is a mad artist called Inchbold,
With whom you must be at a pinch bold,
Or else you may score
The brass plate at your door
With the name of J. W. Inchbold.

[2] Mr. John Brett, R.A., who told me that Miss Rossetti refused him.

[3] A big bound book of blank paper which Lady Dalrymple had presented to Rossetti—the book that once cheered Ruskin through a long wait.

CHAPTER XXXI

I

"REJOICE to hear of your wife's health." So Patmore wrote to Rossetti that Spring.

Those about her knew better. She was only what people called "so-so"—that is, she ate well, took a walk daily, had got out her water-colours and was working hard, "but none the better for it," her husband said, telling a friend of their mutual activities and the new garnishings of their home. Though she was not kept indoors by her complaint, even when the weather was inclement, William, who had talked to Dr. Gull, realised that the disease was running its course and had now got thorough hold. William gave her six or seven years at most to live, and that was a sanguine view, for him.

She knew it herself. Strong-willed, vain, she was determined, before she died, to produce a son to lay, in classic fashion, on the knees of Gabriel's mother and so justify his marriage to an invalid.

It had been one of the coldest of winters : there had been skating on the Serpentine by night, the fire-plug open on the mains. The coming summer promised to be one of the hottest. "Nightingale colds" were prevalent, for people left their windows open to hear these unusual birds.[1] Nightingales or no nightingales they could not do it in Chatham Place, because of the smell of the river—awful and insistent despite the purge of the great and happily devastating fire which, the very night after the Rossetti party, began on the other side, sweeping away any amount of wharves and their greasy, fetid buttresses standing in stagnant water—Cotton's, Chamberlain's, Fleming's, Hay's and Beale's. Compared with *their* usual effluvia, the smell of burning tallow, which had assailed the nostrils for three days and nights, was ambrosial. Gabriel was suffering from an ulcerated throat

---

[1] There may have been some in the Temple Gardens.

with occasional fever and a temper. One of Ruskin's letters to him at this time began, "Dear Rossetti (I had almost written Dear Bear !)." He was working too hard. He had finished a picture for Plint, spurred not so much by Lizzy's monitions as by that gentleman's rumoured infidelities. William had heard, through Scott, that Plint was beginning to "run" Hunt and had given three (or four thousand pounds) for five sketches which used to hang in Hunt's house in Church Street. Gambart had been clever enough to buy them up when Hunt went abroad and knew how to force them, now that Hunt had become famous, on the great Leeds buyer. Mr. Plint, also on Gambart's suggestion, had bought *Christ in the Temple* for four thousand pounds or more, so

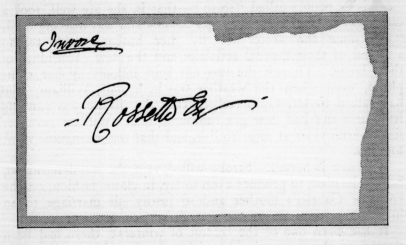

gossip said. Hunt was still away. Gabriel was reluctant to shelve the cartoons illustrating *The Parable of the Vineyard*, seven designs, that he had undertaken for the centre light of The Shop's front door. He had been delayed for want of a number of *The Pictorial History of England*, containing a print of a Saxon wine-press. The opening day was near and he had promised if he could "spare another hour from *Llandaff* to send it on in the evening. Pure labours of love like this were not irksome to his generous disposition, but it seemed dreadful to him to work, as Lizzy was making him work, for money that he had already acquired and spent. And, as it was, bills came pouring in for what he called " necessary debts," *i.e.* for which he was liable to be dunned. He complained to Brown that " all my yesterday has been spent in paying out," and that when he was done he only had left, out of a hundred guineas which had come to hand, about twenty-five. He " anticipated more accounts dropping in " (Who does not?). " And so, my dear fellow, I must be a defaulter to you again." [1] Some of the unnecessary expenditure was for Lizzy or for showy charities, such as seats for poor Robert Brough's benefit—and Mrs. Brough had all Lizzy's jewellery already !

She wanted to get into the country but was up against her own austere programme for Gabriel : the performance of work overdue. " She has to sit to me a good deal." The cottage at Scalands was at her disposal, maid included. Or they could have gone to Mrs. Gilchrist's place at East Colne, which she would have liked less though Gabriel was inclined to it : he thought of her, for once, writing that he wished they could have accepted—" some sun would be good for my wife. We must see."

But something was nearly always found to keep him in town (Fanny, so the wife supposed, or even Kate). Mrs. Rossetti was good and went down to the Morrises at Bexley Heath now and then and Mr. Rossetti joined her there, " for such outs as I am able to make "—posing as the busy man-of-brushes.

2

In July he was faced by " the most difficult fix I ever was in ! " said he. " I told you so," said she, and she had been telling him so all along, like any scolding housemate. It was all his own fault. He had " found it impracticable " to devote himself as was clearly his duty, to the three pictures for which Mr. Plint had paid him in advance seven hundred and fourteen pounds, and now Mr. Plint had died suddenly and the pressure from his executors and their agents began and was, to say the least of it, " inopportune and harassing." Gambart, as London agent to Mrs. Plint with three others, to make the gesture more portentous and insulting, beat up the defaulters and called on the three worst ones, Brown, Jones and Rossetti, to view the pictures " in progress."

They all arranged matters after their lights—of probity. Brown went further into debt to pay *his* debt, Jones compounded with G. F. Bodley and did a replica, " slightly varied," of an important altar-piece he had ready for a church at Brighton but

[1] To Brown.

" really too elaborate to tell its story from a distance," so he sold that and did another and a simpler one and made his peace with both worlds.[1]

In Rossetti's case the pictures were like the Emperor's clothes, non-existent, except for the little *Doctor Johnson at The Mitre*. At any rate, Gambart saw nothing—not even the painter. Rossetti's point was that he refused to show work unfinished to anyone whatsoever and drafted a letter [2] to that effect for the executors which, in default of William (now touring abroad with his mother and sister, introducing the Continent to the latter for the first time), he showed to Brown. It was an offer, within three months of the present date, to name a day for handing over the pictures—" when I shall better know my engagements." *Llandaff must* be got out of the way first. Concerning the probate duty, he said he had already told their Mr. Knight everything that gentleman needed to know, viz. the amount of the commission. With regard to " delay in the *undetermined* delivery of these commissions " that was, of course, the result of his desire to do justice to the estate, for, if they hurried him, the pictures would be bad ; whereas, if they allowed him to take his own time, they would be good. And he refused to see anyone [3] " on business which no interviews can further," and ended with the pleasant proposition that within the space of three months, *fixed by himself*, the trustees shall " hear from him as to delivery."

When William got back he called on Gambart and listened patiently to complaints of brother Gabriel. The dealer hinted that he " and others concerned " had been debating whether to advise Mrs. Plint to administer and so make herself responsible for debts. " If things go on so," she might find herself compelled to leave the creditors to realise without the option of administration. The suggestion leaves Gabriel calm. He will have nothing more to do with Gambart—once his friend but now "so offensive" that he can't be stood at any price. He has made a

---

[1] Alfred Hunt, moved by the destitution of Mrs. Plint, forewent his claim for work done and bought up some of his own pictures for more than he got in the first instance.

The Sale was rather a touchstone : the figures show how, by skilful pilotage, Rossetti was building up his reputation. Hughes' *Belle Dame*, sold at £250, went for £60. Brown's work brought in £550, but Rossetti's *Burd Alane*, sold at £84, pretty nearly maintained its price and represented the triumph of the day.

[2] Was it ever sent ?

[3] *Rossetti, his Life and Work*, Waugh.

Limerick[1] about him to that effect. He will write direct to the trustees, who, he is sure, are not for a moment thinking of going to law. So William is to do nothing about Combe and Garnett, only William *must* be careful to post letters " from where I am not," for Gambart is " quite leary enough to notice postmarks."

He tried to get the trustees to treat, through Ruskin, on his behalf, but learned to his vexation that the upright and tactless Professor had actually recommended these worthies to make use of Gambart's services.

3

Someone taking an interest in Mrs. Rossetti's health in these times of stress wrote to her brother-in-law. " You ask me after Gabriel's wife ? "—he is sorry to say that she was " exceedingly ill some time ago " but hopes that she " has remained better since."

Ruskin was home again, " at least in the place which ought to be home." He had been in Ireland with the Latouches, trying to acquire a cottage near his Rosie, involving himself more and more deeply with Rosie's religious mother, signing wild compacts. . . . His faith was tottering, but she made him promise to make no published avowal of his infidelity for the next ten years, on pain of losing both her friendship and that of her child. There was his own mother too, full as pious as Mrs. Latouche. She perhaps thought of that ?

Gabriel wrote to him to complain of Gambart, who had abused him to William, leading William to think that he had been " acting *wilful* wrong" to Mrs. Plint. It was all owing to the late Mr. Plint's " unfortunate habit of pressing money on him for work in progress "—offers of which he naturally availed himself, having an ailing wife and a child coming. " I *had* to do other work, to live, while I painted them."

In this letter he adumbrated a plan and Ruskin approved, as it was entirely in Mrs. Plint's interests. Yes, if he is referred to, he says he will certainly recommend it. But he hoped that somebody would soon throw Gabriel into prison—" and we will have

---

[1] There is an old he-wolf called Gambart
Beware of him if thou a lamb art.
Else thy tail and thy toes,
And thine innocent nose,
Will be ground by the grinders of Gambart.

the cell made nice and airy and cheery and tidy " and, because of all these amenities, Gabriel will get on with his work " gloriously." His " love to Ida."

He was lost to them as far as any help in him went.

4

" The death of Plint nearly ruined me," Gabriel would say complacently in years to come. In more senses than one, perhaps ! With the queer under-wisdom of the great, he knew. His conduct of these matters had deeply jarred his wife's sense of rectitude and made her morally averse to him whose passions, she for her own purpose and Nature's, was seeking to arouse. She went her own way to work—methods nerve-racking, destroying. She tried jealousy and put up little Swinburne as a possible rival (or allowed Brown to do it for her). But Gabriel refused to object and treated them both like children. They quarrelled over Algernon. She annoyed Gabriel by the example, always held up before him, of the young man's regularity in all that pertained to money matters. Yes, he was a good payer. But did she know, then, that Algernon had a secure income and set his punctiliousness with regard to bills against that ? Yes, for she, too, was of good old English family, the daughter of humble people who were yet so proud that they sent their young daughters out to work sooner than owe a farthing. " And," he would retort, " to defray the costs of litigation." The late Charles Siddall had spent pounds on his fight for the Greaves money. Yes, but when he had all but won the case, young Clara had got hold of the papers and put them on the fire sooner than have her father worry himself any more about them or make the further effort necessary to get hold of the money. A beautiful action !

The fathomless and boundless deep,
There we wander, there we sleep. . . .

They quarrelled babyishly, bitterly, suicidally—until the very centres of life for both of them were involved. The Browns' hearthrug received her convulsed form, flung down, twisting, heaving, shaken in gusts of passion that nothing in the way of comfort and kind words could allay. They just threw a rug over her and crept to bed, to lie awake themselves. Next morning they would give her her breakfast and she would go home, weak as water.

278

For Gabriel, the finer vessel, when all was said and done, there was no recovery. Melusine did her work and La Pia could not save. They would hear him reciting Blake,[1] Dante, Keats—*La Belle Dame*—tags on which the tortured spirit fastened, as a shipwrecked sailor to a spar from the roof tree of his House of Life. A man, now, grave, bluff and sensible, watch-chain looped on opulent waistcoat : to look at, Allingham said, something like a " prosperous citizen of Genoa." Nothing wild or spiritual about him any more except the eyes, so beautiful and tender : brooding and puzzled. A woman, she, bitter, thinning, with shrunk bosom and eyes more prominent than ever ; together they must exist in that doomed house until her time came. Stoically in his drawings he registered, with Pre-Raphaelite truth, the new outline, in sketches of the once beloved head, mostly pillowed, the bows of hair less opulently outspread, the forehead lined ; twists instead of curves in the cynical, sensual mouth of the Blessed Damozel, abusing, pining for the lover she has left behind, leaning out of Heaven and looking down

> . . . . as low as where this earth
> Spins like a fretful midge,

in the attitude of one who yearns and forgives.

5

Quarrels are often merrily incurred by women in whom one set of nerves affected is as good as another, considered as a means to a certain end, but " *Amantium iræ, redintegratio Amoris* " ?— never ! Lovers' talk in the innermost chamber—" *Nay, but the hours, clashed together, lose count in the bell,*" and the voice of love harshened by dismay, raised in anger, can never whisper again.

For Gabriel, now, a difference between the gloomy house at

---

[1] A deep winter, dark and cold,
Within my heart thou dost unfold.

. . . .

Iron tears and groans of lead
Thou bend'st about my aching head,

. . . .

And fill with tempests all my morn,
And with jealousies and fears
Fill my pleasant night with tears.

" Never perhaps," says Rossetti somewhere of this poem, " have the agony and perversity of sundered love been more adequately rendered."

whose base the greasy waters sucked continually, the air about it heavy, resounding many times a day with the clang of many chimes : between this room " so full of books and clamorous work undone," with its innermost chamber that was Lizzy's bower, and that of " handsome Jenny mine ! " Both beautiful, desirable women, with the right hair, golden—Lizzy's the redder and finer—Fanny's the yellower and coarser, sunned and tanned by the wind of the Essex marshes where she was reared. Both with the same full white throat, flung back. . . . Fanny Hughes, a woman lusty and fierce, not weak and wilting : of normal, not nervous, reactions, in sex-moments complaisant without sex-purpose—Fanny didn't want any babies, not she—there was a Mr. Hughes ! And she would be glad enough to sleep the whole night quietly in his arms or, " lazy, laughing, languid " after his embraces, sit up when invited to do so and sip heartily from the glass he would fill for her and let them go to sleep again. What if, like Jenny of the poem, the subject of her dreams was the coin wrapped in the meshes of her hair, for her to find when she awoke and the tactful lover gone ? " A pre-eminently sweet woman," as even sour old Scott, who knew so much about her, owned : kind and motherly as well as eager and passionate, knowing her woman's job thoroughly—when to cajole and when to leave alone. . . . She really seemed to have for her " Mr. Rizzetty " some of the decent mother-love of one of Patmore's " Angels " who would work their fingers to the bone to make him green baize coats to work in, or the wife of Sydney Dobell, who used to lie down across his bedroom door when he was ill. She really felt, or simulated, the tenderness in which poor Lizzy was entirely lacking and would cook for him as well as lie with him ; he was always sure of his favourite dish when he went to see her. Her rounded form was his pillow—she was " The Lumpses," so good to roll over against in the night—so he told Lizzy in one of their quarrels. Her " large, lovely arms " that waited for him were his shelter against the world's rubs and unkindnesses, her Cockneyisms his relief from the well-bred, susurrant accents of the embittered housemate ; her commonness, his refuge against too much refinement and esotericism.

6

Order in disorder ! Gabriel had become a creature of habit—two habits. Lizzy was merely one of them. And his powers of inhibition were so well adjusted that he was actually " nicer " to his wife when he had been with the other; then there was a surcease of quarrelling.

The wife hardly knew where the mistress lived—somewhere, she took it, on the other side of the river—Wapping perhaps—not so very far from her own people? She left it at that. She did not choose to know. She was, for many reasons, afraid. She never spoke of Fanny to him or to anyone except Brown and his wife; not even to Georgy Jones. She never entered the studio when the woman was there, but stole in, after she had gone, to con the lineaments of the destroyer of her peace—if the noisy desert, full of the dust of recrimination in which she lived, could be called so. And to see what had been taken—for Brown and all Rossetti's other friends knew that where Fanny sat, she stole; that where the treasure was, the thing she called her heart was also. Very anxiously Mrs. Rossetti was watching the progress of the red chalk drawing of Algernon which she herself intended to take away and hide as soon as it was done. Artists themselves never can tell that, but Fanny would have a fair idea. She had no taste, of course, but a flair as good as Gambart's or any dealer's for what was saleable and aware that sketches of Swinburne and Browning might be of great value in the near future. While for likenesses of herself she had the usual model's predilection (these ladies always hate to see pictures for which they have contributed the features, by far the most important thing of all, going away to someone who perhaps has never even seen the original!)

CHAPTER XXXII

I

YET

> A little while, a little love
> The hour yet bears for thee and me.
>
> . . . who have not said
> The word it makes our eyes afraid
> To know that each is thinking of
> Not yet the end. . . .

Though Lizzy was now nearly always " so-so," keeping up
with the help of laudanum (that needed brandy or whisky to drown
it), she was often willing to undertake what her husband called
" the adventure of Hog's Hole," especially when Ned and
Georgy were of the party. These little people, unaffected,
unpretentious, loved it all—the arrival at Abbey Wood station
and out, bleared and London-stained, into the " thin fresh air,
full of sweet smells meeting you," the packing into the wagonette
sent for them from Red House—Morris himself perhaps on the
driver's seat—up the hill and then three miles or so of winding
road, and then the friendly porch where the dark-haired, dark-
eyed, dark-skinned, Janey, hatless, looking like an overgrown
schoolgirl, would greet them.

But it had come to be nowadays, somehow or other, a rather
quieter, steadier party. Jones, still badly in debt (with sove-
reigns lurking in the linings of his coat pockets!), about to
shoulder responsibilities to come, had grown milder than ever.
Morris too was less noisy, less bouncing, the backwater of
morbidity that ran alongside with the burly life-stream of this
violent, patient in the main, man, was more obvious than it had
been. He was poorer too, his income, the part of it that was
derived from the copper mines in Cornwall, was beginning to
diminish; he had the Firm on his back and other little things . . .
which he was not allowing to hurt him—as yet. Rossetti, stout,
patient, dullish and darkly sober, looked like a good burgess by
now. . . .

282

In the evenings " Poll " Marshall, accompanied by his Gussy, would sing *Clerk Saunders* to please Mrs. Rossetti and *Busk ye, Busk ye, my Bonnie Bride* for Mrs. Ned, and she would sing in her high wild voice *La Fille du Roi* out of *Échos du Temps Passé*, to please Ned and Top. The world had grown older. Gabriel was thirty-three, Top was twenty-seven and Ned twenty-six. Of the women Lizzy was the eldest. Janey was already a mother, Georgy an expectant one. Lizzy, so regrettably free of matronly solicitudes, joked about it very often, mirthlessly, like the changeling of legend.[1] No more innocent teasing, such as sending Top to Coventry in his own house or getting a rise out of him by erasing his chosen motto, *Als Ich Kanne*, from the shutter where he had cut it and substituting the derisive *As I Can't*. No more hide-and-seek all over the house, jumping out on Janey and making her scream. No, in the evenings they sat, two of them—never Lizzy—on the great settle from Red Lion Square with the three painted shutters over the seat and a ladder up to the parapet and a little door in the wall leading to the roof. Windfallen apples were stored there, but no one now pelted Morris with them and sent him off to Leek next day with a black eye. Perhaps the settle reminded Mrs. Rossetti rather too keenly of the old studio and Walter Deverell. . . . She was indeed a bit of a wet blanket and none of those who were at Red House at the same time as she—Gussy Marshall or the Faulkner girls—ever mentioned her in their happy letters thence.

Yet—" Oh, how happy we were, Janey and I," Georgy admits, driving about, " exploring the countryside," with a map and an old pony. No men with them : Georgy's husband was as bad as Gabriel's wife and " hated expeditions." His little wife found excuses for him—" Like all imaginative natures," Ned did not *need* to be " *made* to feel."

Sad enough already and mortally tired,

> Laden autumn, here I stand
> With my sheaves in either hand.
> Speak the word that sets me free,
> Naught but rest seems good to me.

Lizzy was glad to get back to her city bower, the two doves, the bullfinch, the cosy evenings with the Joneses and, occa-

---

[1] That never cried or spoke except when it saw its earthly foster-mother trying to boil water in an egg-shell—eating hardly anything, never laughing except when alone.

sionally, Swinburne. She would even giggle in her rather wicked way, while Gabriel sketched Georgy, at Algernon rolling in his neat blue serge suit on the floor, making rude Limericks, finding rhymes to difficult names

> . . . Georgy,
> Whose life is one profligate orgy.

A nervous subject, she seemed able to stand what no one else could, the manifestations of this young man's " inner core of excitement," his dancing about while he stood, moving his wrists continually while he sat, making some people feel positively sick. Him, of all Gabriel's friends, she liked best, except of course Brown, who was like a father to her, and the absent Allingham, who ranked as a nice intelligent brother, and Georgy's husband, " more romantic than his name," so Allingham said. Both these men, full innocent, unsophisticated, incurious of horrors and dirt—" *Justine*, unmentionable, one supposes ? " so Ned, politely, of Swinburne's familiar. But *primo inter pares*, the Joneses ! To the very end she talked of a joint household with them. Georgy and Janey were, for the present, Lizzy's only available women companions : her sister was busy getting married.

" I hope you are coming over to-morrow like a sweetmeat— it seems so long since I saw you, dear," so she wrote to her " dearest little Georgy," whom she probably had seen last week ; "Janey will be here I hope to meet you." [1] She is sending a willow-pattern dish with her love and they must of course take Jemima (Dummy of old days) back in the cab with them ! After the meal the three men would leave the women to clear, and wander about in the studio, going over matters, turning canvases round face forwards from the wall while the others waited in the drawing-room for them to finish their talk, or in Mrs. Rossetti's bedroom if she were more " so-so " than usual and had to put her feet up, which it was impossible to do on the hard gilt settees in the drawing-room.

The men's discussions were mostly academic—or about what The Set was doing ; they hardly ever discussed outsiders except to magnificently praise or, with equal vigour, blow up. The problem that interested them, apart from helping artistic lame dogs over stiles, was how to nobble the dealers and get their own " pics " on the market. Jones, the shrewd, would be

[1] *Memorials*, Lady Burne-Jones.

declaring that it was a mistake to let a prospective buyer see things without a frame and, for himself, even if he ever did " get there," he always reckoned on the neglect a man's work might have to undergo at the end of his life, as well as at the beginning and prepared modestly for " public weariness of me." He apologised for himself—" I do things badly because I don't know how to do them well. I *want* to do them well." Top averred that jealousy, not vanity, was the unpardonable fault in an artist. Rossetti, joking, put it to them that Jones was not really modest—" He thinks that even his pictures, when he has done them, are not really good enough for *him* to have painted!" Gabriel certainly was too conceited to be jealous. . . . And so, bullying each other, good-humouredly, they would join the ladies.

Lizzy might have been with Georgy and Janey in the inner room, " trying on " something, or lying on her carven bed : laughing or crying—it depended on the state of her health, she was always more cheerful when she was most ill. But she seldom talked happily even when she was alone with her friend, though to Georgy she was always fascinating, whether she grumbled or exulted, was excited or melancholy, humorous or tender. She was all these by turn. (If William had been there, he would, for sure, have described her manner as " flightier " than ever.) Even Georgy, all tolerance and love, noticed that the moment the men came in the manner of her hostess changed and that, if such a thing were possible, she began to flirt with her own husband. He could rouse or quieten her at his will, putting his finger, as it were, on some jarring nerve or other, waking it and stilling it alternately so that her mood, in his hands, would change from one of excitement to peace—or the other way round—in a moment! She loved the experimentor, the tormentor—so perhaps it was all right?

2

" A painter ought not to be married; children and pictures are too important to be produced by one man! " Nature apparently recked not of the artist's view, for Jones was made a father in the early days of October—a little earlier than he expected—and he nearly succumbed to the emotions aroused, so that the straw provided by Ruskin—one of Philip's god-fathers—might well have been laid down for him. Though trembling in every limb, he proved more practical and efficient than Georgy " of the lion heart," who had been tactless enough to put a pen in her eye just before her time came. Neither doctor nor nurse was to the fore in Great Russell Street : they managed without, till Nurse Wheeler came and put everything right. But from that moment both the Joneses " saw everything through a mist of baby," and Lizzy had to put up for company with the wife of the other member of the Triumvirate—it was a convention of the three friends, that their wives, more or less, sufficed each other for company. Lizzy accepted that convention. She was of course not jealous of Georgy— she herself was again " hoping "—or of Janey now that she was safely married. Kind Emma Brown was away and the hearthrug in Fortess Terrace unavailable so she was willing to go and stay with the Morrises, while Gabriel was in the North chasing commissions—perhaps new loves. . . . Money was tight. The Plint affair was not yet settled although Mrs. Plint had died. There were, Lizzy understood, young children and executors imperious on their behalf. There was, too, a whopping bill for the alterations at Chatham Place—and the double rent ! . . .

3

There were some other rich Heatons near Leeds, unrelated to Miss Ellen Heaton, and Gabriel was summoned to Bingley to paint the very handsome lady of the house as a woman genius, holding in her hand a model of Woodside and the grounds, with swans on a sheet of water in front of it.

Lizzy had promised to stay on quietly with the Morrises at Upton while he was away—it would only be for a week. Suddenly came from Rossetti an urgent letter to Brown—William was out of town—to say that he had not taken Lizzy to Yorkshire with him for two reasons. Firstly, it would have been impossible for him to take her with him to Bingley and, secondly, " the money we have would hardly suffice for my own journey North." And now he hears that she has gone home—" had had to leave Upton in a hurry." And he knows that there isn't such a thing as a halfpenny in Chatham Place for her daily needs. He will be back in a week : will Brown take her some pounds, which Gabriel will of course repay punctually on his return. " Her flight, at present, makes me very uneasy." Brown might

286

MRS. BURNE-JONES AND 'PIP'
From a Photograph by W. Jeffrey

send the " few pounds " by post if he is really too busy to go to Blackfriars, but Gabriel strongly hopes that he will " make time " to look up Lizzy.

Forgetting his usual tact, Gabriel had proposed to call Mrs. Aldham Heaton's portrait *Cor Cordium*. Lizzy's, which he had been thoughtless enough to sell, was named *Regina Cordium*.

4

One afternoon, late in November, Lizzy and Janey made an appointment to meet in Great Russell Street to see the new baby. Lizzy was fairly well, several grades above " so-so." Janey too was blooming, for her, of whom nothing could overcome the olive paleness that spoke of her perpetual anæmia. So that day " The Statue " and " The Picture," two tall beauties, stood over the cradle and surveyed with very different feelings the " separator of companions, the terminator of delights " which was the mother's pedantic little way of saying that young Philip, who ought to have been called Christopher [1] but wasn't somehow, was a bit of a trouble. The three Pre-Raphaelite Queens sat round the beribboned bassinette, in the charming room with the big window looking straight on to the Museum, with a side-view of the trees in Russell Square. It was furnished of course from The Shop and decorated all by the painter's own hands, except the walls, hung with tapestries left by Henry Wallis when he ran away with Mrs. Meredith. The sideboard was painted " with ladies and animals," while, on the piano, modelled on the famous one of Brown—only in plainer wood, covered with a lacquer of domestic provenance, the shade deepened by the use of the kitchen poker—Ned had done an illustration of *Le Chant d'Amour*, and on the panel under the keyboard a gilded and lacquered picture of Death, veiled and crowned, a reminder such as only two perfectly happy people can manage to live with.

" Never was there two such beautiful ladies ! " said Mrs. Wheeler, passing and re-passing at her nursely avocations, leaving the little brown bird of a mistress, who didn't mind at all, out of it. It was one of Lizzy's good days. She and Gabriel had made it up—whatever it was—this time, in view of what might happen. Rossetti, always insulting about the

[1] Christopher was, and for long after into the 'eighties, the pet name for forthcoming infants of members of The Set.

Browns' domestic arrangements,[1] was glad enough to leave his wife with them while he gallivanted about the country painting the pretty wives of his various patrons.

5

Then suddenly all was naught. Gabriel returned in haste to meet a new and important buyer, Mr. Rae of Birkenhead, and found himself under the necessity of apologising to a host for his wife's manners. Brown had come home to find that Mrs. Rossetti had " left his roof " and, feeling sure that Gabriel was somehow in fault, posted off to Chatham Place and found Mr. Rae there in full and fertile consultation. Not daring to speak out lest he spoilt the pie, he left in a huff and it needed all Gabriel's exquisite politeness to calm him down. " I could not mention about Lizzy's leaving before Mr. Rae. She tells me she felt unwell after you went out yesterday and, finding the noise rather too much for her, left before your return lest she should be feeling worse. Many thanks for all your care of her during her illness. . . . I write this as her departure must have surprised you as it did me."

He had and could have no secrets from Brown—this was not for the eye of Mrs. Emma. Brown knew that Lizzy's nerves were in a shocking state and that the explanation she put forward did not meet the case. Gabriel was by now pessimistic about his chances of paternity. Nature did not choose that a living child should be begotten of they twain, any more than Dante could hope to have a child by Beatrice.

[1] " If dirt quite essential, will turn some dogs in." An invitation to Brown to dine at the Rossettis'. Brown was supposed to prefer foreign eating-houses, for the reason set down above.

CHAPTER XXXIII

I

A MONTH later a man she didn't particularly care for died; it upset her and Gabriel too, for it was so sudden and so near. Only a week before he had been present at one of the more informal evenings at Chatham Place for which the invitation had run, " Can Gilchrist look in on Friday ? Anderson Rose, Sandys, Meredith and Val. . . . Nothing but oysters and come in the seediest of clothes."

The illness seemed negligible at first. " Poor old Gilchrist ! " Gabriel wrote in October. " Two of his kids and one of his servants have died of scarlatina." It was not realised by any one that his attack was of a malignant nature. Rossetti, Jones and Swinburne [1] went one Sunday to Cheyne Walk to supper and " never spent a pleasanter evening." Lizzy did not go,[2] as Mrs. Gilchrist, upstairs nursing the children, was unable to appear.

Then the poor, pleasant master of the house went down with scarlet fever and after five nights of agony was carried out, feet foremost, on a wild and stormy evening on the last day of November.

Gabriel " couldn't "—didn't at any rate—go to the funeral,[3] any more than he went to Walter Deverell's. Women were not by way of attending these functions, and Mrs. Rossetti had not even complied with the Public Order for " Decent Mourning " enjoined on the Nation for the Prince Consort (he who had taken the turquoise and vermilion out of the Royal Arms and the azure out of the Garter and got rid of all the beautiful uniforms; and was primarily responsible for the " flowing of all the innocent ugliness under the sky " of the early 'forties).

[1] Swinburne had won his spurs for knightly courage during the terrible cholera epidemic in Newcastle when he was a boy, staying there with the Scotts—fearing neither Don, Devil nor infection.

[2] " Lizzy particularly unwell," on the 4th December, Gabriel writes.

[3] " I am afraid it will be hardly safe for me to go."

These sartorial and other singularities helped to accentuate the eccentricities that kept her lonely. Her old friend Bessie kept in touch with her, but was much in request and out of town a great deal. People like Mrs. Marshall did not call on the Pre-Raphaelite ladies whom her husband doctored for nothing: she considered Mrs. Morris " a beautiful but queer sort of young person," Mrs. Jones negligible and Mrs. Rossetti " a sheer nobody that Mr. Rossetti had picked up, thin, *gauche* and badly dressed." The Ladies Waterford, Dalrymple and Cavendish only put themselves out to go to " clever parties "—given on purpose for them. And anyhow Mrs. Prinsep of Little Holland House always dropped painters when they married.

There were outside amusements of course. They could go and have a good laugh at Bob Sothern in *Dundreary* or have their flesh made to creep over *The Woman in White*, from the novel by the brother of a Pre-Raphaelite. The first number of *Fun* and Christina's poems were out. And Politics! America in an uproar—the Mason and Slidell affair; Italy, with Garibaldi gone to Caprera, and, backing all jealous wives, the ominous, scandalous flight of the Empress of the French to Scotland. They might feel deeply the destruction of old Westminster Bridge or the projected renovation of their own Blackfriars. Some sort of political or social excitement of the kind might perhaps have saved her from coming to be known as Mr. Rossetti's trying wife,[1] peevish, uncertain-tempered and staring-eyed, and to whom he was unfaithful. . . .

2

Woe! Woe! The cry of prophesying Cassandra before the doomed house, " faughing " at the smell, not of blood, but drugs. People began to avoid it. Gradually the human tide flowed back and away from the accursed house by the river mouth; and the *châtelaine* of the vaunted, queerly painted chambers—Numbers Thirteen and Fourteen, with the fair green door for both—became a sour, unwholesome myth, pining and etiolating, alone with her birds and her bottle of laudanum or whatever it was?

Ruskin's dark hour coincided with hers. No one had seen him; everyone knew that he was ill and suffering, and even had he been in England she was not one to send for him. She

---

[1] So my mother and her friends always spoke of Mrs. Gabriel.

had angered the matter-of-fact Morris by her nonsense, and vexed the patient Browns by her vagaries and, now the Jones became of no avail, for Ned got ill and, by Christmas, was spitting blood.

These Pre-Raphaelites never seem to have been able to conduct life unless out of Froissart or Malory! With a blood-stained napkin in her hand Mrs. Ned must needs take a cab to Doctor Stephenson who doctored them all—to find a Christmas party going on and the consulting-room full of hats and coats. Still, she managed to show him " the crimson sign which would tell him more than I could," and he saw Edward and pronounced the hæmorrhage to be from the throat and not from the lungs. Then the baby fell ill and Gabriel's mother, who ought to have known, since she had brought " the most precious of boys into the world," was asked to come and prescribe. But all she said was " It is certain that the child is suffering great agony." And then they found a cheque for twenty (or thirty?) pounds in a dressing-case—where it had been left long for the strange reason that it was crossed! which tided them over the two illnesses.

But, of course, they could neither of them leave the house much that winter, and garrotting was so bad in London that women could not go about the streets alone after dark for fear of being strangled. Gabriel was nearly always out or entertaining men in the studio, at any rate not there to escort Lizzy to Great Museum Street, so she stayed at home and more often than not, had only for company, when Algernon was out of town with his people—Mrs. Birrell and her niece Catherine, and sometimes Red Lion Mary, who had plenty of conversation and was, on the whole, the best of them.

3

By the time that the pale New Year, full of rumours of change and revolution, had dawned, these two, wrapped in the savage artistic isolation that the Pre-Raphaelites seemed to love and endeavour to create around them, were hopelessly, damnably estranged. The man was busy, fulfilling, at his splendid wicked leisure, many commissions; helping Morris with his stained-glass experiments.—The Firm had bespoke a space at the second Great Exhibition to be held this year. Distant but attentive, he was having her Tauchnitzes bound for her, persuading her to buy herself new clothes to be made up by Red Lion Mary, taking her to the theatre to see Miss Herbert (who sometimes came to sit) play at the St. James' in *Le Chevalier de Saint Georges*, and writing to his friend, buyer and confidant, the American, Norton (who had not met Mrs. Rossetti or heard of Mrs. Hughes), letters full of decent concern for " my wife," giving him at the same time news of the progress of the picture he was painting for him—*Before the Battle*—which, in view of the imminent risk of hostilities between England and America, might never get across ? Nervously, deprecatingly, he dilated on Lizzie's health and the beauties of their house (which Norton, of course, had never seen), as it were an auctioneer's catalogue—" I write in our drawing-room, entirely hung round with her water-colours of poetic subjects." He was fully aware that the locality was not the best possible for an invalid and would move at once if he could " find a nice place elsewhere " and hoped to do so before long, but—" there is something so delightfully quaint about our quarters here that nothing but the conviction that they cannot be the best for my wife would induce me to move." [1]

Quaint indeed, and picturesque, London's Maremma wherein this tragedy was being consummated,[2] but the artist is always at odds with the doctor. Nothing worse, from the point of view of health, than those loathsome, picturesque bights, like festering sores, forking up as far as Great Queen Street, less of a blessed harbourage than a breeding-ground of death and discomfiture ; Water Lane and Puddle Dock, just round the corner from Chatham Place, during the hours of a low tide, revealed a brown, sliding plateau of liquid suet, with the upturned green keels resting on it, blown, distended, monstrous, like frog's bellies or dead rainbow trout. And the Fleet river just below the windows was nothing but a sewer, roofed over. The shoreman —the man who " made " the " shores," that is to say, cleaned the sewers—knew his way about below better than he did on top, he told Ellen Macintyre. Lor', you could get in here and come out at Hyde Park! Under the River Room the drains lay so close under the bank that he could take rats quite easily in his hand. He sold them for threepence each—brown rats and grey rats, faugh! . . . Nonsense! There were no black rats now. The brown ones had killed them and black rats were

[1] *Ruskin, Rossetti and Pre-Raphaelitism.*
[2] She died five weeks from the date of this letter.

much worse than brown for pestiferous fleas. Besides, the sewers were cleaned out regularly—every blessed parish was supposed to do its own flushing. She was sure St. Bride's did not trouble. Was he aware that there was a cesspool under their own doorstep?

"Not beautiful now, or even kind." And she spoke her mind, like Tennyson's poor mad Maud, serving up loathsome *on-dits*, exulting in the macabre—so all-pervading now—as he had taught her to do. And why, if the river was as healthy as he maintained it to be, why—tell her that?—why had Walter, consumptive like her, been forbidden by the doctors to accept Gabriel's hospitality in the past? There was some other reason. . . .

There she sat on her low stool in the middle of the River Room alone, mostly all the day, amid the ceaseless, senseless crooning of her doves, silent or talking to servants, like Ellen and Catherine Birrell till dusk, when Gabriel, in his studio, would be heard to throw down his painting things (no such thing as putting them away) and, telling her to put on her bonnet, they would sally forth, the sturdy, hungry man and the thin, fanciful woman, to get a scratch meal in some place " where a lady might go if she ran very fast upstairs." Or to some noisy, more respectable resort, like The Cheese, where you could get a very fair dinner if you weren't particular about the table-linen. They were trying this or that new café and restaurant.[1]

On Monday Swinburne was going to take them to the Hôtel Sablonière, near Cranbourn Alley where Deverell had first seen her. Had she but stopped at that! . . .

The food they got at these places was not nutritious and seldom cost more than two shillings a head. She was growing emaciated, but it was not what she ate, or didn't eat. Gabriel was not blind to the symptoms of her gradual deperishment or callous to her sufferings; he was patient but, æsthetically tired of it all—of the smell of drugs clinging constantly about her and that of the still more odious correctives . . . of the cooing of her doves, of her voice even—querulous, raised—and the oppressive meekness that succeeded or preceded an outburst.

---

[1] Verrey's for French cooking, corner of Hanover Street; Simpson's, The Albion over against Drury Lane, two shillings a head from five till seven. The Divan, 102 Strand; Rainbow Tavern, 15 Fleet Street; The Albion in Aldersgate; Richardson's under the Piazza in Covent Garden and at The Piazza Tavern in the same quarter.

He envied (and said so) " the kind, sweet, blessed life " (in his
letters well rubbed in) of Norton in America and began to stay
out o' nights. And mostly, if they dined together, he sent her
home alone in a cab, and in her sleep of exhaustion she never
knew what time in the morning he sneaked in and lay down
at her side.

4

Mr. Swinburne came every day to sit for his portrait. The
Young Man of No Feeling, in his seer-like way, noticed many
things, heard the burden of the humming misery that was
going on—"dumb tones and shuddering semi-tones of death." . . .
She was still lovely to him, but the author of *The Leper*
could not help noting " the change that finds fair cheeks and
leaves them grey," her eyes no longer like those witching cat's
eyes of Félise, but " as a dove's that sickeneth," and on her
cheeks " where the red was, there the bloodless white." Her
mouth, sweet still, but paler too, and her hair—"all the fine
gold of it tarnished at the heart." The sight of his sweet
friend's decadence it surely was that imported the Pietistic
strain into his verse. She was the morbid streak, the brown
stain on his rose-red philosophy, the Pre-Raphaelite revelation
of Death's lewd ugliness, as it came once to the eyes of the
gay, cheerful Brethren that night at Millais' father's in Gower
Street, in the picture of the gentle knights and ladies leaning
over the necks of their horses to see the purulent Kings in their
coffins. He realised that all her husband's magnetism was
implicitly withdrawn from her and so he now only rendered
her lip-service. Simple as he was decadent, Algernon fancied
that she was dying of love for that husband, consciously un-
attractive now through illness to the full-blooded man that
Gabriel was.

Algernon Swinburne would have nursed and tended her,
as the poor serving-man the leprous lady. Not so Gabriel
Rossetti.

It had been a great passion that was now a-dying. Algernon
had heard of it long before he met them both. He pitied but
dared not condole; she was so deadly proud and let nothing
out, except in impersonal verse, some of which he had been
permitted to scan.

Ah, she had kept her man waiting too long and had been too

pious for him! The boy blamed her (if a-morality knows how to blame) for what had been told him of her procedure during those ten years before marriage—the withstanding—the withholding. . . . Now, but sure, unconsciously, Gabriel was punishing her, even as brutally as did the Knight Des Lorges, the lady who sent him for her glove down into the lions' den.

She did not believe much in the baby, she had always had such bad luck, but she meant to die in harness. She was willing, nay, eager, to pose when she could, gold-crowned, in a green robe with her hair all over it, as Princess Sabra, enthroned on a platform or dais looking out on a crowded square, with her father and the heralds and, prone beside them all, the dead dragon. The hero is bareheaded and Sabra is holding out a steel helmet full of water for him to wash his blood away.

But, when she was not wanted, she sat bookless and workless, entertaining thoughts of suicide. In those days she was well on that bridge " between sadness and madness—made of a single hair " which Tennyson talked of. Little things that William Allingham, the poet and mystic too, had repeated to her as having been said to him by his two best friends were summoned back by her morbid, imperious mentality. That great kind soul, Carlyle, did not consider suicide wrong. He thought that a man might, " in desperate need," invoke the Roman Death, as he called it . . . *Veni, Proserpina!* The Romans did not disapprove of self-murder. Actually, Tennyson told Allingham, a poisonous liquor was kept at Massalia and given to persons who presented themselves before the Senate and gave good reasons for their need to die.[1] And Mr. Carlyle had a notion that the dreadful act itself was not painful whether by poison or otherwise—" more like a torrent of sleep pouring in on the brain. . . ."

Courage, poor heart of stone!

She was not at ease spiritually, not conscious of being saved in spite of the *voulu* religiosity of her verse. No priest—no man—cared for her soul; so she would tell the man who no longer cared for her body. " Living in a darkness that could be felt! " Thus William, a poet too, deeply com-

---

[1] Carlyle, " so plainly serious and discreet and so reliable not to misuse whatever was told him, and all sorts of people were continually talking to him, confidentially, all his life and nobody ever regretted it."—D. A. Wilson in *Carlyle at his Zenith.*

miserating where he would not save—he thought her so bad for his adored brother. She was. And so thought Christina. Here was a chance for nun-like charity. Her neglect of this hapless sister in Christ is a stain on the effulgence of a great and noble woman, deeper far than the projected over-stepping of the convent threshold (poetical periphrasis for the front-door mat in Albany Street) for which she did self-imposed penance for the rest of her life. No particular blame attaches to his two best friends, who did not care for her either. Morris and Jones, loving each other to the tomb and Rossetti, if it were possible, beyond and after, might have saved him and her both—Morris by his nobility and discretion, Jones with the shrewdness and sane, sweet sense, despite affectations and wilful wool-gathering, that was his reserve. But Gabriel, of passions ranker and infinitely stronger, a bull on the leash of civilisation, negatived by his selfishness and heartlessness all they could do. Of their wives, Janey, " subtly of herself contemplative," as an influence was null; Georgy, backed by Ruskin, did think of a rest-cure, unknown technical term in those days.

Her outcries, at this time :—

> Life and death are falling from me,
> Death (and day) are opening on me.
>
> . . . . . .
>
> Lord, have I long to go ?
>
> Hollow hearts are ever near me,
> Soulless eyes have ceased to cheer me :
> Lord, may I come to Thee ?
>
> . . . . . .
>
> Holy Death is waiting for me—
> Lord, may I come to-day ?
>
> How is it in the unknown land ?
> Do the dead wander hand in hand ?
> Do we clasp dead hands, and quiver
> With an endless joy for ever ?
>
> . . . . . .
>
> Lord, we know not how this may be ;
> Good Lord, we put our faith in Thee—
> O God, remember me.

CHAPTER XXXIV

I

THE little Joneses were all agog. Ruskin was taking his "dearest children" to Italy in the spring and Georgy had actually steeled herself to leave baby Pip, but, says she—" First, dark waters had to be passed through."

One foggy morning in February, her Ned breakfasted and settled down to do what he could to his picture in the absence of proper light to see by, when there was a tap at the door and Red Lion Mary called in. There was nothing strange about that : she was a usual Iris between Chatham Place and Great Russell Street and, had it been a Sunday morning instead of a Tuesday, might have come to read Ned choice bits from Reynolds, and wind up the clock and the musical box that lived under his pillow and play his, and her own, favourite tune, *Oft in the Stelly Night*, as she called it. But to-day Mary stood stumpy on the mat and blurted out, "Mrs. Rossetti ! . . ." "Come in ! " they shouted. And she did come in and cried and told them plump that their " poor lovely Lizzy " was dead, of an overdose. (No need to say of what—to them.) It was all over ; but the master wanted Mrs. Jones to come to Chatham Place, where they had been up, all of them, the whole night—since eleven o'clock, when Mr. Rossetti had first found her. He had only just got into the house, he had passed Mrs. Birrell and Ellen in the hall, but had come down in a minute or so to ask them to sit with Mrs. Rossetti while he fetched Dr. Hutchinson, who had attended her in her confinement, a few doors down Bridge Street. Did Mrs. Jones know she was expecting again ? Mary thought it must have been another mishap. She was always having them. She was all black in the face. Mr. Rossetti hadn't seen—he had not been near her since daylight. He was like a madman, refusing to believe it, calling out her name—throwing things about, breaking up all the china in the flat. Mr. Brown was persuading him to lie down. The man was worn out, had been all over the place fetching people—up to Mr. Brown's and Mr. Marshall's and the family—all in opposite directions. Dr. William, Mrs. Birrell had herself fetched later—lucky he was such a punctual man! He was there now, and Mr. James and Miss Clara—the other sister was not able to be about just now. The place was full of people. Mary herself had just happened to go with Mrs. Rossetti's new mantelet to be tried on, that she was making for her against Saturday to wear down to the Red House, a black one with magenta fringe and trimmings. . . . Yes, everything had been done for her. At six Mr. Hutchinson left off using the stomach pump, saying it was no good. There were at least four doctors with her by then, but she hadn't known a blessed one of them, not no one, nor her husband. She had gone to bed with the door open—Ellen had peeped just before he came in. She was snoring a bit then, but not much to speak of.

2

All this was in the bus going to Blackfriars. Georgy had not allowed Ned to come with her; he was ill and might have got his death in the fog and damp, which was sure to be worse near the river. She sat there quietly beside Mary, putting two and two together. . . .

She knew that they had been going to dine with Algernon last night to sample a newly-opened café-restaurant he had discovered, where you could get a really good French dinner. They would dine about six and leave there about ten or eleven. Why had Gabriel needed to go out again, once he got home, especially just now?

Mrs. Birrell met them in the hall. Yes, last night after eleven Mr. Rossetti had come down and begged her and Ellen to go and sit with Mrs. Rossetti while he ran across and got Mr. Hutchinson to come and have a look at her; she was breathing queerly. . . . He seemed to be hours away and it was awful sitting beside her—lucky she had Ellen, she wouldn't have been alone with the lady for anything! It soon got worse and she was honking as if she could hardly get a breath, and fairly black in the face, as they saw later when the dawn came through the shutters that hadn't even been closed over-night. Mrs. Birrell had been up talking to her that very afternoon, about her hair that she was washing for Saturday and all about her mother's that came down to her feet like a sheet though she was old. Yes, her mother had been there on Saturday—quite an event, that was; that and the dove that had got out last week and flown away. She had been worried over it, but Mrs. Birrell had said leave the cage open, and the window, and put a bit of something for it to eat and, ten to one, it 'ud come back. Yes, and it did, said Catherine Birrell, that very morning while they were working at her. Might have made all the difference if she had known! Catherine heard a noise at the window and there was the dove pecking at the pane and trying to get back into its cage, but it couldn't, for someone had shut the window. Catherine had let the poor thing in, but it had died of weakness and she had laid it on the window-sill outside, where it was still—unless somebody had removed it. That *would* have worried Mrs. Rossetti if she had been told, but she was all but gone, by that time.

And then Algernon came to sit for his portrait, and Georgy had had to go down into the hall and break it to him.

3

It was taken for granted that Mrs. Jones would want to see Her. She did *not* want to see her dear stretched out, hands folded on the coverlet, the way they arrange them, on the very bed where she had been used to lie and laugh—not to say giggle—on their lovely evenings that were no more. Nor did she care to see Gabriel, whom she could hear talking to Brown in sodden, plangent tones on the other side of the flat. He must be tired out. The very mileage he had covered between the hours of eleven and six, walking a good deal, which he hated so—cabs were scarce at night! He had fetched James and Clara from the other side of the river and then Marshall from Savile Row and, lastly, had got to Brown's at Highgate, a matter of several miles.

And always at the back of her mind was the question, why had he gone out again and left Lizzy after bringing her home ill? There must have been One of Their Quarrels and he was full of remorse now that it was too late! They said that he had not looked at her face once, since dawn. . . .

Would Mrs. Jones like to speak to Mr. James and Miss Clara? A natural curiosity overcame Georgy to see what Lizzy's brother and the beautiful Clara were like. She said yes.

A sensible-looking, hard, self-contained man came forward to meet her. "I was aroused in the night," he said, "and I went in all haste to take the hand of my sister, but it was cold. I spoke to her, but there came no response." Clara was as different from Lizzy as James, who in a way resembled her. Clara, questioned gently, said that, though the doctor had told her nothing, she was sure that her sister had died from an overdose. She often had to take something to make her sleep and no doubt had done so last night and miscalculated. Miss Siddall had, on arriving, at once sent Gabriel off to fetch a second opinion while Mr. Hutchinson went on with the pump. Then he had tried flushing out the stomach with water—quarts he had used! At six o'clock he had left off trying and gone away, and she had stopped breathing an hour and twenty minutes later.

Georgy felt sick and decided to go back to Ned—she was not wanted here. She had thoughts of asking Gabriel to come back and sleep at their place, for one night at any rate, but the door was between them and she was timid and decided not to interfere as Mr. Brown was with him.

4

"Gabriel deeply troubled about these sad business arrangements, as you will guess," she wrote to a friend, "and so is Ned, and all the men!"

For there had to be an inquest, Dr. Hutchinson said, in the circumstances. Oh, purely a matter of form, for everyone knew how attached Mr. and Mrs. Rossetti were to each other and there was of course no suspicion of foul play. Still—he had found an empty two-ounce bottle labelled *Poison* in the room. Nothing else of any importance.

So Mr. William Payne, the coroner for Southwark, in Her Majesty's name summoned and warned twenty-four good and sufficient men personally to appear before him at Bridewell Hospital to inquire on behalf of their sovereign Lady the Queen touching the death of Eleanor Elizabeth Rossetti, now lying dead within his jurisdiction. A long list of names was furnished him, among them that of Mr. De Keyser, of Numbers Two and Six Chatham Place, and Mr. Henry Benthall of Number Fourteen, who received their rent on behalf of Mr. Duncan and who had liked the dead woman, for it was she who saw that it was paid with some degree of regularity.

No disgrace attached to the laudanum-taking. Anyone might

sell it, anyone might buy it. It was used for all sorts of mild ailments, much as people take aspirin nowadays, so Mr. Keates, Consulting Chemist, who lived on the same floor, did not shake in his shoes. But the law of England then and now treats suicide as a felony, and its penalties were still severe and ugly at the time this woman died. She was in act a felon and would have to be buried, like Ophelia, "with maimèd rites" and, if in consecrated ground at all, on the north side of the garth always filled last. The very merciful formula, "Suicide whilst of Unsound Mind," would have been upsetting to both families : to the two very proud mothers, to the stiff William and the punctilious James alike, while it would have damnified the social existence of Lydia Wheeler and the child soon to be born of her. As for Gabriel—everything was bound to hurt *him* and he deserved it ! His friends— except Georgy, perhaps, in her stable loving-kindness—did not then envisage the " disastrous effect of his wife's death on the greatest of living men."

Gabriel, it appeared, was not sleeping at home regularly but came back some time in the morning. And Brown gave up his precious working days to sit closeted with him, making up a tale. . . .

In the cold, dark and clammy weather, the fog outside deadening the booming noises and cries of the riverside, the boats, from which the tide had retreated, with their dun sails furled, peaking out of the livid, faintly sun-stained mist, Brown, artist and poet, turned business man, because of his love for these two for ever sundered, sat preparing adequate versions, pre-arranging tactics against the dreadful day of the inquest, " when no secrets shall be hid," hoping somehow to direct the trend of thought of all those who had assisted in this drama— as a hundred papers would call it nowadays—into a decent channel for Gabriel. And Gabriel, in the calm of exhaustion, his passion spent, grown curiously apt and business-like, fell in with Brown's plans for his ulterior benefit and answered questions coherently, while William, with his tremendous discretion and knowledge of the world generally, advised from a business point of view. Morris knew nothing; Ned, managed by Georgy, was no gossip at the worst of times and could be relied on. Georgy herself was the discreetest of women.[1] But they must

---

[1] Her account of the death, from the phrase "First dark waters" to "Pray God comfort Gabriel," occupies less than a page and a half of the two volumes of *Memorials.*

be primed—they must all be at one with what they were going to say to-morrow in the Court room in the old Palace, almost next door.

To begin with why, asked Brown, had Gabriel rushed out to fetch Hutchinson in the first instance? What had frightened him? The smell of laudanum about her? He was used to that—all her friends were. She kept a bottle of it under her pillow at Fortess Terrace and it worried Mrs. Emma rather, though Lizzy never let anyone see her take it—nothing so unpicturesque! What about the dinner? What did she eat? Did anything happen at table to annoy her? Where was he going to tell them he went when he left her at nine? What was the very last word he heard her say?

Poor Swinburne was in the next room crying. The slow-voiced, manly Brown, who felt so much more, would deal with him afterwards. He was a bit to blame.

He catechised Gabriel very stringently. She had been all right at starting, "so-so" rather, as usual, but quite pleased with the idea of trying a new restaurant. Their host was to meet them there at six. It was her fault that they were late in starting. About half-way in the cab she had got so queer that Gabriel suggested that he should take her straight home and then go and explain to Swinburne. But she had refused, putting her head right out of the window and bidding the man drive on. He could not prevent it. Brown knew—didn't he?—that she had a fund of obstinacy which was a defect in her character—her so splendid character—and that once she got an idea into her head, nothing would stop her.

They were late, of course. It was nearly seven before they got there—for six; and Algernon had obviously had something to drink. Poor fellow, he always showed it at once! She knew that wine was forbidden him; that Lady Jane had once summoned Gabriel to Eaton Place and begged him to see to it that her son carried out the doctor's orders and drank nothing but water. Gabriel didn't trouble much: Algernon was much more amusing when wine was in him, but Lizzy got it into her head that that was *her* job; that a woman alone could help him. She was so terribly disappointed in Algernon that she scolded him out loud—in fact the waiters might have thought they were a pair of them—nodding her head as if she herself were overcome by drink, letting it drop forward and then rousing herself with a jerk and putting on the flighty manner (Brown knew it was

302

an effect of shyness) that William, used to the demureness of Christina, so much objected to. The dinner was a failure : none of them could ever have gone there again. He was displeased with her and showed it. Oh, God! Now! come, steady, Gabriel! . . .

And she had said nothing, nothing at all, all the way home in the cab, jolting over the cobblestones, quite still, her feet rammed down in the straw [1] . . . it did not rustle. She had seemed frightened, Gabriel said, that was what he minded most now—as if he had kicked a lame dog. And the moment they got in and he had found fault with her behaviour in the restaurant, the quarrel began. They were at it, arguing, from eight till nine, and then she seemed to be utterly worn out and he was too, and he told her to get to bed and he would go out for a breath, perhaps look in at the Working Men's College for an hour—he had promised he would—and they would meet in the morning and forget it all. She had her back to him, standing at the dressing-table taking off her necklace—beginning to undress. . . . She did not seem to believe in the College though she knew perfectly well that he was still concerned with it— had taken over Brown's class there and had been giving a testimonial [2] to someone, or refusing it. . . .

She had not particularly liked his going to the College that night, Brown suggested, pinning him ? . . . Well, no, as a matter of fact she resented it violently. She seemed to have made up her mind, standing there, to show what power she still had by preventing him from going out again. Twisting the necklace round and round in her hand she began to hint— more than hint—at Fanny, trying to keep him beside her with the threat of another miscarriage—suddenly clapping her hand to her side. . . . He was convinced that she was acting, for he did not really believe in her pregnancy and, anyhow, from something Hutchinson had told him last time, he had gathered that she was not likely to have conceived again.

And so on and so on. Gradually Brown tore the truth out of the bleeding flesh of the man, poet and artist, moved as

[1] Bits of the straw off the floor of the cab were sticking in the hem of her dress that she had no care to shake off.

[2] January 14th, 1862. G. Rossetti gave a testimonial to —— who wrote back to ask if the terms of the recommendation might be " altered to higher praise." D. G. R. declined to do so, saying that he had already gone against his conscience— " this genius seeming to have taken up art as a calling, for the usual reason of unusual incompetence."

Brown had never seen him moved except perhaps when his father died. He got the very words used between them a few hours ago and her cry, "Stay with me, Gug, stay with me!" to be remembered by the poor, remorse- and morphia-sodden wretch on lonely nights in Cheyne Walk in his bed, thick-curtained, "hung with masks of mockery," his sheets "watered with the wasteful warmth of tears." No tears from her—she never wept—but much, oh, too much "damnable iteration." . . . And his back was up because of the vulgar scene in the restaurant. He would not, curse him, he would not stay, and made to leave her, saying he must go to the College if only for an hour—it was his night there.[1] Half undressed she followed him to the landing and stayed hanging over the banisters; any of the other lodgers might have heard the frantic partner of his bed shriek out as he passed down the stone stairs with his head bowed as under a storm—"Go then, and you'll kill this baby as you killed the last!"

5

Soothed and satiate, he had come back a few hours later, táken the key from under the mat, let himself in and called her. Getting no reply, he thought she was sulking and languidly groped for matches. She was in bed and asleep and he felt glad that the matter had been settled so. He did not go near her at first, but then her breathing began to puzzle and frighten him. He stood still a minute, with the candle raised, looking at her; then went downstairs again and told Mrs. Birrell—who luckily was still up—and by her advice went out and fetched Hutchinson.

Where did *she* think he was off to that night? Brown, a man of the world, thought it was to Wapping. Fanny was the only person that Gabriel "knew well enough," as the children say, to leave thus cavalierly whilst half the love-night was still unspent.

As regards the alibi, Brown meant to accept the College explanation. Everyone in St. Martin's Street would, at a pinch, back their ex-chief.

Gabriel had hidden the bottle that lay on the little table by the bedside when he came in, but Brown made him put it back. Someone might have noticed it, he told Gabriel, and for

[1] No, it wasn't.

him to have removed anything might prejudice him if there were any suggestion of foul play in the minds of the jury. But, indeed, Brown had seen and handled that which would certainly exonerate Gabriel from a charge of murder, but would lay Lizzy in a felon's grave. He was on thorns to know if any eye had lit on it before his own. The women would certainly have produced it. But it was still dark when Brown got there and her nightdress was white and would not show a piece of paper pinned on the front. Read out, it ran :—

"*My life is so miserable I wish for no more of it.*"

6

Brown resolved to withhold the darker knowledge that was his until he could discover whether or no Gabriel shared it with him. He was pretty sure that none of the others had noticed the piece of paper before he came. . . . He was not so sure of the doctor who had been first on the scene and was insisting on the inquiry ? He made it his business to pay him a visit, but could not draw him and realised that he must remain terribly anxious on Gabriel's behalf until the inquest was over to-morrow.

There were compensations. Brown had the pleasure of telling Ruskin, on the mat, that Gabriel was not well enough to see him.

It would be in the papers—the son of a baronet dining with an artist and his model in a French café-restaurant in Leicester Square the night before. . . . Swinburne must be given his piece. Brown went to him, in the drawing-room hung round with her poor, wooden little drawings. He was alone and crying— he could stand pain but not strain. He had adored her and she had been very fond of him . . . but Passion, on the red head of him, was impossible.

It was quite another thing tackling Algernon : there was all the difference between his gentlemanly reserve and Gabriel's businesslike communicativeness. Between sobs and Don't Re-members Brown got very little out of the young man. He knew perfectly well that all was not right between the lady and her husband, but do you think he would admit such a thing for a moment ? Invited, delicately, by kind Brown to try to describe her behaviour on the night of the dinner—that was only last night, and she his honoured guest ! No, he had not observed anything in particular . . . she might perhaps have been a little more fatigued than usual, but then she always did seem tired nowadays. It was still " nowadays," and he wept again ! She was, of course, annoyed with him for taking too much wine; she was good enough to care a little what happened to him. . . . In short, Lady Jane's son was too much of a knight and a gentleman to be of much use in building up a defence for Gabriel, should any come to be needed. And he might, in his own mind, though he made no such hint, have considered that Gabriel deserved some punishment.

Brown's imagination got to work. Looking at the white forehead of Algernon and the blue and yellow bump on it, slowly fading out, he was reminded of a scene a few nights ago when the poor fellow had had more than half a glassful of wine and had suddenly caught sight of his own face in Lizzy's little *Cinquecento* mirror and, fancying that the reflection was mocking him, had smashed it with violence and fallen with his forehead on the corner of the table. She had forgiven him, queenly, as she would not have perhaps forgiven Brown or Gabriel if they had broken her looking-glass ? . . . She had a certain power of invective.

Brown's invention was superior to his acumen. . . . He had it ! The Drugged and the Drunk ! She knew of her knight's foible and deplored it : he, on his own showing, was totally unaware of hers. She had gone to the dinner fortified with an extra dose of laudanum in brandy ; and the sight of her protégé's backsliding, combined with her own bemused condition, had been too much for her and she had taken more when she got home—to make her sleep. He must work this explanation up and have it ready for the people who, knowing something of the life of Gabriel and less of poor Lizzy's, would accept it—the superficial Hardmans, the horny-hearted Merediths, the W. B. Scotts of the world.[1]

7

On Wednesday morning—as no post-mortem examination was necessary, the members of the Jury—(Mr. Benthall of Fourteen Chatham Place and Mr. De Keyser of Two, Six, Seven and Eight New Bridge Street, whose names were among

[1] William undertook to write to Scott in Newcastle and tell him exactly what he was wishing him to know, but, answering the letter, Scotus placed the onus with fatal accuracy.

the twenty-four citizens empanelled, had managed not to be included)—mounted, with their heads respectfully down, the steep stairs to the second floor of Chatham Place and were permitted to view *in situ* the body of " Elizabeth Eleanor Rosetti " lying on her own bed, "wonderfully quiet and peaceful-looking, poor thing ! " (so William admitted, as if she had no business to be). Her serene face framed as usual in the oriole wings and upspringing bows of her hair, looked so coloured and beautiful that one of them [1] could not believe that she was really dead until he timidly touched the forehead and experienced " the feel " which convinces—like a mound of stone, cold beyond Arctic dreams . . . like nothing else in the world. Even Brown, earlier in the day, in that deceptive hour when " the rose is seen above the mould " and the flesh fills out as if some new ichor of life had been poured into it, had rushed across to Hutchinson and asked him to come and have another look : it might be one of the Poe-like trances with which Gabriel's reading aloud had familiarised him.

8

Missing their dinners, the gentry from the upper storey, Rossetti, his brother and Swinburne : from the basement, those important witnesses Mrs. Birrell, her daughter and Ellen MacIntyre the housemaid ; while from the other side of the river, Clara Siddall, dark, splendid and frowning as usual, who could not, would not, have helped her red red lips, supported by brother James, silently converged and met at the door of Bride-well Hospital a little higher up the street on the same side. A sad, silent troop, they entered the old House of Correction " for strumpets and idle persons : for the rioter that consumeth all ; for the vagabond that will abide in no place." And there, it seems, must she too fare for a space who is suspected of "wilfully seeking her own salvation."

Through the strong but finely wrought iron doorway picked out with gold, through dusty passages and ante-rooms with shelved walls and tables from which pale-faced clerks and scribes stared up at the rather unusual " cloud of witness," and so into the great panelled Hall with the high, straight windows on

[1] Henry Watts of the *Melbourne Argus* and, later, of the *Standard*, later author of the *Life of Cervantes* and editor of *Don Quixote*. An ugly pock-marked man, as plain as she was fair.

the south-west side looking towards the green meadow on the river bank where once the Templars jousted. In obedience to a whispered direction they stopped, sheep-like, under the big brass chandelier suspended from the ceiling, partially lit this dark day; and in silence, under the eye of the Law of which, for the nonce and at all times, some of them went in fear, humbly bestowed themselves along the walls, waved thereto by a gesture from the beadle, until such time as they should be called to go forward and up between the hollow square of the two long tables, to speak foolish, incriminating words that might be drawn from them by the modern representatives of the rack and the thumbscrew. The Jurymen sat at a long table at right angles to the Coroner and the Witnesses at another long table against the wall. Friends of the dead—there were none! And the Officials were allotted place along the sides of the gangway leading up to where the Coroner, dressed in his so brief authority, sat in the President's immense chair backed by the gay, resplendent arms of Bridewell. Over his head crowded canvases deliriously stooped, so as to be seen even at the risk of a twisted neck, from near the top of the ceiling. They were not Cupids and clouds—they were portraits. Over Mr. Payne's head there was that of a white-faced boy smothered in ermine, handing a Charter of Endowment to the Mayor of London, painted by Holbein who had managed to insert his own likeness into the head of a bystander, and a full-length by Lely of Charles II and a George III after Reynolds. Hung thus deplorably high, they were yet well worth an artist's craning notice. All "pieces"! The chair on which the Coroner sat was by Chippendale or at any rate Hepplewhite.

It must have been the first and the last time in his life that Gabriel Rossetti entered a show-place without looking at the pictures or considering an example of antique furniture, but perhaps he remembered it his whole life long.

> From perfect grief there need not be
> Wisdom or even memory.

Brown, sick, sad and sorry, found himself adumbrating a sonnet, one of a series, which he worked up afterwards for a new love.[1]

Mrs. Birrell, the responsible caretaker of Chatham Place, was examined first, perhaps so that the educated explanations of

[1] See Appendix.

308

her betters should not influence her. Then Clara Siddall was called and sworn. The evidence of James Siddall, for some reason or other, was not taken. Yet the brother and sister of the deceased were the first persons, outside the household, who were with her husband in those trying moments before Brown got there !

It was made clear that Gabriel had gone out again immediately to find a doctor : he had procured four of them before he had done.

Clara Siddall, of Eight Kent Place, black-veiled, weeping through the mesh, charily gave her sister's age next birthday, but did not seem to know the date of that. Yes, her sister had taken a few drops of laudanum in brandy *and water* that very night before she went to bed.[1] She did not suspect any foul play. So far her evidence was all to the good, except that she had added the water. But she reminded the wretched man of his wife's last words by her unnecessarily qualified answer to a straight question—" Any family ? " " None—*alive !* " No, she knew of no enemy—no person intending harm to her sister, nor did she suspect any. . . .

She was led away weeping and, rolling rather, his growing *embonpoint* seeming circumscribed between the two narrow forks of the gangway formed by the table, Gabriel Rossetti passed up, to admit that the deceased was his wife and that her name was Eleanor Elizabeth Rossetti. And that only yesterday she had seemed perfectly well and eager to go out and fulfil an engagement to dine with him and Mr. Swinburne at a new café-restaurant in Leicester Square. But that actually before they started she had turned so queer that he had wanted to stop the cab [2] and tell the man to turn round. But she was set on proceeding. Mr. Payne then gently asked him to describe her manner, and this was the part he had rehearsed with Brown so carefully the day before, but he had forgotten most of the points *he* had to make and those he was to prevent *their* making. He said " Something between flightiness (William's word pursued her thus beyond the grave) and drowsiness." A little excited, was she ? Yes. Had she eaten anything at the dinner to disagree with her ? Mr. Rossetti was afraid he had

---

[1] How did she know ?

[2] " Out in the carriage," says the *Daily News*, and spells the name throughout, as most people did, with one *s*. That and the proper observance of the single *d* in her maiden name were Gabriel's sore point.

not noticed. At any rate the meal was soon over. They had come straight home, having only been in the place an hour.

The Coroner seemed to take it for granted that the anxious husband had stayed with his wife, but Gabriel without prompting from him, said that he had left her at nine, while she was undressing, getting ready for bed, and "right as before." He spoke so naturally that he was not asked where he had gone and put under the necessity of lying, as Brown had dreaded. He was asked how he had found her on his return and at what hour that had taken place? Half-past eleven, and she was then in bed and snoring. Then what had made him fetch Mrs. Birrell and the doctor? Because he had tried to awaken her but had found her "utterly without consciousness" and there was the half-empty phial on the table by her bedside marked Poison. He had not seen it before? Yes—but . . .

The notion of suicide, already pretty nearly dispelled, prompted Mr. Payne's next question. Had she spoken of wishing to die? No. (*But of a dead child in the womb.*) She was engaged to go and stay with friends in the country on Saturday and had ordered some new clothes for the occasion— he understood that she had bought a mantle only the day before (which happened to be a Sunday!) But he would naturally be a little confused about dates, poor fellow!

Simple, manly, business-like, giving his evidence without reserve and seeming anxious to assist the law, though properly distressed (Mrs. Birrell had spoken to their living happily together; the sounds of brawls had not descended—even Xantippe would not be heard a floor or so below), Mr. Rossetti even acquired merit with the Coroner and the Jury, who knew a gentleman when they saw one, even if it was one of those randy artists! He dilated rather copiously on the disposition of the deceased to take laudanum at all times and seasons (showing something of the aversion of a new addict to the habit that was being inculcated in him by the partner of his bed and board), his speech slightly informed with the bitterness which was, to those who knew, part of the *fons et origo* of their estrangement, taken in conjunction with his connection with Mrs. Hughes. Yes, his wife was in the habit of taking very large doses: he had known her to take as much as a hundred drops at a time; there was the brown kind that was cheaper and less calculable in its effect. . . . That was a good stroke, Brown thought. (Gabriel was beginning to know a lot about drugs. His own special anodyne, his friends knew, was already chloral.) He went on to say it was his opinion that, without opiates of some kind, she could not sleep or, at times, even swallow food. And that the neuralgia which had obliged them to come home early had become so intense that night (brushing aside Clara's polite fiction of " in water ") that he thought she must have taken it neat to quieten her roaring nerves, without, however, any idea of injuring herself. . . .

He protested too much, and Brown was quite glad when the Coroner asked him to retire in favour of the next witness.

During the rest of the examination the drug *motif* was kept up as well as that of the husband's devotion, and this was all Brown's handiwork. Brown had known how to deal with those malleable worm-witnesses downstairs, only half cognisant of and wholly despising the way of the eagles perching high above in their aëry hung with dirty gobbets of brocade and faded silks and velvets, carpeted with dirty threadbare rugs, peacocks' feathers [1] stuck about and " orts " out of curiosity shops, gilt chiffoniers set with broken potsherds and kitchen stuff which they called " good " china. Actually they were quite quiet people. Mrs. Birrell had known Mrs. Rossetti for nine years, officially for two, when she began living there as his wife. That got out. Too late to matter, but she would have disliked it. When did they last see her alive ? On Monday afternoon—quite cheerful, for her. Mrs. Birrell had not known when they went out nor when they came back, but Mrs. Rossetti was asleep by eleven— that she knew for certain. She was never so surprised in her life as when Mr. Rossetti called down to the basement, and at the queer tone of his voice. He said, Come and sit with her while I run for the doctor. Where was she ? In bed, and quite black in the face when they took a candle to see her. The doctor came very quickly. *And* he attended to her. It was still dark. Did the witness fancy anything wrong ? No, she knew of no hurt to her nor suspected any. Would she say they were a united couple ? She would say they lived very comfortably together.

Francis Hutchinson, called next, honestly believed that the deceased had died from the effects of an overdose of laudanum, a fairly large one ; he had found in the room an empty phial marked Poison and the smell was very distinct. She was then,

---

[1] What the Rossettis called their feather-brooms.

already, in a comatose state; quite unable to swallow. He had done all he could to empty the stomach out, but after a while he had had to give it up and leave her in the care of a friend, Dr. Marshall. He had attended her in her confinement last year—a female child still-born—but he had only seen her once since in the street. She had hurried past him and seemed altogether in a very nervous state, perhaps owing to the habit she had contracted. . . .

Catherine Birrell said she never got less than a shilling's-worth for her and always took the same bottle to get filled. The one produced was it? Yes. She waited on her? Yes—but she never once saw her swallow any of it. She had not bought her any for six months.

Again Brown was glad when she retired in favour of Algernon Charles Swinburne, whose evidence was nugatory and who got himself dismissed almost at once, for he had one of his attacks of St. Vitus's Dance and could not stand still, which confused the Coroner. No, he had noticed nothing unusual about the deceased on Monday night, except that she seemed a little weaker than usual. Exactly what he had admitted to Brown. *Bon sang ne peut mentir*, but it can at least manage to be consistent. . . .

He did no good but no harm and the evidence of Ellen Mac-Intyre with her " She told me that she had taken quarts of the stuff in her time ! " was a clincher. Like Catherine Birrell she did not mention having bought any laudanum recently for her, but by now they knew all about Mr. Keates, Consulting Chemist, handy on the next floor.

" And all doubts of suicide were disposed of," said the City Press. The verdict was *Accidental Death*. William sedulously omitted to record the proceedings in his so opulent diary and, except for a Sheffield paper and the paragraph in the *Daily News—Death of a Lady from an Overdose of Laudanum*—the case was not reported. Perhaps Mr. Henry Watts was responsible for that ? And for the carriage to the Sablonière Hotel.

CHAPTER XXXV

I

JONES was too ill to leave the house and Georgy was nursing him. Lizzy's people, excepting her mother, stoical and vain, who lived to be ninety-two, were abased to the very ground. The friends of Lydia Wheeler ever after hinted at a "constitutional melancholy." She never would talk of her sister; between the events of that dreadful week and her after life, full of thought-deadening, useful child-bearing, a curtain was drawn.

The scene, of course, was lightly dressed for Anne, Janey, Georgy, and delicate females generally, while Gabriel's men friends generally spoke of "the woman at Wapping, or somewhere on the other side of the river," as filling the bill.[1]

Of his own family, William was the most affected because of his brotherly love—and a tinge, perhaps, of remorse for neglect of her. Scott, the friend of his boyhood, had to take him off to the Continent as soon as his work at Chatham Place was done. Both men of the world, these two did not adjudicate the blame;[2] loving Gabriel nearly as much as William, Scott, more cynical if anything than he, blamed Lizzy and was of opinion that Fanny, Gabriel's *dæmonia* from the very beginning, had grown to be more in the nature of an easement than anything else and that the matter-of-fact mistress prevented the husband from going

---

[1] Little Georgy would describe a street-walker as "one whose goodness was in abeyance," but Anne Gilchrist and Miss Heaton were of sterner stuff. Ruskin, before he went away, wrote to the latter telling her that B. J. was so depressed "about Rossetti's wife's suicide," and over his own work, that if she would buy something of him she would be doing a kindness—and "would not be getting a third-rate work, by any means."

[2] "Heard of the death of Mrs. Gabriel with sincere sorrow and grief for *him*. The *circumstance* you mention and which we hear from other sources has been the cause of some notoriety, adding to the mutual pain of such a parting."—Scott, *Reminiscences*.

The use of the singular points to Scott's cognisance of the real facts, which he obviously was pleased to possess.

313

mad when the wild wife died. She had, invited or not invited, come to sit as usual next day. Who was there to forbid or mind?

2

The inquest safely over, it was all out. Everyone knew how badly Mr. and Mrs. Rossetti had been getting on together and considered that it was the man's infidelities which had driven the woman to her death. Yet his behaviour after the inquest when he had, as it were, settled down a little, whether premeditated or accidental, dictated by prudence or merely characteristic, did not foster the idea of remorse at all, except perhaps for a letter to Mrs. Gilchrist, beautiful, patient, full of self-abasement; that, and his refusal to look on his dead wife or even [1] go into the room where she must lie until Thursday. But then the portrait in the green robe with the yellow hair falling over it, for which she had posed less than a week ago, all the time confronted him in his studio as he sat, and when they considerately put its face to the wall he turned it round again.

William of course made himself responsible for the funeral arrangements.[2] Another plot of ground was bought, near the grave of Gabriele Rossetti, under an aspen tree in the haunted western corner of the cemetery—Number 5779. William ordered the coffin and dictated the name-plate and fixed the date of burial for Thursday. Meanwhile Gabriel slept, God knows where, and none of them dared to ask; but William let it be understood that he went to them in Albany Street. Gabriel never left the house in Chatham Place at all now, until after dark; it would not have been a friend's part, when the little green garden gate on to the street clashed, to look to see whether he turned northwards, to Regent's Park, or southwards towards the river. During the day he was to be found in his studio, ready to come out and speak to all, issuing like a prince into the ante-room where suitors wait.

The women of his family did not need to meet Fanny; she was a mere studio piece. They came every day and sat with friends in the drawing-room, telling them what they wanted them to know. That is to say, Gabriel's mother and his sister Maria:

---

[1] In this he was not altogether singular among these semi-*détraqués* who are our great men. Tennyson refused absolutely to look on his mother's corpse, so Mr. Allingham told me.

[2] A famous bookseller avers that he paid the funeral expenses.

314

Christina did not offer to accompany them in their daily pilgrimage to Chatham Place. Her soul's salvation did not lie that way and she was too honest to come and vex the unhappy dust she would not save. She put on mourning for her sister-in-law (Allingham saw her in it) and kept it on till August. But Janey Morris, "tall, wonderful, in white bodice and yellowish skirt," came quite soon to Chatham Place, but did not stay very long. She had not known the dead woman so very well.

There were things to do, and coming and going in the house over the river. Green, the frame-maker, was sent for and there was a sound of knocking in the desolate rooms. He packed *Before the Battle* and despatched it to Norton in America. Then he was bidden to go and ask old Mrs. Rossetti if she could find the cradle which only a week ago young Mrs. Rossetti had got out, to put on fresh bows and loops of ribbon. Now, this was to be sent just as it was, bedclothes and all, to Mrs. Joseph Wheeler at Number Ten Barnsbury Street—Mr. Rossetti wrote the label himself. Not even Mr. Brown knew that just before Green began cording it up for Pickford, Mr. Rossetti had sneaked out on to the little landing when no one was about and had laid a five-pun' note between the two tiny pillows.[1] Someone—Clara, when she came back after the inquest to fetch her bag?—had cut off a lock of hair for the unavoidably absent sister, and a good bit for herself. But there, poor Liz had enough and to spare! Aunt Day always said that the masses of it had weakened her—but then it was so light and loose. . . .

Gabriel would not see Georgy, but he sent, both to her and Red Lion Mary, photographs of Mrs. Rossetti from his own drawings of her, and a nice letter. He told people that he had several times attempted to have Liz photographed from life, but that she always came out so badly it was no use keeping them— the gold hair always came out black or blue. . . .

The only thing of hers he cared to keep was her long gold watch-chain. The family might have her " things."

Aunt Day took her brown and black striped silk[2] and her work-box with the two letters she had once received from Maria and Christina respectively lying folded in the bottom of it, and

---

[1] None of Lydia's children turned out to have golden hair and Gabriel took no further interest in them.

[2] Her best. I have seen a bit of it. She was wearing it when she was photographed at Hastings. Dresses were of such good material in those days that they were long-lived for careful people.

the little table easel on which she had painted most of her drawings.

Fanny took the Swinburne, and Gabriel was too miserable to miss it.

3

Presently Gabriel saw a few men—Meredith, of all people, Morris of course and " his little Northumbrian friend " and hers, with whom he had already arranged to live. But Ruskin he would not see. It was William who led Ruskin, all bowed and stooping, into the bedroom to say good-bye to his beautiful protégée of other days. And his most arrant failure ! (But he had failed with all women.) He had done his best for Lizzy, but the bone-dust, the subsidy, the fees to Acland, the sojourns at Hastings and Clevedon and Nice and Paris even, had not availed to save this most wilful of all women, who lay now, still and static, weighed down, but not oppressed by the Eternity into which she had entered ; mute-faced—" as though the hills were on her eyelids piled "[1]—safe in Heaven—instead of his own very Calvinistic Hell.

" Marvellously calm and beautiful," so William, reluctantly, of her who in life had always puzzled and confounded him. He could not call her " flighty " now, yet the old grievance was still uppermost. " *Secretum meum mihi*." . . . Still she evaded him and the rest : her secret more than ever was her own, her life's withdrawal which had vexed and estranged them all, for ever sealed.

And poor deeply grieving Allingham wrote, thinking of her :—

> Her face is very pale and fair,
> Her hooded eyelids darkly shed
> Celestial love, and all her hair
> Is like a crown around her head.
>
> Yet now is silence. Do not weep.

No one did but Algernon. For, as even William could bring himself to say

> ——with her was such very humbleness,
> She seemed to say, I am in peace.

Yet, how dared she ?—Ruskin was saying in his Calvinistic heart, though, by her looks, God had spoken. She had not presumed on His mercy ; yea, she who had taken her own life had been permitted to enter the Everlasting Rest. Ruskin's tottering

[1] T. Gordon Hake.

316

faith, undermined by the 'haviour of his own cruel little Love, for ever died as he looked on Rossetti's, in full possession of unmerited Beatitude.

Ruskin, poor dear, who had never gained any woman's confidence, knew all : his psychological flair, always there but sometimes inhibited by pedantry and didacticism, told him what the Blessed Damozel had done and yet been allowed to take her place in Heaven. And Gabriel, in his eyes, was now utterly damned. He knew the nature of the unholy relief that the man was finding, in these early hours of loneliness, from his intolerable remorse,[1] nor would he in this hour have denied the poor wretch the rough-and-ready consolation of a woman's breast. . . . He was aware, too, that the days of their great friendship were numbered and that Gabriel, conscious of his terrible perspicuity and intolerant of his usage of the right to lecture, would, sooner or later, pick a quarrel with him on that account.[2]

4

On Wednesday afternoon, late, the undertaker was expected to come and finish. Gabriel's mother, sister and brother, and a friend or two—Brown, Swinburne, Anne Gilchrist and young Luke Ionides—were assembled in the room next to the one where, alongside the carven bedstead on which she had died, the coffin stood on its trestles, not yet closed down. All had taken their formal last look at her except Gabriel. Would he, now—his first since Tuesday? He was moving restlessly about among them, hardly speaking. Presently he went to his study and returned, looking ugly with his large, distended nostrils and loose lip, carrying in his hand the little green book they all had handled, into which, evening after evening last winter, he had been copying his poems. He made for the bedroom which he had not entered since Monday, saying in a low voice, without looking to the right or left : " I have often been working at these poems while she was ill and suffering and I might have been attending to her, and now they shall go ! "

[1] " *Natural* sorrow does not destroy strength but gives it, while an *irregular*, out-of-the-way, sorrow kills, according to weight."
In writing this, he was, of course, thinking of himself and Rosie.
[2] Within a month of the death Rossetti was worrying Ruskin on a matter of business. He got him written to, to say that he was under the impression that drawings by himself and his wife were being sold by Ruskin. Why, in Business' name, not?

He had beckoned Algernon to follow him.

When they both came back after a few moments Gabriel's hands were empty. He passed into the other room and Algernon stayed behind and told them what Gabriel had done. He had lifted the tiny, thin, lace-bordered napkin that undertakers bring to cover the face with and laid the book on the left side, between her hair and her cheek, sedulously averting his eyes, like a child that has been scolded.

It was the one gesture of Gabriel Rossetti's life—to be rendered void, at the behest of the caitiff Howell.[1]

She had won her woeful victory. For her sake he was a painter, no longer a poet, his credentials buried in a dead woman's hair.

5

More than the book was buried with her. A few hours before they all arrived, Catherine Birrell had crept in, carrying the dead dove off the window-sill, and laid it at the thin end of the coffin, like a dog at the feet of a Crusader. It took no room to speak of—no more than Lizzy herself had taken in this world.

---

[1] " Fallen in the practice of a cursed knave," he never, in the opinion of his brother artists, painted a fine picture again. With Howell as a guide, he went deep into Spiritualism.

FRONT VIEW 14 CHATHAM PLACE
JUST BEFORE DEMOLITION
From a photograph

CHAPTER XXXVI

IT has been said [1] that Remorse is the easiest passion of all to live down : Rossetti never did. His own fierce and sentimental personality would not let him forget, and Society forthwith started the legend that was to hound him to his passive, drug-ridden death, strangled by the hank of golden hair that hung on the bell-pull of his bedroom and the dreadful onus of the recovery, by dull, swart, gravediggers, of his last oblation to her.

" Let him, it does him honour," his brother had said when told that Gabriel had laid the little green book under her cheek. But Brown, an artist, had not approved of this confiscation by Death, of work that might enrich the world. And later the man himself allowed the haunting fear of blindness to nullify and render vain this one fine motion of his spirit. Yes, one can dictate a sonnet, but not a picture, and he was soon got to think that actual publication of masterpieces addressed to her would be a surer tribute than that last alteration and obliteration of the grave. So there were great flares by night, [2] in the western corner on the haunted side by the aspen tree in Highgate Cemetery, and Mr. Tebbs who, with Howell, was Master of these Ceremonies, lay abed three days in his home in Aubrey Walk with a sore throat. . . .

And the joke of it all was that the best of these poems were enshrined in the memories of The Faithful who had heard them so many times. Brown, Swinburne, Alaric "Attila" Watts, Tebbs, down to my mother, could have reeled them off at a sitting, and did very often. And besides, who wanted to recover " Dante at Verona " or even " The Staff and Scrip " ?

Clara alone, of Lizzy's relations, was able to be at the graveside. She was not told of the exhumation, so that on the appearance of " Poems and Ballads " she swore that recovery of these masterpieces was impossible, since she had with her own eyes seen the coffin let down in its bands and " the earth over her."

---

[1] By Leslie Stephen, of Regulus.   [2] In 1868.

319

At first, stunned, Gabriel was noisy. Then he settled down into a drugged and sleepy monomania. The carven bed was moved into the sitting-room and made into a couch. He never slept again in Chatham Place, though he painted there a little. But a month after her death he could not bear even to do that and took some chambers on the first floor of Number Fifty-Nine, Lincoln's Inn Fields. For a time his work was feeble and unremunerative. Scott had to be his banker. Ruskin had gone out of town on the very day of the funeral, and then Rossetti got it into his head that the Professor was selling his drawings by Lizzy and the little quarrel, foreseen by the other, took place.

Of the family, Lyddy would not see him and the mother was too ill, but kind Clara, whom they fondly called Tump, went to see him sometimes, to talk to him about Liz, reminding him of nice things connected with the days that were gone, which helped his tardy tears to flow. And Tennyson was nice, and an American called Whistler. And Allingham, shocked, but very pitiful, thinking of "The Cold Wedding," written after the first time he saw her, and another poem, more deeply serious, "Mea Culpa" (nothing to do with them), which he had once shown in manuscript to Gabriel—"Very fine, my boy!"

In July he had come over as usual and met Gabriel at a great affair at the Parkes' ("Bessie as usual an excellent hostess"). And William and his sisters (or did his eye deceive him?) were "in mourning for poor Mrs. D. G." The family were proposing to live all together and maybe a Polidori—and of course Gabriel must have Swinburne "to inspirit" him—in an old house in Chelsea "built in Elizabethan style" with great bow windows (?). It would be possible, Gabriel said, to make a studio of the old hall and a fanlight might be cut over the door to make one see better coming in. . . .

Next year Gabriel had his first epileptiform fit. Later, he went to Newcastle, taking Fanny with him, to look up her relations while he hobnobbed with his best buyers, Mr. Leatheart and his son-in-law Rae. Mr. Rae bought a little oil picture of Mrs. Hughes, looking tragic, as harpies can—her blunt features somewhat sharpened, perhaps, by the terrible happenings in which she had been art and part.

While, in the other camp, Lizzy's mother, the dignified, handsome old lady, recovered some or all of her spirits—she was a bit of a fay too—and went out often to tea, letting her wonderful hair down as her wont was, so that it lay like a draught of silver fishes over her shoulders, right to the ground. She would be fetched home by her two tall deferential sons, James and Harry. James in Cator Street, carefully preserving his dead sister's marriage lines, lived longest, kindly remembered by the neighbouring tobacconist. Gabriel kept both brothers. It was the least he could do. Clara, alas, died in an asylum.

Barbara Bodichon, she who at Hastings had engineered " The Cold Wedding," much later, to please Allingham, went to see Mr. Rossetti " in a friendly way." For " I am so sorry for him— I like him so." Ten years after this she did not even recognise him, until he spoke.

Gabriel let Boyce have Chatham Place and Boyce slept there and used the studio, so full of ghosts, until the whole block was pulled down. In 'sixty-eight my mother had tea with him in Number 14 and sat on the carven bed on which Lizzy had died.

Gabriel never saw her grave and left instructions that he was not to be buried in Highgate Cemetery in any circumstances whatever.

MEA CULPA

At me one night the angry moon
Suspended to a rim of cloud,
Glared through the courses of the wind.
Suddenly then my spirit bow'd
And shrank into a fearful swoon
That made me deaf and blind.

We sinn'd—we sin—is that a dream?
We wake—there is no voice nor stir;
Sin and repent from day to day,
As though some reeking murderer
Should dip his hand in a running stream,
And lightly go his way.

Embrace me, fiends and wicked men,
For I am of your crew. Draw back,
Pure women, children with clear eyes.
Let Scorn confess me on his rack,—
Stretch'd down by force, uplooking then
Into the solemn skies!

Singly we pass the gloomy gate;
Some robed in honour, full of peace,
Who of themselves are not aware,
Being fed with secret wickedness,
And comforted with lies: my fate
Moves fast; I shall come there.

With all so usual, hour by hour,
And feeble will so lightly twirl'd
By every little breeze of sense,—
Lay'st thou to heart this common world?
Lay'st thou to heart the Ruling Power,
Just, infinite, intense?

Thou wilt not frown, O God.   Yet we
Escape not thy transcendent law;
It reigns within us and without.
What earthly vision never saw
Man's naked soul may suddenly see,
Dreadful, past thought or doubt.

WILLIAM ALLINGHAM.

ROSSETTI PEDIGREE

GABRIELE ROSSETTI = FRANCES MARY LAVINIA POLIDORI
B. 28 Feb. 1783
Italian Patriot,
Author and Poet
D. 26 April 1854
Burd. Highgate
  Cemetery

B. 27 April 1800 at 42, Broad
  Street, Golden Square, London
Marrd. 10 April 1826
D. 8 April 1886, aged 85
Burd. Highgate Cemetery

MARIA FRANCESCA
ROSSETTI
B. 17 Feb. 1827

DANTE GABRIEL ROSSETTI = ELIZABETH ELEANOR SIDDAL
B. 12 May, 1828
D. 9 April, 1882, at
  Birchington-on-Sea

Marrd. 23 May, 1860
D. 11 Feb. 1862

WILLIAM MICHAEL ROSSETTI = LUCY MADOX BROWN
B. 25 Sept. 1829
D. 1919

B. 19 July, 1843, at
  Paris
Marrd. March 1874
D. 12 April, 1894, at
  San Remo

CHRISTINA GEORGINA
ROSSETTI
B. 5 Dec. 1830
D. 29 Dec. 1894

SIDDAL(L) PEDIGREE

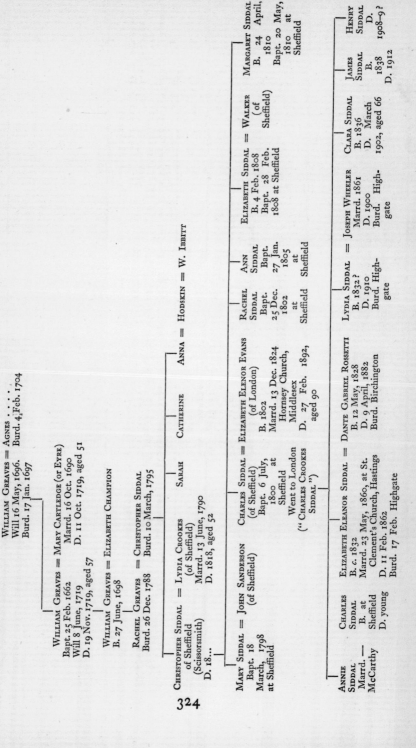

WILLIAM GREAVES = AGNES . . . . .
Will 16 May, 1696. Burd. 4 Feb. 1704
Burd. 17 Jan. 1697

WILLIAM GREAVES = MARY CARTLEDGE (or EYRE)
Bapt. 25 Feb. 1662   Marrd. 16 Oct. 1690
Will 8 June, 1719   D. 11 Oct. 1719, aged 51
D. 19 Nov. 1719, aged 57

WILLIAM GREAVES = ELIZABETH CHAMPION
B. 27 June, 1698

RACHEL GREAVES = CHRISTOPHER SIDDAL
Burd. 26 Dec. 1788   Burd. 10 March, 1795

CHRISTOPHER SIDDAL = LYDIA CROOKES   SARAH   CATHERINE   ANNA = HODSKIN = W. IBBITT
of Sheffield   (of Sheffield)
(Scissorsmith)   Marrd. 13 June, 1790
D. 18...   D. 1818, aged 52

MARY SIDDAL = JOHN SANDERSON   CHARLES SIDDAL = ELIZABETH ELENOR EVANS   RACHEL   ANN   ELIZABETH SIDDAL = WALKER   MARGARET SIDDAL
Bapt. 18   (of Sheffield)   (of Sheffield)   (of London)   SIDDAL   SIDDAL   B. 4 Feb. 1808   (of   B. 24 April,
March, 1798   Bapt. 6 July,   B. 1802   Bapt.   Bapt.   Bapt. 28 Feb.   Sheffield)   1810
at Sheffield   1800 at   Marrd. 13 Dec. 1824   25 Dec.   27 Jan.   1808 at Sheffield   Bapt. 20 May,
    Sheffield   Hornsey Church,   1802   1805   1810 at
    Went to London   Middlesex   at   at   Sheffield
    (" CHARLES CROOKES   D. 27 Feb. 1892,   Sheffield   Sheffield
    SIDDAL ")   aged 90

ANNIE   CHARLES   ELIZABETH ELEANOR SIDDAL = DANTE GABRIEL ROSSETTI   LYDIA SIDDAL = JOSEPH WHEELER   CLARA SIDDAL   JAMES   HENRY
SIDDAL   SIDDAL   B. c. 1832   B. 12 May, 1828   B. 1832?   Marrd. 1861   B. 1836   SIDDAL   SIDDAL
Marrd. —   B. at   Marrd. 23 May, 1860, at St.   D. 9 April, 1882   D. 1910   D. 1900   D. March   B. 1838   D.
McCarthy   Sheffield   Clement's Church, Hastings   Burd. Birchington   Burd. High-   Burd. High-   1902, aged 66   D. 1912   1908–9 ?
    D. young   D. 11 Feb. 1862   gate   gate
    Burd. 17 Feb. Highgate

324

APPENDIX I

MARRIAGES solemnised in the Parish of Hornsey, in the County of Middlesex, in the year 1824.

Charles Crookes Siddall, Batchelor, of this Parish, Elizabeth Elenor Evans, Spinster, of this Parish, were married in this Church by Banns with consent of this Thirteenth Day of December in the year One Thousand eight Hundred and twenty four

By me, J. Bluck, Curate.

This Marriage was so solemnised ⟮Charles Crooks Siddall.
between us   ⟮Elizabeth Elenor Evans.

In the Presence of ⟮Wm. Henry (Batten ?)
No. 348.   ⟮Mary (Cookman ?)

   Extracted from the Register Book of the said Parish this 13th Day of Decr. in the year 1824

325

APPENDIX II: *THE THELEMA PROJECT*

From *Railway Reminiscences* : G. P. Neale.

The Monastery of Mount St. Bernard is situated on the borders of Charnwood Forest; we arrived there by way of Coalville, and drove to the door of the Monastery. It was a new sensation to be received by the Guest Master in his white monkish costume, and to be invited to enter the convent premises. While all the other Members of the Confraternity have "silence" enforced on them, the Guest Master has a dispensation in this respect. . . .

The Guest Master explained to us the extent of the Monastery grounds, the whole farm being cultivated by hard labour. There were two bodies of monks—one called the Choir Brethren, the others the Lay Brethren: the latter wore dark robes, the former wore white vestments; the rule of "silence" applied to all alike, but the Lay Brethren were mainly occupied in the day in the field labour, tending the flocks, and other portions of outdoor agricultural life, while the Choir Brethren were free from these engagements.

· · · · · · ·

We came to the doors of the interior quadrangle; on them was posted up "No woman is allowed to pass through these doors." . . .

"Silence!" "Eternity!" met us at every corner, and at intervals along the cloistered walk. In the centre of the quadrangle were the graves of various Members of the Confraternity who had entered into the silent land, and had exchanged their opportunities of time for Eternity itself; each had been laid there, without any coffin, simply wrapped in the monastic garb. It had been customary to keep an open grave in this central spot in readiness for the next brother who might in turn fall a victim. . . . It was a relief to follow our Guest Master out into the open fields, and walk through the pastures where the sheep were so tame that they moved not away in the slightest degree at our approach; they allowed themselves to be handled like domestic animals. Here and there we saw the Lay Brethren; they took no notice of us as we passed them on the pathway, they kept their eyes on the ground, lost apparently in contemplation, and so indeed did those few Choir Brethren we came across in the cloisters and passages. . . .

The Abbot wore a garment much like the other monks, he was girt with a long chain of beads and a cross pendant from the chain, he . . . seemed pleased to answer any inquiries. . . .

He told us that he had given orders to dispense with the Trappist rule of the open grave, as there had been unpleasantness connected with their burial customs in this respect, and had decided to abandon the practice.

We took our leave, first of him and then of the Guest Master, and placing our contributions in the monastery alms box left St. Bernard's with many striking memories, none more permanent than the . . . notice at the entrance of the quadrangle, " Silence ! " " Silence ! O Eternity ! "

APPENDIX III: *MS. DRAFT OF BROWN'S SONNET*

Hopeless Love.   Sonnet 6.   Absence.

My mistress one dark night passed over sea.
(. . . . . . *this dark hour is on the* . . .)
O may the gales deal gently with such freight
. . . *might the gales her softness* emulate)

(And on my sleeplessness did visions wait)
By turns, each saddening and each one she
(. . . *each sad of face* . . .)
Till one not her in mien . . . approaching me
Told how, bewept by kindred desolate
She lay at point of death, her mother strait
(*She lay* . . . . then sought I straight

Her mother, love armed—spurning secrecy.
The half lit chamber faint with drugs I scanned

The blackened lips, the wan white brow and the trace
(The wan white features *dark lipped and the trace*
(*The wan white dark-lipped features and* . . .)
Of pain on eyes fringed still with loveliness
(. . . . . . *fringed round*)

Till agony of sobbing as a wand
Waved back my phantasy's strong fever and
Left but the tears that wetted still my face
(*Of all left but some tears along* . . .)

DG

Note.—The holograph initials *DG*, set against line 14 by Mr. Brown, surely refer to the circumstances of the death scene in Chatham Place on that day in February, 1862. V. H.

APPENDIX IV

London
and
Southwark

AN INQUISITION indented taken for our Sovereign Lady the Queen at the Precinct of Bridewell in London on the Twelfth day of February in the Twenty-fifth year of the reign of our Sovereign Lady Victoria by the Grace of God of the United Kingdom of Great Britain and Ireland Queen Defender of the Faith before William Payne Sergeant at Law CORONER of our said Lady the Queen for the City of London and the Borough of Southwark in the County of Surrey on view of the body of Elizabeth Eleanor Rossetti now here lying dead within the jurisdiction of the said Coroner upon the oaths of the undersigned Jurors good and lawful men of the said City who being now here duly chosen sworn and charged to enquire for our said Lady the Queen when where and in what manner the said Elizabeth Eleanor Rossetti came to her death say upon their Oaths that the said Elizabeth Eleanor Rossetti being a female of the age of twenty-nine years and the wife of Dante Gabriel Rossetti an artist on the tenth day of February in the year aforesaid at Chatham Place in the said Precinct and City Accidentally took an overdose of Laudanum by means whereof she the said Elizabeth Eleanor Rossetti then and there became mortally sick and distempered in her Body of which said mortal sickness and distemper and of the Laudanum aforesaid so by her accidentally taken as aforesaid she the said Elizabeth Eleanor Rossetti on the Eleventh day of February in the year aforesaid at Chatham Place aforesaid did die   And so the Jurors aforesaid upon their Oaths aforesaid do say that the said Elizabeth Eleanor Rossetti in the manner and by the means aforesaid Accidentally and casually and by misfortune came to her death.

IN TESTIMONY whereof as well the said Coroner as the said Jurors have to this Inquisition set their Hands and Seals the day year and place first above written.

Wm. Payne Coroner	Hy. Watts	George Rider
T. S. Capel	H. J. Andrew	
James Spicer	Charles Coulson	
He. Miller	Wm. Tuff	
John Hart	Thomas Martin	
Charles James Thicke	J. T. Teasdale	

To the Beadles and Constables of the
Precinct of Bridewell in London.

By virtue of my Office of Coroner of our Sovereign Lady the Queen, for the City of London and the Borough of Southwark in the County of

329

Surrey, These are, in Her Majesty's Name, to charge and command you, that in sight hereof, you summon and warn Twenty-four good and sufficient Men of your Precinct personally to appear before me on Wednesday the twelfth day of February one thousand eight hundred and sixty two at ½ past 1 of the clock in the afternoon precise time, at Bridewell Hospital in the said Precinct and City then and there to do and execute all such things as shall be given them in charge, and to enquire on behalf of our Sovereign Lady the Queen, touching the death of Elizabeth Eleanor Rossetti now lying dead within my jurisdiction, and for your so doing this shall be your Warrant; and that you attend at the time and place above mentioned, to make a Return of the Names of those you have so summoned, and further to do and execute such other matters as shall be then and there enjoined you; and have you then and there this Warrant, Given under my Hand and Seal this Eleventh day of February 1862.

Wm Payne   Coroner.

The Execution of this Warrant appears by the Panel hereunto annexed.

The answer of

Thos Oxford   Beadle.

LIST OF NAMES FOR THE CORONER

Mr. John Hart
Mr. John Campbell Junr
Mr. John Sheppard
Mr. James Spicer
Mr. John Rider
Mr. Thomas Spencer Capel   Foreman.
Mr. Ishmael Fisher
Mr. Charles James Thicke
Mr. John Walpole
Mr. Henry James Andrew
Mr. Henry Watts
Mr. William Horsford
Mr. Henry Miller
Mr. Ralph Charles Price
Mr. Charles Coulson
Mr. James Thomas Teasdale
Mr. William Tuff
Mr. Thomas Martin
Mr. Henry Benthall
Mr. Thomas MacNally

Mrs. Sarah Birrell, housekeeper
Catherine Birrell, daughter
Ellen McIntyre, niece
Clara Siddall, sister to Mrs. Rossetti
Mr. Swinburn, friend of Mrs. Rossetti

14 Chatham Place   witnesses.

330

FANNY HUGHES
From a photograph by Downey of Newcastle

Sarah Birrill 14 Chatham Place Blackfriars says I am Housekeeper says I knew the deceased Mrs Rossetti. I have known her 9 years, she has lived there about 2 years. This happened on Monday night after she was in bed. I saw her about 4 in the afternoon. She was quite cheerful then. At 11 she was asleep. I was called up about $\frac{1}{2}$ past 11 by her husband. I saw her then in bed. She looked very blank (? black) in the face. A Doctor was sent for he came directly. And he attended to her. She died at 20 minutes past 7 on Tuesday morning. She used to take laudanum occasionally to produce sleep for the last twelve-months I saw a Phial of it was under her pillow. I knew of no hurt to her nor dont suspect any. Her husband & herself lived very comfortable together.

Clara Siddall No. 8 Kent Place Old Kent Road says the deceased was my sister her name was Elizabeth Eleanor Rossetti. Her age 29 last birthday. I saw her on Saturday evening last she seemed in tolerably good spirits then. I have heard of her taking laudanum to produce sleep. I was sent for and saw her about 3 on Tuesday morning. She was then alive but quite unconscious. I know of no harm to her. I dont suspect any. I heard she had taken a few drops of laudanum in brandy and water before she went to bed. She had no family alive.

Dante Gabriel Rossetti of No. 14 Chatham Place Artist says that deceased was my wife & her name was Elizabeth Eleanor Rossetti. On Monday afternoon she was perfectly well, about 6 or 7 we went out to dinner, but before we started she appeared drowsy and when we got half way in the cab I proposed going home again. She wished to go on and we dined at the   in Leicester Square with a friend. She seemed somewhat between flightiness and drowsiness, a little excited. We left there at 8 and came straight home. I went out again after 9 leaving her just going to bed. She seemed as right as before. She was in the habit of taking large doses of laudanum. I know that she has taken a 100 drops. I thought that she had the laudanum in brandy. I returned home again at $\frac{1}{2}$ past 11 and then she was in bed and snoring. I found her utterly without consciousness. I found a Phial on a small table by her bedside, it was quite empty. The Doctor was sent for and he attended her she had not spoken of wishing to die. She had contemplated going out of town in a day or two and had bought a new mantle the day before. She was very nervous & had I believe diseased heart. My impression is that she did not do it to injure herself but to quiet her nerves. She could not have lived without laudanum. She could not sleep at times nor take food.

Francis Hutchinson of Bridge Street M.D. says I knew the deceased and attended her in her confinement in April or May last. The child was born dead and had been dead for a fortnight before it was born. I have only seen her about once since then, that was about a month ago in the street. I was sent for on Monday night about $\frac{1}{2}$ past 11. She was in a Comatose state—we tried to rouse her, but without any avail. She could not swallow anything. I used the stomach pump but it had no effect. I then injected several quarts of water into the stomach and washed the stomach out. The smell of laudanum was very distinct, 100 drops is a large dose. I staied with her till 6 in the morning. I left her in the care of Mr. ? Mable a medical friend of hers I believe that she died from the effects of laudanum which must have been a very large dose. The Phial found in the room was about a 2 oz. Phial. It was labled " Laudnum Poison." She was in a very nervous condition when I saw her. Her husband appeared very much attached to her.

Catherine Birrill says I had not bought any laudnum for the deceased for 6 months. I bought a shillingsworth. The Phial was about half full. The Phial found was the one she generally used. I never saw her take any. I know of no hurt to her. I waited upon her and they lived very happily together.

Algernon Swinburne 16 Grafton St. Fitzroy Square at present says I have known the deceased and her husband. They dined with me on Monday, I saw nothing particular in the deceased except that she appeared a little weaker than usual.

Ellen Macintire says I live at 14 Chatham Place says I was with the deceased on Monday evening about $\frac{1}{2}$ past 8. She seemed cheerful then. I did not see her again till Mr. Rosetti called me up at $\frac{1}{2}$ past 11. She told me once that she had taken quarts of laudanum in her time. I have seen the Phial with laudanum in it.

Taken on oath $\}$ Wm. Payne. Coroner.
before me

INDEX

334

335

INTIMATE LETTERS FROM TONQUIN

By MARSHAL LYAUTEY

Translated by MRS. AUBREY LE BLOND.
With an Introduction by V. C. SCOTT
O'CONNOR, author of *The Silken East*, etc.

With a Frontispiece Portrait and three
Maps illustrating the Campaigns in
Tonquin.

15s. net.

Hubert Lyautey, Marshal of France and Member of
the French Academy, is one of the greatest figures of
our time. These letters, written before he had
become famous, to an intimate circle of friends between
1894 and 1896, cover his journey out to and period of stay
at Tonquin, when he was attached to the Headquater
Staff there under General Galliéni. They are delightful letters, written with a gift for literary expression
rare in a man of action, the letters of an ardent and
ambitious personality who was keenly interested in life.
They will also give English readers an insight into the
development of a colonial empire and into the methods
adopted by the great French administrator.

JOHN LANE THE BODLEY HEAD LTD., VIGO ST., W.I

JOHN CROME OF NORWICH

By R. H. MOTTRAM

With Eleven Illustrations and a Map.

12s. 6d. net.

"A biography of great charm, written with intimate knowledge of the scene of Crome's life, and with a sympathetic understanding of the painter's character."—HERBERT READ (*Listener*).

"To the lucky the book will be of absorbing interest—it is a labour of love."
BONAMY DOBRÉE (*Spectator*).

"A delightful and original study—it is at once more and less than a critical biography."—*Punch*.

"Mr. Mottram's 'John Crome' is a living being . . . he has succeeded in presenting a more probable John Crome than we have yet had."
Times Literary Supplement.

"It is not often that we have a book about an artist so firmly founded . . . this is a solid piece of work of an unusual kind."—*The Times*.

JOHN LANE THE BODLEY HEAD LTD., VIGO ST., W.I

THE
STREAM OF TIME

A Study of Social and Domestic
Life in England 1805–1861

By MRS. C. S. PEEL, O.B.E.

With 83 Illustrations.   18s. net.

" I warmly recommend this volume to all those
who wish to learn exactly how the men and women
of one hundred years ago lived and felt."
> HAROLD NICOLSON (*Action*).

" You get the whole atmosphere of the period . . .
absorbing; an admirable piece of work."
> J. M. BULLOCH (*Sunday Times*).

" I am gladder of Mrs. Peel's " The Stream of Time "
than of the majority of Victorian biographies issued
in the last year or two."—STET (*Week-end Review*).

" A valuable vivid picture . . . it would be difficult
to find a more comprehensive picture of the time."
> HUGH DE SELINCOURT (*Everyman*).

" Containing a mass of facts, this book is not only
excellent but extremely easy reading, and one which
does much to place the Earlier Victorian era in its
proper perspective."—*Manchester Guardian*.

JOHN LANE THE BODLEY HEAD LTD., VIGO ST., W.I

HARLEQUINADE

The Story of my Life

By CONSTANCE COLLIER

With a Preface by NOEL COWARD.

Illustrated.   15s. net.

"This book does give a living portrait of Beerbohm Tree and another of Miss Collier . . . in the early part the picture of the Gaiety girl is admirably effective. Miss Collier sets out to be her simple, remarkable self, with the result that she has produced a book which genuinely diverts the plain reader and which no student of the social history of the last forty years can safely ignore."

ARNOLD BENNETT (*Evening Standard*).

"This Life-story of a distinguished actress is one of the best pictures of theatrical life, its squalors and splendours, that have appeared for a long time."

Manchester Guardian.

"Few more readable books have appeared of late years than 'Harlequinade.'"—*Sunday Times.*

JOHN LANE THE BODLEY HEAD LTD., VIGO ST., W.I